Virtuoso

Virtuoso

Film Performance and the Actor's Magic

Murray Pomerance

BLOOMSBURY ACADEMIC

NEW YORK · LONDON · OXFORD · NEW DELHI · SYDNEY

BLOOMSBURY ACADEMIC
Bloomsbury Publishing Inc
1385 Broadway, New York, NY 10018, USA
50 Bedford Square, London, WC1B 3DP, UK

BLOOMSBURY, BLOOMSBURY ACADEMIC and the Diana logo are trademarks of
Bloomsbury Publishing Plc

First published in the United States of America 2019

Cover design: Louise Dugdale
Cover image: Film, *North by Northwest* (1959) Directed by Alfred Hitchcock,
shown: Cary Grant / Photofest

Library of Congress Cataloging-in-Publication Data
Names: Pomerance, Murray, 1946- author.
Title: Virtuoso: film performance and the actor's magic / Murray Pomerance.
Description: New York, NY: Bloomsbury Academic, 2019. |
Includes bibliographical references and index.
Identifiers: LCCN 2018048922| ISBN 9781501350689 (hardback: alk. paper) |
ISBN 9781501350672 (paperback: alk. paper) | ISBN 9781501350689 (hpod) |
ISBN 9781501350702 (ePDF) | ISBN 9781501350719 (xml-platform)
Subjects: LCSH: Motion picture acting. | Motion picture acting–Case studies. |
Motion pictures–History. | Motion pictures–History–Case studies.
Classification: LCC PN1995.9.A26 P66 2019 | DDC 791.4302/8–dc23
LC record available at https://lccn.loc.gov/2018048922

ISBN: HB: 978-1-5013-5068-9
PB: 978-1-5013-5067-2
ePDF: 978-1-5013-5070-2
eBook: 978-1-5013-5069-6

Typeset by Deanta Global Publishing Services, Chennai, India
Printed and bound in the United States of America

To find out more about our authors and books visit www.bloomsbury.com and
sign up for our newsletters.

A bit of drama is an aphrodisiac.

IAIN SINCLAIR

to

William Rothman

CONTENTS

ACKNOWLEDGMENTS

In a wide variety of ways, many generous people have helped me in and out of performance. I wish to thank the late Reginald Bedford and Evelyn Eby (Hamilton), Lisa Bode (Brisbane), the late John Browning (Lenox), the late Henry Bumstead (San Marino), Rolando Caputo (Melbourne), the late Aldo Ciccolini (Asnières), Matthew Cipa (Brisbane), Alex Clayton (Bristol), Ned Comstock (Los Angeles), Brandon Cronenberg (Toronto), Adrian Danks (Melbourne), the late Donald Davis (Toronto and Buffalo), Nathaniel Davis (Toronto), Evans (Evans) Frankenheimer (Beverly Hills), Lisa French (Melbourne), Jean-Michel Frodon (Paris), the late Assheton Gorton (Montgomery), Elliott Gould (Los Angeles), Louise Hilton (Beverly Hills), Jason Jacobs (Brisbane), Patricia Ward Kelly (Los Angeles), Mark Kermode (New Forest), Andrew Klevan (London), Bill Krohn (Los Angeles and Long Beach), Dominic Lennard (Melbourne), Gillian Leslie (Edinburgh), Norman Lloyd (Los Angeles), Elliott Logan (Brisbane), James MacDowell (Margate), Magdalena Maj (Toronto and Kraków), Jonathan Miller (Toronto), Jerry Mosher (Long Beach), the late Earle Moss (Toronto), the late Jesse Nishihata (Toronto), Florence Oba'Elle (Toronto), Christopher Olsen (Los Angeles), Anaïs Peli (Toronto and Marseille), the late Victor Perkins (Coventry), Stephen Rebello (Pasadena), Andy Rector (Newhall), Sean Redmond (Melbourne), the late Ian Richardson (Toronto and London), Jenny Romero (Beverly Hills), William Rothman (Miami), Dan Sacco (Toronto), the late Rudolf Serkin (Saratoga Springs), Robert Sinnerbrink (Sydney), Douglas Soesbe (Los Angeles), Jonathan Soja (Toronto), Matthew Solomon (Ann Arbor), James Spader (Toronto), George Toles (Winnipeg), Angela Tuohy (Brisbane), Daniel Varndell (Southampton), Constantine Verevis (Melbourne), Linda Ruth Williams (Southampton), and Jennifer Yared (Brisbane).

I am especially grateful to my colleagues at Bloomsbury Publishing, working with whom has been a thorough pleasure: Katie Gallof, Erin Duffy, Rachel Singleton, Leeladevi Ulaganathan, Abdus Salam, and Louise Dugdale.

Inspiration has come to me from many sources, none, I suppose, warmer or more unforgettable than the late Leon Pownall, who helped me cross the border between watching performance and doing it.

Nellie Perret and Ariel Pomerance have been guides in the dark, virtuosos of kindness and understanding, and providers of invaluable moral and intellectual help.

OVERTURE

After a painful absence, during which he has undergone treatment for a severe nervous disorder, a brilliant and sensitive composer returns home to his wife, who in the interim has fallen in love with another man and is now on the point of marriage. "Let me come back to you," the man begs, with all the feeling in his heart. "Take me into your life again." This is John Barrymore (1888–1942) with Billie Burke (1884–1970), in George Cukor's great masterpiece *A Bill of Divorcement* (1932). "Let me . . . only . . ."

Burke could not make it plainer, through the way she turns her head down, moves toward and swiftly away from him with her eyes, holds her breath, that (a) not only is she still completely swept away by this man but (b) he is something of a force of nature, and so compelling in this way that she is on point of being driven mad by her need for freedom now caught against her enduring affections. Further, (c) he has amazing powers of persuasion, surely an amazing voice for uttering (as might anyone who writes rhapsodic concerti for piano) and also (d) in her eyes there is no doubt that he is *in extremis*, lonely, frightened, aging, adoring, fearing, quivering with doubt. As to Barrymore, here in what may be the truly supreme moment of performance of his cinematic career, he is both noble and beautiful (as should be any dream vision of a composer of rhapsodies) but also broken and decayed. Something has disempowered him utterly. His need for Meg is more than a need, it is an obsession born of the summation of all his creative powers and all his hopes. She is his future. She is his Statue of Liberty, with that towering eminence, that beckoning voice, and he is her tired, her poor. Indeed, he feels himself low, and in the screen moment, after stumbling awkwardly from the door over to the wing chair in which she sits in her last wave of poise, he stumbles, hesitates, crumples. His body literally crumples inward, a mere bladder (out of Shakespeare) from which the air has been kicked. At the critical juncture, the instant that converts her, shining the light once again but also showing the entrapment of her dream, he falls to the carpet at her feet. He knows she would show mercy to her dog, and might she not show at least as much mercy to him? "Little things . . ."

Not love but mercy.

Might she not show at least as much mercy to him as to her dog, so that, with his voice now (artfully) cracked (his operatic voice) and his posture disassembled he might indeed resemble nothing so much as her dog, her faithful loving dog, the dog who will never abandon her, though she may see fit, in a flicker of feeling, to kick him into the kitchen. Yes, though he may be kicked bluntly into the kitchen, thence to be kicked through the servants' door onto the pavement outside. Outside, where some passerby might even kick him into the street.

Cukor's greatest strength as a filmmaker was knowing when to leave actors alone, as, notably, he does here. In the action I describe above his camera is there simply to make observation, not to emphasize through close-ups or other tricks, not to suggest an "angle" through which we might critically witness the event. Here in their fragile, their expressly existential moment, the Cukorian camera observes Hilary and Meg wide-eyed, a child confronted by a catastrophe, so that finally, invested with the vision of them on the precipice, we may catch our breath to wonder and surmise and never, once having seen and heard them, forget. But having sketched the scene only too briefly—it runs for several minutes—let me here pull away to note several features of Barrymore's and Burke's work that are simultaneously present and inseparable onscreen:

- Performances are of the body and from the body, expressed by way of the body, here on both sides of the conversation. Yet in cinema bodies are also foreign, absent, to us. We sit embodied, then lose our sense of the body as we hover, in onlooking engagement, over the behavior of simulacra. But those flickering images result from the presence of real bodies, too. We are seeing the trace of real life, preserved (see Bazin) in so magical a way that every nuance of life is here but for the palpable presence of the flesh itself (that is given onstage, yet at a forbidding distance). We must find our way toward and into these bodies, especially these bodies offered at such an apotheosis of feeling and being. The recognizable face is a central aspect, not only for our appreciations of feeling and identity but also for Hollywood's business machine.

- The expressions of both characters are entirely confluent with what has happened in the film so far for each of them (and what will happen hereafter), but at the same time the fluidity of the film—its carefully edited passage from before until later by way of here and now—does not overwhelm or hold back the emergence and glow of this moment. What we see stands out but without breaking away from its context. At the same time it is valuable to note the obverse, that what we see is tidily embedded in its context yet achieves a special, standout glow that makes our experience of the scene utterly radiant. This moment is no blemish, but we cannot take our eyes from it.

- Neither of the two instrumentalities—Barrymore's presence, Burke's presence—overwhelms the other, yet each is emergent and spectacular. Call this directorial balance; call it performative etiquette and grace; call it aesthetic modulation. There are numerous very notable performers who have never yet shown onscreen the capacity to hold back from taking over by the power of their personalities and gestures. In the cases of Barrymore and Burke we have two exceptional talents with immense range, and either could easily have made the scene a self-promotion.

- The actors both remain in character and transcend character. That is: Barrymore is always as present as Hilary is; Burke as present as Meg. But, the Hilaryness of Barrymore and the Barrymoreness of Hilary are not at war or in struggle, and we are not led in this scene to wonder about the actor's life. Watching Barrymore here is gaining a great lesson in the technique of characterization and cinematic movement and presence, with each flicker of gesture a telltale indication of Hilary's sensibility at the instant and also of the actor's method of indicating it. In listening to the stage dialogue of Oscar Wilde pronounced by John Gielgud (on Broadway in 1947) or that of Chekhov pronounced by Raul Julia (1977), to the pianistic modulations of Liszt or Rachmaninoff accomplished by Aldo Ciccolini or John Browning, to the vocal sensitivities of Strauss in the voice of Jessye Norman one has a like sense of doubling, of catching the composition and the performance indivisible together.

- Technical skills are in use that eclipse the knowledge and perception of the ordinary spectator. Yet the spectator never feels diminished in capability as she or he watches. By contrast, many effects are produced that give the actor no special challenge (given training and experience) yet seem to the viewer astonishing achievements.

- Both performers in this scene must seem to "fit" into the more globalized, ongoing career being established by each, in film after film. Barrymore in particular, the more widely known of the two, must never so uncontrollably dive into Hilary that his presence as Barrymore is effaced, yet in this moment he does appear to dive this way. And Hilary must never do anything, feel anything, or behave in such a way that the John Barrymore whom audiences know and love, the John Barrymore who gained their undying allegiance could not reasonably do, feel, or behave. Barrymore's dive into Hilary and Burke's into Meg must be, in short, recuperable, whatever depths it leads to; and recuperable whether or not it seems to be.

- The estimable technical virtuosity involved in giving performance of this kind must not "give the show away" by revealing itself as such, by making plain to the viewer's eye nothing more than a bag of tricks that the actor dutifully schleps around from job to job and reaches into for a moment's help. The performance should not seem technical. Yet of course it is technical, as is all work diligently done.

- The feeling generated in the scene must have a genuine quality, but at the same time—and with feelings of great extremity, such as here, this is of central urgency—it must be produced by people working on a contract that could require them to retake the scene (for any of a dozen good reasons) again and again. It might well seem logical to think that the more extreme the feeling as performed the more vitiating the work, yet for film actors it is vital never to be unable to keep going. Involved in the tumbling of the work, then, is a kind of acrobatic roll. Whilst we do not see the actor's reserve of energy and tension, she is constantly aware of it, constantly maintaining it against the continually incalculable odds of a long, hard day.

- Here and in almost all films, the performer is not in control of what the final screened scene will look and sound like, since the sound recording, the camera work, the editing, and the use of ancillary effects are all in other people's hands. When onstage an actor makes a posture with the body, it can be known what the human form thus constructed will look like from various points in the auditorium. But with film it is the camera's position and movement, and even more the lens, that shape the body's form in the frame; and it is the editor who shapes the character's tempo and duration.

There are numerous other contingencies of acting of the sort one sees from Barrymore and Burke in this scene, acting that I will refer to, because of its purity and extremity, its power and its idiosyncrasy, its delicacy and the supremeness of its expressive effect, as "virtuosity." I think it rather unlikely that every actor is capable of virtuosic performance; yet at the same time I suspect it very likely that many more actors are capable in this way than we have come to know, many more than have been given opportunity to show what they can do when brought to a height. And we must remember that sometimes it is cinema itself that shapes and configures the virtuosity of a performative moment. And remember, too, that screen narrative works because many moments are happily enough *not* virtuosic.

Many other things about cinema, the way performance is magnified in it, the way performance can flame, will come to view in the exploration I hope now to begin.

For those who must know, Meg does take Hilary back, giving up her dream of release. And he does, at a very satisfying moment, sit at the piano and complete his long-unfinished concerto.

1

A Brief History of the
Virtuosic Moment

FIGURE 1 *Richard Burton in John Gielgud's production of* Hamlet *(taped in Electronovision) (Theatrofilm, 1964). Digital frame enlargement.*

Writing about the hand in culture, Frank Wilson reflects on prodigy: "Musical skill provides the clearest example and the cleanest proof of the existence of a whole class of self-defined, personally distinctive motor skills with an extended training and experience base, strong ties to the individual's emotional and cognitive development, strong communicative intent, and very high performance standards" (207). Some notes about these standards and this class:

First, acting works like musical performance (moving as they do through harmonic space and across rhythmic time, actors are musicians[1]). And secondly, as Wilson himself notes, "very high performance standards" are a relatively modern addition to the repertory of an artist's strengths. With both music and acting, the professionalism we associate with extreme levels of performative articulation followed long periods of less intensive, amateur activity (activity deriving from enthusiasm), in which people made music and occupied the stage—the "stage": a specialized area summoning concentrated attention—because they loved to do so, or felt a calling (a *vocation*), or needed a moment of expression, but in any event for fluid, personal and unorganized, possibly religious reasons. If Greek drama was impressively declamatory, requiring vocal strength for long projection in an open-air *odeon*, it was also practiced by citizens who had not necessarily developed body and personality, through struggle and training, for the challenge of wearing the mask. The audience required only sufficient clarity of projection for the voices and postures to be received and interpreted straightforwardly; the prodigy of the drama lay in a text spoken, *however* it was spoken. When *Oedipus Rex* was played, Sophocles was the virtuoso: "Count no man happy until he has passed the final boundary of his life secure from pain."

The major cultural change in music, Wilson tells us, came with Franz Liszt (1811–1886), who, living and working at the same time as Charles Darwin, was similarly concerned with competition and life experience. Both saw the elaboration of technique as vital to success. "Where do we find the *selection pressure*," Wilson wonders, "that explains the descent of musicians?" and, with Liszt and those who followed him, explicitly the descent of brilliant musicians who beyond interpreting a score could put on a show by reading it in a spectacular fashion. To Liszt, Wilson reminds us, is attributed the exclamation, "Le concert, c'est moi!" From the brilliant musician it is but a short leap to the brilliant performer onstage or onscreen, who also declaims, "L'acte, c'est moi!" Before Liszt, the celebrated actor was in service of the script; afterward, with the invention of virtuosity in performance, the script could be seen as serving the performer.[2]

---

[1] I mean the phrase "actors are musicians" metaphorically, not descriptively; poetically, not occupationally; although the links between film, filmmaking, film performance, *and music* are intrinsic ones, as many observers, including Alfred Hitchcock, have noted (see my *Man Who Knew*). Hitchcock often regaled listeners with an odd little tale about a man who gets up in the morning, brushes his teeth, gets dressed, picks up his satchel, walks out of the house, heads to work, arranges himself in the percussion section of an orchestra, and, during the performance, hits one single beat; then afterward packs up, goes back home, and goes to bed: action and music!

[2] In his masterful performance of Dickens's *A Christmas Carol* December 24–30, 2001 at Broadway's Marquis Theatre, Patrick Stewart outshone Dickens.

No natural wellspring, the artistic prodigy had endured "specialized educational practices" (Wilson 228) geared to strengthen certain sinews, attune certain sensitivities, focus the mind on delicate muscular manipulations, and the like. Here is grounded the startling aplomb of Sarah Bernhardt, the magical transformations of John Barrymore, the noble gracility of John Gielgud[3] and flamboyance of Laurence Olivier, the cagey concentration of Derek Jacobi and his pupil Kenneth Branagh, the high-cheeked flush of Edith Evans, and the ineffable sadness of Laurette Taylor, whose playing of Tennessee Williams's *The Glass Menagerie* on Broadway in 1945 so stunned audiences, but especially actors who paid over and over to see her, that her moments endured for them as eternal memories of greatness. According to accounts, she *simply was*, on the stage; no affectation.

To distinguish the script from the speech, one might note Hamlet's too famous self-mocking "To be or not to be" and its many orators. Gielgud's Hamlet differed from Richard Burton's and Laurence Olivier's and Maxine Peake's. One thinks of Gielgud's voice as having quaver and resonance, like a great organ, his intonation sepulchral and secret, a phantasm's; so that when with this great soliloquy Hamlet wanders through the forest of his mortality we feel we are in some stark, whispered privacy with him, perhaps inside his soul. Olivier used facial muscles, knowing that his Hamlet would be seen in close-up, so that the shifting eyes, the relaxing and tensing lips, the hollowed cheeks when the head was turned would all sum to neurotic sensibility losing its way. Burton had been gifted with a voice like cut diamond, and when he spoke (I saw his performance in a theater of 3,500 souls, where the words swam in the air before me) one could hear something akin to a trumpet being played in all its registers, softly or with force, and with unbounded power to shift moods even in the middle of a syllable. This Hamlet sang his pain, was an undiscovered artist whose fate darkened because of his artistic power. Peake used a clipped matter-of-fact tone, drawing the audience to her as friends, but also staccato pauses to gain attention.

Professional artistic culture, suggests Wilson, "created its own archaeological context for defining and then reciprocally *redefining* the fitness" of the performer (216). The performer's fitness, for both audience attention and the special illumination of the stage or cinema, became an issue for criticism. Francisque Sarcy, a theater critic for both *L'Opinion nationale* and *Le Temps*, adjudicated Bernhardt: "She carries herself

---

[3]Which, by August of 1969, was enough to set Richard Burton off:

J.G. said he'd been to see [Peter Brook's *Marat/Sade*] three or four times and thought it was miraculous or marvelous or whatever the latest adjective was that he'd picked up that morning as he passed T. S. Eliot in St James' Park on his way to the nearest public lavatory. . . . John, as Tony [Quayle] or I suggested, had deliberately become a send-up of himself. "I am just a child of nature, I don't know what I'm doing. Give me the words and I'll get on with the job. Is the war over, I'm so glaaaaad" (317).

well and pronounces with perfect precision. *That is all that can be said about her at the moment"* (Skinner 37; my emphasis); the virtuosity she promised apparently required more still. And reviewing the same Burton performance I saw (more or less, because now the cast, including Hume Cronyn as Polonius, Alfred Drake as Claudius, Eileen Herlie as Gertrude, Linda Marsh as Ophelia, as well as George Voskovec, George Rose, and Barnard Hughes, had moved to the Lunt-Fontanne Theatre in New York) the *New York Times* was overwhelmed by its capacity and girth: "Richard Burton dominates the drama, as Hamlet should. For his is a performance of electrical power and sweeping virility. But it does not burst the bounds of the framework set for it by John Gielgud's staging. It is not so much larger than life that it overwhelms the rest of the company. Nor does it demand attention so fiercely for itself that the shape and poetry of the play are lost to the audience" (Taubman). Two essential provisos for brilliant performance: (1) do not overwhelm your circumstances; (2) do not obfuscate the script. "It is clear early on that Mr. Burton means to play Hamlet with all the stops out—when power is wanted. . . . I do not recall a Hamlet of such tempestuous manliness." *With all the stops out:* the reviewer is showing himself experienced, has seen acting with "stops left in," has heard tones muted but here and now made sonorous and deep.

Prior to Gielgud's modern-dress staging with Burton, fifty-nine productions of *Hamlet* had found their way to Broadway, perhaps most famous the 1922 John Barrymore offering, which, if it also stunned the *Times,* created, it seems, a more ethereal, even ghostly effect. Barrymore also possessed an orchestral sound, although of the two voices Burton's was the jewel with more carats:

> The atmosphere of historic happening surrounded John Barrymore's appearance last night as the Prince of Denmark; it was unmistakable as it was indefinable. It sprang from the quality and intensity of the applause, from the hushed murmurs that swept the audience at the most unexpected moments, from the silent crowds that all evening long swarmed about the theatre entrance. It was nowhere—and everywhere. In all likelihood we have a new and a lasting Hamlet.
>
> Mr. Barrymore disclosed a new personality and a fitting one. . . . This youth was wan and haggard, but right manly and forthright—dark and true and tender as befits the North. The slender figure, with its clean limbs, broad shoulders and massive head "made statues all over the stage," as was once said of Edwin Booth.
>
> Vocally, the performance was keyed low. Deep tones prevailed, tones of a brooding, half-conscious melancholy. The "reading" of the lines was flawless—an art that is said to have been lost. The manner, for the most part, was that of conversation, almost colloquial, but the beauty of

rhythm was never lost, the varied, flexible harmonies of Shakespeare's crowning period in metric mastery (Corbin).

If the virtuosity of Burton was operatic,[4] the virtuosity of Barrymore's Hamlet had a cousinly charm, that of a handsome young articulate who chatted his lines, watched his rhythms, posed with sculptural grandeur. Burton, by contrast, was terrifying, slouching in his open-necked jet-black work shirt.[5]

Even when she is enunciating a deeply meaningful and very poetic script, the body and presence of the performer enunciate themselves with special force in virtuosic acting, just in the way that, before the performance began, they had promised to do (leading strangers to pay good money for the experience of catching a view). If in music, during the Romantic era,[6] artists effectively competed with one another by giving public performances of the same "classic" (read, canonical) concertos—the Grieg A minor (1868), the Tchaikowsky B-flat minor (1875), the Brahms D minor (1858), any of the five Beethovens (1795–1810), the Lizst No. 2 (1861)—so that what the listening audience finally received was an idiosyncratic *version* of a text already *known*, similarly onstage *Hamlet* was an already known score, and the competitive performativities that lent themselves to it were taking opportunity to show personal, often entirely quirky ways of saying words and phrases everyone knew other performers had already said, in their own ways. Which words or syllables would gain emphasis? Where would pauses be inserted? Where stage business undertaken? What gestures of the face and limbs might express emotion? In the early 1990s I attended an enchanting lecture by the great British actor Ian Richardson,[7] about Shakespeare's soliloquies. He made it quite plain that as far as he was concerned the way to do it was to read the exact text, with five stressed beats to the line, *counting silently to oneself and doing business whenever a line had fewer than five iambs.* He demonstrated and, indeed, his logic was flawless. Other performers, of course, enjamb the lines, pause in mid-line, raise their pitch on eccentric syllables, often try to divine the meaning of the text so as to convey it to the listener rather than assuming the text has the meaning already and the listener will hear.

---

[4]In the review of Burton in 1964, as of Barrymore in 1922, criticism persistently revolved around gender-performance of suitably "masculine" Hamlets. (For a fuller analysis of the politics of gender identity as mocked up in fictions, see Goffman's *Gender Advertisements*, Butler's *Gender Trouble*, and Lehman's *Running Scared*, among numerous other studies.)

[5]Slouching in figure only: during the Toronto run, on a quick side trip to Montreal, he married Elizabeth Taylor.

[6]A convenient way of dating it would be to begin with Frédéric Chopin (1810–1849), although one could go back to the Beethoven Concerto No. 1 (1795).

[7]A founding member of the Royal Shakespeare Company.

Once the age of virtuosity has dawned, writers and composers begin to design materials ideal for the display of a performative self: rich meaty verbs (Joe Pesci in *Goodfellas* [1990]: "Fuck you, you fuck!"), character action strange enough to seduce the eye (in *Woman of the Year* [1942], Katharine Hepburn trying hopelessly to cook breakfast for Spencer Tracy). Scripting in both stage work and film attends rigorously to performative possibilities: eccentric and highly visualized action (Sam Shepard's *Operation Sidewinder* [Vivian Beaumont Theatre, Lincoln Center, 1970] had a small tribe of Native Americans, in full regalia, literally disappear from center stage); fabulously unpredictable language (Olivier in toga to almost naked Tony Curtis in *Spartacus* [1960]: "Do you eat oysters?"); marvelous choreography (the cattle shoot in *Hud* [1963], in which Melvyn Douglas gives an unforgettable virtuosic turn by standing stock still in defeated silence). Materials produced much earlier, for less ostentatious display or display with an entirely different kind of ostentation—Shakespeare's plays, Dickens's novels—are reinterpreted with new, self-declarative voices: Ethan Hawke doing a slacker *Great Expectations* (1998), Helen Mirren playing Prosper(o)a in Julie Taymor's *The Tempest* (2010). Dramatic renovations offer almost unlimited opportunity for virtuosic playing, since the presence of unexpected personnel has the capacity to make every tiny gesture seem significant, enriching, and special (as, between April 19, 1979, and June 28, 1981, with David Bowie taking over the lead in Bernard Pomerance's *The Elephant Man* from Philip Anglim, at Broadway's Booth Theatre).

"Musicians had always spoken to and for people's feeling," writes Wilson, but "the Lisztian declaration—a new formula for survival—profoundly transformed the relationship between musicians and audiences, and in so doing transformed the definition of musical skill" (215). What was the "new formula" wedding actors to audiences, then?: formal audiences who might sit in vast swathes in the darkness or smaller audiences, who might torment the privacy of the dressing room or hotel suite? Here is Sarah Bernhardt's (1844–1923) own reflection, my added italic drawing emphasis to her hyperbolically repeated hyperbole even as she remembers the virtuosic feelings of a moment long past:

> When I arrived at [New York's] Albemarle Hotel I was tired and *very much* in need of solitude. I *made haste* to lock myself up in one of the bedrooms, in the suite of rooms reserved for me. I closed *all the doors.* One of them had *neither lock nor key*, so I *pushed* a piece of furniture up against it and *forcefully* refused to open any door.
>
> In the drawing room there were about *fifty* people, but I was *overcome* by the kind of *extreme* fatigue that will *drive* you *to violent extremes* to obtain an hour of rest. I wanted to *stretch out on the carpet with my arms folded*, my head back, and my eyes closed. *I did not want to talk any more, smile any more, or look any more.* I *threw* myself down on

the floor and made *no response* to the knocking on my door and [her secretary] Jarrett's pleas. I did not want to enter into *any* discussion. I did not say a word. I heard the buzzing of visitors outside and the muttering of Jarrett as he tried to hold them back. I heard a piece of paper being slid under the door and then the whispering of [her friend and assistant] Mme. Guérard.

"You don't know her, Mr. Jarrett. If you force the door that she has jammed, she is quite likely to jump out of the window." (253)

What a picturesque dramatization is Mme. Guérard's knowing supposition!: one can imagine the movie scene, with Paul Giamatti forcing the door against the wishes of the dutiful Meryl Streep, and hyperexhausted Helena Bonham Carter indeed throwing herself out the window, arms raised to her face, lips as pallid as ash.

Virtuosity need not inhere in a performer's look. Bernhardt's follower Eleonora Duse (1858–1924), unequivocally virtuosic by all accounts, wore little makeup according to her biographer, and "made herself up *morally*. . . . She allowed the inner compulsions, grief and joys of her characters to use her body as their medium for expression, often to the detriment of her health" (Winwar n.p.; my emphasis). A later Italian genius of performance, Anna Magnani (1908–1973), was called a "living she-wolf symbol" of the screen, "the volcanic earth mother of all Italian cinema" (Monush n.p.). Roberto Rossellini, for whom she made the astonishing *L'Amore* (1948), thought her "the greatest acting genius" since Duse (Johnson 194). To watch *L'Amore* is to be swept away, distanced from shore by an oceanic force.

Virtuosity can be self-distancing. Richard Burton, no big fan of "To be or not to be":

For some reason English people adamantly believe that acting in the theatre is superior (what a funny word) to acting in the films or TV. I've done all three with considerable success, and I'll tell you, . . . that they are all difficult but with the difference that after, shall we say, 10 weeks of playing *Hamlet* on the stage one's soul staggers with tedium and one's mind rejects the series of quotations that *Hamlet* now is. Has there ever been a more boring speech, after 400 years of constant repetition, than "To be or not to be"? I have never played that particular speech, and I've played the part hundreds and hundreds of times, without knowing that everybody settles down to a nice old nap the minute the first fatal words start.

. . .

[An American lady] said that she had seen me as Hamlet in New York, and actually asked me how could I possibly remember the lines. I told her that I never did actually get them straight and that some of my improvisations on speeches which I hated and therefore could never recall would have

been approved by the lousy actor-writer himself. I told her that once I
spoke "To be or not to be" in German to an American audience, but
she obviously didn't believe me. I told her there were certain aspects of
Hamlet, I mean the man, so revolting that one could only do them when
drunk. (291; 224)

Burton's admission here in print, that he "never played" the "To be" speech,
brings a shocking recall of memory to me as I now reread it, because the
year I saw his performance I was a senior in high school, spending five or
sixth months on an in-depth study of *Hamlet* for an extensive final paper
in English, in the course of which project I saw more than half a dozen
productions live, including his. And I suddenly remember that indeed he *did
not play* that speech, but merely sat at stage left and spoke it: spoke it as if
telling someone of a speech Shakespeare had written, with an "It goes like
this . . ." elided first. The voice was a glory, but the feeling he conveyed as
a disturbing, unhealthy, alienated flatness, a perfect mark of Hamlet at this
despondent moment of his life. Burton was giving Hamlet *life*. If through
her every breath Bernhardt suffered, Burton's Hamlet, so introverted, only
invokes the idea of suffering. The *Times* swooned, "Mr. Burton . . . reads the
'To be or not to be' soliloquy with subdued anguish, like a man communing
painfully with himself."

In both Burton and Bernhardt we can find exceptional vocal refinement,
careful gestural shaping and grace of movement, and a dancerly accuracy
of placement. The composer Reynaldo Hahn saw the structural significance
of the "gowns made famous" by Bernhardt (27), her garment being a vital
component of body display. She was distinguished onstage because of the
way she contrived to look. Victoria Duckett suggests that "Bernhardt's
turning and twisting body, as well as the spiraling material folds of her
costume, were not just an unusual part of her stage performance. They were
inseparable with her identity and so worked into the many portraits made of
her. Becoming an integral part of Bernhardt's reproduced image, her curved
and sinuous body came to symbolize the corporeal shape of art nouveau, its
manifestation in human form" (33).

The body can have its own natural grace, and the aspiring actor learns
how to recognize, then permit it. In the winter of 1953 Peter O'Toole went
with a cohort of friends to watch Burton ("hailed as the new Olivier")
play the Bastard in *King John* at London's Old Vic: "When Richard Burton
strutted his Bastard on to the stage, he fetched with him a virility and poetry
which neither before nor since have I seen matched in any playhouse" (Sellers
28). Characteristically, and inspired by Burton's poetry, O'Toole poeticizes:
"fetched with him" is a curious and wonderful phrase, an acknowledgment,
perhaps, of what only an actor habituated to playing masculinity before
the critical eye could see. Burton, O'Toole teaches, had the virtuosic power
to summon, to "fetch" virility along, and poetry, too. He could beckon the

spirits to come along with him. O'Toole desired that vocal power. He said that he and his friends didn't want to talk posh, "we didn't want to talk like the Royal Family, we just wanted when we got into the theatre to talk like Olivier, or Ralph Richardson or Gielgud, actors who spoke beautifully, we all wanted to do that" (27). When the performance was done, O'Toole and company hit a nearby pub,[8] to which Burton and some other cast members shortly thereafter retired. O'Toole distinctly recalled "Burton catching sight of his own gaze and staring back with a grin, 'as big as it was friendly. He raised his glass to me, to my friends, we raised our glasses to him, and then with the grin still on him he ambled away'" (28).

---

[8]The Old Vic is on Waterloo Road, across from Waterloo Station.

2

Showing Off

FIGURE 2 *Kenneth Branagh as Hercule Poirot in* Murder on the Orient Express *(Kenneth Branagh, Twentieth Century Fox, 2017). Digital frame enlargement.*

From an audience's point of view, virtuosic moments can seem excessive: "too loud," "too strained," "hammy," "over the top," "out of tune," specifically in a performer's being perceived as working harder than should properly (naturally) be necessary for demonstration. "Hamming it up" derives from ham fat, which was used once as a makeup base and makeup remover; "hamming it up" meant wearing excessive makeup—pushing one's act further than was needed. (I have also seen numerous exceedingly accomplished actors slur and mumble their lines, that is, go in the opposite direction, "ham it down" as it were.) Actors are audiences, too; they watch their scene partners at work whilst working with them. Indeed, many teachers of acting stress that listening is the most important thing: listening, attending, letting the other person frame one's consciousness to a significant degree. And an actor observing a virtuosic colleague up close might privately frown at the other's bombastic overstatement or grandiose gesture, might regard it as discourteous upstaging, a tactic for purloining viewer attention.

Glen O. Gabbard has noted actors' envy, how in watching others at work they have a tendency to be hypercritical of the skills in play (433 ff.; cited in Aaron 121).

But the problem of expansiveness in virtuosic performance has deeper roots than resentment or jealousy, embarrassment for the actor in his labors or the unaesthetic ruin of dramatic balance. If in a culture critical of sham all performance were regarded with suspicion; if any acting at all might too quickly seem reprovably disingenuous, then acting of a sort that drew special attention because of its magnitudes—the bellowing tone of voice, the brazen tilt of the head, the vaunted thrust of the arm—could only seem problematic in a very extreme way. Viewers of acting, from the audience and from the stage, are always especially sensitive to its tonal and figurative balance and proportion, whilst at the same time understanding that moderation is only sometimes valuable: the moderate performance is not so easily seen. In some arrangements it takes very little stress, if any at all, from a performer to signal an arrogant self-importance that undoes dramatic engagement. This is one of the characteristics Hamlet criticizes in warning the First Player not to "saw the air too much."

In all acting, the performer employs technique to a purpose. Overacting can be the employment of too much technique, or the overemployment of even a modest technique, or even, when there is broad suspicion of technique altogether, doing anything perceptible to work up a character. "Working up" itself is seen as wrong. There is suspicion of technique in cultures of authenticity, where "proper" action is thought spontaneous, natural, unaffected, pure. Any performative situation involving period settings or costumes, specialized makeup, or characterological impairments or special talents would fail at naturalness and seem contrived. Thus, in Kubrick's *Spartacus* (1960), when slave after slave stands up to the Romans and declares, "*I am Spartacus!*" the moment seems as false as a dildo. Ditto the garish banquets in *Marie Antoinette* (2006), the unavoidably glary appearances of Alec Guinness in *The Man in the White Suit* (1951), Ian Holm's blithering disembodied head in *Alien* (1979). Clown acts are similarly difficult for virtuosity (we will see an interesting case later), as are playing in fancy costume or hairdressing (*The Wizard of Oz* [1939], *The Hunger Games* [2012]), acting by mo-cap (*Lord of the Rings* [2001]), and other perforcedly visible, thus hardly unaffected kinds of performance. The extremity of performance is a structure, not an achievement.

Social arrangements disparaging performance have been in play for a very long time. Reflecting in *Fangs of Malice* that the idea of acting as hypocrisy "was a constant in moral pamphleteering in the seventeenth and eighteenth centuries in England and France" (xi), Matthew Wikander strikes at a fear of theatricality deeply embedded in the West. Performance is taken to be "false at the level of the profound heart" (xi) in numerous tracts, such as William Prynne's *Histriomastix,* where one can read of "Hypocrites,

Stage-players, as being one and the same in substance" (Prynne 158, qtd. in Wikander xii). A popular early and "profoundly anti-theatrical" idea, with life to carry it well into the twenty-first century, holds that "a true self, an own self, a sincere self, is unplayable," which is to say, any acting at all is charlatanry and nothing else (Wikander xiv). The quest for authenticity that centered so much attention in the Renaissance and centers so much attention now (a quick look at the condescension of internet surfers toward Johnny Depp's lucrative performances as Cap'n Jack Sparrow will provide confirmation) is incommensurate with performativity, that troubling Machiavellian darkness, and it is easy to imagine how, if performativity itself is in question, performance that calls attention to itself through virtuosity is seen as especially worthy of damnation.

(It is wise to remember that all of interactional life—like all of acting—is "showing off." We can exist with one another effectively only by making displays of intent, so that conscious display is not inherently strange.)

It is perhaps from Jean-Jacques Rousseau (1712–1798) that our treasuring of the unplayed "real" emerges. Wikander offers Rousseau's fable of a mountain community near Neufchâtel—"utopian because there is no theater there," says Wikander (70)—the inhabitants of which are, as Rousseau has it, never idle and never bored. Then a theater is established. What happens?:

> [Rousseau] enumerates five "disadvantages": "slackening of work," "increase of expenses," "decrease in trade," "establishment of taxes" (to build roads and make up for trade deficits), "introduction of luxury." Here women will strive to outshine one another in dress, the sumptuary laws will fall into disregard, and husbands will be ruined. (Rousseau xxv, qtd. in Wikander 70–71)

Immediately with organized performance, then, the attention of not only the eyes and ears but the entire working spirit is distracted, waylaid, kidnapped. Economic misfortunes follow in train. Finally the triumphal reign of appearances is acknowledged widely, and the custom of guising oneself is made popular and uncontrollable. Resources are squandered on maquillage and costumes. The more entrancing the performance, the more virtuosic may be judged the performer in carrying off his fictional charge, the more deeply is the penetration of influence upon the innocent population, the more anti-utopian the arrangement.

Is Rousseauan anti-theatricalism not, perhaps, at the heart of the contemporary penchant for realistic performance, performance that seems like actual being? Our estimation of screen acting in the age of action film, for instance, places very high value on performers who submit themselves so completely to the rigorous armature of the effects design they are imperceptible doing so. Brilliant acting can nowadays mean being strapped into a harness and cloaked in sensor markers, set into an empty soundstage before a green screen, and miming out the gestures of some strenuous and complex activity—an activity that will exist onscreen, to be sure, but manufactured post hoc on a computer screen: waiting alone in a high-walled arena, say, as a pack of velociraptors prepare to chew you to pieces. In cases like this one a number of actors, all decked out in sensor suits and sometimes partial costumes, mime together. Faces, facial expressions, as well as grosser gestures, can all be overlaid in the graphic "skin" that the sensors make it possible for designers to construct. In this motion capture work, the brilliance of the brilliant actor resides in his or her passivity, fitting movement precisely into a predesigned grid and forming expression exactly on cue and as requested. Here, then, the actor, who is not already really expressing a self of any kind, cannot overexpress a self, cannot make a statement that is too loud. It's a perfect style for an anti-theatrical culture. But of course, action film is only one of the venues of contemporary "real" performance.

In domestic dramas onstage, onscreen, and on television we find close-contact scenes—nowadays very typically set in a bed, with a small number of actors nude or half nude and either on point of sexual encounter or just recovering from it—where performance is constituted by alternative casual whispers, long pensive forward gazes (indicating thought), and casual physical touch. The sexual act being taken in our culture as a fountainhead of authenticity, privacy, and sincerity, most of this exact kind of casual interpersonal action embedded in a performance will seem inherently real and natural, merely because of its setting. Here, virtuosity becomes oddity, since there is no way to exaggerate the realness of reality but one can suggest action with which audiences are unfamiliar. A virtuosic turn might consist of an actor doing absolutely nothing when a pungent line of dialogue is delivered into his face (Helen Mirren and Rhys Ifans are both expert at this "deadpanning"). Except in limited dramatic circumstances, the production of emphatic gesture or speech in very private moments is disproportionate on the face of it, so the scene controls the behavior. In other sorts of scenes, such as occur at offices or in public transportation, the action is all "business," and the performances are restrained "civilly" to fit in with an "accurate" depiction of the, for audiences, well-known social circumstances. Action is again geared to modest and self-effacing efficiency, to relative quiet, keeping the decorum and tone of the setting principally in mind. Special excitement is manufactured by the script and by actors submitting themselves to the rigors of the plot, as we see with Jake Gyllenhaal, for example, in *Source Code* (2011); the train explosion in which he is caught up is a sensorily overwhelming excess, precisely the kind of thing authenticity arguments put down in human behavior, but it is redeemed by being arcanely technological and tightly stitched into the script. If we focus on the Gyllenhaal character we find that he is relatively unexpressive, "normal," reduced in display, perfect for the contemporary world.

Two interesting examples come to mind, one austerely exemplifying this principle of self-effacing, "naturalistic," anti-theatrical contemporary performance and one delightfully violating it.

In *The Bourne Supremacy* (2004), our hero Jason Bourne is arrested and trapped in an Italian office. His minder there is a very green officer of the CIA. The room is bare but for a desk and small file cabinet. Bourne sits in abject silence while being questioned: such an operative *might behave this way* in such a circumstance (and to effect the behavior the actor is quite literally *doing almost nothing.*) Bourne's silence merits special note: peppered with simplistic questions, he not only holds his voice back but restrains his body, becomes a statue, thus marking and mocking the agent's attempts to suck information from him as hopeless from the start. But now the agent's cell rings and as he takes the call, turning away from his prisoner, we note Bourne's astute regard, his measuring every angle of the agent's pose. In a cutaway to Langley we find on the other end Pamela Landy (Joan Allen), a high-level controller who has been plotting to locate Bourne and now informs her callow agent how dangerous his prisoner is. Terminating the call with the smile now wiped from his face he is in process of turning toward Bourne when the prisoner mounts an alarmingly swift and effective attack, against which the young man has no opportunity to defend himself. In less than five seconds of screen time, he has been wholly disabled and rendered unconscious, Bourne has fished out the keys to the handcuffs he's been wearing and, having extricated the SIM card from the agent's phone, has made his escape.

While efficient movement is a necessity of the plot here, and has been choreographed carefully between the performers and the camera, the quiet virtuosity in Matt Damon's work lies partly in his stony poise and partly in the (literally) split-second transition into high-gear motion. When a great cat leaps we see the pose that sets up the angle and attunes the muscles, in short the preparation; but when Bourne leaps there seems no preparation at all. Or: the preparation is all mental, without visible muscular ripples, without shifting of posture, without setup, all this possible, of course, because the director, Paul Greengrass, shoots the action over and over from many different angles, then cuts very small pieces together to give an illusion of continuous motion. Visible in Damon's performance, too, and caught in close shots by the camera, is a very different kind of action than what one saw in westerns of the 1930s, 1940s, and 1950s, or in police procedurals, or in crime films, adventure films, or sci-fi films, action that replaces gross muscle movements (twisting, leaping, dodging) with tinier finger gestures and manipulations, the removal of the SIM card in *Supremacy* accomplished almost without a pause. Here, virtuosic action performance is cooked as fully by the cinematographer and editor as by the actor, offering up what will appear as "exceptional" trained capacity. Much of Damon's labor— undertaken with diligence and care—is a refusal to express, an interior immersion blocking every flicker of presence. If there is no way to watch this thinking, "There is no contrivance," there is also no gap in which to detect the put-on. Damon's Bourne has art, to be sure, but is without artifice.

Enjoying *The Bourne Supremacy*, then, is not incommensurate with deploring performance, extolling "naturalism" and authenticity, or being revolted by performative excess because one privileges the "reality" of the everyday. Damon's difficult work is done in such a way as to be entirely invisible. No loud, brazen, decorative, colorful, exoticized, emphatic acting here; no showing off.

A profoundly different, in some ways hilarious, virtuosity was performed in the everyday world, gaining spiciness and dramatic weight just by virtue of the venue. On the Manhattan A train one morning in the early 1970s, I sat among five or six strangers in a too brightly lit car, gently rocking as the train hit the points. Next to me was a woman holding a tiny tot, perhaps two years old. Somewhere near 72nd Street, on shuffled a tall, somewhat disheveled man in a white t-shirt. I thought he looked familiar. He sidled up, holding the support rails, and was soon standing in front of the woman with the kid. He watched them for a moment, then slowly, smoothly, bent down so that his enormous face was in the kid's line of vision. I suddenly clicked. It was Al Lewis (1923–2006), known to me as Captain Schnauzer on *Car 54, Where Are You?* (1961) and recognizable to multitudes as Grandpa on *The Munsters* (1964) but also a film veteran who had performed in *They Shoot Horses, Don't They?* (1969), *They Might Be Giants* (1971), *The World of Henry Orient* (1964). He put his large fleshy hands into the corners of his supple mouth and pulled to the sides, in order to make a gigantic maw; opened his eyes wide and made them cross; then stuck out his tongue. Big mime show for tiny audience, and the audience squealed. He stood up then and became a normal human being, looking away, bored and alone. This was essentially a display of the physiognomy by way of facial musculature and masking. It did not seem as though any of the other passengers recognized Mr. Lewis at all, and when he got off they looked at one another quizzically, as though relieved from the imposition of a madman show-off.

What was unmistakable about the Lewis performance, after all, was its open announcement of construction, its implicit indication of a private self, and its strident focus upon playing a face to a receptive looker. "This is show business!" Rousseau would have hated it, would have pulled away from the utter vulgarity of the geste—its distance from the Renaissance ethos of "distaste for theater" (Wikander xv). With his mouth and eyes, Lewis was "sawing the air." Hamlet's mentor Polonius gives the appearance of having a distaste similar to Rousseau's when he tells the young prince to be true to his "own self"; and many who play that crucial scene or teach it to students love to focus on the character's celebrated speech as a sermon urging a proper and fruitful way of living life, a way that Hamlet would apparently do well to apprehend and make his own. In short, as we are often led to believe, in his anti-theatricality Polonius is giving off a "good" message here, and much of Hamlet's trouble stems from his woeful inability to avoid "being false to any man." But Shakespeare is far craftier than this. Polonius is himself a masquerade being put on by a cheap liar, first for the audience in general and secondly for this princely audience in particular. Very soon later, we are given plenty of reason for understanding him as a model of "falseness."

If in an anti-theatrical culture performativity is false and damnable, performance taken to excess must apotheosize falsity and trouble, if not evil itself. Thus, with Al Lewis, one could think, "Wouldn't a little smiling wink have been quite enough? Why the crazy face?" And with Damon escaping we could wonder, feeling the need to see naked reality, "Isn't this a little rehearsed (that is, manufactured)? Wouldn't he fumble just a little? Wouldn't there be some slip-up?" The scenic smoothness as Bourne leaps around the tiny office seems balletic, exceedingly lubricated (long practiced until muscle knowledge takes over). Starkly contrasting is the straightforward scene work of John Wayne, who positions himself securely, gives his line, stares at his scene partner, and no more. He does not ornament his performative moment with any turn of body or gesture of face or hand that might call for the camera to linger and reveal. He does not fancy himself. But if we look at Kenneth Branagh as Hercule Poirot in *Murder on the Orient Express* (2017), we see a voluminous catalogue of facial, gestural, and locative tics, all meant to sum toward the "real" eccentricity of the character (which particular characteristic is enunciated in Agatha Christie's texts, if somewhat curtly; and developed onscreen in various incarnations, with almost religious devotion, by David Suchet, Albert Finney, Tony Randall, and Peter Ustinov—all actors whose careers suggest their eminent promise as either *ticeurs* or exaggerators of affect). But Branagh openly demonstrates demonstration. In his Poirot, a great deal of virtuosity is attributable to the elaborate—I think Rousseau would have thought pointlessly elaborate— moustache and his various ways of playing with it (as only an actor would play).

In watching *Orient Express* we wonder: is this Poirot, who shuffles and gesticulates so, an authentic fellow? Are there people like this (or were there, early in the twentieth century)? (Yet, what would we artlessly be doing pretending to travel to the twentieth century?) Or is this Poirot an artful marionette? And of Branagh: is he working properly and adroitly to construct what is effectively a complicated realism? Or is he showing off? Could he, for instance, speak more directly and with less embellishment? Could he leave the moustache alone? But of course no: the already established Poirot culture demands an expressivity that is attenuated and repetitive, precisely what Branagh is *realistically* offering. The character has taken on a life that the actor merely borrows a ticket to inhabit, this because the film is standing upon presumed memories of, and therefore reference to, earlier Poirot texts onscreen. In a like way, it would be difficult to view as "showing off" an actor's doing "To be or not to be" in what seemed a state of blue depression, there being already in the air a received typical—too typical—reading of the speech as depressive (as Richard Burton noted with irritation).

Clearly, an actor entertains a tenuous relation with the character as scripted. In any scene the character may be scripted to behave with such expressivity or without sufficient reserve, so that some hypercritical observer could disparage the moment as overinvolved. The character could suddenly become transparent, for example, revealing not only an actor beneath but an actor too flamboyant. In such a case an actor could be in process of giving a modest and faithful rendition of what is called for, yet fall prey to the accusation of pointing to himself too much: the showing off is actually part of the character. I think we have this feeling of watching what could be called affectedness in some of Gladys Cooper's scenes with Bette Davis in *Now, Voyager* (1942), yet far less in her scenes with Rex Harrison in *My Fair Lady* (1964): the business of *Voyager* flows from the writer, Casey Robinson, not Cooper. Cooper is a master performer and part of the "nakedness" of Mrs. Vale in *Voyager* comes from directed focal moments insufficient to cover the actor's blossoming talent; it is not that she protrudes but that the normal camouflage of her character temporarily, as though in a gust of wind, recedes. Yet with Cooper here, instead of believing to catch the naked actor flailing we have the transformative experience of feeling that *Mrs. Vale's* social façade drops away and we see her soul. *Mrs. Vale's* soul, not Gladys Cooper's.

We often feel that showing off is using technique to no intrinsic purpose, but what if the performer/character has purposes the audience has not previewed or yet perceived? Thus, "showing off" may be an idiosyncratic reading some viewers are sometimes prone to make, couched as an objective allegation.

3

Effacement and Allure

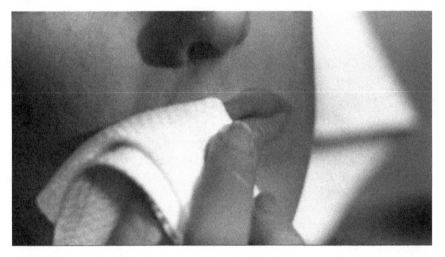

FIGURE 3 *Close-up shot of Kim Novak in* Vertigo *(Alfred Hitchcock, Paramount, 1958). Digital frame enlargement.*

An elemental truth of cinema, often reiterated and as soon forgotten: that in the theater the actor's face is knowable to only a few members of the audience, but in cinema the face is available for all.

With the invention of the close-up (most often credited to David Wark Griffith in his small 1903 film *The Gay Shoe Clerk*), it became possible for the actor's face (or, as in the case of *Clerk*, hand) to literally take over the screen. Some of the very first filmic material I watched, as a tiny child and knowing nothing of the name or content of the piece or, indeed, of cinema itself, consisted of giant faces looming radiantly before me in silvery black and white. These films could well have been from the 1930s or 1940s, even the very early 1950s. In cinema, I learned without knowing that I was learning, the face is everything. In cinema, the face can be a virtuosity itself.

Of course it is also a virtual virtuosity, because—contrary to what I thought in those early days—it is not there: not behind the screen, near the screen, actually somehow on the screen. The face is not there but it seems to be there, and in its power lies the expression and evocation of emotion, speech, momentum, intent, alignment, memory, and hope. "The great face," Stanley Cavell calls Alfred Hitchcock's revelation of Cary Grant in *North by Northwest*, in the scene where he climbs on Mt. Rushmore, that paean to great faces.[1] But faces are cinema much more than because they swim across the screen, explode, and flicker. In the earliest days of the studio, and then with notable intensiveness after 1930, management organized financial investment in motion pictures around the "star power"—read, box-office power—of principal players, and producers knew that as far as the public was concerned, the principal player was the principal player's recognizable face. More than his or her personality, more than muscles, more than shapely curves, more than athletic capacity, more even than her birthright to riches, it was the face of the star that the public came to know and adore. It was the face of the star that sold the movie. That sold movies altogether.

The facial portrait became a vital calling card, and face shots were used to dot film posters and to adorn the covers of fan magazines such as *Photoplay* (see Higashi; and McLean, "Wedding Bells"). The Hollywood face became legendary—any one of them was almost always made up and lit to seem related to others—whether hooked to the name Clark Gable or Tyrone Power, Claudette Colbert, Barbara Stanwyck, Joan Crawford, Errol Flynn, Dick Powell, Irene Dunne, Veronica Lake, or Judy Garland. It was because audiences could see the Hollywood Face as a promise of pleasures to come, and because, once the movie was unspooling, the Hollywood Face centered the action and stretched itself to form the interpersonal bonds that sealed the plot, that facial appreciation became central to moviegoing and facial construction became central to studio work. Look again at the marvelous scene in George Cukor's *A Star Is Born* (1954) when Esther Blodgett (Garland) is being remade as Vicki Lester by the erstwhile experts in the studio's makeup department, or in Hitchcock's *Vertigo* (1958) at the scene where Kim Novak's Judy Barton is having her makeup and hair altered to suit the taste of James Stewart's Scottie Ferguson. It is not only that the face, hardly only natural, must be constructed for the screen; it is that the constructed face *is* the screen when it comes to the movie business.[2]

---

[1] Cavell's piece is in his book *Themes Out of School*. See as well "A Great Face" in my *The Horse Who Drank the Sky* 62–85.

[2] These fictional cases are based in studio realities. David Halberstam writes, for instance, of Marilyn Monroe, a star whose every presence onscreen was a virtuosity in itself: "With studio help, her hair became blonder, and plastic surgery was used to make her more photogenic. Her teeth were straightened, some work was done on her nose to slim it down, and additional work

Almost all shots of film characters are made with the face turned at an angle to the lens, so that over the course of audiences' exposure to stars a certain biased view comes to be taken as natural and genuine. Encountering an actor off the screen, seeing him face-on, can be disorienting (while, of course, this is how scene partners see him most of the time). In the rare dramatic circumstances where the performer turns to face the camera directly—Gloria Swanson in that celebrated "ready-for-my-closeup" shot from *Sunset Blvd.* (1950) or Robert Montgomery's characters speaking directly to us in *Lady in the Lake* (1946)—we find the performer oddly unrecognizable, just for a moment, oddly merely human, and with those telltale features re-proportioned and made so indelible at an angle now re-set. With CinemaScope (1955 and onward) new setup styles made for new angles of linkage between performers onscreen (some of the dynamic parent-child argument scenes in Ray's *Rebel Without a Cause* [1955] are strongly illustrative), but in typical cinema before that, with the 1.33: 1 Academy ratio image, when over-the-shoulder setups were required to show both sides of a two-person conversation (that staple of film drama), viewers invariably saw beloved giant creatures at an angle. Actors worked in such a way that if they were subject to a face-on shot (there is a striking one of Charlton Heston driving his chariot in *Ben-Hur* [1959]) they would angle the head, or else, pointing the head straight forward create an angle by pointing the eyes askance. Anthony Hopkins is absolutely masterful at creating, varying, emphasizing, and shifting angularities between body placement and eyeline when his character poses in front of the camera, clear evidence of which is in *Howards End* (1992).

However the virtuosic face was turned, it aligned with audience expectations formed through earlier viewing of the same actor, earlier in the present film or in others, and through the machinations of publicity. Theaters touted the films they exhibited with photographs and lobby cards posted for passersby to ogle before paying for entry, and newspaper advertising worked through posterizations that conveyed the principal attributes not only of the story and setting, graphically through pose and line, but also of the main players, through expressive orientation of their faces (see Haralovich). Most fans who followed the trail of publicity had a reservoir of preconceptions about the stars they would pay to see, and much of the appraisal of films—"good film/bad film"—rested on the precarious connection between what the big faces did and what people watching them already expected when they came into the theater. Vision-by-expectation accounts for many structural moments in classical cinema, arranged through oft-repeated conventions (the clinch, the showdown): conventions offer at

---

was done to refinish the contours of her chin. But the studios did that with hundreds of other young women . . ." (567).

least some guarantee of success, because they have a track record. When in the late 1940s and early 1950s certain performers struck out to deviate from convention in order to produce more spontaneous (and, for them, serious) performative work—people like Montgomery Clift, James Dean, Marlon Brando, Marilyn Monroe—they could seem to be inventing cinema anew, and their every move could seem virtuosic merely because such a thing had not been seen—in this way—before. Monroe traipsing down the train platform in *Some Like It Hot* (1959); Brando's intense physicality in *A Streetcar Named Desire* (1951); Clift staring lovingly at the lens in *I Confess* (1953); Dean imitating an ambulance siren at the police department in *Rebel*.

The star's face was a composition of readily recognizable and easily interpretable expressive features, very like the face of a dear friend; but it was also smoothed and aesthetically extended by way of makeup and, most importantly, lighting, so that its relationship to everyday life was thinned and finally evaporated, its iconicity hardened. Every star was made to seem somehow unique, yet also perduring, so that films of the early career and the late could be joined as a foundation for the persona's personality. Personality was the hallmark, emphasized and stretched to such a point that the star mask became a virtuosic indication, a performance of style and attitude, self-conceit and emotion that seemed to float above mundane reality, both for viewers and for actors themselves. The actor's actual personhood— paying taxes, getting cash at the bank, dining in a restaurant—disappeared into the inscrutable forest beneath the canopy of the star image, which had constancy, brilliance, and stunning idiosyncrasy. For each star, a sense was manufactured and maintained that *this being is like no other person now, or ever*.

No other person now: now, that is at this single moment of viewing, when the star's virtuosity lights up the screen in some definite setting and with some particular accompaniment, but also in the strange and wondrous extension of present time that seems to fall back to an indecipherable eternity and to broaden itself across all the terrain of present and future consciousness. Now and forever. Jack Palance slowly dismounting in *Shane* (1953). This virtuosic magnification of quality, this heightening of viewers' experience, helps citizens drop into a state of shock when a famous virtuoso shockingly leaves the scene. People with ordinary responsibilities experience birth, growth, and death but in the popular imagination (a specific cultivation of the star system, that flowers for profit) stars exist outside of ordinary time, and their virtuosic presence is beyond both the capabilities and the limits of ordinary humanity. "By detaching the image from the person," writes Danae Clark,

> the studio could reconstruct the relation between the two into a unified subject position called the "persona." Changing the names of actors

was one way of establishing this control. By erasing an actor's previous "identity" (name, personal history), the studio could create a new image and identity. An agreement of sorts was made: in return for the actor's physical body (*as bearer of an image*), the studio would attempt to generate for her or him the wealth and social prestige of star ranking. (23; emphasis mine)

But a problem plagues the virtuosity of the star face. No part of the cinematic production, no one face, can announce itself so boldly that it enshadows everything else. Stephen Aaron notes the inherent risk that at any instant performance might fall off key; what Erving Goffman calls "calculated unintentionality" might be marred by an audience's glimpse of labor. "Maintaining the character is, in itself, a very fragile affair," writes Aaron:

It demands of the actor a series of highly complex, intrapsychic transformations. As we have seen, there is the unique problem of the performing-actor: hiding and showing at the same time. The actor's conscious fear is not that he will make a mistake but that the audience will see something it is not supposed to see, namely, his fear, his stage fright. (59)

This blossoming from the problem of showing and hiding expressly *is* the stage fright, a condition that occurs on a "stage," that is, before the eyes of watchers liable to detect anything and everything. Actors in the theater, who gesture more with their bodies than with their faces, so as to reach the distant crowd, must worry about grace, and can sense the watchers palpably watching in their presence (yet, a presence that is officially denied). Actors in cinema, by comparison, know that only the camera is watching them, but that it is the silent factotum of a great multitude. They know, too, that the face more than anything is captured on film, so that all of the muscles above the shoulders must be capable of being calmed or activated at will. A marvelous tiny moment in *Their Finest* (2016) has Bill Nighy as the fading old star Ambrose Hilliard alone in his room, practicing facial expressions before a mirror. To achieve this kind of virtuosic fluency in the face of a probing camera is a feat. Luigi Pirandello about actors, in *Shoot!*:

They feel that they, too, are slave to this strident machine, which suggests on its knock-kneed tripod a huge spider watching for its prey, a spider that sucks in and absorbs their live reality to render it up an evanescent, momentary appearance, the play of a mechanical illusion in the eyes of the public. (68–9)

And Aaron reflects that "primitive man and superstitious people are often afraid of the camera's eye" (97). The working actor is reaching into reserves of memory and feeling, surely employing a toolkit of carefully rehearsed techniques and gestures, and is thus both modern and primitive at once, both a beneficiary of inventions and tactics derived in the spirit of the technological age and a delver into the long-lost history of situations and responses. Actors are notoriously superstitious. Film actors will very commonly spit out a mantra or oath before a take—identically before *every* take. We see much of the same kind of superstitious adherence to routine with virtuosic baseball players when they come up to bat, that is, make an "entrance." Jerry Lewis apparently prepared to walk onstage by chatting with the stagehands (see Pomerance, "Twelve Memoranda").

The tension between allure and effacement is a constantly ongoing problem for actors. The more skilled and transcendent they may seem in their work the more acute is the stress. The virtuoso in any artistic field is performing something of a high-wire act, and the more elaborate his maneuverings above our heads the more precarious his position. Cinema is often able to self-reflexively make this very point. Tony Richardson's *The Entertainer* (1960) with a galvanizing performance by Laurence Olivier is a textbook. Gene Kelly's 1956 *Invitation to the Dance* begins with an episode called "Circus," in which an aerialist (Igor Youskevitch, from the Ballets Russes de Monte Carlo) is in love with a circus performer (Claire Sombert), who is also yearned for, ardently, by a clown (Kelly). In something of an homage to the ancient ritual of the Priest of Nemi described by Sir James George Frazer in *The Golden Bough,* the high-wire artist is challenged on the wire at a critical point by the not-sufficiently-capable Clown, who plunges to his death. One of the many pleasing ironies of this little ballet (with music by Jacques Ibert) is Kelly's seeming athletic deficiency, since already by the mid-1950s he had defined himself as the supremely athletic dancer-performer in Hollywood cinema: this turn on the wire was a self-declaration by the dancer of his own terrors and difficulties, that one does not merely *effect* the kind of athletic dancing we keep seeing onscreen (in *The Pirate* [1948], *An American in Paris* [1951], *Singin' in the Rain* [1952]) but *labors* intensively to achieve and maintain it. Kelly and other virtuosi show off their talents and achieve a glowing allure, but in order to produce "unintentionality" they must self-efface to a degree. In this little sequence, for instance, Kelly never uses his facial expression to exhibit self-regard or self-estimation, pride for a bodily achievement; it is his Clown's emotional life that he shows. The virtuosic actor always seems much too busy in energizing the continuity of performance to pause for consideration of his or her actions. The performance is all-consuming. For the virtuoso, who draws viewers in to special depths, the performance might seem even to devour the performing self.

Allure draws us to the performer's face: that and its notably heightened powers of being and expressing (Martha Raye's or Jerry Lewis's mouth; Barrymore's voice; Carole Lombard's radiant face; Lucille Ball's hair;

Tom Cruise's teeth). Cinematic being and expression, after the close-up, re-originate in the face not the body. And with self-effacement it is the face that is tucked away, moved "into the wings," the actor withdrawing presence by moving out of camera range or, even more potently, suffering the face to freeze: go "blank to action" by being unmoved and unmoving, backgrounded, neutralized. The star cannot always be spotlit, after all; there must be reflective moments when the audience is permitted to catch the breath.

It is also possible to think of effacement—tuning down the face—as, finally, an indication of the screen itself, our umbilical connection to the art, the thing we choose not to notice when we watch movies, and that Michel Chion has called *la toile trouée*. Because of the allure of the faces it holds, the screen has gained our orientation and attention, has beckoned while being but a part of the darkened cube into which we have inserted ourselves, seems to have come alive. What, then, if glowing and radiant upon that screen, shining on that screen, that screen that is effacement itself, there should arise a form viewers would expect to find alluring, when it is instead as empty as the screen itself—an emptiness posed upon an emptiness, an invisible thought in an invisible shade? The gaze withheld, as with Cary Grant in his first appearance in *Notorious* (1946), where we get the back of the head.

Affirming the vital expressive powers of the eyes, George Toles reflected to me a personal observation I find profoundly meaningful: "I suspect that if I were talking to James Stewart in 1959 at a table situation like this, I would not be able to find his eyes." He went on to say that a kind of opacity exists, a screen, indeed, that prevents us from fully and unconditionally getting at the performer's gaze. Some actors work by maintaining this screen, which finally becomes a kind of self-reflection for them, a conscious awareness of *self in scene,* and acknowledgment and hiding of the operations necessary for performance. But some actors open themselves to their scene partners, offering a streaming presence. When eyes meet eyes in this way, a living passion is produced, emanating outward with such profusion that it can be caught by the audience. Frank Sinatra achieves this emanation in the train duet with Janet Leigh in *The Manchurian Candidate* (1962); Montgomery Clift with great bravery in *From Here to Eternity* (1953); Ingrid Bergman torn within, in *Stromboli* (1950) and *Gaslight* (1944). And, today, Andrew Garfield (trying to put one over on his professor in *Lions for Lambs* [2007], suffering mortally in *Breathe* [2017], failing to understand another culture in *Silence* [2017]). When eyes are revealed time seems to stop.

The eyes unlock the face, make the face take shape. Eyes in the absence of the face are always seeking, always hungry, never at home. Consider this: Christiane, a young woman who has been in a car accident caused by her surgeon father, is sequestered in his estate and operated on by him, using face transplants taken from kidnapped young women. In the end, her eyes

shine through the plain pallid slick mask that is all her face has become.
This is Georges Franju's *Eyes Without a Face* (1960), released in France
nine days before the inauguration of John Fitzgerald Kennedy, eight months
before *Psycho*. The girl can have no future, no present. She has become a
mannequin, this tale being the inverse of *Pygmalion*, in which a desperate
man made a sculpture come real. Here a desperate man makes a real person
into a sculpture. Is Franju's Dr. Genessier a monster—one might say, a mere
monster—another Moreau with beasts, a Dr. Frankenstein playing at the
boundaries of flesh, when he plunges into his horrendous experiments? And
if inside the narrative we are brought to a strange and forbidding place,
cinema itself has become strange and forbidding, a zone where, as Adam
Lowenstein avers, "modernization offers no real escape" (40).

The horror of *Eyes Without a Face* is a compound one. We are confronted,
first, with the agony of the injured women, with the horrible mutilations of
the young people being used as *materiel,* with the naziesque physician, the
crisscrossing desperations and sterile surround, the perversion of familiality,
the utter violation of femaleness, unconscionable in itself but set in the
greater context of moral violation beyond measure. She is condemned
to "recognize both herself and the dead she is responsible for in her own
disfigured face," writes Lowenstein (43), discussing the mutilated Christiane
as an allegory of the Holocaust and the Occupation and recalling Sartre's
postwar judgment, "Now when we raise our heads and look into the mirror
we see an unfamiliar and hideous reflection: ourselves" (43, citing Sartre
xxviii).

But another, deeper horror lies beneath what the story tells and shows.
When, usually, we watch the star face at play on the screen we are always
seeing a rhythmic alternation between the polarities of allure and effacement.
The face draws us to recognize, to adore, to patiently attend, to move across
in languid, careless, polymorphous play, but then in tranquility to wonder
over and question. The actor swims in the river of the character's expressive
feeling, but must also become still, to breathe, to re-attune to the charged
current of commitment but also ward off the fear that leads to overacting,
the blotching stain. The stillness in which the actor's momentary self and the
character's narrative truth are united is a kind of effacement, a losing of the
celebrated face in the name of a great search. In his disturbing vision, Franju
produces that stillness, that effacement, making indication of it not only
inside the film, by the twists of the story, but on the surface of film itself, by
presenting in star position not a star's but a featureless face through which
the hungry eyes never stop staring.

4

Follow the Money

FIGURE 4 *Advertising poster for* Ninotchka *(Ernst Lubitsch, MGM, 1939). Album / Alamy Stock Photo.*

Until the mid-1950s or shortly thereafter—the time, roughly, of Cecil B. DeMille's *The Ten Commandments* (1956)—audiences went to the movies to see stars. Stars, not tricks, messages, or ideas. Nor moral tales. Nor production values. Nor some albeit interesting node in the history of American culture or filmmaking.

Not only were star names featured in extra-large font in advertisements (printed: there were no other kinds of movie advertisements at this time), often, as in *Ninotchka* (1939) above the title; and not only were star faces wonderfully stretched to exaggerative effect in the drawings (typically artists' representations, not photographs) that went along; but movie reviews featured judgments about star performances (then, as now, but far more centrally since aside from telling the plot there seemed little else to say). In such discourse as existed about films—mostly until the 1960s a casual trade of experiences after seeing a film, part of longer conversations with friends and intimates—commentary was offered about how stars performed in notably impressive or disturbing scenes; what they wore and how healthy or beautiful they looked; the exotic places they (their characters) visited. The movie was a star vehicle through and through.[1]

Star fantasies are bluntly referenced in Nicholas Ray's *Rebel Without a Cause* (1955): when Jim Stark (James Dean) first shows up at his new high school he passes Plato (Sal Mineo) combing his hair in front of an open locker inside the door of which he has affixed a star shot of Alan Ladd. Soon later Plato will admire Jim in a similar way, this gesture having a double meaning, since not only does the diegetic Plato admire the diegetic Jim but the very young New York actor Mineo adulated the older, magnetic Dean. Metaphorically, the planetarium in the Griffith Park Observatory stands in for the ineffable heavens, as the lecturer (Ian Wolfe) makes plain over and over, but also for the movie business, emphatically the movie screen which, like the night sky, is studded with stars. In one shot Ray allows the "night sky" projected on the planetarium ceiling to fill the screen, so that the "sky" and screen become coextensive.

Since movie stars, particularly their faces, were virtuosities not only in their respective talents but also in Hollywood's business model, they were intentionally cultivated as principle resources in studio film production. It was the star's face the viewer was paying to see, with the storyline functioning as hardly more than a string from which to hang the star images.[2] Lobby cards and vitrine photographs that touted films, as well as advertising, completely eschewed the kind of macro-close-up facial images to which one would be treated in the film itself: to see these, the face made gigantic and superhuman and desirable, one paid money.

Many films in the classical period (as now) relied on genre formulas: melodramas, westerns, police procedurals, war films, sci-fi films, crime films. Genre formations made film production smoother, less expensive than it might have been had each film been a wholly unique creation, because

---

[1]Notwithstanding the work of filmmakers who used stars in order to make significant philosophical observations about the world: Fritz Lang, F. W. Murnau, Alfred Hitchcock, Yasujiro Ozu, Nicholas Ray, Michelangelo Antonioni, Ingmar Bergman, for some examples. The work of most of these did not circulate in North America, by and large, until the early 1960s; and someone like Hitchcock was seen as little more than the "Master of Suspense."

[2]When travel for location shooting became popular (by the late 1950s), it was customary in studio filmmaking to return to the soundstage for star close-ups. There, lighting—the most invaluable tool—could be controlled and shaped carefully and deliberately; a scene could be shot without distracting location sound or expensive insurance costs; stars' labor on location (a matter of contract negotiation) could be usefully reduced; and the studio's in-house experts in star photography could play a role. Backgrounds were often supplied through rear projection.

plots could be rehashed and minimally modified, sets and costumes reused, well-learned technical moves repeated, editing patterns copied, advertising predesigned for an audience that was already primed and prepared. The technicians who designed, wrote, edited, and scored films knew the expected patterns for different types of scene and could easily and swiftly complete work assignments based on earlier experience. Once one was involved in a Greto Garbo picture,[3] for instance, one knew that the ideal cinematographer was William Daniels, and knew, too, well in advance of principal cinematography, that he would be likely to light the Garbo face (to *create* the Garbo face) in particular ways to draw attention to the smoothness—the snowiness—of the cheeks and the sharpness of the mouth. It was Garbo and only Garbo the audience was hungry to see even though in the hands of directors like George Cukor or Josef von Sternberg stories could resonate. But the Garbo presence was what audiences carried away, the feel of closeness to her, notwithstanding that for her adorers Garbo was only an entity called "Garbo." The Garbo beneath "Garbo" was unknown, unmet, uncherished from start to finish: a blank canvas of sorts upon which every member of the audience could limn a distinctive portrait. What was the film you saw last night? "Oh, that new Garbo thing." On the set people called it "the new Garbo thing," too.

It is interesting that so many crime and detective stories, at least since Howard Hawks's *The Big Sleep* (1946) and surely including motion pictures and television productions today, involve agents of law and order searching for *de facto* "stars," that is, persons of particular, perhaps notorious interest. Using a panoply of instruments of surveillance and detection[4] the protagonist and his friends try to sift through the confusing mess of a huge population (exciting dramas are set in highly populated areas such as London, Los Angeles, and Hong Kong) in order to find one person who seduces attention by virtue of peculiar action, definitive relation to other character(s), or recorded police history detected on some computer screen. Here, then, the fascinating villain: Alan Rickman in *Die Hard* (1988), Gale Sondergaard in *The Letter* (1940). Audiences participate in the organized search, the target helpfully elevated in some way (elevated even if the role is played by a character actor working on a day contract). But the narrative is

---

[3]Garbo is not the only case in which a star could alone be the basis of a genre, a phenomenon that dissolved in the mid-1950s, when many actors took to developing their careers by *not* playing the same type again and again. The "Garbo picture" had its own qualities; as did the Marlene Dietrich picture, the Irene Dunne Picture, the John Wayne picture, and very largely the Cary Grant picture, among other forms.

[4]Some recent television shows, like *Scandal* (2012–), imply secret agencies practicing surveillance in a wholesale manner, gathering and storing records of all telephone calls across the United States; or global positioning information on anyone, anywhere, anytime. And many productions, such as *The Blacklist* (2013), involve "experts" who can rapidly find and project chemical analyses, fingerprint scans, personnel dossiers and the like on massive screens.

pyramidical, and at its apex stands one and only one crucially identifiable agent, one and only one principal biography, history, and set of motives isolated and magnified: the noble hero. The presumption has long been that audiences don't come to the cinema to see the villain, fascinating as he or she might be.[5] Yet the myth reified in this narrative pattern is that the villain is a charged and interesting personality, a warped psychology, a ruined childhood proto-monster now grown out of control. Producers of cinema and television work *against* that myth. They searched in the earliest days of film, and are still searching now, not for persons as personalities but for *the face*: a face that instantly rings a bell, instantly seems appropriate to a prescripted scenario. Glenn Close in *101 Dalmatians* (1996); Jack Palance in *Shane* (1953); Judith Anderson in *Rebecca* (1940); Jack Davenport in the *Pirates of the Caribbean* films. The producer's scrutiny was aimed at finding the right face, either in the portfolios of agents pressing at his door or out there, by happenstance, in the wide wide world (Schwab's Pharmacy at Sunset and Crescent Heights). And having "discovered" that face, convert its owner into a star by way of the star treatment, the star surface, the star mode of presentation (so carefully shaped and controlled).

The apparent supreme self-confidence of the movie star was due to a structured mode of public appearance, facilitated by strict control of situations in which the public could have access to the performer. At each instant of behavior before the lens, the star was prone to suffering fear of the sort anyone might experience when subjected to scrutiny. She had been neither born nor educated in early life to think of herself as an object of intensive study, after all, or to feel obligated to be in presentation mode for extended periods of time: having an adored aunt pinch your cute cheek is one thing, having uncountable strangers scrutinizing your every breath is another. The many-eyed monster was out there, would always be out there, picking at flaws and raving about—well: here was the rub. The actor in a successful performance is often in no position to know what it is that made for success; what it is that people liked. The star with a large audience can see by the trade reports that a picture is wildly successful, even that he or she is being touted as a major reason for the success, without having information about what (what *exactly*) the applause was for. What gestures, styles, mannerisms, postures, vocal tones, then, to repeat next time? The actor in a star role must take direction, and (alone or with help) choose the right scripts; and the history of Hollywood movie-making has legion examples of cases where this didn't happen.

Being before the lens is dangerous, the moment of acting a dangerous moment, and the virtuosic turn is dangerous supremely. To guard against

---

[5]In other genres there are notable exceptions: horror films present lovable monsters, melodramas have truly execrable villains but they are often played by stars.

falling from a height, every actor who is soaring has a personal method or talisman, mantra or rule-book. At first, relaxation comes; but after years and years of walking the tightrope the fear swells. Find a face in the mirror and subject it to the monster. When the monster pulls away make arrangements to cover the loss. The editor can cut around such retreats most of the time, and may be obliged to by stars powerful because they have brought their producers money. On the stage or the soundstage, the actor herself must work hard to learn how to manage fighting the fearsome monster, because every gesture of battle is a giveaway of the monster's presence, that is, a message to the audience that the star knows they are there watching; but doing nothing only exacerbates the sense of perilous height. In all forms of actorial display, the audience must never ever be told that it is there: *even when the actor turns and speaks to it.* Even when the actor, speaking, pointing, says, "You . . ." The "You" is only a character we play as we watch, a screen behind which we hide ourselves. The viewer can be told *someone* is there, *someone who is like you,* but not actually, definitively, you. In much the same way, as I write this I am addressing someone very much like you.

The stars were the precious jewels, at any rate, and precious jewels stand out from their settings. Profiting on an investment, therefore, meant having the virtuoso photographed apart from the surround, no matter how intriguing or exotic the surround. Until the late 1950s there were very few films using setting, extras, or other production features in so spectacular a way they could possibly steal attention from the face. DeMille's *Ten Commandments* was very costly for its time, for instance, but Charlton Heston and Yul Brynner dwarfed the pyramids. But by the 1960s, say with Robert Wise's *West Side Story* (1961), one began to see the story and its placement of action, the set or location, the realism of costume and makeup, the supporting players in their character roles—all in synchrony and tension with the star performances; all helping the stars shrink, the star faces becoming more and more like the faces in the surrounding crowd. In 1958, Charlton Heston had starred (with Janet Leigh, Akim Tamiroff, and Orson Welles) in Welles's *Touch of Evil,* and here, although the setting of the tawdry Mexican border town absorbed a signal amount of the evocative black-and-white photography, still the star performances are continually drawn to the foreground, Heston's no less than Welles's itself. This was the 1950s. In *Ben-Hur*'s (1959) lengthy chariot race sequence, an important transitory moment between 1950s and 1960s American cinema, balancing the face against the setting was a challenge. The action is deftly cut between (a) portrait shots of the star Charlton Heston and supporting player Stephen Boyd, (b) long shots of the chariots in movement, (c) close shots of the beautiful horses straining for the lead, and (d) occasional long shots of the arena, the vast crowd, the brilliant sunshine streaming down. But with the movies of the 1930s and 1940s, it was almost always a full concentration on the star persona, the star *face,* that organized the work. By the late 1990s and 2000s, the star presence is usually inutile unless attached to a fabulously complex rhythmic, scenic, and propulsive arrangement: a clockwork.

Praised when a film went well, blamed when it failed, the star figured in a central formulaic relation between face and tone. Audrey Hepburn: the gazing waif. Bette Davis, the superior schoolmarm. Melvyn Douglas, the suave meditator. Bruce Willis, the smart alec. Gene Tierney, keeper of secrets. Kristen Stewart, magnetic magician. The system takes up and creates the invocation of qualities that, framed and specially lit, cultivate our desire. We all turn to the light. When the body was principal in film, light hit the face. When special effects are principal to a film, light is made to emanate from situations, not characters, and the setting becomes the new face. The constructed star's inherent virtuosity, a special glow but a manufactured one we count on, very like the inherent virtuosity of special-effects planets, space fights, and monstrosities, differs in its fundamental qualities from the unanticipated moment of virtuosic performance that always comes as a gift, not as part of the contract. Money does not—cannot—pay for the virtuosic moment, however close the bank.

5

"I Am Acting"

FIGURE 5 *Gary Cooper (l.) and Fredric March in* Design for Living *(Ernst Lubitsch, Paramount, 1933).*
Digital frame enlargement.

Typically, the actor considers himself or herself "an artist who possesses a
mysterious artistic gift setting him apart from all other people. Possessing
this gift, he should be free from control by outsiders who lack it. The gift
is something which cannot be acquired through education; the outsider,
therefore, can never become a member of the group." So writes Howard S.
Becker about the jazz musician as artist, thus invoking a close cousin of the
actor, who also has a gift and who also recognizes "outsiders" (85–6). The
actor's outsiders buy tickets, become fans, are to be addressed through the
extremely recognizable mask of a famous self. In stage acting, actors and
audience are, in the end, merely people who in like fashion are temporarily
living at an address (the actor in character actually being, breathing, passing

time with his viewers), but the fiction maintained in the theater is that through immeasurable and inconceivable power an invisible wall separates them one group from the other; they do not touch, they do not mutually know the other, they are and are not alive together. Moreover, it is through the audience's willful participation that the stage line is maintained: desiring contact, the viewer exercises restraint, this exercise being a vital part of the wonder of the moment. The audience, at any rate, does not (usually) cross the stage line. And if, as, for example, in the Broadway musical *Hair* (1968), audience members are hauled up willingly onstage, ostensibly to participate in the action, they find that they do not stand in the same gravity, and flaunt badges of the same membership, as the actors around them.[1] In cinema, production personnel and audiences never routinely share the same space, but a space is imagined and framed for the audience's participation, and the placement of the camera shapes that space in relation to the diegesis. Film actors are alone in their own space, always already. If in the theater the threat of disintegration is energized through the continuing physical possibility and staving off of contact, in cinema disintegration of performance can occur not because a proximate audience comes too close but because an audience positioned at an ineffable distance, that cannot be summoned to come nearer, is not apparently invoked in the actor's imagination—that is, not played to.

A conviction widely shared by actors, and often so thoroughly taken for granted it gains little open acknowledgment in their conversation with one another (and in interviews they give to outsiders), is that whilst one performs one should never use such magnified declarative and gestural force as would draw attention *to the fact of the performance.* "I am playing to you but I am not screaming that I am playing to you." One should never be caught at covering a "true" civilian self. The open-faced impostor is always a painted figure: painted with makeup so as to make technically possible the exaggeration of facial gestures for readability at a great distance; painted with too much spirit, overflowing embarrassingly; painted with the bloated gusto that declares self-consciousness and provokes the viewer's shame. But also: painted by someone who paints, the actor himself or herself, the make-up artist, finally the Spirit of Production who never takes an eye off the audience and its expectations. Painted by an agent of the audience, then: the audience that must never be invoked or seen.

To declare oneself an actor, while in the process of being one—to "give the wink," as actors say—is thought ruinous. Professionalism dissolves. The

---

[1] A condition that may have applied as well with the Living Theatre performances (from 1947) of Julian Beck and Judith Malina and troupe, and the Open Theater work (1963–1973) of Joseph Chaikin and his collaborators, who would occupy audience space quite as readily as stage space.

scene collapses, if only for a split second—but a split second is enough. Watchers lose their delicate touch with the character who charmed them, a figure now, suddenly, shockingly, replaced by no more than an everyday stranger crassly paid to erect that character. Since the backstage or off-camera zone, with all its properties and furnishings, is itself declarative evidence of guyed-up performance within it, it must be kept hidden and inviolate. Thus the disruption produced if the off-camera world leaks into the pictorial frame.[2] While living in front of the audience through, and in the name of characters, actors as workers live far away. Keeping cloistered their backstage or off-camera lives—what is true for them beyond the perceptible confines of a clear-cut performative boundary—actors generally attempt to secure for their presentations the imprimatur of the real, real even if made seriously, avowedly dramatic. Since the facet we see of the character seems to be seeing only what is enacted before her eyes, her eyes and what audience members' eyes can see that her eyes can see, she is, as much as audiences are, blocked from detecting the support structure that facilitates that enacted seeing. As she believes in it *audiences believe in it*, and for them, as apparently for her, it is the truth. The truth, at least in the moment of perception, when acting does its alchemical work.[3]

However:

There come moments when a particular act might, to be completed, require self-acknowledgment and when the stage/camera boundary must knowingly and artfully be compromised for the best effect. At such moments we may find a charading actor openly giving the signal "I am acting" to other characters, perhaps to the viewer as well, and thus producing a fascinating dilemma for the actor at work and an even more fascinating one for those of us who watch. Should the viewer acknowledge the signal as such, in this way subjecting the entire fictional structure to compromise, yet a compromise that would resolve itself inside the drama? Or should the signal be treated as private, as disattendable: professionally private, as when one performer cues another in such a way that no one else is offered a view; or dramaturgically private, as, for example, in the soliloquy (about which, more to follow), where the actor bluntly addressing the audience openly confirms his knowledge of their presence, and thus his knowledge that his status in front of them is that of the sort of person who would be talking to an audience, in short, an actor.

---

[2]In *They Might Be Giants* (1971), for one example, a somewhat elaborate diegetic fantasy is broken into by a stray boom microphone dipping into frame. In the early days of traveling mattes, a thin line (the *minus*) would surround the matted-in figure, and be detectable to those wishing to find it.

[3]In cases where audiences or other characters see something one character does not see, the *not-seeing* is taken just as seriously by those who watch, and what is not seen is taken as true for the moment.

Reference to the performative self, made openly and intentionally, is inherently destabilizing. Hamlet disparagingly bellows about the Chief Player, for instance, "What's Hecuba to him, or he to Hecuba/ That he should weep for her?" (II.2.1631–2), but in doing this he positions the Player as real in himself, an actual old thespian arrived at Elsinore (even though he is, in Hamlet's estimation, a fake, like all actors who invent thin nothings and pretend credence to them) and at the same time, since he is speaking this to the paying viewers, positions himself as outside the Player in two key ways. First, more authentic than a mere watcher he is a veritable critic of acting, and a critic who happily lives in the world of fictional Denmark. But at the same time he is no citizen of Denmark at all, he is a familiar of ours (since he can direct himself to us), a figure who lives in the fictional zone, the same place as we temporarily but with full commitment inhabit.

Lives in the same place—yes, here in the arena of the drama: Elsinore, the Wild West, the pirate village, Middle Earth. But also, therefore, here, right here, where viewers are watching. Watching for real. If in some sense it is the onlooker in us he speaks to—that personage, that familiar we "become" while engaged in the drama—in another he also stands back as the critic, and by listening to his critique, though we are strangers we become critics along with him, agreeing that the Player is a bit of a fool, if kind-hearted and committed to his foolishness. (There is no way for us to disagree without losing the thread!) To the extent that Hamlet tells us to, as it were, "watch this man evaluatively, the way I am watching him," he treats the Actor character not as such but as an actor, an actor in the way that the person playing Hamlet is an actor. Thus he is acknowledging acting; acknowledging that the Player is acting but also that *he is, too*, that he owns the identity of actor, the selfsame identity as is owned by the person playing him. If he is as much an actor as *his actor*, at this instant, *he is that actor*, effectively. Theatergoers, who recognize "play," "stage," and "script" know they are in the presence of actors (while onlookers do not [see Goffman, *Frame Analysis* ch. 5]). That he might be addressing us in both these ways, as Hamlet the Prince (in whom we believe) and as Hamlet our theatergoing friend (with whom we are skeptical), through speedy alternation, does not change the issue: even by fluctuating he announces "I am acting." "Acting sometimes," after all, means acting altogether. In the very fluctuation we take notice of the actor energizing the movement.

Certainly the confession "I am acting" can be sent out as an advance warning—Hamlet confiding to Horatio that he plans shortly to be putting on "an antic disposition": keep an eye on me, you will see that I change into an actor putting on a false "I." Then, at least when that false "I" comes on, we recognize that we are watching someone we were advised about, who claims by his every word and gesture, as we were told he would, "I am acting"; and Shakespeare has arranged this whole thing as a drama, so that this claimer will be . . . an actor! The open confession might happen *in medias res*—John Barrymore's "bearded old gentleman" on the railway platform in *Twentieth Century* (1934), at first only a senile dotard but, because he is on camera just a little too long speaking at a little too great a length, recognizable soon enough as Oscar Jaffe in masquerade, and then of course as Barrymore masquerading as the masquerader.

Since virtuosic performance works by standing out—if there is nothing exceptional about the performative moment it is hardly virtuosic—there is something about it always that may well offer the signal "I am acting," unless the performer takes special pains to hold back that signal, for instance, leaping swiftly to some bit of business that distracts attention and makes the viewer hurtle forward (Tommy Lee Jones in *The Fugitive* [1993]), or playing dramatically pungent moments with a calculated casualness, even dullness, that covers technique by apparently making it dissolve away (Glenn Close in *Fatal Attraction* [1987]).

The signal "I am acting" is structural. It points to the play-within-the-play. "I am acting" means, "I am *now* standing on a platform doing a performance that I was not doing before (when I was not to be understood, performing, as doing a performance); and so *this* is the performance, nicely framed *within the grosser event taking place all around more naturally*." It can also be desirable that audiences should identify this mini-fiction of performance-within-performance, and also the very explicit acting that comprises it, only retroactively, as has become customary in much action drama where a stunning sequence occurs *before* we are let in on the "backstage" secret that it was all a setup, a fiction-within-the-fiction, a play-within-the-play (a textbook example being David Mamet's *The Spanish Prisoner* [1997]).

While the play-within-the-play is an openly declarative formula for self-acknowledged performance, a related but different situation is to be found when characters don't expressly put on their masks as we watch, don't expressly turn to the camera as Michael Caine does in *Alfie* (1966)—dancing out that turn—but instead offer us their superlative work surreptitiously. The frame in which their acting is visible seems to be unknown to, or unrecognized by, them. This is virtuosic acting that does not self-indicate; indeed, the actor's wink at the viewer might not emanate directly from him or her at all.

In the opening meeting-cute scene of Ernst Lubitsch's glorious *Design for Living* (1933) Miriam Hopkins has entered a railway carriage where two old chums, Fredric March and Gary Cooper, are dozing side by side, head to head. She sits across from them, swiftly opens up her sketchbook, and begins to draw. Close shots of the boys' sweet but goofily out of touch faces from her vantage point. She, by contrast, is a paradigm of optical acuity, not only having open eyes but using them to seize a vision for posterity. She draws extremely well (we will soon examine her delightful sketchbook) but knows how to scout with her eyes and snatch with her hand (evidencing that observation of Balzac's that artistry is tied to a "quick grasp" [Benjamin 41]).

This female optical acuity is contrasted onscreen by the models' dopey slow-wittedness. Pretty to look at, these two are hopeless in a pinch. Lubitsch has classical rigor: Hopkins's smart gaze will have heroic ramifications as the film winds on; and the two young men will never see anything as quickly, deeply, or tellingly as she does.

This sleep routine plays out precarious circumstances, since the boys do not know and do not dream they will meet this girl who is already meeting them. What could happen if and when one or both of them awoke to the reality we already see? If a spy would detect signs the observed subject does not wish or intend to emit, a voyeuse detects signs the subject does not realize he is emitting. Because she is working her vision in a territory outside of what they know to be their performance space, their consciousness, this female is a voyeuse. The pleasing irony here, offered by Lubitsch for our inspection, lies in the fact that one can still perform while sleeping, or while "sleeping," as long as an audience is placed to watch.

Hopkins, at any rate, soon wearies and slides into a nap herself. A titillating, late pre-Code, sexual possibility (of a ménage) spices the action as Cooper wakes up, sees the pretty girl, and nudges his chum. March swiftly tidies himself, makes himself look "the presentable young man," Cooper directly following suit. Now *they* are in *her* backstage, a musical repetition of the earlier irony for clarity and emphasis: to be enjoying someone's privacy when they don't know it.[4] Backstage of Hopkins now, the boys may eagerly finger her sketchbook—it is something of a secret trove, like the purse of the girl on the New York subway being fingered by Richard Widmark in *Pickup on South Street* (1953)—slowly uncovering, of all things, a pot-bellied Napoléon who proceeds, page by page, to lose his clothing. March and Cooper eagerly pleasure themselves with this "Emperor's New Clothes" routine, emphatically turning forward to what promises to be Napoléon stark naked. March even hungrily licks his fingers before flipping the page. But instead of Napoléon nude they find . . . themselves, snoring together, framed as in a cinematic double close-up.

Let us return to our memory of an earlier moment of the scene: was Fredric March really asleep, and Gary Cooper with him, as they lay shoulder to shoulder with eyes shut? I mean to ask, were they sleeping *in actuality*, as the camera turned. Was Lubitsch himself a voyeur, and had March and Cooper, exhausted by long work that day, snuck off to this corner of the set for a catnap so that catching a glimpse the director whispered to his cameraman to hurry and snag the shot? If we think casually about March

---

[4]Cinema is filled with repetitions of this trope for ironic, dramatic, suspenseful, or joyous purposes. See Richard Todd examining the desk in Marlene Dietrich's apartment in *Stage Fright* (1950); 'Tippi' Hedren checking out the drawer of Mariette Hartley's desk in *Marnie* (1964); Melvyn Douglas on the telephone discovering who his wife really is in *Two-Faced Woman* (1941); or any heist film.

and Cooper sleeping with Hopkins's Gilda seizing the moment to sketch them before they wake, the voyeuristic idea of spying on sleepers—Gilda spying (by way of shots intercut); us spying on her spying—may hardly seem strange in itself, indeed may hardly seem like voyeurism. But what if March and Cooper, and later Hopkins, only *mock up* sleep by giving the artful appearance of surrendering control? What if they are acting? (Because if any one of these people is not *actually cat-napping,* that person is pretending to be asleep for our delight.) It would seem as we watch the "sleeping" March and Cooper, and then the "sleeping" Hopkins, that they are confessing, telling us, as actors, "We are acting sleep," a dictum that would liberate us from the charge of voyeurism in appreciating cinema. (To watch a sleeper sleeping is often thought to be stealing a view.) We would no longer be prying into privacies, watching real sleepers sleeping,[5] but would instead be watching performance, quite as in narrative displays we always do.

Let us focus on Fredric March and consider this last possibility, that, accomplished actor, he has *created the impression of* Tom sleeping by pretense, very skillful pretense; by playing possum on camera. What in that possibility would prove valuable to the spectator who embraced it? If March isn't really sleeping but acting—March the actor, not his character— he is putting his action up for view so that our watching it becomes both acceptable and morally right. Further, since, with eyes closed feigning sleep, he doesn't see us seeing (the film actor never sees us, but he does see our agent, the camera), since he isn't watching us watching, we may feel a special comfort catching an actor who is proclaiming "I am acting" in apparent contravention of all the rules of the game, because he is apparently not watching us (the camera) catching him saying it. "Watch me hamming it up!" Here is a kind of protection for our sacred pleasure, the pleasure we often steal; and for relaxed room in which to conjecture. We know, for instance, that March's declared acting relieves any concern about actuality, in this case the supposition, at this point recognized as false, that an estimable actor like Fredric March actually became tired and fell asleep during a take. We can recognize that it is only by thinking the actor thoroughly unprofessional— he is the sort who falls asleep on the job—that is, by having a pejorative consciousness of him, that the thought of March really sleeping could make logical sense, and his silent vow, "I am acting" legitimizes our certification of him as *non*-unprofessional. Indeed, not only is March not actually asleep

---

[5] I leave untreated here the interesting philosophical question of whether prying or infringement of privacy is truly involved when we watch a sleeper sleep: whether such a person is always, of necessity, in private space. We are all aware that we do not disappear from view when we sleep, but that, away from the everyday in our personal zone, we are nevertheless physically visible to outsiders; that, asleep, we can always at least potentially be on show. Another way to say this: that we cannot see ourselves (I do not mean dream ourselves) does not mean other people can't see us.

but instead we are encouraged to note his gesture here as a tiny performative *cadenza* in which, magnificently exceeding the norm, and stepping out gracefully on a dangerous limb, he can do something actors don't typically do—close his eyes at the lens. Here then is the much-recognized Fredric March doing a fabulous trick, being fully awake *but pretending sleep.* (The somnambulist of course is fully asleep but pretends to be awake.)

As most everyone knows how easy it is to do this trick, a child's game, yet a construction nevertheless, here, we note, is an esteemed performer playing that child's game, feigning "sleep," but in this case as commitment to, not escape from, his professional labor. As March performs we can know him performing—"What you see isn't real, it is an act"—yet remain caught up, completely caught up, in the performance. As Tom Gunning has put it, "I *know,* but I *see.*" And as to a grown adult wearing the guise of a child, I am reminded of listening as a child myself to the great Artur Rubinstein playing, as encore, the "Twinkle twinkle little star" variations, *Ah, vous dirai-je, maman,* by Mozart. Easy as pie, one might think.

But to continue, a half twist:

Laying Fredric March aside and picking up the Tom he becomes: March's Tom, our sleeping Tom, could be *feigning sleep* whilst we take him to be sleeping really. We *do* take him, and Gary Cooper's George, to be sleeping really—really diegetially—since the joke of Hopkins's Gilda snatching sketches seems to us empty if they are conscious, but let me emphasize: *seems to us.* In taking Tom to be sleeping really we could in fact be duped. (If March can feign, are we to think Tom less human than March and less capable feigning too?)

Tom could be feigning sleep, yet the tendency for viewers watching the scene is to deny this possibility. Tom is *really* asleep, and *it is March, and only March, who is feigning.*

There are two distinct ways this awake March feigning a sleeping Tom here announces, "I am acting." First, quite normatively, through Tom's simple, direct presence: that the character is believably here before us, not a work in progress: a Tom, in fact this Tom, this Tom who looks like March *but is not* March (because he is Tom): "I, March, am putting up what you, the audience, witness being put up, that is, sleeping Tom, or, more basically, Tom (who happens at this moment to be asleep)." The very continuing presence of Tom sleeping, then, is a continuing confession of the presence of Tom at all, and a statement from March, "I am acting." Because Tom can be present only if March is acting him. March is acting whenever we perceive Tom (because—this point cannot be emphasized enough—without March *there is no Tom).* This formula is in regard to any actor's creation of any state of being: awake, asleep, inebriated, anxious, tortured, in love.

Then secondly: "I am acting" (claims March) referring not to Tom's existence but to Tom's sleep (the sleep that is only "sleep"). Tom's perceived behavior of the moment is being enacted, not merely being, because in order for Tom to merely *be,* March need only sit in front of the camera. "I am acting not just the fact that this guy exists but also the fact that he is asleep, *and also,* therefore, the way a person like this would sleep when and if he were sleeping." March is acting Tom, but Tom in particular action: Tom sleeping.

Again, just for clarity: I am leaving entirely unelaborated at present the character Tom's possible craftiness, that possibly March is faking a faking Tom. No, no: let us continue with the assumption that March must be faking a genuine Tom. The type and style of sleeping that Tom is doing, as "acted" by March with such fidelity to form, instantly invokes ways of acting awake. And this raises the interesting, if here untreated, issue of characters' apparent consciousness in almost all film scenes, as related to the waking consciousness of the performer. Are the character and actor both conscious, and conscious in the same exact way? How many ways are there to be conscious? When in *Born Yesterday* (1950) Broderick Crawford plays gin rummy with Judy Holliday, slapping the cards down with irritation as he deals, is he acting through the technique of a fully or partially automatic routine (between February 4, 1946, and December 31, 1949, 1,642 times Holliday had done this routine on the Broadway stage, but Crawford was here doing it for the first time), or is he actually thinking about dealing playing cards as he deals? Thinking about the cards, his fingers, playing gin, and not being Harry? Or, since Harry is playing gin, is thinking about his fingers on the cards a wholly useful way for Crawford to be thinking about Harry? When actors go through a lovemaking scene onscreen, are they thinking about lovemaking, is lovemaking happening, and if so, what kind of lovemaking?[6]

When the two men's heads cant together in their doze, they transmit the message, "We are acting," but in order that we might avoid seeing their acting work, their mere choreography for camera, and be led to detect instead a natural pull of gravity drawing these objects together in space, we must disattend their message. If they are not rank amateurs, these two can be doing nothing else but acting, but if we focus on that, we lose touch with their delicious sleep. We thus achieve engagement with Lubitsch's story by paying no heed at all to something that is being bluntly announced within it, something that is part of that story. All acting raises the possibility of this deep riddle—that we receive and also do not receive the message, "I am acting"—but by opening his film with a moment of "sleep," which can call out performance in such a way, Lubitsch raises the ante on the viewer's credulousness, seriously challenging our convictions about pretense and

---

[6]For three perplexingly different takes on the performed love scene see *Gone Girl* (2014), *Devil in the Flesh* (1986), and *Can Heironymus Merkin Ever Forget Mercy Humppe and Find True Happiness?* (1969).

reality at the very moment we need to abandon them if we are to enjoy the film. Film openings are transitional for viewers, after all, the moments in which we slip away from our everyday selves into the invisible presences who hear and watch.

To be sure, a waking admission of acting while pretending sleep turns out to be central to the structure of this moment. "I am only pretending; I am only acting," the actor silently announces; do not mistake that you have actually caught me on vacation. As his Tom awakens, the apparently awakening March effectively announces to the viewer, "Just a moment ago I wasn't actually sleeping, I was acting Tom being asleep." I do not sleep on the job. Just as I am here for you now, I was here for you then. Here, and fully here. And more: just as I was here for you then, I am here for you now. Then and now, "asleep" and "awake": *I am always here.*

But to turn the screw still more:

Because the sleeping moment is now visible as performative—"I was pretending to be asleep"; or, "That was me a moment ago, whom you saw 'sleeping'"—the present indicative moment, the one in which we are being told: "I am telling you about that previous moment, from beyond it," is apparently intrinsically *not* performative. *That* was performance, *this is not.* That sleeper you saw was *put on* by me, the "me" who is now directly "telling" you that. "I am *pointing back* to acting, not acting that I am pointing back." But opening his eyes and looking forward, March *is* acting now; *is* acting that he is pointing back, and, as is usually the case in performance, is doing so without declaration. "A moment ago I was acting Tom asleep; but now here is Tom." But not, but never: "I am acting that I am pointing back to a moment in which I was acting." The pointing here and now is for real, the finger of the pointer is a really, truly, authentically, believably trustworthy living finger.

Regarding the sleeping boys as a play-within-the-play, Hopkins is as much the audience for their "show"— as she certainly takes it to be—as we are. But it is vital to recognize that Tom's "actual sleep" and Fredric March's pretense to sleep were simultaneous and coterminous, Tom's sleep appearing authentic only because we had no visible grounds for thinking it otherwise, only because he had not yet awakened to signal us of someone's actual conscious being. When Cooper and March awaken, we are now suddenly confronted with presence that brings to light the authenticity or fakery of that sleep; we read that sleep not only presently, while it is happening and Gilda is watching it, but retroactively against the more solid truth of the consciously awake men. "We *were* sleeping." Not quite fully present for us until now—fully present, that is, present in verifiable consciousness, ours and theirs—March and Cooper have suddenly arrived. One could go so far as to say these stars "make entrances" by opening their eyes. These stars, not these characters. (Although the characters have the same eyes.)

Further, it helps to be mindful of Goffman's poignant dictum, worth a great deal of repetition, that when "audiences" on a stage find themselves struck by a play-within-the-play—*Hamlet* is of course the most celebrated example—we may be led to think of those "audience members" (Claudius, Gertrude, Polonius, Laertes, the court) as being like us, that is, people seeing and being caught up in the artificiality of some performance. But the members of that onstage audience are *not* people like us, they are characters. We are duped by a structural arrangement. In a similar way, although one may be struck with the feeling of encountering Tom as he awakes, one is really doubly confounded. First, since this newly conscious Tom was the very March who slept as Tom, we have all along been confronted by this selfsame being, and if his awakening assists us to navigate the social business between the characters as the scene proceeds, it has no real effect on our estimation of performance: this "Tom coming to life" isn't real. But also, March neither slept nor woke, "Tom" did: even the sleep wasn't real. March was animating both sleeper and waker, himself never asleep and not now awake for us, in the way that Tom is. March has been pulling Tom's strings all along, the strings that pulled Tom's eyelids up and the strings that, earlier (before we saw), drew his eyelids closed. March is awake in a way that is quite beyond Tom's wakefulness. He thought about it before, and decided how he would play it.

On Tom's arousal, he can be taken as saying, effectively, "I have been elsewhere (in Dreamland) and now I'm here with you," *you* being both his chum George and their new visitor Gilda, and surreptitiously, in the secret compact of filmgoing, us. As well, March could be taken to mean (as I am taking him to mean), "I was acting sleep, and now I am acting awakeness." Since *waking consciousness* is the zero-state of mind of viewers entering the theater and also of actors doing their work (we are all alive in the same sense of "to be alive" and when we are conscious we are all conscious in the same sense of "to be conscious" regardless of the mode of consciousness: conscious is conscious), for March to say, "I am awake" is essentially for him to say nothing beyond, "I am. I am here for you to look at. I am a film actor at work. Light is falling on me. And you, dear viewer, are witnessing all this." But all of this ostensible confession was understood in advance, on the face of it. We always understand this in cinema and theater, on the face of it, because this is always what is deeply, essentially *real* about the circumstance of watching acting, especially virtuosic acting like this. Thus, the deeper gist of March's admission as his eyes open is, "This is *real*, and I am *real* in it, *just as you are* (George and Gilda)." My sleeper may have been a dreamer, but I—I now see and recognize him for what he was. In sleeping he was less than I am looking back. "I am here" *not* "I am acting being here." This moment is an everyday moment, a moment of comparative actuality. Whether my former sleep was feigned or real, says Tom, I engendered it just as I am engendering this more *present* state of actual being. But Tom is not experiencing a state of actual being. As we watch him, the only person experiencing anything actual is utterly invisible and unknowable to us. When we interact with others in the everyday we consider them real, too, we don't think they are performers performing "reality," yet of course, as far as we can know, they are. All the men and women are merely players.

Although the actor's actual body and present experience are not absent from the embodied performance he allows us to see, we understand that real body and experience to be hidden within, behind, or around. When during a performance the actor explicitly or implicitly makes the statement, "I am acting," we must seek to know in what way the behavior—the body, the presence—now on show differs from the behavior that led up to it. In the case of *Design for Living*, what we actually have is a moment of March acting with his eyes closed followed by a moment of him acting with his eyes open; his character seemed at first removed from engagement with his surround and now is immersed in such engagement. Is this also true of Fredric March in some way? For instance, when his eyes were closed he did not see the camera facing him but when his eyes were open he did. Are we being given a tiny clue to such a person's variation of commitment to the present? Perhaps the limiting case of "acting" is the performance of any limiting condition, such as blindness, deafness, paralysis, sleep—as in the case of March here—or death. My own first performance was as a corpse in a live theatrical situation, and I later played one on film. Holding one's breath is of course the major requirement, but it also helps to have the eyes closed and to think of something else so that one's attention is removed from the gross presence of one's own body, since that body should not appear to move, which is to say, demonstrate awareness of itself.

Most dramatic moments, onscreen and offscreen, call for actors to manifestly avoid making the claim, "I am acting," or even the telltale claim "I was acting before," which could lead any viewer to conclude, "Then you must still be acting now." Playing in a film that requires multiple transformations of character, the actor must maintain vitality with, and fully inside, each new incarnation; earlier incarnations can be abandoned without note, and the fact that they *were incarnations* in this way obscured. Think of how Orson Welles moves through *Citizen Kane* (1941) without ever losing the power to give each present instantiation of Kane an idiosyncratic vitality he could have only if the same actor had played the same character, albeit it in a wholly different way, just minutes ago (screen minutes ago), that is, *had acted. Citizen Kane* is a chain of declarations, "I am acting," in which no one of the declarations is taken so seriously by those who watch the procession that changes in Kane are disruptive to the film.

The unbounded confluence of the actor's body and the character's presence during performance suggests that outside the precincts of the character there is nowhere for the actor to hide. The character is thus, in one flash, the actor's stage and also his dressing room. As characterization becomes elaborate, highly dependent on décor and mannerism, on emotive extremity or on special photographic effects, the actor at work might seem increasingly palpable, the articulation "I am acting" a more and more truthful and holistic statement of affairs. "I am acting" suggests manifest, ongoing, and intentional contrivance: Claude Rains's invisible man; Ricou Browning as the stunning creature from the Black Lagoon; Cary Grant as a Nubian in *To Catch a Thief*; or any James Bond incarnator winking through his tuxedo; but it is also, finally, presence—indeed riddling presence. But presence is always a riddle.

6

"I Am On Show"

FIGURE 6 *Fred Astaire (l.), Nanette Fabray, and Jack Buchanan singing "That's Entertainment!" in* The Band Wagon *(Vincente Minnelli, MGM, 1953). Digital frame enlargement.*

An awkwardly stimulating, possibly embarrassing moment, at some distance from virtuosity:

Doing "I am acting," the actor momentarily points to a self that has been put on display, but points in such a way that audiences are invited to lean back from engagement and consider, not the details of a playing-out but, the fact of the playing-out itself, and the fact of its happening in a mediated context. The viewer feels, "Here I am, watching something that has been made for me to watch; and watching it unobtrusively." The doing is being done before the audience's eyes; I am seeing this being done; I am seeing this being done onscreen. Produced here is a piquant multiplication of presences, a kind of performative cubism, because at once, as we see it: (1) the actor is the character, but (2) the actor is an actor acting the character, and therefore (3) the actor is not just announcing himself acting but doing an act in which he announces himself acting, that is, setting out to destroy the illusion. Say, in a medium shot made in wide angle so that the gun barrel aimed toward the camera seems to flare monstrously, Clint Eastwood chews out, "Make my day." We can see his ("Dirty") Harry. We can also see Eastwood possessing, manipulating, playing out that Harry. And we can see Eastwood's play to camera, thus, in effect, the camera itself.

But there is always one more turn of the screw:

Doing "I am on show," the actor points not only to the self but also to the audience. Not, "I am here not really (or not only) doing this but acting doing this," but in its place, "You are there looking at me, me, here in this especially visible context. I am aware that this is so, and as you watch I watch you watching, by projecting your attentiveness in my actions as in my thoughts." (I speak exactly the way you would expect me to speak, and I can do this because I know what you expect.) But because the audience was not warned that it would be invoked in such a way, abruptly, fully, and because it is being invoked suddenly in the flash, it is made sharply self-conscious. Not self-conscious in social-class terms: Look at me, I can afford a ticket and also to spend my time being regaled with fictions (which is to say, I have dispensable cash and time). But self-consciousness as a viewing persona: Look at me, I am looking, it is for my benefit this material I look at is played out and arranged—arranged, in fact, expressly to facilitate my having a point of view. "Look!," beckons the performer, but notes as well, "I am making it possible for you to look."

In order for an audience to be invoked it helps if there is an audience substitute within the diegesis, a substitute that can be the target of an express invitation. The viewing audience can feel that through the substitute the invitation is directed to them.

This particular form of self-referential indication is central in many stagings of choreography and singing that one can find in the classical Hollywood musical. I take as exemplar the vivacious, comical, spirited "That's Entertainment!" number from *The Band Wagon* (1953)—a film very widely recognized as an epitome of the film musical form. The key to the "I am on show" style lies not in the song lyrics:

A clown with his pants falling down
Or the dance that's a dream of romance
Or the scene where the villain is mean.
That's entertainment!

but in the way the performance of the song is staged (by Michael Kidd, the film's choreographer, and Vincente Minnelli) for camera.[1] Kidd here employs a strictly conventional staging technique, one in prolific use in the genre. He neither invents nor inadvertently falls into the staging method we find here:

Tony Hunter (Fred Astaire) has been looped by his old chums Lily and Lester Marton (Nanette Fabray, Oscar Levant)—a scripting team meant to call up thoughts of Betty Comden and Adolph Green—into at least trying out the thought of doing a new musical they have written, with the participation of the Broadway phenomenon Jeffrey Cordova (Jack Buchanan), a preposterous egoist but also a man of vast performative talent. They are on a rehearsal stage. Cordova has been cajoling and persuading, urging and insisting, telling them what the show could be. (It will tickle readers unfamiliar with the film to know that the show is, from its very inception, a guaranteed failure.) Cordova's argument reaches its apogee after he has done a little tap routine on the stage, has fallen off, has been picked up by his friends, and proclaims in melody:

Everything that happens in life
Can happen in a show.
You can make 'em laugh,
You can make 'em cry
Anything . . .
Any-thing! . . . can
Go!!!!

And the song proper begins.

But as "That's Entertainment!" is performed we begin to feel an awkward, even irritating sensation, mounting all the way through until, by the climactic moment, we are cringing. This climax has the four performers in stationary pose, wrapped together, enormous smiles pasted on their faces, staring out at *a presumed enraptured audience*, that is, an audience that has been following the whole song and dance move for move with increasing excitement and *is now, at least metaphorically, applauding in hysteria*. But onscreen there is no audience at all.

---

[1]Production practice in classical Hollywood, as very often today, has the choreographer, not the film's director, actually staging all shots that are part of musical numbers. Vincente Minnelli, who directed *The Band Wagon*, had astute musical taste and often participated in camera placement and direction (see my *Eyes* 185–186 for details of just a small spate of time during the filming of the "Heather on the Hill" number of *Brigadoon* [1954], itemizing the number of takes Minnelli took on various shots with the dancers, whose energy maintenance is particularly sharp).

It is as though the figuration "song-and-dance routine," used by characters "backstage" to negotiate their involvements together, has osmosed through the cell wall of their staging area into the consciousness of the viewer. They are doing a "routine"; they know they are doing a "routine"; and we know they are doing a "routine"; but the only audience they could be doing it for isn't there. (This is of course an authentic enough representation of actual rehearsal technique, where performers must get into the habit of grinning at the audience that will eventually be watching them; except that in this bit of film, the singing dancers are *not* in rehearsal, they are *doing a performance*.)

Mercifully the editor dissolves away from the quartet as the last note trails off so that there is no horrible moment when they must realize they are alone, and that trailing off is what, finally, sells the song. Part of what makes the situation so uncomfortable for us is that clearly they are alone—they know, we know they know—and suddenly they are behaving as though they are not alone. We are there approving them. *But where did we come from?*

We came from the performers' mental idea of "the audience," an idea everlastingly present for those who go "on show," but not an idea audiences carry about themselves; nor do audiences think that performers carry this idea while they are being audiences.

When a "routine" like this is on show in a musical as part and parcel of an interior musical-within-the-musical, as one of the "acts" (often prefaced by a camera view of the program showing the upcoming "routine"), the onscreen audience is explicitly shown, either before the "routine" begins, while it is ongoing, or when it concludes, and they applaud ravingly (never merely politely): an arrangement that allows the real film viewer to remain incognito. That is performance in the stage frame, thus performance that can be thought to be performance. But when the "routine" is performed in a rehearsal space *with nobody else present, by knowledge and intent*, the only possible "audience" that can be present for the arms-out, chin-up, overtly grinning, high-pitched final note didn't knowingly intend to be there: nearby, perhaps, but not quite there.

For whom do these people think they are performing?

We see them smiling outwardly either at the camera or offstage right or left into an "audience" we know is absent. We see constant viewer checks: "You watching my little act of genius? . . . Did you see that one?" The bodies, we note, are always turned out so as to present an ideal view for some "watcher" sitting roughly where we are sitting, yet no one is sitting there (because when we watch cinema we are not there watching). We are *here* watching, in the theatre, instead.

Are these entertainers, these people committed to entertainment for its own sake (as they indicate melodically) and wrapped in the belief that "anything, anything can be a show," all . . . psychotic? Might they all four share a professional psychosis, indeed? And at the end, when they embrace us (as by their opened arms they seem to do), are we exposed to catching the psychosis by contagion? Is it in fear of that contagion that we "pull away" rather than "moving toward" the cluster?

Or take the celebrated "Trolley Song" from *Meet Me in St. Louis,* where Judy Garland is singing a vivacious number to a chorus of girlfriends and boyfriends on a moving streetcar. (It is 1903, streetcars are prevalent.) She attends to their expressions throughout, as though using the lyrics to communicate to them the history of some actual experience of hers that she wishes to recount. (The song seems to be functioning as a "conversation.") But at the conclusion the group find themselves posed in a kind of sacred triangle, with Garland at the apex, and no longer interested in them. By the second and third final lines, she is centered onscreen, looking—not at her friends, but—up and away (to the heavens? to a balcony?), just over our heads, with bright gleams in her eyes. This is, at once, a young woman living out her dream, thus looking up to "dreamland," but also a movie performer gazing out at her quite uninvoked audience, an audience we are suddenly aware we have been forced to become. In the song's final line the boy from next door (Tom Drake), having raced to catch up, has materialized at her side and just before the final word she notices him, her eyes open wide into his face, and she demurely backs up a little. Back into the action.

Buzz, buzz, buzz went the buzzer
Flop, flop, flop went the wheels
Stop, stop, stop went my heartstrings
As he started to leave
I took hold of his sleeve with my hand
And as if it were planned
He stayed on with me
And it was grand just to stand
With his hand holding mine
Till the end of the line!

Back into the action, but not before giving a performance that, in its culmination, can seem nothing other than a PERFORMANCE. "I am on show. I am on show *for you!*" What she is performing is her adoration of that boy, and she allows him to blush and perform his fascination with her, but *to us,* not to each other. We are presumably evaluating and adjudicating this potential couple.

Typical of the form is the casting of at least some (or one) of the performers as a diegetic "performer" of some kind—singer, dancer, painter, writer—someone who knows how to "put out" for a receptive audience. In our cringing, part of what disturbs us is the matter-of-fact awareness that a person like this, professionally conscious of audiences, seems entirely *un*conscious here, unconscious that no one is watching him make a display to watchers. Even if the performer character is so wrapped up in the moment

that he or she has lost presence of mind, has been drawn into a waking
dream, a dream in which a magical audience can participate with pleasure,
still, the finale moment, the moment of closure, when a cadence is delivered
in bravura style to utter emptiness (an emptiness we must perforce fill so
as not to embarrass the performer), destroys such an illusion. This is not
waking from a dream, this is convincing oneself one is "onstage" when one
is manifestly not. (Except that one *is* on a diegetic stage. And one *is* on
a film screen.) I suspect that when one is confronted with a performer at
other times thought virtuosic, the sort who really does inhabit audiences'
consciousness—Fred Astaire, Ann Miller, Garland, Ethel Merman—the
embarrassment we feel is augmented.

The receptive cringe can eventuate when anyone "acts out" in a social
situation without gesturing realization that the "acting self" has been invoked,
"invited" to perform. Highly exaggerated, decorative, and impossible to
miss as such, performance itself seems strange, deranged, and unsocialized
without some legitimized form of staging. Normally in musicals, and
whatever their exact diegetic placement, song-and-dance routines are shown
as conventional for their moment, as with Charles Foster Kane's cavalierly
singing along with the chorus girls when he returns from abroad—but not
before demurring that this is a song about him: "You buy a bag of peanuts
in this town, you get a song written about you!":

> There is a man—a certain man
> And for the poor you may be sure
> That he'll do all he can!

We balance the question, "For whom do these sudden performers think
they are suddenly performing?" against the pure pleasure for which the
performers make room. Because some of the very greatest musical numbers
in Hollywood history are set up this way. In "That's Entertainment!"
however carried away we are by the gusto of the song and the enthusiasm
of the singing some trace of that gusto and enthusiasm still melt away at the
finale, leaving us to feel, oddly, naked, not cloaked by our normal invisibility.
In some "I am on show" routines the performers direct their bodies and
gazes explicitly at us; in some they direct themselves offscreen at an angle, as
though someone over there (whom we believe in but cannot see) is watching
carefully. Our cringing, however slight, makes us happy the song is over.

As to that cringing, however, and that apparently relieving happiness:
In these open, climactic moments when performers appear to say, "I am
doing this for you!," our refusal to accept what is being offered betrays a
certain critical denial of pleasure, even an asceticism. The gates to pleasure
are opened before us but we turn away. The pleasure rejected is the thrill of
presence before the ebullience, plain and simple; and typically in film musicals
the ebullience is truly there. What "embarrasses," finally, about "I am on

show" is exactly the performers' declaration that we are there to watch, that heightened displays such as these merit our being there. Heightened: singing always exceeds speech, and this is eloquent and harmonic singing, singing with verve, singing on key. Dance always exceeds other movement, but here is splendid, almost imaginary dance, movement of the body we can glory in watching. *We sing and dance in an especially notable way,* the performers proclaim, and *we do it for you.* Albeit there is no "you." And there we are left, pulling away from their offering.

So as a culminating taste or feeling, withdrawal from this musical pointing to ourselves—rejecting sentimentality—brings shame. What should enchant we think tawdry instead. Since singing and dancing (music and movement) are cinema's essence—the sound of music, the music of sound; the image of movement, the movement of the image—the viewer's withdrawal is also a denial of cinema, or certainly a denial of cinema as pleasure. Rationalizing such a withdrawal is a belief that cinema should be instructive, as in: reflect reality, journalize. Whereas to plunge without inhibition into moments of song and dance is to let oneself enter the poetic world, where sounds and images flow (regardless of where the performer's eyes are pointed).

When the performers stop and reveal themselves without hesitation or regret as having just performed; when they indicate "I am on show!" with feeling and joy, we teeter at the supremely challenging moment of either taking, or not taking, cinema for what it most deeply is.

7

Charisma as Commodity

FIGURE 7 *James Dean in* Rebel Without a Cause *with Ann Doran (l.) and Jim Backus (Nicholas Ray, Warner Bros., 1955). Digital frame enlargement.*

In his helpful book about Britain in the 1930s (a territory with little frivolity), Robert Pearce gives a clear illustration of the power of Hollywood films to influence behavior, well outside the United States, hinting at a certain domestic effect:

> It was said that Hollywood "movies" were influencing the way [many people] tried to look (as well as the way they walked and talked and smoked). Many women wanted to be glamorous—to look like Gloria Swanson or Jean Harlow or perhaps Greta Garbo—and the way to do this was to buy a "film star frock" and to apply lipstick, face powder, rouge and eyebrow pencil. The frock might be daring and reveal amounts of flesh that to the older generation bordered on the scandalous, but no longer was "a glimpse of stocking" looked upon as something shocking. In the words of the Cole Porter song of 1934, "Anything goes." It was said, not always quite accurately, that all women could look like film stars. (46)

Not always quite accurately, indeed! All *women* couldn't manage to look like film stars, but many *film actors* couldn't, either. And this stardom that stars achieved—through physical manipulations of the body and mass-market publicity—achieved and put to special show, was, in itself, a virtuosity. The deep point and self-justifying merit of the "star look" was virtuosity itself, a notable and distinctive formation that stood out from, elevated itself over the context of, normal performance.

But the virtuosic face of the star did (and was designed to) inspire an itch for imitation. It wasn't only the star identity but the virtuosic aura attached to it that fans wanted to possess. The clothing the star wore, the way the star sashayed, strode, or slid, the piquant dialogue that came out of the star's mouth (always piquant because always written to be piquant) could all work for fans as marketable accompaniments to the celebrated face. Very little has changed.[1] If one can't manage to get whisked off to Hollywood, one can spout character lingo, often in rank imitation: "You're gonna need a bigger boat"; "Here's looking at you, kid"; "I don't think we're in Kansas anymore"; "I'll be back"; "Make my day." One can fix the face: ringlets, a bandana, and golden tooth caps while you say "Arrrgh!"; mustache, bowler hat, and cane while you wiggle; pigtails and a gingham dress while you call Toto; fedora with moistened trenchcoat when you go to the airport. The red windbreaker purchased at Mattson's for James Dean in *Rebel* (Frascella and Weisel 119) became a fast-selling commercial item. In the latter part of the 1950s, many young children across North America had to have a Davy Crockett hat (yes, author included). Gestures were made both indelible and grammatical, they spawned progeny at least onscreen: Vivien Leigh's swoons in *Gone with the Wind* (1939) more or less established a paradigm for further filmic romances, and, no doubt, for what happened in plenty of cocktail bars and bedrooms; Errol Flynn's swashbuckling was reborn with Luke Skywalker and Darth Vader. Copycatting abounded in everyday life: weekend dancers using John Travolta's Tony Manero (*Saturday Night Fever* [1977]) as *teacher*; teenagers using Tom Cruise in *Risky Business* (1983) as a guide to being a "teenager pretending to be a rock star." For previously staid British women, "anything went" once they had seen that "everything went" for their screen favorites. "Good authors too who once knew better words/ Now only use four-letter words," thanks to Cole Porter. And considerably more: "If Mae West you like/ Or me undressed you like/ Why, nobody will oppose."

Virtuosity fires up imitation, then. And in imitation, the main idea is to not be entirely convincing. Nobody putting on the Garbo look wants anyone

---

[1] In Emir Kusturica's *Arizona Dream* (1993), Vincent Gallo plays a young man so obsessed with movies he has literally memorized the dialogue so that, watching one on television, he can come in half a beat before the actors do.

to think she *is* Greta Garbo: Garbo didn't attract friends, she had calculated remoteness, untouchability, unfamiliarity, actual non-presence. In procuring and putting on a "look," a kind of clubbish affiliation was achieved, an open claim of admiration and desire but not a personal transformation (the kind of transformation the actor accomplished in character virtuosically to start with). The radical capitalization of makeup and fashion worked by playing to the unbounded hunger of consumers who knew that, regardless of their efforts, they would have to keep on trying, keep on buying, "climb ev'ry mountain, till [they found their] dream." Following Pearce, we can see how, in its generation of a tidal wave of economic frenzy, the popularity of big stars outside America—their cash value in London, Paris, Berlin, Tokyo, Rio de Janeiro, Stockholm—was considerably greater and deeper than even the fan's desire to see films. Consumerist reproduction trumped the image.[2]

Many virtuosic performers became iconic "types": Gloria Swanson (as in Leo McCarey's *Indiscreet* [1931]), Jean Harlow (as in Victor Fleming's *Red Dust* [1932]). In a chain of films (Edmund Goulding's *Grand Hotel* [1932], Rouben Mamoulian's *Queen Christina* [1933], George Cukor's *Camille* [1936], and Ernst Lubitsch's *Ninotchka* [1939]) Garbo stunned and mobilized world audiences. But virtuosity does not monopolize. Simultaneously present on screens were Katharine Hepburn's more awkward but galvanizing femininity (in George Stevens's *Alice Adams* or Cukor's *Sylvia Scarlett* [both 1935], Cukor's *Holiday* or Howard Hawks's *Bringing Up Baby* [both 1938]) and Barbara Stanwyck's at once tough and vulnerable variety in John Ford's *The Plough and the Stars* (1936) and King Vidor's *Stella Dallas* (1937), or Claudette Colbert's chic and insightful woman in Frank Capra's *It Happened One Night* or John M. Stahl's *Imitation of Life* or Cecil B. DeMille's *Cleopatra* (all 1934). Irene Dunne! Gail Patrick! Carole Lombard! Miriam Hopkins! Here was *the* epoch of classically glorious stardom, and the British women of whom Pearce writes were calculating in seizing images to copy: beyond being masters of "screen performance" these virtuosic performers handed over designs for living. And the iconicity of the performance, far from accidental, was a basis for capitalization.

One may well ask: Is the viewer's desire to connect with the star, to have the virtuosity rub off, even in the vaguest way, just a yen to wear the same kind of socks and hairstyle, nothing more than a superficial, dissipating response to the display? Or does one stretch to "touch" the virtuosity because standing out, it is the element of screen form most easily, most thoroughly, seen, the one that feels closest? Or again, resting on some more democratic belief that the star's qualities, more than being striven for and labored at with genuine concentration can be found anywhere and everywhere, that

---

[2] A reading of Walter Benjamin will provide much more elaborate discussion of the power of reproduction.

with enough closeness we might somehow productively participate—stars
ourselves, if undiscovered ones? All of these possibilities add up to a single
riddle: Is screen virtuosity to be thought contagious?

The belief in contagious magic is a very old and very elemental social
form, deriving from societies described by Max Weber as being organized
around charismatic leadership:

> In economic sub-structure, as in everything else, charismatic domination is
> the very opposite of bureaucratic domination. If bureaucratic domination
> depends on regular income . . . charisma lives in, though not off, this
> world. This has to be properly understood. Frequently charisma quite
> deliberately shuns the possession of money and of pecuniary income
> *per se,* as did Saint Francis and many of his like; but this is of course not
> the rule. Even a pirate genius may exercise a "charismatic" domination,
> in the value-neutral sense intended here. Charismatic political heroes seek
> booty and, above all, gold. But charisma, and this is decisive, always
> rejects as undignified any pecuniary gain that is methodical and rational.
> In general, charisma rejects all rational economic conduct. (Gerth and
> Mills 247)

The rejection of all rational economic conduct: the booty is shining icon,
not bankable resource. Thus, the commercialization of the charismatic star
image, surely overt and greedy economic conduct if ever there was, must
be kept more or less clandestine, presented as only a related side effect
disconnected from the strictly bounded screen image of the star, which image
is entirely the property of the producing studio in any and all manifestations
in any and all venues, without limit.

A very tiny example: the Montblanc Special Edition Greta Garbo pen
(selling today for roughly six hundred dollars!) does not look or behave
like Garbo onscreen, and could never be mistaken for Garbo herself or any
version of her appearance ever marketed in connection with any film, but the
name serves to bind it. Exploitation contracts are now quite commonplace
for star characterizations: t-shirts, bobble-head dolls, Hallowe'en masks,
not to mention video games, posters, paperback spinoffs. But the fiery
embers of the 1930s star's charismatic power were blown upon by a
commercial exploitation that never announced itself in direct proximity
to the screen; you didn't walk into the lobby on your way to the street
and find someone hawking Garbo pens or Jimmy Cagney souvenir dolls,
nor did you find such things next door at the toy store. The thought of
exploiting virtuoso-dolls began in 1948 with Howdy Doody. Howdy, albeit
a puppet (created by Frank Paris and remodeled by Velma Wayne Dawson),
was a bona fide star. Any ready-made star could appear and reappear in
commercial constructions entirely tangential to the ones the studio was
putting in place.

The *tangentiality* of its star image—and by direct association, the person beneath it—could make the commercialization "reject all rational economic conduct" connected to the stardom itself. Rationalities were hidden. The star salary was never a matter of public knowledge at the time (and didn't become so until the mid-1980s when Carolco had to strike multimillion-dollar deals for Sylvester Stallone and Arnold Schwarzenegger), whereas today, of course, one often hears how much a star is being paid for a deal long before the deal is complete and the characterization makes its way to the screen (Johnny Depp being widely reported as having signed for $64 million to do Cap'n Jack Sparrow the fourth time). Garbo, Stanwyck, Hepburn, Swanson, Colbert, Harlow—they worked for nothing, as far as their fans knew. Or else they were paid "a fortune, so much it was beyond conception." Stars were not thought of as being in and of the world, participants to the ceremony of life, as were their fans; their profit did not come by rational economic conduct, the everyday, the grind of a job, but was more magical, as inexplicable as it was wondrous.

As to funds, "frequently charisma literally shuns the possession of money": if we concentrate we can see a mental vision of the wealthy star lavishly endowed with luxuries but all of whose bills are paid by an invisible factotum. The offscreen presence of a real, civically minded, routinized person, a worker who earns recompense, was uninvoked and therefore unimaginable. The star's home was a fairy castle (see the postcards of Pickfair). The car was a chariot. The family was a royal entourage. Offscreen, celebrity was rarely seen at all, and almost never seen face to face by fans in normal circulation outside of structured, tightly organized studio premières at Grauman's, the El Capitan, the Fox in Westwood (and today the Arclight on Sunset Blvd.). As we see depicted in the finale of John Schlesinger's *The Day of the Locust* (1975), fans would crowd in legions to cheer at a première, and would crane to catch a glimpse of the favorite, now diminished in size and fully embodied yet at the same time got up in splendid, even preposterous garb, upon a plush red carpet. The star was the glowing image, and this image was economically sacrosanct, effectively cut off from trade, from exploitation, from the very capitalism that engendered it.

The fan's unconscious mode of appreciation, her near engorgement of the star image, her unmitigated (and apparently unmediated) delight and rhapsody in seeing the star face's gigantic superhuman magnitude, all summed to a loyal and untrammeled allegiance—inviolable, unquestionable—with the star as nexus. Fan response (*fan*-aticism) essentially constitutes the relinquishing of critical judgment, certainly in the realm of the aesthetic, where the star reigns as monarch; but also in the economy, where money is spent to gain access to the star but the star has no truck with money. This is how the star-charisma "always rejects as undignified any pecuniary gain that is methodical and rational."

An essential—and endlessly interesting—aspect of virtuosic star performance is Hollywood's careful distancing structure, its tightly scheduled and rigorously maintained practices of keeping the movie star away from the fans who might, like the Bacchae, tear him to shreds out of the desire for contact. A delicate structure because in order for the fan to believe that contact was possible, thus to take her own desire as sane, the star, while being removed, couldn't be *so far removed* as to be astral. One's grasp should exceed one's reach, but not by such a degree that the desire to grasp withers. To touch the figure so that the essence could somehow flow, is the passionate longing diffused by a publicity machine and system of exploitation that substituted photographs, clothes patterns, souvenir trophies, and other colorful paraphernalia (or paying a few bucks to have oneself selfied next to the "Cap'n Jack Sparrow" impostor on Hollywood Blvd.) for the impossible human relationship. Fetish as substitute, but tactile substitute. To have the selfie (formerly the 8 x 10 glossy), to have it instantly available on one's phone (mounted on one's wall), for real. Or the movie poster.[3] Or the ticket to a special screening, the stub of which can be preserved as a sacred relic.

Very typically, major studio virtuosi would make publicity trips to catch audiences across the country (with heavy local publicity). Meticulously scripted and deftly organized, these adventures, involving radio interviews, personal appearances (the smiling face while the hand signs one's autograph book), and associated other promotional ventures involved people like Cary Grant, who stepped onto a stage in my home town (while I was too young to know) and spoke—from a charged distance—to the fans who adored his films. A star who made such appearances, or public appearances anywhere, stood as a pale substitute for: not what he was, a mere human, paid to act in the movie showing here tonight and to stand on a real physical stage as breathing emissary, but the image that would not disappear from the screen. The personal appearance gave audiences opportunity to meet the closest possible friend of the virtuoso they adored, a friend as intimate as could be found and met.[4] Friend, confidant: if not the virtuoso herself

---

[3]Fan behavior and experience is itself incorporated into star display from the 1970s onward, as part of the more generalized self-reflectiveness of cultural materials. Take for one example Tony Manero's bedroom in *Saturday Night Fever* (1977), decorated with an enormous image of Sylvester Stallone as Rambo and another, simple portrait pose, of Farrah Fawcett Majors that titillates Tony's father (Val Bisoglio) quite as much as it does him. A popular favorite of television viewers in the 1990s was Dawson Leary (James Van Der Beek), whose bedroom, until a critical turning point in *Dawson's Creek* (1998), was decorated with a lavish chain of posters from Steven Spielberg films.

[4]Performer responses were themselves carefully stage-managed, scripted, planned in advance of the questions that occasioned them.

then the exceedingly intimate doppelgänger.[5] The actual virtuoso was kept inaccessible, charged precisely because visible and unavailable at the same time. Thus, any sense of proximity a viewer feels may ultimately sum to a sense of virtuosity. A situation of contact might seem virtuosic in itself, though no thought is given by the performer to achieving supremity of any kind. In this sense, the performative virtuosity is an extension of the audience's fascination, to some degree a product of it.

An eleven-year-old boy meets his adored screen hero face to face:

In the spring of 1998 I brought my family to Paramount for the studio tour, but at one moment ducked away with my son to scout through a gaggle of trailers parked on the lot. One of these had an open door and gingerly we stepped up to it. There inside, not two feet away, and sharing mugs of coffee from the automatic machine that rested near the door, were Patrick Stewart in costume as Capt. Jean-Luc Picard and Brent Spiner, in full Data makeup. They paused to give us a look, especially my son, with broad, welcoming smiles. Stewart bent down from his perch (the trailers are elevated) to have a few friendly words and to give a full-on Picard smile. Stunning, of course, yet also perhaps confusing. It wasn't just that the real person was emerging from *behind* the character, it was that the character himself was emerging from the TV world and making an entrance into real life. Was real life a stage, then? Even a double strangeness, because instead of "Tea, Earl Grey, Hot" our "Captain" was sipping black coffee just the way my son had seen his father do. If the trailer had been the bridge of the Enterprise, my son might have thought himself on a star voyage. Stewart of course took great care to make no gesture unbefitting the cherished Picard.

They shook hands, Jean-Luc and Ariel, and whatever contagion could happen, happened.

---

[5]Many performers did publicity tours by way of the military, USO shows, and the like. Bob Hope, Bette Davis, Ray Bolger all did patriotic war work from 1940 onward. An interesting cinematic rendition of the star-fan relationship in this context can be found in Mark Rydell's *For the Boys* (1991).

8

Outstanding

FIGURE 8 *Elizabeth Taylor as Martha in* Who's Afraid of Virginia Woolf? *(Mike Nichols, Warner Bros., 1966). Digital frame enlargement.*

Structurally speaking, the central problem virtuosity must resolve is perceivable elevation. Virtuosic display must rise above the emotional, tonal, gestural, and figurative plane of all else that is going on within the embedding complexity. If the virtuoso doesn't stand out, performance continues but virtuosity fails. But if the virtuoso *only* stands out, the scene fails. A linked advancement and retreat are required, since rising above the general array has its most emphatic effect if it is but temporary, then converted into a graceful, almost unobtrusive fall-back, a rejoining of the crowd.

Can a single performer manage to accomplish more than one virtuosic turn inside a drama, without taking up too much space or causing viewers to lose sight of other things? In *Rebel Without a Cause* (1955), James Dean answers this clearly in the affirmative, (1) virtuosically handling a knife fight (with Corey Allen) at the Planetarium in Griffith Park; then (2) virtuosically standing upon a precipice looking down into the surf by night; then (3) virtuosically lifting a milk bottle to his face; then (4) virtuosically splaying himself upside down on his parents' sofa; then (5) virtuosically spreading his arms upon the staircase as he bleats at them, "You're tearing me apart!"; then (6) virtuosically stomping out of the house placing his foot through a framed oil painting that rests on the floor; then (7) virtuosically throwing himself into an empty swimming pool; then (8) virtuosically nursing the dead body of his pal Plato. There are almost no moments by Dean in this film that are not virtuosic in some way, partly because of his astonishing screen presence; partly because of his invention of gesture; partly because of his musical voice. Yet he always falls back to a base moment of normativity from which he can rise in spectacle again.

There are interesting interactive implications, since part of the fabric of our engagement with a story is woven from our noticing, considering, and evaluating the putative relationships between characters, their estimations of one another, their level of regard and esteem, their feeling of attraction or repulsion. When one character becomes exceptionally noticeable, in performative virtuosity, others nearby can hardly behave as though nothing has happened: should they do this they would seem tuned out. We typically watch interactions, not only individual characters, and beneath or behind these interactions it is not hard to imagine—in a world of publicity it is too easy to imagine—actorly interactions as well. When characters "act out," become momentarily virtuosic, the actors performing those characters are visible to, and open to the judgment of, actors watching them from very close up. An obvious example: in Mike Nichols's 1966 *Who's Afraid of Virginia Woolf?*, audiences were witnessing the bickering marriage of George and Martha, played, as everyone had plenty of reason to know, by the not-long-married Richard Burton and Elizabeth Taylor. These two came together in 1964, having met more than a decade previously while Burton was filming *The Robe* (1953) and having trysted some in 1963 while Taylor was being Cleopatra (and he, Mark Antony) for Joseph Mankiewicz in Rome. Theirs was Burton's second wedding, Taylor's fourth (the marriage lasted a little more than ten years, and was reprised soon after the 1974 divorce). Nichols's film was made in late 1965 and early 1966. Here onscreen for all to digest was the real thing, then, the inside of the privacy. Here was the raw sinew. And because of Edward Albee's language scripted by Ernest Lehman, it was a Wagnerian mode of relationship that caught audiences' attention, entertainment here flowing from Burton and Taylor's careful work to balance each other's virtuosic moments, with neither trying to outshine the partner. If Martha and George have a vituperative marriage, they believably remain a union: a deep mystery of the play and the film. But Burton and Taylor must each not only act but watch the partner acting, too. If the virtuosities are to seem in competition, by intent, each swagger must be observed and met with a bigger and bolder one. In general, when a character ascends in a virtuosic moment the actor ascends, too, and not secretly. In the virtuosic moment, the actor has a view from "above" his coworkers. Lest the effect degrade into what perceivers would consider mere arrogance, the virtuosic turn should be as brief as it is expressive, as carefully shaped as it is bombastic, as ironically as restrained as it is expansive.

Fred Astaire's many filmed dance numbers, generic in themselves, are much-celebrated moments of virtuosic display (by a figure who spent a very great deal of his off-camera time assiduously practicing). If virtuosity here originates in setting, costume, and camera tricks no less than in the dancer, still the routines are designed around, intended to exemplify the improbable, unearthly talents of Astaire, and so they are always, no matter what else, of, and about, him. Astaire shows classic grace in bravura partner choreography with such as Eleanor Powell, Judy Garland, and of course Ginger Rogers, who can be seen to ornament the routine while Astaire's movement gives the structure. But typically at least one Astaire routine will be a solo demonstration of special, apparently quite difficult work, usually set in a location where the audience will be astonished to see him able to dance at all. (In these routines the complexity and problematization of the dance, being scenic, extend far beyond the body of the dancer, far beyond athletic taxation which Astaire must endure and for which he masters his techniques. The staged environment is almost always invisibly and especially guyed to support the special movement effect.) The sand dance, "Top Hat, White Tie and Tails" in *Top Hat* (1935); the astonishing slow-motion "Steppin' Out with My Baby" in *Easter Parade* (1948); the "You're All the World to Me" dance on the walls and ceiling in *Royal Wedding* (1951) are only a few examples of Astaire's virtuoso style and ability. While he can infect a partner, and she him, with a kind of contagious virtuosity, as in the intoxicating pas de deux, "Night and Day" in *The Band Wagon,* where with Cyd Charisse he dances in a dreamy Central Park, he tends to step away from his company and to a "higher plane" in his effects routines. Other dancers see, and cannot imitate; and also do not show regret.

Virtuosic exertion might color the performative presence not momentarily or spontaneously but genetically, filling each instant of a highlit figure's presentation. With arbitrary brief pauses, to give the audience relief, the "extended virtuosity" is treated as a "phenomenon," less a normal presence temporarily extended than one whose expressive tools are highly tuned all the time, in every circumstance. Such a presence was to be found in the stand-up comedian Robin Williams, who, although in privacy he was quiet and reflective, onstage or before the camera often neglected to pause his extreme articulation: extreme in content, in amplification, in musicality, in breathiness, in spontaneity—even when, as in *Aladdin* (1992) he does nothing beyond vocal animation. Another fascinating and telling cinematic case is Meryl Streep's performance in Stephen Frears's *Florence Foster Jenkins* (2016). Her remarkably vulnerable characterization in this film (based in fact)—a very rich woman who is infected with the belief that she can be a great opera singer, notwithstanding her inability to stay on key—begins in full force and continues with only the tiniest abatements—given over, usually, to her costar Hugh Grant—through the hour-and-fifty-one minute duration. The marvelous effect is to see Jenkins as both mad and heroic, both hopelessly incapable and incredibly brave, and to see Streep as generating all of this, unrelentingly and in an ascending arc. In virtuosic moments it is ideal that audiences actually witness the artist raising a self up to supremity, *taking off in flight*. In this light, the brilliant John Hurt's playing John Merrick the Elephant Man for David Lynch (1980), a triumph of characterization since both extreme pain and extreme receptivity to love had to be conveyed together, failed as virtuosity because the acting was perforce cloistered in makeup; the discernible presence of the actor rising was lost. The covering was perhaps not a problem as Hurt saw it, because vital to the role—Merrick was strikingly malformed—but it could not be a pathway to the actor in the *act of achievement*. One might thus consider Hurt's stellar work in this film, modest. With Streep's turn as Jenkins, a downkey opening set the performer up for a swiftly ascending and enduring flight. She *dons* eccentricity.

Cinematic performance can be mistaken for filmed stage performance. The progression and continuity of stage performance cannot be achieved when an arc is sliced into fragments, the fragments labored at sometimes repetitively and in a temporal order unrelated to what will finally be cut together, and the actor's ability to show the self always mediated by the technical features of the camera's lens and the camera's framing and movement. With Streep's Jenkins, for instance, one finds a beautifully "drawn" curve of character expansion, emotive amplification, and physical degeneration together, but an actor must be ready to shoot a film like this out of sequence, thus being challenged in plotting out the character's developing state over the whole script and finding the self for every discreet scene only through arduous concentration. In a film performance, the virtuoso is hard at work providing the pieces out of which other people will fashion the "role." Pieces crafted in advance to cut together logically later on.

Grounding is vital to elevation. The virtuoso must climb above some base level clearly understood by the audience as quotidian and normal for the character. In an ascent, the virtuosic turn can seem *not* normal: bounded away and worthy in itself. This diffuse mode of distracting attention from the performer's talent, bringing special light to the neutralizing background frame—without such neutralizing light the virtuosic turn floats in a vacuum—can be effected in many ways: the action of the story can be accelerated, or seductive visual effects used to further it; the supporting cast can mass together in an aggregate bond, a kind of chorus, that drowns the voice of the venting star; advertisements, in their graphics, can highlight features of the story that make it generic, which is to say, instantly and repeatedly recognizable. The setting can be made to gain attention as realistic, even while it subtends a virtuosic moment, so that it is palpably there for the performer, upon finishing, to reinhabit, be swallowed up in. In *The Bourne Identity* (2003), Matt Damon's Jason Bourne is in a Paris apartment when he suddenly engages an adversary in hand-to-hand combat which is unquestionably virtuosic in speed, deftness, savagery, and surprising climax; but the modern apartment, with its various slick conveniences, explored first and also afterward, becomes a hermetic envelope that contains the vital energy of the virtuosity. Or the Astaire dance number: it always springs, like the songs in a musical, out of some totally commonplace, even nonsensical everyday action like crossing a street, walking into a park, coming back to one's hotel room. Florence Foster Jenkins has her loyal manager (Grant), a splendidly sedate and cultivated man who maintains an air of pleasant, but not in any way marked, decorum; after each of her manic turns at virtuosity she returns safely to his tender, also comparatively tedious, care.

While virtuosity elevates the excitement and engagement of the audience, often in surprise, it will not come unannounced to the virtuoso, nor need the virtuoso be excited by it. One practices. One builds one's chops. To declaim or pirouette becomes as effortless as whispering or standing perfectly still, but only after really working the voice or the leg muscles. After all, the virtuosic moment is a working moment like any other, except that a different range of talent and, typically, an augmentation of force are required. In actual performance conditions, the performer knows when the turn at virtuosity is coming up, knows where in the event as a whole the moment will be placed and therefore how high a climb will have to be; how far away that climb is from the present breath; and thus how much time is still available for preparation. In filmmaking, one travels to the studio or location fully aware that today's work will include a step beyond the norm, a moment that will be adjudged extreme. The performer is thus prepared for what the audience is not. Though fans may look forward to something exceptional from their hero, they never know when it will come.[1]

As the performer prepares for takeoff, energy is mustered and the body re-envisioned as a site of particular placements, the balance struck with a posture, the costume arranged, and the supporting cast made fully ready to avoid, at all costs, any display that could show them off in a too-distracting light. In short, virtuosity, most notably onscreen, is collaborative, and a matter of complex and devoted arrangement. When John Wayne speaks, the surround is silent, but not by accident.

---

[1]In some action films, the protagonist takes off in a spectacular display of physicality right off the bat, even before the opening credits, thus catching the viewer off-guard: until the fan viewership becomes accustomed to this ploy and comes to expect the explosive opening. The model everyone is following here is Orson Welles's *Touch of Evil* (1958), accomplished with a tremendous musicality.

9

Virtuosity Superimposed

FIGURE 9 *Cary Grant* in North by Northwest *(Alfred Hitchcock, MGM, 1959). Digital frame enlargement.*

To see how a performance containing several moments of virtuosity can have been structured from without as well as within, how the directorial influence, the design, the script, and the cinematographic vision can work to draw an actor's work to the foreground of the audience's consciousness, thereby more or less superimposing virtuosity upon it, we may find help in studying one particular case, the much-celebrated Cary Grant in Hitchcock's *North by Northwest* (1959).

How does he manage to be so persistently astounding and glorious in this film, scene after scene (the scenes here are not filmed in sequence)? Conversing with the alluring, sophisticated, and curious Eve Kendall (Eva Marie Saint) in the dining car of the Twentieth Century Limited, coy, handsome, nervous, but also utterly desirable, especially in his shy meekness and with those tickling sunglasses. The wary but genteel hesitation as he circles around a Long Island study with James Mason, the two of them eyeing one another like cobra and mongoose with a beautiful framed landscape behind their heads. Plied to excess with bourbon, Roger put behind the wheel of a car on a curving hilly road, which he now navigates in a total stupor, surviving because the Fates are with him. The very well-known cropduster evasion, where, standing all alone, effectively naked in his expensive gray suit, surrounded by endlessly stretching fields in all directions, he must endure a machine-gun attack from the air: the consummate, the ultimate victim, heroically desperate. Then attending and, with truly prodigious calculation, disrupting an art auction. Then, ascending the cantilevers of a South Dakota mountain aerie, improbably finding a way by moonlight into Eve's upstairs room: a quintessence of silent and beautiful athleticism. Finally, of course, fumbling his way with her hand in his, over the faces of Mount Rushmore: stellar bravery, daunting courage, humble aplomb as he squints up into the evil face of Martin Landau: "Help me!"

What extraneous forces help mold these many virtuosic moments?

Face-off

A number of factors bolster Grant in the Townsend study scene: that his scene partner is one of the great screen actors in Hollywood history, whose jibes, so oily and sweet at once, counterpoint Grant's querulous silences. That Grant's Roger has no idea what broth he has been dropped into, and we with him, so that attention is raptly focused on each syllable, if only to facilitate demystification. That the room is designed to seem luxurious and pleasant, a powerful man's study overlooking a great lawn through splendid mullioned windows: the elegantly suited Grant seems to belong, quite as much as his interlocutor (who has, we will learn only later, purloined this location).[1] We are at home and not at home in the same breath. As is the convention in numerous cinematic confrontations between heroic and villainous types—a convention in the development of which Alfred Hitchcock played a signal part—the dialogue, particularly that of Vandamm, is riddled with gracious politeness and yummy *double entendre*. The more etiquette, the more danger.

And, too, as a way of bringing us into engagement with the moment, as well as aligning us with Roger's disturbed curiosity as the scene progresses, Hitchcock puts movement into our perception by using the camera to pan in a circular fashion, so that the shots of Vandamm eyeing Roger and those

---

[1]Grant and Mason are in their own clothing here, Grant dressed from his own collection and Mason having paid a London tailor and been reimbursed for the expense.

of Roger eyeing Vandamm can be intercut in what will come to seem a diabolical circle. Not only do they circle one another but we circle the pair, sharing in Roger's doubt and Vandamm's conducting.

Hilly Drive

Roger is not just drunk, he is blasted. His vision is blurry, his hand-eye coordination is sloppy, he is barely awake. Further, he did not bring himself out to Long Island, we saw him kidnapped and limousined there, so this is manifestly not his territory and he doesn't know the road. He is in a car that has been stolen from "Helen Babcock" so the controls are not familiar to him, nor have we seen Roger, a quintessential New Yorker if ever there was one, driving a car at any point.[2] This moment in the car has been established by the preceding scenes, then, as one in which he has no reason to feel comfort, even sober. The actor is receiving considerable assistance from the architecture of the script.

The road is notably precarious,[3] seems, in fact, endlessly twisting and endlessly precarious. Even without the bourbon, a neophyte driver could have difficulty here. The scene is photographed using rear projection which has been thrown just a tiny bit out of focus in some shots, so that we cannot see the road ahead any better than Roger can. And—this is one of Hitchcock's very favorite techniques—because we feel we are positioned as drivers, yet cannot control the car at all, our sense of paralyzed conviction is intensified by the focal trouble. We are trapped, like Roger, in an uninterruptible vision of a space that cannot be navigated. For continuing to exist at all behind the wheel of this car Grant seems virtuosic, and this is a negative virtuosity, constructed entirely from outside. "Negative": not rejection or denial, but reversal. If Grant sits and stares, the photography will do the rest, and he will seem the luckiest man on earth (virtuosically so).

Lunch on the Train

A completely sociable moment (at least on the face of it). The speed of the scene is slowed down. Bright, sparkly sunlight streams in through the window, bouncing off the white linen tablecloth. Both partners are dressed nicely, and seem to like one another, so that nothing in their relationship calls the moment into question. They discuss the food: "How's the trout?"

---

[2]Most residents of Manhattan, especially tony ones like Roger, taxi or walk rather than driving or owning cars. We met Roger in full stride, gliding backward as he approached.
[3]The sequence was shot on one of the curling approaches to Griffith Park Observatory, Los Angeles.

. . . "Trouty." Strangers who do not presume to know each other yet agree to abide by the rules of etiquette. With cleverness abounding: Roger offers an alias but Eve quickly sees through it, remembering that his face is on the front page of every newspaper in America (he is thought to have killed a diplomat, and is therefore in flight). Allusions are made to interpersonal excitements, a dramaturgical requirement since we are watching the male and female leads of a romantic adventure film and they are now having a first meeting; these allusions tickle sensibility and warm us to the encounter. But in fact, since we have been set up to require this little island of sociable peace in the sun, Grant's (Roger's) virtuosic charm is coming as much from the scenic support as from personality.

In the previous scene Roger was under scrutiny obtaining his ticket for this train. Before that, we saw him from a high position atop the U.N. racing from the location of the killing. Before that, he was meeting Lester Townsend in the U.N. Delegates' Lounge, and learning that Townsend had not been at his Long Island house for a long while, therefore that the man at the Long Island house had not been the Lester Townsend who owns it, this before a knife found its way into Mr. Townsend's back and he expired with Roger leaning over him clasping the handle tentatively while someone snapped a picture with a flash. Before that was the kidnapping sequence, the confrontation in the study, the bourbon, the car ride, and at its end Roger crashing into a police vehicle and showing up in a courtroom still tipsy. All of this action was borderline comic, borderline troubling, borderline disorienting, borderline confusing, and endeared Roger to us while also showing that he was in some kind of trouble, a trouble that surrounded and dwarfed him, a trouble he could neither predict nor control. We arrive in the dining car, then, needing at least the same respite he does, with an overmothered, harried, kidnapped, taxed, threatened, perplexed, and terrified Roger, who persists all the while in showing suavity and self-possession he cannot possibly possess. The scene binds us to him, lets us discern his every syllable of endearing coyness and boyish play, here at lunch with Eve, as momentarily virtuosic. But the virtuosity of the performer comes from the virtuosity of the character by contagion, and the virtuosity of the character is produced largely by the continuity of the film. Albeit Roger Thornhill seems to be Cary Grant!

Lest one be distracted: the exterior—the Hudson River near Ossining—is seen through rear projection, beautifully shot to effect a real passing landscape, the scene being principally portrait shots of the diners in alternation (made in studio, where the lighting can be very carefully modulated to round out the star personae). As with Hitchcock's sets quite generally, the railway car is an utterly faithful rendition of such locations at the time, to such a degree that the film plane vanishes and we feel we are looking at a real encounter, live, but magically enlarged.

The Cropduster Scene

Roger will seem virtuosically heroic in this scene if he can survive. Hitchcock provides several aids. The opening crane shot shows the vast extent of the denuded territory, with the narrow road cutting through (this is in California, not far from Hitchcock's ranch). Long portrait shots of Grant waiting at the roadside emphasize his lone status, and when a bus pulls up and a stranger climbs on, Grant's tiny conversation with the man leads him absolutely nowhere. We must believe that he is threatened, so intensely that in the theater seat we wish to flee from the approaching cropduster (while being pinioned: affective paralysis). For this, the plane is shot previously on location and then rear-projected into a studio where the foreground is set up for Grant's run. He appears to be running away from, and then diving away from, the approaching plane, and because it is produced this way the plane can seem very close to him indeed, as long as the rear projection is shot with technical virtuosity—which it is. The culmination of the scene is Roger in the middle of the road as an oil tanker comes barreling toward him, halting just at the tip of his nose. Again, rear projection, this time shot with a telephoto so that the camera can be further from the truck than it will seem; and in reverse action, with the truck backing up (later, projection is reversed in the optical printer). The plane crashes into the truck, fireball, Roger steals a pickup and (with miraculous talent) drives away. (The fire is carefully controlled and some of the effect is created by blown black smoke and a prop partial aircraft.) Here we have virtuosic physical action set up and fostered by complex visual effects flawlessly carried off.

The centerpiece of the sequence is Grant in his Madison Avenue gray suit, an expensive and elegantly tailored suit that fits him like a skin. He looks clean, professional, and dignified. The action will require him to endure self-abasement in the dirt. He will try conversation and be rebuffed, he will run from the plane in his leather brogues on a paved road, he will throw himself into a ditch as bullets land all around him, he will enter a corn stand and be cropdusted from above, brought to the point of choking, he will run onto the road and withstand the threat of being mown down by an advancing truck. And finally, indignity of indignities, he will save himself by driving the sort of vehicle in which no smart-looking Madison Avenue advertising man would ever be seen (again: even if he does somehow know how to drive). Roger's prettiness has elevated him some, and the step-by-step degradation in this sequence lowers him, makes him more familiar, takes some of the Cary Grant sheen off and shows us a simple man trying to save his own life. Given the complexity and brutality of the threats aimed at him here, his coming through alive evidences an extremity of endeavor, a virtuosic heroism. Grant virtuosically gets dirty so that Roger can save his own life.

When Roger is challenged by the advancing truck, Hitchcock knows
that his audience will sensibly trust that he has no intention of eliminating
his star performer; on the other hand, the audience must be driven to fear.
Hitchcock makes use of the "looming response," a phenomenon in evidence
from the earliest days of cinema which is based on the human withdrawal
from objects advancing toward the eye. Intercutting shots of Grant's terrified
face, Hitchcock offers an expression of his character's wish to withdraw, but
if Roger backs away to let the truck pass he loses his only opportunity of
escaping the situation. By showing the truck coming directly at the camera,
he involves the audience in withdrawal. Yuri Tsivian has dubbed this
"anxious or panicky reaction to films of approaching vehicles" as the "train
effect"[4] (see further on this, Bottomore.)

At the Auction

I have elsewhere given a detailed analysis of the dramaturgy of the auction
house scene, especially the social import of Roger's linguistic gestures in both
their quality and their timing (*Eye* 29–38). Let me add that Roger's social
manipulations of the captive (bidding) audience, in order to obtain a safe
exit, play upon our already received notion—our charmed expectation—of
Grant's social agility and couth, that the actor behind the character *is* the
paragon of manners and grace he so often epitomizes onscreen (perhaps
with great emphasis in George Cukor's *Holiday* [1938]). His origins in
a working-class English background are elided in the construction and
reception of his star persona. Predictably, Roger Thornhill has the gracious
mannerisms we take to be Grant's. And at the auction house he uses verbal
skill both to project his high social position relative to the bidders (he's
from New York, they're from Chicago) and to undercut it (and them). He
constructs a mentality gone off the rails (a direct rendering by Hitchcock,
with the brilliant assistance of Ernest Lehman's script, of Hamlet's "antic
disposition"). Here from Roger is a virtuoso performance of insanity, which
is to say, a performance from Grant of a "performance of insanity"—
unrelentingly and fundamentally inappropriate to the scene as "gallery
patrons" know it, while at the same time showing us—because we are in the
know—only exceeding verbal and social skill: he disrupts the proceedings,
but with personality not violence. Or, he exercises the violence of personality.
Grant's ability to play each accreting moment with perfect attunement,
perfectly aimed enunciation, and perfect innocence is evidence of extreme

---

[4]In acknowledgment of the Lumières' *L'arrivée d'un train en gare de La Ciotat* (1896), during
early projections of which it is rumored watchers pulled away. See Chapter 11 below.

virtuosity, this long scene being one of the really virtuosic (as well as truly hilarious) moments in American cinema.

Climbing to Vandamm's

Grant's job here is to pose with extraordinary grace—something he is always, and predictably, good at. Most of the work is being done by the camera, which frames the diagonal struts of the house (apparently an architectural marvel, roughly à la manière de Frank Lloyd Wright) in such a way as to suggest that Grant is very high off the ground. He is in fact in a studio set, extending downward not more than a few feet beneath him.[5] His arrival by way of the balcony at Eve's room is of course a little homage to *Romeo and Juliet*. The exceptional quality of the sequence flows from Grant's pressed trousers and nappy white shirt seen against the wooden struts at twilight. He could be modeling.

Mt. Rushmore

(For technical details, see my *The Horse Who Drank the Sky*, ch. 3.) Roger and Eve are not on Mount Rushmore. Some setup shots were made there, at considerable expense, in order that the monument appear in crisp sunshine, and with Grant, Mason, Leo G. Carroll, and Saint in proximity. But the scaling sequence is produced entirely in MGM's Stage 27, an enormous and very high facility in Culver City, where, combined with an extensive painted backing lit variously for different parts of the twilight, and with Styrofoam rock formations built to match it, Roger and Eve "scramble," with mounting fear of falling, to evade Licht and Valerian who are chasing them to the death. Views of the monument are framed from various angles, to give the impression we are resting upon the Great Faces, but these are really rear-projected stereo (still photograph) images made by the designer Robert Boyle in advance, on location, using a boswain's chair (property of the Parks Department, and used normally for cleaning or repairing the actual faces). Much of the scene, the part, indeed, that gives the strongest sense of Roger's (Grant's) heroic athleticism in descending while protecting Eve, is made with long shots in which the two bodies are tiny by comparison with the enormous stone faces, and the set they are working on is rather high. Emphatic is the apparent magnitude of the terrain and thus the characters' physical difficulty in managing a descent. Safety seems a long

---

[5]Matthew Yuricich's splendid (roughly 30" x 24") matte painting of the Vandamm house helps a lot with the visual trick here, establishing the scene.

way off, and by way of very dangerous paths. Roger's identity as an ad man (that is, a word guy) and his aplomb managing the steep rocks seem entirely incompatible, once again a source of wit but at the same time a legitimation of the extremes to which he must go in order to succeed.

The Grant of previous films had in fact established his "fabulous" screen identity largely with feet on the ground, maneuvering through social situations with the slickness of an acrobat but hardly confronting geographic, geological, physical danger and mastering his body to face it. Stage 27 is eighty feet high and he was sometimes near the top, clinging to scaffolding. Energy was required, because many shots were taken and retaken, but there was no threat of falling from the monument (or, for insurance reasons, the set). The sequence suggested a virtuosic athleticism from a major star, a derring-do of great proportion as he put himself in "harm's way." By the late 1950s, very few Hollywood stars had been accustomed to showing off physical agility and strength: Charlton Heston's undoubled shots in the chariot race of *Ben-Hur* (1959) constitute a rare exception (he spent considerable time learning how to drive the team that pulled his chariot), as do Burt Lancaster's routines in *Trapeze* (1956), *The Train* (1964), and *The Gypsy Moths* (1969).

In each of the scenes I have discussed, Grant accomplishes some virtuosic work that easily goes unseen, because it is superimposed upon him, not emanating from him, and because its primary content is emptiness: he avoids doing something that might ruin the scene. Consider the manifest invisibilities in this film, sequence by sequence:

The Townsend Study

The actor is carefully (and invisibly) attuned to the scene partner so that the tonality of expression is responsive and works as a kind of accompaniment. This attunement is fully apart from what the script says and implies: it's not what you say, it's how you say it, bouncing back what your partner is saying to you in a particular way. If we juxtapose this scene, for example, with one of the scenes of Grant with Roger's mother (Jessie Royce Landis) (or even with his robustly skittish tone with Katharine Hepburn in *Bringing Up Baby* [1938] or his robustly confident tone with Rosalind Russell in *His Girl Friday* [1940]), we find wholly incompatible tonal duets; the Roger who is talking to "mother" cannot be the same Roger as the one talking to Vandamm ("Townsend"), and neither of them flows from the same Grant who is putting together a dinosaur or writing a news column. In the study, Grant is obliged to imitate James Mason just a little, enough so that the two belong together yet not so much as to seem mocking or mirroring. Grant picks up the level of Mason's voicing and phrasing, the way of speaking while slowly circling. There are other cinematic scenes where one might find this labor, but one tends not to because it is out of sight whereas here it is at the center.

Driving Downhill

How convenient to perform inebriation. The body sways without balance control; sounds, incoherent, emerge from the mouth; the driver yanks the wheel this way and that way to extremes, guiding the car almost off the road. But for this scene to work well, Grant must hold back from trying any of these tricks: they would all lead attention to him, not to Roger's predicament, for concentration on which the viewer must focus upon the hard-to-focus-upon background. What rolling, seasick-inducing motion is needed will be produced technically, through the advance filming of the rear-projection plates: Grant will have to submit to the roll, in fact, rather than making it. The rear projection will effect such pronounced apparent movement of the car on that road from left to right and back, that Grant's real preoccupation must be to contrive his hand movements in such a way that what we see at the steering wheel matches the gross movements as built through the image composite. Roger must seem to have a body out of control, yet not so much out of control that the coherence of the overall visual orientations is lost, *and these orientations are largely created through rear projection, too.* As we look at Grant, what we see behind him must be visually coherent with the way he moves, *yet (like all actors on the rear-projection stage) he cannot see what is behind (here, ahead of) him.* In fact he may not even see the projections in front of him as well as we do because they are set to a particular focus *for the camera,* not for him. Given that he has to perform in such a *guided* way acting this drunk driving madly down this hill he has to be as sober as can be.

Lunch on the Train

This scene is constructed of alternating portrait shots to establish the rhythm and décor of a seductive conversation. Each actor must play solo while simultaneously working to accompany the action of the other (through lead-in and follow-up). But because the camera will be composing the shots tightly, far less gesture can come into play than might in ordinary life. The actor lets the dialogue carry much of the weight, and works the face and hands for minimal gestures of accompaniment. Actors like Saint and Grant are aware that because of their status as film actors, they are already noteworthy in portrait shots. Audiences will be scanning for the slightest detectable move, thus great focus upon gestural technique is required; even a slight gestural emendation or correction would throw off the tone of the instant. Think of a scene like this as a typical boy-girl conversation intensively magnified, so that the slightest tic, now made huge, bodes disaster.

A second problem is created by the camera setups here. Interspersed among the portrait shots are angle shots of each character giving body posture and facial expression but also, simultaneously, revealing the world that is swiftly passing by outside the train window. An interesting technical feature of rear projections of this sort, involving travel seen from the side, is that the viewer's attention is momentarily thrown past the characters to the interesting terrain. The terrain is only there, after all, to add realistic interest. And so one is interested in that interest. But every flicker of gaze at the passing river, the telephone poles, or the trees is a flicker stolen from the characters, who must sustain one's involvement if the story is to unfold. What is called for from the actors is a kind of intensified casualness, confident if the viewer's eye wanders but relaxed and self-effacing if it does not.

Cropduster

Grant's Roger must here seem to feel that his life is imperiled, in a way that builds and then climaxes with the action. But because this is Cary Grant, not some other man at the roadside, the main job is a kind of psychological removal from the dangerous territory. Were an actor to behave *realistically* as though he thought his life were in danger the scene would fly off the rails. For Grant, the cropduster must offer a perfectly controlled, even, for him, pleasurably rhythmic enactment of terror. The scene will be imposing a tremendous pressure, and Grant must let the viewer see that if Roger senses that pressure (the airplane machine gun) he is not collapsed by it, even though he must physically fall. Think of the acrobat's trick of "taking a fall" in such a way as to rebound instantly with high energy—a trick Grant knew from long practice.

Auction

Roger must here seem not mad but contrivedly "mad," expressly not so unhinged he doesn't know how to control himself. Through facial gesture and the refined modulation of vocal tone he provides a symphony of "control loss" kept sharply on key if continually boding disaster; the symphonic quality convinces us of the actor's virtuosic control, as, further, does his carefully holding back from showing so much shaping power as to leave us the impression that Roger's "losing control" is definitively being faked: we surf through the scene wondering, and only slowly losing the wonder, whether our character has really gone off the rails. Finally, at the character level, the fakery must seem clear and intentional: Roger is being wily, not anti-social. But much of what Grant can accomplish is generated and bounded by Ernest Lehman's script for the scene and its setting, the film as a whole: Roger at first almost always perfectly social and sociable, even under trying circumstances; then losing balance a little, as with Mother; now, facing off with the auctioneer, someone who knows how bidding is done. Thus, Roger is a man whose awkward style is a put on, but also a spontaneous someone who could blurt something he might otherwise refrain from saying. Grant is expert in playing the lines of dialogue Lehman has written to set up this progression, but his expertise would evaporate without the lines. The actor knows, too, that his Roger is playing a scene with a number of secondary characters whose brittle obedience will brilliantly illuminate his every move. His luminousness is thus circumstantial, from the action around.

Ascending the House

We see another precarious balance there, between agility and fear. Roger constantly pauses to check his balance (fear of falling) while pulling himself up the angular struts with real strength (purposive agility). If Grant, who can have no trouble with the movement itself, shows too much agility, we will not fear for Roger and the scenic architecture will fall flat. If on the other hand he shows too much fear, Roger's making it to the balcony will disturb the realism, and *we must* find him there next. If Roger shows no agility, we won't believe he could be doing this at all. And if he shows no fear, Roger will seem like a man who thinks he's a movie star on a set, not a Madison Avenue executive trapped in South Dakota.

Mt. Rushmore

For long shots made in Hollywood before the use of traveling mattes (today, blue- or green-screen backings), the simulation of height was difficult. While some shots in this sequence required Grant and Saint to be high off the soundstage floor, they were perched on a ladder, and posed against Styrofoam not rock. Part of the virtuosity of the scene, then, is just plain everyday working courage. In all the shots, however, Grant has to give Roger the quality of a man dangling but somehow not losing his characteristic Grantian insouciance. At the same time, he is constrained to read the lines of the script and to be seen doing this as the director, cinematographer, and set designer have contrived. The character in this scene is a resultant of outside forces converging on the body to effect an illusion of perfect, and entrancing, vulnerability.

* * *

Many who view acting think the performer works by pretending to put himself into a situation. Here, for instance, Grant is pretending to dangle from Mt. Rushmore. It's hardly that simple. Anyone pretending to a fictive circumstance *with no reservation* will be caught up in it, thus unable to show a self being caught up and transcending through virtuosity. Further, it's not the circumstance but the lens with which an actor is embedded. Not where you are, but how people will see you being there.

10

Spontaneity

FIGURE 10 *James Cagney (r.) in* White Heat *(Raoul Walsh, Warner Bros., 1949). Digital frame enlargement.*

Nicholas Ray advised actors, regarding their lines, "Say it as if for the first time or the last time, but never in between" (3). What he was looking for—even a cursory review of his films will show this—was a kind of spontaneity, a sense that the moment was blooming out of itself without extrinsic organization and without plan, without contrivance. Conditions perpetually change, and one's actions should respond to conditions. As Paul Goodman says in *Speaking and Language,* talk is one's way of being in a situation.

Spontaneity is central to viewers' expectations of the virtuosic moment and to their ways of finding satisfaction in it. While the performer must store and use capacities and strengths to produce the moment—a unique voice (Albert Finney), astounding breathing and range (Katharine Hepburn), a body that draws attention (Bill Nighy), an ability to pose and move with grace (Audrey Hepburn), emotional force (Elizabeth Taylor), expressive punctuality (Humphrey Bogart)—this storage and use, insofar as they are to be taken as spontaneous, must not show evidence of self-awareness or design. In point of fact it must be staged—open to a view from one side only—as with any other dramatic material; but staged, of course, as unstaged. The deeply affecting moment must seem merely to happen, "for the first or the last time but never in between."

One may conceive the towering difficulty raised by the requirement for spontaneity. It is one thing to respond with urgency and directness to the events of everyday life—scream in pain when scalded by coffee—but quite another to *give the impression* of doing this when one is neither engaged in nor surrounded by everyday life—when the coffee is just brown-tinted tepid water and the camera is trained close on your face. With real coffee, the heat itself produces a nervous reaction, a spasmodic reflex which may be part of the instigating force behind the scream; this is absent when the liquid is tepid. Further, because in making a film actors have the script in possession and have read it beforehand, they tend to know the action that will precede this moment in the final edit, and the action that will follow it. More: they are in a position to know how—and when!—the story will end. Thus, each felt moment is part of what professionals call an arc, in which there will be rises and falls "mapped" and thought through, very bright and very dark moments, moments of frontality and confrontation and background moments when the character stands and watches. For mounting and sustaining a virtuosic moment there is a certain necessary energy—physical and emotional, mustered personally by the actor—and the actor must be in position to summon that energy, appropriate to the dramatic moment; hold it for as long as the director takes to make the scene; and judiciously (but also spiritedly) marshal its use. A shot could have to be retaken for numerous reasons, many involving work outside the actor's purview. Being used, the performative energy may need to be regained quickly for use again.

The greatest moments of virtuosity do give the appearance of springing from nowhere.

For a sterling example, consider James Cagney in *White Heat* (1949). His Cody Jarrett is a hardened criminal and a hardened man: impossible to know which came first. In crime he is rough, in speech abrupt, in social relations by and large a bully. But he has a mother (ironically boss of the crime gang) (Margaret Wycherly) to whom he is passionately devoted, and to whom he shows tenderness and protective love. Cody goes to prison. One day at lunchtime, he sits at a long table crowded with inmates to the left and right of him. An establishing shot of the area from a high perch shows dozens of such tables, with hundreds of men chatting loudly and a team of guards on the prowl monitoring them. We come upon Cody stuffing food into his mouth, head down. He is concentrating on his own space, a recluse drawn into a protective territorial bubble. But then, stealing a glance to his right, he asks his neighbor whether that isn't Lefeld down there?, Nat Lefeld?, and has he just come in? Yes. So, Cody mutters, "Ask him how's my mother."

In what resembles a game of "telephone," we see the man lean over and ask his neighbor, mouth to ear, and then the neighbor ask his neighbor, and that neighbor ask his neighbor, and so on. The target Lefeld leans to his left (screen right) and whispers an answer, that we have trouble lip-reading because his face is in profile to the camera. The loud din of the prisoners covers the whole acoustic space of this action. The message is passed back, as the camera slowly glides rightward to find Cody again. With the last iteration, we are able to hear, "Dead."

Jarrett now goes entirely out of control in the dining room, leaving his place, hitting guards, racing around as he screams, "I have to get out!" But the manner in which Cagney produces this eruption is something to see and hear. He begins by doing two things more or less in tandem: emitting a soft whine, like an animal in pain, and leaning forward in an effort to raise himself out of his seated position. The upward climb continues until he is standing, head bowed—in what, reflection?, helplessness?, respect?— and fists on the table for support. All through this, with inhalation after punctuating inhalation, the whine grows in amplitude until it has become a hysterical scream. He begins to smash the table, then to climb upon it, climb over the other prisoners, raising the pitch on the scream and throwing his arms around without direction. As he hits the floor and runs off to punch the nearest guard, he is screaming without bound, and the other men have become silent to watch, their little gesture of course aggravating the intensity of Cody's voice (which echoes, too, because the room is cavernous). We retreat to the bird's-eye position again as he is finally cornered by a gang of guards and carried, twisting and screaming, out of the scene.[1]

The extreme modulation of Cagney's vocalization and movement, before and after he clears the table, is plenty logical for Cody, but virtuosity lies in Cagney's idiosyncratic method of moving from meditative silence through distaste and anger, through pain and mounting pain, through the need to burst with feeling, to the point of the actual explosion. He achieves a perfect crescendo of feeling and movement.

To think through what the performer must be ready to do, in order that this scene can be played:

Any one of the half dozen character actors next to Cody might make a gesture that ruined the shot; and in the general surround there are hundreds

---

[1]Considerable emphasis is added to the carrying movement by the actor's screaming and evocative twisting, as we see reprised in Harold Becker's *Mercury Rising* (1998) with Bruce Willis carrying the "autistic" Miko Hughes away from danger.

of extras pretending to eat their lunch and loudly talk, all of this raising the chances that the shot might have to be redone; so Cagney must "expend himself utterly" without actually expending himself utterly. To add trouble, the guard action must be precisely choreographed with Cagney's, so that the mutual pummeling, actually unreal, will seem real: and any of this might spark a need for retakes. And Cagney's initial maneuver, in which he shifts Cody from a childish mewl to a killing rage, is taken in one uninterrupted shot. In short, the filming is precarious for technical reasons, entirely unrelated to what could be going on personally with the star as he works. Cagney must have this vocal and physical routine—it is nothing less than a song and dance—carefully rehearsed, but not in such a lively way that his voice gives out. The voice must sound very powerfully, at both ends of the acoustic spectrum, and also with great control (and that tactical reservation, just in case). Remember that when an opera singer gives a concert, each song needs to be sung only once, and each difficult passage, once it has been sung through, becomes history. In filmmaking, there is no history.[2]

Added to the gross configuration of Cody's loss of self, we hear tiny declarative riffs inside Cagney's utterance. That opening tiny bleat of pain is sounded through an exhalation, quite as though the character is sighing with some ultimate resignation, using his last breath, dying in response to the mother's death: the sound is even etiolated and shrunken, coming out of a body that has reached, as Sophocles wrote, "the final limit of his life" (perhaps by returning to infantilism). One anticipates a full body collapse, a fainting withdrawal from the circumstances. But the whine expands and picks up volume (an engine starting up), takes on a quality of repetition, tribal, vengeful, terrifying, the natural expression of some animal on the hunt. Soon, because he stands the way students do to be heard in the classroom, we realize that Cody needs to enunciate his pain, but decorum is swiftly brushed aside as he climbs over his neighbors onto the table. A full-blown catastrophe ensues. Whilst *crescendo* is the overall form of the moment we experience it as an enjambment of increasingly demonstrative instants. And Cagney is responsible for producing each and every one of those instants—producing: which is to say, preparing to produce, enacting the production, and recovering from it so as to be able to move on to the next moment, not to say the next shots on the schedule.

There are many explanations for the kind of work involved in mobilizing spontaneity. Konstantin Stanislavsky wanted his students to be able to mount the stage and simply sit in a chair: simply, *just* now. Not *Sit In A Chair*—declaration, irony—but merely do the thing that is done by millions of people in the spontaneous everyday, the effortless thing, the thing one

---

[2]This curious aspect of cinema is put up for affectionate parody in Harold Ramis's *Groundhog Day* (1993) and Doug Liman's *Live. Die. Repeat (Edge of Tomorrow)* (2014).

does without self-awareness as object of the critical gaze. In achieving such simplicity the performer brings an effusive energy, derived largely from relaxation, being in the body purposefully but without particular concentration. Aid may come from some (in this case, limited) use of memory, the act of reaching back and inside for a repository of true feeling, yet not in such a way as to mar the naturalness of movement. When we sit in a chair we do not remember how we sat yesterday, and how there was feeling; and we do not foresee what will come afterward. On a bare stage this spontaneous action can be a daunting task, but on a film set the designer and cinematographer are working to provide enormous help. The actor must inhabit the set, not only placing but also accommodating his body to the shape of the space so that it seems to be his actual space, the space in which he has memory and aspiration and sensibility, here, now, at this instant and also before; yet again, *not* the set *as it really is* but the set as it will appear on camera, which is, after all, another space altogether. "It is necessary," Stanislavsky wrote, "that you really believe in the general possibilities of [the character's] life, and then become so accustomed to it that you feel yourself close to it. If you are successful in this, you will find that 'sincere emotions,' or 'feelings that seem true' will spontaneously grow in you" (55). To feel *close to* the character, not to inhabit the character, since plainly that is not possible, the character being only a construct in the first place. To inhabit is to live inside; but to be close is to hold an image strongly, with feeling.

When we see Cagney climb onto the dining table we sense that he has eaten at this table countless times, that he is sitting at his own place there, the place he always occupies. And the plate from which he is scooping food is not *a* plate but in fact *his* plate, the one he has appropriated (and always appropriates) for himself.

Uta Hagen reflects on seeing the great Laurette Taylor: "I went to see her again and again as Mrs. Midget [in *Outward Bound*] and later as Amanda in *The Glass Menagerie*. Each time, I went to study and to learn, and each time I felt I had learned nothing because she simply caught me up in her spontaneity to the point of eliminating my own objectivity" (5). Hagen taught that "self-glorification and narcissism block the spontaneous behavior, the genuine give-and-take of any actor" (20).

Sanford Meisner's method is interlocutive and somewhat mysterious, if also alluring:

"Now, what did I just do?"

"You found a reaction in yourself, something that was big enough—"

"Spontaneous, right? Tell me you're going to invite me to dinner when you finish decorating your dining room, and that the main course is going to be artichokes."

"Sandy, when my dining room is finished, I'm going to invite you to dinner and the main course is going to be artichokes."

Again, from looking pleased, on hearing the word "artichokes" Meisner's face contorts with displeasure.

"You don't like artichokes?" Bette asks.

"That's quite clear, right?" Meisner asks, and again the class laughs. (145–6)

Nicholas Ray's instruction about delivering lines is part of the method he uses. He was also interested in having actors find the spark of spontaneity in the placement of any one moment inside a phrase that itself might occupy a far greater spate of dramatic time, beginning in some earlier scene (earlier in the diegetical plan) and culminating in a later one. For a singular example: in *Rebel Without a Cause* (1955) a teenager played by Sal Mineo, a shy, sensitive, lonely boy, accompanies his two friends Judy and Jim (Natalie Wood, James Dean) to a deserted mansion late in the film, and by night there, as his friends cuddle and pretend to be married, he lays his head back on Jim and pretends to be their son. Plato (Mineo) is effortless, completely and nakedly genuine in this move, but the meaning rests on his memory of having met Jim in a school hallway much earlier in the film, having admired him on sight, and later on having been harassed by a gang and retreating to a sumptuous parental bedroom. The building of the boy's need for affiliation, for touch, for unification with others has been growing steadily scene by scene, and here it reaches an apogee, yet an apparently natural apogee, so natural that we would be dismayed if the gesture had been withheld. The arc will be completed in tragedy, as at film's end Plato lies dead in Jim's protective embrace.

For Ray, when the actor entered the scene, the question would immediately be raised, "Why are you here? What are you trying to do?" This focus on purpose, the project of life, gives frame and shape to action. Are you trying to apologize, antagonize, make friends, get information? What is your purpose, underneath the script, in your territory only.

A spontaneous moment from Natalie Wood, in the same film. She is at home in her parents' middle-class house. The dining room. Dinner time. Her father (William Hopper), strict and repressing, is at the head of the table. Suddenly she is at his side, bending, giving him a kiss that comes out of nowhere. He pulls away, angry and repulsed. She leads us to think she has not really thought through doing this: expressing love for the father directly. But she is a teenaged girl, not an adult, deeply self-conscious and especially of her body. She has on a tight sweater that emphasizes her bust line just enough so that when he saw her out of the corner of his eye we could have no trouble reading his gaze as both lustful and self-censored. It is a sexual daughter who is planting those red lips, seen from outside; yet for Judy the red lips are nothing but her lips, the body nothing but her body. If we see her offering herself, she is still vague about what "offering the self" might mean.

Is Wood acting out of nature here? When she moves to kiss Hopper we have the sense, by the clumsy swiftness of her gesture, that the thought has just come to her. A moment with its own possibility. To show him affection on the spur of the moment, out of the air, in so physical a way, can mean nothing good. In a much earlier scene, while we stared at the jarring red lipstick she wore against the red of her coat, she complained of how her father didn't like the lipstick and tried to rub her lips off.

11

In Dreams Awake

FIGURE 11 *Marlene Dietrich with Jane Wyman in* Stage Fright *(Alfred Hitchcock, Warner Bros., 1950). Digital frame enlargement.*

Discussing early audience "astonishment" at cinema and the legendary "terrorised spectator" of the Grand Café,[1] Tom Gunning takes to task an argument of Christian Metz:

> Contemporary film theorists have made careers out of underestimating the basic intelligence and reality-testing abilities of the average film viewer and have no trouble treating previous audiences with similar disdain.

---

[1]The first film screenings, by the brothers Lumière, took place at the Salon Indien du Grand Café, Boulevard des Capucines, Paris, 28 December 1895.

The most subtle reading of this initial terror comes from Metz.. . . . Metz describes this panicked reaction on the part of the Grand Café audience as a displacement of the contemporary viewer's credulity onto a mythical childhood of the medium. Like the childhood when one still believed in Santa Claus, like the dawn of time when myths were still believed literally, belief in this legendary audience . . . allows us to disavow our own belief in the face of the cinema. *We* don't believe in the screen image in the manner that *they* did. (115)

The early magic theater, Gunning argues potently, "labored to make visual that which it was impossible to believe. Its visual power consisted of a trompe l'oeil play of give-and-take, an obsessive desire to test the limits of an intellectual disavowal—I know, but yet I see" (117). This is a compact and revealing statement of the viewer's position with figments of the screen, a position in which information and effect merge to create a strange understanding. Partly because of this wild marriage, films are like dreams for us, and watching in the dark theater is like dreaming. We can be, as Thoreau warned, and following Caliban, "in dreams awake."

In the dream one can be confronted with a passageway into a space that, for one reason or another congruent with the story, cannot be entered. A doorway into a restricted holy space, a world of taboo. In this way the dream mirrors cinema, where viewers are offered a moving, coherently fashioned spectacle at the same time as they are pinioned in a zone designed for them only, a reception zone opened to address. That zone buffers them, keeps them away from the privacy in which the production was prepared and mounted. The "stage line" of the theater or the "axis" of cinema keep us distant from what entrances, while at the same time rendering entrancement possible. Entrancement in viewing has the quality of one of those dream moments (but substantially extended in time) when a gate paralyzes and reveals a forbidden territory.

(At the end of *Rear Window* [1954], when Thorwald bursts into Jeff's apartment, I am terrified [quite irrespective of Jeff], and want, hopelessly, to escape.)

That the forbidden space is present to the eye works to verify its very existence, just as the palpable silence of the untold secret works to convince that it is not, in reality, nothing. The boundary of the space reveals both it and those who work there, invisible to us. Here, then, is the package of our knowledge. Yet, at the same time that we recognize a production space, *thus a production*, a production that is catching our attention *now*, still we see! Knowing that cinema works to sweep us away, still we are swept away.

A particular charge of excitement and pleasure lies in "behind-the-scenes" movie musicals, as well as other similarly "revealing" films that "show" production: *Gold Diggers of 1933* (1933), *Gold Diggers of 1935* (1935), *A Night at the Opera* (1935), *A Double Life* (1947), *Summer Stock* (1950), *The Band Wagon* (1953), *There's No Business Like Show Business* (1954),

White Christmas (1954), *The Entertainer* (1960), *8 ½* (1963), *Contempt* (1964), *Inside Daisy Clover* (1965), *Alex in Wonderland* (1970), *Day for Night* (1973), *The King of Comedy* (1982), *Passion* (1982), *The Dresser* (1983), *Noises Off . . .* (1992), *Birdman* (2014). Here "the show must go on" but some irresolvable problem obstructs (keeps characters away from one another emotionally). As the "problem" is resolved, the perceptible "show" gets healthfully underway. And in this way the illusion is struck and fostered, developed and enriched, that we are seeing both the front of the entertainment and its back, both the presentational side and the productive. We go into the wings (as, in the concluding shot of *The 39 Steps* [1935], where a poor performer perishes but our lovers find one another in bliss, backstage).

Central to the "backstage" illusion is the inevitable scene in which we find ourselves in the dressing room. *The Blue Angel* (1930). *Yankee Doodle Dandy* (1942). *The Red Shoes* (1948). *White Christmas*. We feel we are seeing the entire machine, all of its parts, the grinding of the mechanism and its beautiful product. Yet of course, as Goffman warns about the play-within-the-play, no such arrangement is in place at all. The backstage or off-camera space we see is actually only a "backstage," or "off-camera," mounted from a backstage or off-camera entirely closed to view.

In the Central Park "Dancing in the Dark" routine from *Band Wagon*, in a strange and fascinating way, the dressing room and the performance area, the front and back of the structure, seem to be present at once. The scene is prefaced in Tony Hunter's (Fred Astaire's) sumptuous rose-pink hotel suite at the Plaza, where Gabrielle Gerard (Cyd Charisse) has paid a visit to make a somewhat insincere apology. She comments on the reproduction paintings framed on the walls, only to be told they are not reproductions at all: a clumsiness he forgives without a thought. She accepts his invitation to go for a ride and see if they can get along (in diegetic terms, manage to dance together). A horse-drawn carriage brings them to a secluded nook in the Park by night. They move through a public dance area where oblivious strangers are locked in one another's arms (reflections of the audience), to a wholly private, empty place. A bench, some rocks in the background, high trees, and beyond that the New York skyline lit up. This setting (by Preston Ames, under the supervision of Cedric Gibbons) is at once, and very movingly, artificial (a set design: the perfectly danceable flatness of the ground) and realistic (actual New York: the correct street lamps and quality of nocturnal light, the size and quality of the space, the skyline, the trees). One knows but one sees! This is an extended dressing room, as it were, where secretly, unseen by the world (!), the two protagonists who later, on a stage, will be seen as stars find time to "rehearse" in "total privacy."[2]

---

[2]A charming homage to this scene is provided by John Travolta and Karen Lynn Gorney in *Saturday Night Fever* (1977) as they try dancing together in a rented studio, watched by a camera that dances, too.

Yet the lighting, the choreography, the unheard supra-diegetic orchestral rendition of Cole Porter's song, the matching costumes, the elegance of the two dancers in all their moves sum to a pair of virtuosic accomplishments, one diegetic and one not: Tony and Gaby on one side, Astaire and Charisse on the other, joined invisibly by the entire off-camera crew. This "backstage" moment tags the present unseen "off-camera" world obliquely, because whilst this is manifestly a dance it is diegetically not a dance but only a practice to see if later on a dance will be possible. The scene also enriches us with something utterly fictive, something magically touching, as no real performance onstage could manage to do in our sight, although any such "real" later performance would be just such as this present real (performance-as-) rehearsal already is; would be, but isn't, since this is the only version of the routine we ever see.

Between knowledge and enchantment there operates a kind of mental switch that can toggle our consciousness, hum us to sleeping dream or alarm us to awaken. The filmmaker is in a position to acknowledge and control this figurative switch. Consider Marlene Dietrich and Jane Wyman near the conclusion of Hitchcock's *Stage Fright* (1950). It is to be remembered that beyond being a master of cinema, Hitchcock was a master of dramatization altogether, and knew how to position and frame actors and performance for ultimate clarity and revelation.

Dietrich's Charlotte Inwood (a famous stage performer) and Wyman's Eve Gill (secretly an acting student at the Royal Academy of Dramatic Arts, no less) are alone together inside the star's dressing room. It's late in the day, the star is dressed to go off for the evening. Caught up helping the police catch a murderer who is believed to be associated with Inwood (I labor here to avoid spoiling), Eve has been masquerading for some time as the star's Cockney dresser "Doris," putting on an accent and taking care to comport herself beneath her actual social station. It is "Doris" facing Inwood here, nor just some unknown who is named Inwood but "Charlotte Inwood" *the* elegant star, "Charlotte Inwood" the internationally famous, Charlotte Inwood with a cigarette poised between her fingers, a fur wrap around her neck, and a somewhat disdainful unfocussed gaze in her eyes. The much-accomplished stage performer has been utterly taken in by the girl's act so far and, because it has been going on for some time, in a way so are we, at least in this scene. Inwood actually deigns to offer "Doris" some money as a parting tip, with a very sweet tone and a genuinely encouraging, even chummy voice: "Go ahead. You've earned it. Go and buy yourself something." But now "Doris" seems to be blocking her exit from the room. "You're in my way." Not a sound or motion from the girl, so a more peremptory voice, colder: "Step out of my way or I'll call the police."

At this instant the mask drops off, in order that a dramatic confrontation (on which the plot will revolve) may be triggered. Eve, in her forthright, real accent, showing plainly that "Doris" was fake: "Yes. Call the police, Miss Inwood."

"You're no dresser!"

This is a virtuosic moment in several ways at once. First, Wyman handles the flip with a sharp, instantaneous change of speaking mode, but without any noticeable physical posturing. It's the voice alone, indeed the accent—that aspect of the English language that to residents of Britain is so signal a clue as to identity, place of origin, and culture. Charlotte is taken completely aback, first that "Doris" really doesn't exist (and she's been duped: she, a doyenne of the stage) and secondly that while she thought she was safe in private space with her dresser she now realizes she is vulnerable in public space with a manipulative stranger. Let us say that Charlotte abruptly awakens from her dream. And to some—ideally, limited—degree so do we. We must be alerted to a grounding beneath facade, yet not so alerted as to detect Wyman or Dietrich beneath Eve and Charlotte. ("Yes, call the police, Miss Dietrich!"—"Then I will, Miss Wyman!") In dropping their faces so slickly, Wyman and Dietrich are virtuosic.

And Eve can hardly be ready for the defensive anger Charlotte now displays, so that if Charlotte is now awake to mortal danger so is Eve. Young at the game, Eve perhaps didn't guess how rough play would be once she was in it. She has taken a giant—and naked—step closer to the thing called murder, now seeing Charlotte converted on the instant—through her own tiny but potent virtuosity—from charmer to schemer. It would be easy to go too far and feel that we, too, had been awakened: to a "true" reality, the theater, even this one, a gigantic cavern where the movie is playing just for us. In the shadow behind the well-lit front, evil may spring. (That long tradition in the West, again, holding that theatricality is an evil danger.)

But:

Our reality is not up for grabs here. We are watching Eve and Charlotte awaken to *their* reality, with makeup and costumes laid aside, the bare selves revealed. Their new view only partially dismantles the scene for us because still, as long as the celluloid unspools, we see the "bare" selves of only characters, however fascinating and fleshed out. Oblivious we remain to whatever vital state of affairs might lie in the dressing room we may not visit.

12

A Feminine Mystique

FIGURE 12 *Glenn Close as Albert in* Albert Nobbs *(Rodrigo Garcia, Mockingbird/Trillium, 2011). Digital frame enlargement.*

Writing of anxiety in the Victorian age, Nina Auerbach addresses the virtuosic social structure we may call "theatricality":

> "Theatricality" is such a rich and fearful word in Victorian culture that it is most accurately defined, as Carlyle uses it, in relation to the things it is not. Sincerity is sanctified and it is not sincere. Reverent Victorians shunned theatricality as the ultimate, deceitful mobility. It connotes not only lies, but a fluidity of character that decomposes the uniform integrity of the self. (pg, qtd. in Wikander 75)

Matthew Wikander claims about Auerbach here that she echoes Jean-Jacques Rousseau's "vision of a feminized world of performance" (75), a deep-seated conviction in performative acumen, especially virtuosity, as a gendered thing. The "femininity" of the world of performance seen in these early approaches consists, for Auerbach, of deceit, fluidity of identity, and fundamental opposition to entrenched value. We can presume that the corresponding "masculinity" implied stability of identity, open-faced honesty, and celebration of sincerity and directness, a complete negation of performance. The male who exhibited what might turn out to be a "false" masculinity, that is, a masculinity detected as performative, could be ostracized.

Sarah Bernhardt considered performance the woman's domain, too.

> I think that acting is essentially a feminine art. Indeed, to make up one's face, hide one's true feelings, try to please, wish to attract attention, these are the faults of which women are often accused, and for which they are forgiven. These same faults are odious in a man. And yet the male actor has to make himself as attractive as possible, whether it be by means of makeup, fake beards or toupees. . . . Perhaps the perpetual suppression of himself gives the actor a more feminine nature. (230–31)

The deceit of performance is here made specific: to cause the face to look different *from what it naturally is*; to make a display of feeling that is inauthentic to the truth of the moment (for instance, to hide one's pain and humiliation under the guise of decorum or "seemliness"); to seduce attention by a fawning subservience of manner and fastidious devotion to heightening one's visibility. For an audience to experience virtuosity in the Victorian age, Bernhardt's age, would have meant bearing sight of really extreme manifestations of "the feminine" in these respects. The voice, for instance, might ring powerfully, both making declaration and guaranteeing a focus of attention.

In early cinema one frequently sees male actors using broad—in ordinary terms overexpressive—gestures of the upper body and face, especially in the 1910s when the tableau shot, in which faces were unrecognizable, was replaced by long shots, medium shots, and close-ups. Even into the 1920s, with such virtuosi as Charlie Chaplin, John Barrymore, Lillian Gish, Gloria Swanson, Mabel Normand, Harold Lloyd, Buster Keaton, Marie Dressler, Rudolph Valentino, Janet Gaynor, Lon Chaney, Douglas Fairbanks, and Louise Brooks one could see extremity of gesture and caricature of the face. The Astaire-Rogers dance routines of the early 1930s extend this hypergestural form in choreography—note, for one example, in the "Cheek to Cheek" duet of *Top Hat* (1935) the signal use of the polished limb extension or attenuation of pose, the pointed foot, the perfectly calculated spin, the embrace stretched for noticeability. Rogers wears an astonishing (ostrich feather) gown that moves in space as though alive. In "Cheek to Cheek," as the characters' romance begins the two figures continually mirror each other in physical moves; their commonality is based in an ability, and willingness, to stretch themselves toward the visible.

In screwball comedies and noir epics, one finds a neo-Victorian gender propriety, in which male performance ceases to be physically decorative and the physical decoration of female performance is extended. A male wearing discernable makeup or clothing that draws attention, or speaking with an odd manner, is off-center, the comedy relief: often in screwball films Ralph Bellamy grumbling in loud-patterned jackets, in musicals Edward Everett Horton's tuxedoed garrulous confusion. Heroic females show off in expensive or outlandish garments (Irene Dunne in the publisher confrontation scene of *Theodora Goes Wild* [1936]; Katharine Hepburn in the martini scene of *Bringing Up Baby* [1938]; Carole Lombard at the scavenger hunt in *My Man Godfrey* [1936]), use the voice with an extreme range of tonality (Alice Brady in *Godfrey*; Mary Nash in *The Philadelphia Story* [1940]; Agnes Moorehead in *The Magnificent Ambersons* [1942]), emphatically style their expression (Barbara Stanwyck in *Stella Dallas* [1937]; Veronica Lake in *Sullivan's Travels* [1942]; Judy Garland in *Meet Me in St. Louis* [1944]). Noir films, by and large, ushered in the era of "street performance," in which males and females behaved functionally, holding back expressive gesture that could be seen as decorative. If we watch Humphrey Bogart and Lee Patrick in *The Maltese Falcon* (1941) or Robert Mitchum and Jane Greer in *Out of the Past* (1947) or Charlton Heston and Janet Leigh in *Touch of Evil* (1958) we find down-to-earth, emotional but relatively practical and straightforward behavior. Other genres play the gender game in various idiosyncratic ways, sci-fi tending to project currently fashionable modes into a hypothesized future (wooden Leslie Nielsen and svelte Anne Francis in *Forbidden Planet* [1956]) while westerns exaggerate the helplessness of women and the directness of men (Joanne Dru and John Wayne in *Red River* [1948]; Natalie Wood and Jeffrey Hunter in *The Searchers* [1956]).

Parody is possible. In *Rio Bravo* (1959) Howard Hawks has burly, sturdy, hypermasculine John Wayne, a taciturn and capable strongman broadly acknowledged in the popular culture as such, playing a scene with the Texan/Latino actor Pedro Gonzales Gonzales. Sheriff John T. Chance is in the hotel run by Carlos, who indicates eagerly that a package has come. He brings it up to the Sheriff's room and they open it together. A flaming red negligee, not only the epitome of female couture of the time but optically so brilliant it literally takes over the scene. At Carlos's playful urging, Chance actually holds the thing up in front of himself so his friend can get a rough idea of how it will look on his wife, to whom he intends to gift it. We are confronted with a full-body medium shot of Wayne, a blushing smile on his lips, holding up the negligee as Angie Dickinson happens to come through the door. Her broad smile is full of ambiguity.

For Wayne this exemplifies what might be called "career virtuosity." The actor is risking his career image, that public, studio-constructed face by which he is known throughout the (ticket-buying) world, in order that a playful declaration may be made. The actor is saying, "I am acting," but also, "You know that this is *not* the me I usually pretend to be," and also again (of some actors but, I think, not Wayne), "Yet perhaps it is the *real me*, you'll never know!"[1] (With his bluntly staged self-masking in *Pillow Talk* [1959], his telegraphing to a loyal audience that he is capable of wearing a mask at least some people don't see through, Rock Hudson accomplishes a secret career virtuosity, invisible as such until 1985, when it was declared that he had AIDS and this facet of his talent came to the fore.)

Nowadays there are numerous films, studio-produced and independent, with male characters masquerading as female ones, pointedly putting on the declarative emotionalism and the solicitation of attention to which Bernhardt pointed (that is, both playing to conventional binary form and pointing to a contradictory underself). We find this in *Some Like It Hot* (1959), *Dressed to Kill* (1980), *The Crying Game* (1992), and a noteworthy Alfred Hitchcock film mentioning which would spoil it. The French comedian Michel Serrault's work in Édouard Molinaro's *La Cage aux folles* (1978) is a well-known example (see Stevens, for a careful analysis of this performance), including a remarkably complex scene in which his (rather notably effeminate) Albin takes a lesson from his lover Renato (Ugo Tognazzi) in how to walk "like a man."[2] Serrault, who off-camera walks the way his male co-actors do needed here to show precise, tightly focused difficulties the character would endure, much of Albin's "trouble" having to do with foot placement and rhythmic leg movement. Because the scene is played for open farce, the audience is subtly ensnared into close attention, in order that the tiny tics intended for producing hilarity (that is, for satisfying them) can be detected and enjoyed: gestural comedy often works this way.[3] The subtlety of the ensnaring further feminizes—indeed clandestinely feminizes—Serrault's actions in that he is cornered reaching out to command a view as, for Auerbach and Bernhardt, males would never properly do. In scenes such as this one, Albin is openly, visibly male yet has failed to learn masculine cues conventional in his cultural frame. There are other scenes in the film where, at the nightclub he runs with Renato, we see Albin in full travesty, on a tiny stage, theatrically lit and in front of an enthused audience.

Gender revelations in cinema, open acknowledgment that a secret masquerade is now terminated, can constitute a dramatic virtuosity, can seem to burst with illumination and opportunity for understanding, perhaps because our calculation of gender identity, important as deeply central to personality, is put in jeopardy. Often the decay of the disguise is produced

---

[1]The masculinities of *Rio Bravo* are given explicit and complex treatment by Peter Lehman.
[2]This moment of gendered walking is given homage as Matt Lintz struggles into the role of a female, for police purposes, in *The Alienist* (2018).
[3]Works, that is, by having very small signals magnified sufficiently as to become pleasantly perceptible but not so much as to slide into dominance.

by the script or the camera, but the performer is given credit, at least to the extent that he or she lingers in the viewer's mind because of the centrality to the fictive embodiment (as with Jaye Davidson in *Crying Game*). As well, a quality of sincerity attaches to the removal of the "costume," the "de-feminizing" of the actor's work and his return to the domain of the "real" (as we see with a scene of the stripping Sabin Tambrea in *Berlin Station* [2016]).

A different construction is involved as a male actor "becomes" female for a role. In Tom Hooper's *The Danish Girl* (2015), Eddie Redmayne's initially male character submits himself for a transgender operation and lives thereafter as a female. The game being played in dramatizations of this sort involves the viewer's straining to catch, beneath the lipstick, styled hair, and dress, beneath the soft voice and the softened gestures, some discernable trace of two males at once: the character Lili's male *anlage*, who was dissatisfied with his life as bound to that categorization and therefore underwent the surgery; and the actor Redmayne, officially and publically male, here performing both sides of the character and as such the basis of fan fascination. In *Hairspray* (2007), the masquerade is far less meticulous. John Travolta's travesty is explicit, an obvious dressing-up, part of the "fun" of the moment: his virtuosity depends on maintaining our awareness of, yet still seducing us by, the travesty, and the same is true of Dustin Hoffman in *Tootsie* (1982). When we see a woman onscreen typically, we do not find ourselves straining to see some possible male hiding inside a persona that we are taking as false; we take the given display as authentic, if, as Auerbach has noted, authentically and interminably "inauthentic." A question many people asked their friends who had seen *Danish Girl*: "Does Eddie make a good woman?" If Eddie were to make such a very good woman that no one could tell or remember that he was a male Eddie making a very good woman, he would finally *be* a woman, as gender binarists would define it. He can offer the performance *as performance* only by remaining himself, his "truly" male self, somewhere in the folds of the garment.

The flip side of these performances has its own fascinations. A female actor takes up a role in which she is called upon to guise herself as a male, for a small or large part of a rendition. In Liliana Cavani's *The Night Porter* (1974), a scene intended to be fascist-erotic and confusing in itself has slender Charlotte Rampling in a club full of Nazi officers gaining the attention of Dirk Bogarde with "Wenn ich mir was wünschen dürfte," a song recorded and popularized by Marlene Dietrich. As she coos in a low, breathy alto voice, in the Dietrich style (Dietrich was well known for gender impersonations of varying degrees), her tiny breasts become first visible and then invisible, depending on how she arches her bare back and on the exact profile she offers to the lens. At some instants as a hand rises to cover a breast she turns partly away from the camera, so that in her tidy cap she becomes, effectively, a "boy"; then she turns again and, showing the breasts eagerly, becomes a "girl." One hand slides down her dark pants, self-pleasuring. She falls into a chair and crosses her legs, ankle upon knee. Yet this gender play can be rationalized in terms of the scene.

Katharine Hepburn famously made an early sound-film foray into this territory with *Sylvia Scarlett* (1935), albeit with her pose as a boy (a masque to evade authorities, finally undone by the plot) substantially advertised in advance—"a woman who almost waited too long . . . before she dared admit that she was a woman!"—and inutile, therefore, for giving audiences the pleasing pique of discovery. One topical lobby card of the time had an artist's rendering of the figure sitting by a vanity, a knee lifted, and an accurate enough simulacrum of the Hepburn mouth vaguely smiling. Curled up on the bed behind was a grinning blonde. Notable in this hand-colored drawing is the reddish-brown hair on Hepburn's head, cut with tiny sideburns to reflect masculinity more completely than she manages in the film. The idea entered popular consciousness, at least, of a "daring" woman laying on masculine poses and gestures, bodily styling, and attitude—the idea, that is, that these characteristics do not entirely belong to men. The romantic plot toggles the deeply female Hepburn (fan magazines in 1938 would label her one of those *female* stars "'too intelligent' for their own good" [McLean 42]) between Brian Aherne and Cary Grant. Seven days after the film opened at New York's mammoth Radio City Music Hall, the *New York Times* reported, without enthusiasm, "Katharine Hepburn dons trousers." Julie Andrews's performance as an out-of-luck young woman who under the tutelage of the cheerfully gay Robert Preston masquerades as a male singer, in Blake Edwards's *Victor/Victoria* (1982), seems similarly unconvincing. Both the style of her performance and the logic of the script demanding some characters' gullibility notwithstanding we never for a moment fall into the conviction that "she" is really a "he." Barbra Streisand's *Yentl* (1983) suffers similarly, although the *politique* of the script is far more encouragingly feminist in its declaration that women should not have to masquerade in order to study philosophy. But as a "man" she is constantly visible to us as a woman, so that Mandy Patinkin seems besotted with a dream in failing to grasp.

Decisive masking, thus decisive awakening occur finally in—-SPOILER ALERT!—-Rodrigo García's *Albert Nobbs* (2011). As introduction to a virtuosic unmasking we have Glenn Close—openly declared as present and accounted for in posters and advertisements, and the star of a stage version of the same story in 1982—covered up as a quiet and genteel butler at Dublin's Morrison Hotel in the late 19th century. Covered up, it is important to say, so very effectively and thoroughly that we have trouble recognizing a recognizable Glenn Close inside: a tremendous construction here not merely through facial makeup and expressional formatting, through carriage, and through garments clearly shown as constraining even before the gender secret is "given away." A young man, Hubert Page, shows up at the hotel and befriends Nobbs, indeed they become close, a particular boon for the very lonely, very isolated, very closeted (and chaste) butler. The film's final scenes, however, work with bravura flourish to dislodge us from what has by now become a complacent acceptance of Nobbs's adjustments under social pressure (that is, a complacent familiarity with the increasingly popular trope of gender-switching inside film plots) because he is forced by circumstances to visit Hubert's home and there discovers a remarkable secret. Close and her costar Janet McTeer were nominated for Academy Awards for this film. What we finally come away with is a doubly virtuosic punch: first, an awareness, to new depths, of the pain and suffering endured at the turn of the twentieth century (and still today) by many people whose gender blocks their pathway to success; and further, the ease with which, given passionate intent and some skill, gender performance can be achieved: in other words, the ease with which most of us achieve our own gender performance on a regular basis, all of this bluntly spelled out through actions and visions onscreen.

An illuminating irony: male actors putting on female face tend to be shown as not doing it particularly well, so that their "femininity" is bluntly a masque, not a personal quality (female is acting). Or, viewers are prevented from judging the quality of the masquerade because the producer's publicity machine has ground out a clear impression of a gendered star behind the magic, an impression that abides with viewers when they watch.[4] When the male face is worn by a female performer, there are at least brief moments, if not extended passages, when the transformation is wholly credible, in fact invisible (acting is female). Was Sarah Bernhardt essentially right? In any case, virtuosic gender performances of all kinds show that since actors know and choose which exact expressions, poses, and attitudes to adopt in achieving masquerade, they *have already learned how to do this knowing and choosing*. In short, gender identity in virtuosic acting—and very likely in everyday life as well—is not only something put on and successfully worn but also a particular concoction for persuasion, the recipe for which is precise and widely known, even mechanical, but hardly a natural secret.

---

[4]The same way that for Ang Lee's *Brokeback Mountain* (2006) the publicity machine over-informed us of Heath Ledger and Jake Gyllenhaal's *real* heterosexuality, in contrast to what the film would suggest.

13

Tortures

FIGURE 13 *Fred Astaire, Nanette Fabray, and Jack Buchanan performing "Triplets" (on their knees) in* The Band Wagon *(Vincente Minnelli, MGM, 1953). Digital frame enlargement.*

Because I had just seriously broken my leg and thought that if ever I were going to write about this film, now was the time—I did a piece in 2003 about *Rear Window* (1954) and chose as epigram a Confucian saying, "Misfortune comes from having a body." It seemed to me ironic enough to address my condition and pithy enough to address the film, since, as goes without saying, *Rear Window* is about a distinctly embodied state of misfortune. The body in pain is of course less than fluidly mobile, and partly because of this actors can perform pain by altering the fluidity of their movement. It is also true that pain can be involved in producing the performed moment, a taxation not often complained of.

Stanley Cavell makes an interesting observation of the "cool" young males of 1950s cinema and their inheritors:

> The rebirth of unexpressed masculine depth required the rebound of culture that created the new possibility of the cool; the young Montgomery Clift and Marlon Brando are early instances of it; James Dean and Paul Newman and Steve McQueen count on it; its latest original was Belmondo. Conviction in their depth depends upon their being young, upon the natural accuracy of their physical movements (like athletes between plays), suggesting unknown regions of physical articulateness and endurance. . . . the body is not unhinged from the mind, as in the brute. (*World* 67–8)

As in the brute, or, one might add, the afflicted, or the elderly. With young people Cavell seems to find in normative movement some "unknown region" of physical articulateness and endurance, call it grace, so that when one detects the marked absence of such articulateness and endurance, one thinks to be encountering the *not-young*.

Look at the quality of action in the group scenes of Francis Ford Coppola's *The Outsiders* (1983), with Matt Dillon, Ralph Macchio, C. Thomas Howell, Patrick Swayze, Rob Lowe, and Emilio Estevez; and then in the group scenes of Clint Eastwood's *Space Cowboys* (2000) with him, Tommy Lee Jones, and Donald Sutherland creaking along. In older characters the articulateness and endurance reside in personality and kenning, not movement. (Watch Melvyn Douglas in *Theodora Goes Wild* [1936], then in *Ninotchka* [1939], then in *Hud* [1963], then in *Being There* [1979]).

Being a more than normally forceful piece of work, the virtuosic moment demands a reservoir of energy and strains the muscularity and stamina of the performer if not also the intelligence and spirit. In declamatory performance, the voice must be trained and warmed up in the way that a singer's is before a concert; for dance, serious exercise, practice, and warm-up are mandatory: Fred Astaire revealed to Ronald Davis that he almost never stopped practicing off-camera. Classical pianists need to have strong fingers and wrists, and they do exercises for this: close position, ascending and descending octaves, ascending and descending four-note chords, arpeggios. The virtuosic stand-up comic needs to be able to control breathing, not unlike the operatic diva. The actor, too, may do all of these things, because in performance the body, notably the lungs and the spine, take stress. One learns one's body, how far one can stretch and pause, then fits the performance (as a chain of requirements) into the embodied frame that will be giving it. Unlike that of the writer who creates his character, the cinematographer who pictures it, or the filmmaker responsible for the overall vision, the actor's body is perpetually on view while she or he works; it is never something not to be concerned about.

I have noted elsewhere how for many of the Godzilla films the actor Haruo Nakajima had to spend long hours locked into a stifling rubber suit, and how, making *Edward Scissorhands* for Tim Burton, Johnny Depp had a similar entrapment (see *Moment 96*; 105–6). Though one knows one's body, the performance dictates unforeseen extremity. When he made *Spacehunter: Adventures in the Forbidden Zone* (1983), as he told me in 1986, the makeup and costume in which Michael Ironside had to spend six hours a day thoroughly stole away his real face, so that when he "looked in a mirror I couldn't find myself." Jeff Bridges had to wear a strange and uncomfortable mo-cap suit filming composited scenes for *TRON: Legacy* (2010): one may accommodate oneself to the net of sensors stuck on one's self but that net is an imposition nevertheless. As the monster in *Frankenstein* (1931) Boris Karloff had trouble eating (a compulsory affiliation with the role, since the monster didn't eat either). Examples pile up.

Generally in the romantic film of the classical era the female lead had to wear, at least in one scene if not the whole film, a spectacular garment in which she literally could neither sit nor lie down to rest, so that off-camera breaks had to be endured on a "dress board," a plank set at forty-five degrees, on which she could lean.[1] When he filmed Sportin' Life in Otto Preminger's *Porgy and Bess* (1959), Sammy Davis Jr. was put into a suit that fitted his entire body like a tight glove. The interface of capitalism with aesthetics brings on a special exploitation here, in that the performer might abuse and degrade his body to make food money; thus in Hollywood as in other labor the worker is positioned to have fewer life advantages than the owner. In some circumstances, drama requires that the identity of the performer be entirely camouflaged in order that the characterization be realized, in which case the actor gets relatively little recognition from appearing onscreen (since he or she, famous or unknown, actually does not visibly appear) and must rely on hearsay to further a career. Since more and more films are now interested in narrativizing monstrosity and technology, roles are created for which only some types of performers can suit: we have come a long way from midgets in Munchkinland when we have Daniel Richter in an ape suit and performing with a troupe of chimpanzees as Moon-Watcher in *2001* (1968) or Kenny Baker stuffed into a tin can as R2-D2 or Andy Serkis in a "monkey suit" in *War for the Planet of the Apes* (2017).

The Scottish music-hall performer Jack Buchanan (1891–1957) appeared in more than three dozen films, beginning with silent cinema in 1917. His professional face is best known in North America because of his bravura supporting role in Vincente Minnelli's *The Band Wagon* (1953), where he

---

[1] If you could sit in the dress it was clothing, not costume. That meant that if, after filming, you purchased the garment (as many stars did, at substantial discount), it was a taxable value. If you couldn't sit, it was a tax-deductible property (costume).

is Jeffrey Cordova, the ultra-divo actor-writer-director-producer and self promoter, who is taking over Broadway.[2] In this film Buchanan is involved in several strenuous musical numbers, in which he sings and dances with perfection: "That's Entertainment," "I Guess I'll Have to Change My Plan," and the taxing "Triplets," this last performed entirely on the knees by Buchanan, with Fred Astaire (whose knees were vital elements in his dancing career), and Nanette Fabray (who generally suffered severe hearing loss). The performers' travails were invisible. Imported to Culver City from his residence in England for a limited period's work rehearsing and filming his scenes, Buchanan was a very long way from home, thus away from physical care, and he suffered from debilitating arthritis. As he mounts a giant stairway in his tuxedo, singing his heart out, one would never know. And it happened that during the production he was also suffering from excessive tooth pain, yet could not see his local dentist. The virtuosity in the singing and dancing, then, is built upon a deeper virtuosity, the ability and will to let the show go on—"That's entertainment!"—at all costs; the choice to positively banish debility.

For his work in *What's Eating Gilbert Grape* (1993), Leonardo DiCaprio had to present the everyday normality of an American teenaged boy, whilst being an American teenaged boy. Arnie has what would today be called a developmental challenge. His family is close-knit and protective, but Arnie's repeated (and apparently uncontrollable) antics have become suffocating. The nineteen-year-old DiCaprio, who had by the time of filming made three movies and appeared in seven different television shows, was as yet far from being very well known, and for viewers seeing him for the first time here the performance is so thoroughly articulated as to seem a non-performance. Arnie's spastic enthusiasm, his irrepressible gaiety, his innocence, his beauty—all these are conveyed as though without a thought on the actor's part.

Taken as a whole, the DiCaprio performance in *Grape* has a strange equivocal feel: it seems utterly virtuosic in retrospect, every instant and flicker of the fingers a profound achievement; yet as we watch, Arnie seems to be only and wholly himself, not a character played by an actor. Thus, as brilliant and immeasurable seems DiCaprio's work it is also invisible as work. Often in virtuosity performers indicate themselves laboring—Luciano Pavarotti's extraordinary, long-held high G at the finale of Puccini's "Nessun Dorma" or Larry Kert's in the finale of Bernstein's "Maria": equivalents to filmic stunt effects—and DiCaprio entirely forebears to show work this way. He is a "natural." But there is one scene in which Arnie goes further, seeming

---

[2]This scripting may be a knowing reference to a small transitional passage in Michael Curtiz's *Yankee Doodle Dandy* (1942) where a pan of theater marquees on Broadway indicates boldly that virtually every show is a George M. Cohan hit.

to emerge from the screen into the chilling atmosphere of real life, and this displays shocking (and presumably painful) virtuosity.

Arnie's older brother Gilbert (Johnny Depp) has met, befriended, and become romantically attached to Becky (Juliette Lewis), a young woman traveling across the country with her aunt, and they have agreed to meet one night and have a campfire together. But the boys' incapacitated and domineering mother (Darlene Cates) has insisted Gilbert has to give Arnie a bath. The two proceed to the bathroom, where Gilbert runs the bath, and gets Arnie established in it. He then says he'll be back shortly, and ducks out to meet Becky. We follow him on his romantic adventure. It is a quiet night, the stars are out, the campfire is soothing and beckoning. The two young people embrace and start to make out. Before we know it they are bedding down under a blanket. Gilbert heads home, and drops into sleep on his bed. In the morning, he drags himself into the bathroom to rinse his face, but there is some sloshing going on behind him.

He turns.

Arnie has been sitting in the bathtub all night, waiting for Gilbert.

As Gilbert, apoplectic, helps him up we see the sopping wet, extremely slender nude frame of the boy trembling uncontrollably with cold as he falls into Gilbert's arms and the waiting towel. The full-body trembling does not cease. It is possible at this moment—something very rare in film—actually to sense the quivering of the frail body affecting one's own corporeality. Arnie appears out of control, not a mask meticulously put on by a talented, motivated force. The actor could have achieved this effect by sitting in a lukewarm tub naked for a very long time, and one way to do this effectively would be to use the actual set and just occupy it long in advance of the shooting session. We are certainly not seeing a *semblance of* trembling produced through moaning and stuttering, we are watching a body that cannot shape itself. Arnie is as though intoxicated by self-denial. "In real life," wrote Michael Caine, "a real drunk makes a huge effort to appear sober. A coarsely acted stage or film drunk reels all over the place to show you he's drunk. It's artificial" (6). DiCaprio, at such an early age, has learned already how not to be artificial, how not to reel as he collapses inwardly.

In *Marathon Man* (1976), Dustin Hoffman ran laps around Central Park in order to exhaust himself so that in Laurence Olivier's dentist chair he was *really* disintegrating.

While the case of *Gilbert Grape* invokes consideration of performance as articulation or confession—Arnie's apparently true condition revealing that of the player beneath—some tortured virtuosities are covered by the camera. John Wayne was at war against cancer as he filmed *The Shootist* (1976) and inevitably in a degree of pain the camera never shows. The same can be said for Robert Ryan shooting *The Iceman Cometh* (1973) for John Frankenheimer and for Ingrid Bergman, dying of breast cancer when she filmed the title role in *A Woman Called Golda* (1982). Some actors struggle and negotiate to give even the simplest show of normality onscreen, for example Herbert Marshall, all of whose characters are performed by a man wearing a prosthetic leg. In *Trouble in Paradise* (1932), Marshall three times races up a long curling staircase and one time races down, three of the four moments seen in a single take and the fourth viewed in a mirror: in every case, an acting double is used, the shot neatly cut into a medium close-up showing Marshall "catching his breath." Montgomery Clift struggled to finish his scenes in *Raintree County* (1957) a bare two months after an almost fatal car accident. The shining performances of Vincent D'Onofrio—a psychotic soldier in *Full Metal Jacket* (1987), a cockroach in *Men in Black* (1997), Orson Welles in *Ed Wood* (1994), Abbie Hoffman in *Steal This Movie* (2000), Pooh-Bear in *The Salton Sea* (2002), and many distinctive others, including Goren on *Law & Order: Criminal Intent*—are given by an actor with Autistic Spectrum Disorder.

Notwithstanding all of these cases of suffering or debility masked in the name of characterization, virtuosic performance can also involve painful torture for the character, whether the actor is discomfited or not. We are left only to imagine whether the pain or debility in front of us is real on the surface, or through and through; to wonder about the connection between torture, pain, and labor onscreen and off. A voice is stretched beyond normal limits (Linda Blair in *The Exorcist* [1973]), a body hangs in space (Richard Harris in *A Man Called Horse* [1970]) or climbs to strange heights (Clint Eastwood in *The Eiger Sanction* [1975]), muscles stretch beyond their limit (Griffin Dunne in *An American Werewolf in London* [1981]). As we think about performances of pain and torture, the secret body comes paradoxically into the light.

14

Secret Virtuosity

FIGURE 14 *Trevor Howard and Celia Johnson (r.) with Everley Gregg in* Brief Encounter *(David Lean, Cineguild, 1945). Digital frame enlargement.*

The most bravura virtuosity can go unrecognized and unlauded by viewers, who seem to perceive nothing remarkable (more on this to come). Further, it can be especially difficult to achieve a virtuosic delicacy in which performance is neither glorious nor daredevil nor absolutely central to narrative. On the surface, an action may appear commonplace or elementary when to prepare and accomplish it a performer must master the most exigent challenges to mind and body. Here is virtuosity as architecture, all of its fundamental support structures kept out of view.

At the keyboard, for example, we find ourselves easily impressed with huge chord constructions played triple fortissimo, or with very, very rapid passages where the fingers move in a blur, but these sorts of things are not especially difficult, especially if one is playing a concert grand with very good action.[1] What *is* a true virtuosity is the ability to play a perfectly smooth scale, and in filmic pianism we basically never see it. Many pianists cannot at all, or cannot quite, do this; some notes get a little more emphasis than others. The muscles of the hand must be exercised with the greatest care and patience in order to make possible what may seem an "effortless" scale, which glides up and down the tonal range like a breeze touching the surface of a pond. A good scale also suffers for being visually bland.

Another serious challenge is playing with feelingful, tender sweetness and faithfulness to a melody: in Atom Egoyan's startling film *Remember* (2015) there is an unprepared, unexpectable moment when Christopher Plummer sits at a piano and plays Wagner, shot in such a way that we can see him (full body, in medium shot) at work and watch his hands; he is giving an extraordinarily musical performance, as, one might now see in clarified retrospect, he did in Robert Wise's *The Sound of Music* (1965) singing "Edelweiss." In most cinematic pianism, the performer cannot play the instrument at all and the effect is produced through camera angling. In *Hangover Square* (1945), by notable contrast, Laird Cregar did all his own performing, and the effect—musicality compounded by climactic drama—is staggering.

In acting, especially for camera, a difficulty of equivalent value and taxation is: doing absolutely nothing in character. Simply being before the lens, without a flicker of expression, without any attempt to *seem* to be. Being but not acting being.

An actor who does considerable work in both film and television confidentially shared some of his challenges in this respect. An interference or interruption called *tells* causes a particular infection of performance:

> Staying still is extremely hard, because of your ego. Everybody has *tells* to compensate for being watched, to hide themselves. A *tell* works for and against the actor. This is important especially when emotion comes up. One has mannerisms when one is watched and these "out" you as being false. Actors are subconsciously afraid they're going to be boring. Using your real voice is hard. We all have socialized performative mechanisms

---

[1] The concert grand piano is a full size longer than a salon grand, so that, with top raised or removed—conventional concert procedure—the projection of sounds, both quiet and loud, is facilitated by the instrument itself. "Good action" refers to a number of features of the keyboard including a "touch" the pianist finds accommodating and a speedy rebound from striking. Much is inherent in the quality of the individual instrument and is not open to adjustment. As to touch: Rudolf Serkin's concert piano had an amazingly heavy touch, which was incomprehensible until one shook the man's hand: it was like a side of beef, with enormous musculature. Glenn Gould's rehearsal piano had a very delicate touch, and, as is well-known by those who watched him, he played by bending over the keyboard and placing his face near his fingertips.

(like raising the voice) that give away that we know we're being watched. You have to try not to TELL things to the camera. The genius of the medium is how much is communicated in passivity.

"Actors are good liars," he concludes paradoxically, "but in front of the camera you have to tell the truth." You have to *tell the truth* without using a *tell*, without *telling* that you are telling.[2]

Comedic pratfalls work best without *telling*, and give a nice entry point for studying profound virtuosity hiding beneath the inadvertent. A gesture's flamboyance captures the audience's full attention, diverting it away from the (telling) work at hand: balance, choice of contact point, trained relaxation. Jerry Lewis, for a prime example, spent most of his early career falling down on his face, sometimes in a flat fall forward, sometimes in a more awkward kind of catastrophe. Because his body slammed into the ground, he later in life suffered debilitation and required Perkodan, to which he became addicted. His audience, meanwhile, was convulsed laughing, to a degree that any suspicion of his pain was eradicated. For example, Julius Kelp (in *The Nutty Professor* [1963]) collapses helplessly to the floor of his laboratory when he has digested the foaming pink liquid that will convert him into Buddy Love. There are other moments in Lewis's films where he openly parodies bodily torture: Julius is in a gymnasium using barbells, for example, but the weight is far too heavy; once it's at chest height it falls to the ground, carrying his hands with it: thus, his arms are stretched double their normal length. Kelp gives a bewildered expression (which adds to the piquancy), but in the succeeding shot we see him sleeping in bed, his feet sticking out from the bottom of the blanket and his hands sticking out right beside them. The gag functions to indicate that in other films, and without visual pointing of this sort, he performs physical virtuosities worthy of comment (yet received in the "silence" of plain laughter). Further, in all this work Lewis is pointedly the focus of viewers' attention, therefore he knows he is being looked at (not just because he is on camera). But there are no *tells*. Indeed, part of the humor he produces flows from the insouciant quality of the action: that nobody is looking but he's falling apart anyway.

Trevor Howard (1913–1988) has a moment of summative, yet barely visible, virtuosity at the climactic moment of David Lean's *Brief Encounter* (1945). He and Celia Johnson, having met accidentally in a local town, have come to adore each other and are carrying on an entirely chaste, yet deeply passionate, affaire there. But one day he lets her know that he

---

[2] It is sometimes impossible for a performer to avoid telling that she is telling. Note, for example, extremities of "star" cultivation for attraction: Elizabeth Taylor in *Father of the Bride* (1950), Lassie in *Lassie Come Home* (1943). Every moment, every shot, is a "tell" because beautification bluntly signals "conscious of being looked at," regardless of any actual (undetectable) consciousness.

has accepted a medical appointment in South Africa and is to leave very soon. Both crestfallen, they agree to meet the following week, but that day something holds Alec up at the hospital and Laura, waiting and waiting for him, despondently, has no choice but to head to the station and catch her train. She is in the waiting room with a cup of tea when who should barge in upon her but the infernal gossip Dolly Messiter (Everley Gregg), too garrulous and too curious. Lean fades Dolly's voice out at one point to show how Laura isn't really listening to a word she says. Suddenly Alec shows up, full of apology and explanation. He graciously brings Dolly tea, and sits with them in polite silence. He and Laura must pretend now to be mere acquaintances who have little say to each other, who would never touch, never embrace, never linger in one another's arms; all with Dolly prating and watching, babbling and squeaking. Then a bell sounds. The approach of Alec's train. "Well, that's my train," says he, quietly. *Far too quietly.* The opportunity for a loving farewell has been lost. We note a chill passing through Laura's body as Dolly coos sympathetically to him. He stands quietly, excuses himself courteously to Dolly, and says in Laura's direction, "Well, goodbye," stepping away slowly behind her, *and with one hand very gently touching her shoulder.* Then he is gone. Gone forever from her life. (Gone without telling.)

The delicacy of the moment, set up by Gregg's exquisitely sharp turn, lies in the quietness of Howard's exit, not merely vocal (against Dolly's blubbery expression) but physical, the sense that he inhabits a mere body capable of locomotion. His entirely subdued, disciplined, genteel tone makes every step indelible. Howard did considerable character work in his long career, notably in Carol Reed's *The Third Man* (1949), Jack Cardiff's *Sons and Lovers* (1960), Lewis Milestone's *Mutiny on the Bounty* (1962), Tony Richardson's *The Charge of the Light Brigade* (1968), Lean's *Ryan's Daughter* (1970), and Luchino Visconti's *Ludwig* (1973), among dozens of other films, but in all his celebrated growling, mewling, hissing, blustering, pompous, destitute, or noble moments there is nothing to match the way he stands from that little table and walks away from Laura to his train.

15

(In)credible Belief

FIGURE 15 *Jessica Lange in* Tootsie *(Sydney Pollack, Columbia, 1982). Digital frame enlargement.*

In Sydney Pollack's *Tootsie* (1982), Michael Dorsey (Dustin Hoffman) is a too-outspoken actor who cannot get work until he disguises himself as a woman. As "Dorothy Michaels" he lands a character part on a popular soap opera and soon becomes the talk of the country, celebrated on the cover of *Time* and elsewhere. His castmate on the show is Julie (Jessica Lange), an up-and-coming actress of distinguished talent and great personal beauty. The inner Michael is smitten by her, and so the outer Dorothy becomes her bosom pal. He can be near Julie only if his "she"—the "she" that has always been buried deep inside him?, the "she" that he is concocting out of thin air?, the "she" who is an amalgam of his lifetime observations of women?— takes over, since it was when he was Dorothy, not Michael, that they became acquainted and it is, he deeply fears, only as Dorothy that Julie will know, recognize, and accept him up close. Dorothy offers plenty of the kind of sage (if casual) wisdom young women profit by, lots of career advice about how to avoid the obnoxious come-ons of the show's director (Dabney Coleman) and male star (George Gaynes), and is, to boot, the absolute quintessence (by design, and almost to the point of cloying the audience) of sweetness, amiability, and sincerity.

Julie invites Dorothy to come home with her for a weekend in Vermont.

A paradisiacal forest-bound setting. A great old clapboard house. In the presence of Julie's warmhearted father Les (Charles Durning), Dorothy finds a kind of home herself: certainly unmitigated hospitality and a jovial atmosphere. Of course Les is taken with Dorothy, too—a plot twist that needn't be entertained here since the moment I wish to discuss, a Dorothy-and-Julie moment, has them in bed together, Julie with her night facial on, Dorothy in curlers and a hair net (Dorsey sports a wig he cannot remove, lest the jig be up). They share "girl talk." And Lange gives a stunning portrait of innocent credulity, wholly buying into Michael's disguise (what we easily see as a somewhat overdone complex of adjustments and accoutrements, very out of temper with fashion and wholly artificial) and, with the greatest possible simplicity of commitment, the greatest openness, relishing the private moment with this newfound, exceedingly generous and sensitive friend. Julie, in short, *trusts*.

How does this little show work—since if Julie doesn't seem to trust *really,* there can be no touching quality? Through a pair of carefully articulated strategies, on the part of the whole team. (a) A brazen background behind (b) an unpresuming object of great beauty. First, the circus surrounding Lange is filled with caricatures played broadly for comedy: the leering old male star, an insatiable codger; we know from the start that he'll get nowhere with Julie and nowhere with Dorothy, on both of whom he hits, and we can surmise that his career history is larded with petty conquests of the innocent. The show's director, little more than a meek toady, incapable of genuine sentiment. The producer (Doris Belack), harshly cynical. Michael's agent (Sydney Pollack), helplessly uncomprehending. Julie's father, a roly-poly maestro of American bucolic sentimentality and true gentleman, as sincere as sincere can be, a sweet caricature of sincerity. And Dorothy herself, in Michael's desperate hands, working hard to survive every living moment, and so: Be nice, be nice, be nice, be nice, be nice!

Against this splashing backdrop, any relatively tranquil and relatively pallid looking girl might pick up an additional quality of tranquility and paleness. Lange's Julie is a definitive blonde with long, sumptuous tresses. She dresses plainly and simply when off-camera, with no self-consciousness as a beauty but simply as an honest young woman who knows what she likes— knows even that, at this time in her life, she is too young to really know who she is. Vocally straightforward and honest, she is never categorically expressive. And most importantly, in her responses to Dorothy she is the wide-eyed picture of genuine innocence. The world is what it claims to be, notwithstanding that in the television studio everybody pretends at being someone else. Dorothy being aligned with her against the pressuring forces all around, Julie responds with unaffected receptivity. Lange has here erased any tick of performance that might clue us that deep down she knows she is Jessica Lange, any hiccup of self-aware self-protection at being so fully seen. She merely exists where the camera points, and breathes like a person would breathe who was alive and happy. A young and vibrant person, alive and happy in youth.

This is remarkably self-assured performance on the actor's part. It calls to mind another splendid, if bizarre, Jessica Lange moment, from the Dino De Laurentiis production of *King Kong* (1976), where in a powerful cut-off shot we see her standing in Kong's open palm. He makes bold to breathe on her gently, and the breeze from his giant off-camera ape maw causes her thin dress to flutter, both naturally and evocatively. She is again only herself at this moment, in this place, gazing upward, receiving the attention of the central icon of the story. There is something here, and in *Tootsie*, of Lange's ability to simply stand still and exist in her natural form that charms; perhaps her clear conviction in what we easily recognize as false. She is a fawn in the great forest. And as the quite masterful Jessica Lange is anything but a fawn, her construction of Julie's innocence is a virtuosity accomplished in collaboration.

At a flashing moment in Antonioni's *Blow-Up* (1966) the photographer (David Hemmings) has a strange woman (Vanessa Redgrave) in his studio, up against his mauve seamless, she in a gray skirt and black, white, and gray checked shirt, and with sparkling red hair. "Let me see how you stand," says he. Do nothing, just rest. I will watch. And she does for him merely, only, exactly what he asks, a form without a personality, a beauty without an angle, albeit only for a fragment of a second, because she is also a bundle of nerves. "You've got it," says he bluntly, perhaps to soothe, surely to praise. Of course it was manifestly true offscreen that Redgrave "had it," having worked, before this film, onstage with Edith Evans, Albert Finney, Charles Laughton, and Laurence Olivier; and true of Lange, too, who had danced in her early years at the Opéra-Comique in Paris. As Lange lies abed with Dorothy—flannel nightgowns!—all we can reasonably expect from Julie is all we directly get: a sense of strangeness at this proximity, followed by a sense of trusting relaxation and openness. She is there, warm with the warmth. She makes no calculations, has no questions, sees no tomorrow. Any miniscule hint of kenning in this girl, any hint that she might be attuned to guile—her own or anyone's—would ruin the entire construction.

Lange's and Redgrave's openness at these moments signals that the character not only believes: in the "real" circumstances—for Julie her baby, her apartment, her previous experiences painful or not—but also that she holds as real and unaffected the persons nearby, for Julie, Dorothy and for

Redgrave, the photographer. She believes because she honestly and without qualification takes the object of her belief to be believable. In both cases we are watching a character in the act of fully absorbing as real another character we know assuredly to be capable of fakery (we watched Michael guising himself as Dorothy; and David Hemmings's crafty business, early on, at "working" with his camera secretly in a doss house). Dorothy isn't in that bed just because Julie has invited her to be, though she has; and the photographer isn't studying the woman just because she looks good, though she does. But of these matching guiles there is no suspicion, and from them there is no holding back of the sacred jewel.

To focus on Julie: in her credulous acceptance of Dorothy she is lowered from the stage of her fame (Julie's, because of this soap opera, not Jessica's), where she would naturally be conscious of makeup, put-ons, fakery, and fiction, and attributed the status of an audience, just such as the one we have joined where, as performance rolls on, we give up our skepticism and adopt a pleasuring belief, too. In her accepting Dorothy, Julie becomes like any one of us accepting her accepting. We know we are in the presence of an actor at work, yet nevertheless see—because of the desire to see—the actor vanish as the character emerges. More: we earnestly wish to avoid seeing the actor avoiding the opportunity to vanish. Julie has never seen Dorothy in any other context except "on" (yet of course, like the actors beneath the characters we watch, Dorothy must have a private life of some kind, not visible now and for Julie inconceivable; a private life that would make the performing Dorothy a put-on, and only a put-on). Raptly engaged in her warm friendship, is Julie a fool?

(Under Pollack's direction, Hoffman is careful to make it clear that the on-camera Dorothy in the studio and the off-camera Dorothy nestling in Julie's bed are more or less identical Dorothies. And Julie, who in her personal space is quite different than she is at work, doesn't seem to grasp this, so faithfully does she believe and wish to believe.)

No, Julie is not a fool. She is like anyone in the everyday world, only a person, fully rounded, complete, honestly herself, notably so in that she doesn't go through the day skeptically doubting everything and everyone. She is unaware that her daily reality has been turned into theater. She isn't searching for manipulations duping her, and so she isn't duped. That is, duped, she doesn't feel duped.

Julie's remarkable vulnerability (perhaps *the* telltale characteristic of a Lange performance) brings logic and clarity to her abrupt and very powerful turn at film's end, when Michael has been forced to drop his disguise and confront her as a man. They are on the street on the Upper East Side. "I was a better man with you as a woman than I ever was with anybody as a man," he confesses as she coldly stares through him. We may be stunned and impressed by Michael's confession, but Julie walks away.

16

Touched by the Camera

FIGURE 16 *Kim Novak in* Vertigo *(Alfred Hitchcock, Paramount, 1958). Digital frame enlargement.*

That stunning moment in *Vertigo*: Judy Barton (Kim Novak) now made over to resemble the Madeleine he lost to death steps out of a bathroom toward James Stewart's Scottie. She seems to materialize out of a cloud, materialize so evocatively that we remember it for all time. Not only remember, but iconize as a shining talisman that bespeaks the entire (complex and deeply involving) film. There are plenty of other visually powerful moments in this work, such as Stewart clinging to the eavestrough; the span of the Golden Gate with a distant Madeleine dropping into the Bay beneath; the climb up the staircase of the tower at San Juan Bautista—but none of these chill the consciousness and excite the emotion in the way that this shot of Judy emerging manages to do. The room is suffused with a kind of aqua-green fog, and she steps out of a bathroom the door of which is trimmed with pale green, and we cut to him turning to look, and then back to her (as she is closer there is a little less fog); back to him staring, and now to her

up close, in clear focus. Is it the incredulous look on his face that makes us
concentrate so, that brings us toward an attachment of the sort Scottie has?
Is it the gradually lifting fog (the fog of San Francisco, the fog of the past,
the fog of the present, the fog of existence)? Is it her gloriously graceful way
of moving, like a model on a runway, to show off the gray suit and the hair
pulled back and the made-up face? Is it the color green?

The green suffusion is meant to be read as Scottie's hallucination unfolding,
Scottie's way of viewing the woman. Green for spring and rebirth, greeny
blue for the ocean (of life), and then the simple, unadorned, pale green of
a great parkland in which one roves without end, mortal green, the green
of the boundary between life and death. Madeleine, Scottie's present vision,
died some time ago, and she is now emerging from the dead, presenting
herself again.[1]

Is the moment virtuosic because of Kim Novak? Is this a virtuosity on
her part? I mean to focus quite intently on this slender moment of passage,
in which Judy walks toward Scottie and we see her approach in three
discreet shots with variant focus. It is plainly evident that there is a broad
film holding this, and that Novak has done pointed work in figuring her
characterizations until now. Her general credentials in *Vertigo* are not
in question. But in this transformative moment, surely the only thing we
are seeing is a woman walking. Walking toward us, but walking. There is
extreme grace in her movement, she walks "well," but again: she walks. Is
the power, the virtuosity, the lift out of the baseline of story and realism a
matter only of these steps she takes?

(The shot is made several times, and each time she must walk toward the
camera fluidly, with perfect smoothness and perfect posture, so that when
the sequence is cut together her movement will seem coherent and smooth.)

I think it can be argued that here we see the camera's work as virtuosic,
the camera as our point of contact with the scene. Notwithstanding that the
camera is always our point of contact with a film scene, it does not stand
out and announce itself that way, and so we neglect it. But here the device
cannot be neglected. The camera—which is to say Robert Burks's use of the
lens and manipulations of focus—couples with the lighting (and with some
adjustments achieved in the color timing) to lay the ethereal effect *upon*
Novak's presentation. She not only walks like a model on a runway, she *is* a
model on a runway at this instant, needing only to unselfconsciously move
forward. Scottie's reconstituted Madeleine, his Judy hiding away inside this
character, is a pure figuration, a mannequin upon whose body a "skin" can
be placed that qualifies and defines our experience of her. Scottie is absorbed
(and we with him) by this superimposition. (Judy Barton, of course, is
superimposed on the model Kim Novak. Kim Novak is superimposed upon

---

[1] *Vertigo* is drawn from Pierre Boileau and Thomas Narcejac's novel *D'entre les morts* (1954).

Marilyn Pauline Novak.) The artful photographic effect directs us to account for superimpositions, to recognize in Judy walking toward us, transmuted, her modeling, her amazing act of porting identity.

Scottie worked with and upon Judy to transform her into this stunning "Madeleine," or "Madeleine II," but he is amazed at how well his efforts paid off. Amazed that what he dreamed would be possible, is possible in fact. While for him the softness and the greenness pointedly invoke the past, the past invoking death, death invoking separation, the effect as we watch it invokes a sharpening of attention to the figure herself and her strange, slightly displaced character. Like every model in a fabulous garment, she is beside herself (*ecstatic*). Sometimes the glory of a garment can work to transform the model wearing it into a star herself. In this case what I call the "garment" is both costume and camera effect, a layering onto the actor's performative capacity of design elements beyond her invention or control. As we watch the green haze we find Judy made into a Madeleine, and Kim Novak—at times having given off a plainer, less stunning appearance—now glowing with presence.

To act for film is to submit oneself always to the possibility of being transformed this way, and to a condition of never knowing with certainty what is happening until a long time after it has happened. The shot chosen, the method of its insertion, the decision as to what exact image will lead to and flow from it—all these the actor cannot know with clarity while acting; nor, usually, what lens is being used; nor, beyond rudimentary frame limits, what the cinematographer is selecting with his all-powerful eye.[2] Novak's movement here is unforgettable, but also somewhat natural for her, trained but somewhat artless. It is fascinating that a virtuosic moment might be constructed from elements that are not in themselves inherently virtuosic.

---

[2]Jerry Lewis's invention of the video assist, when he was making *The Family Jewels* (1965), pointedly abbreviated the time lapse between a performative moment and its evaluation by a director or actor.

17

Improvise

FIGURE 17 *Frank Sinatra and Janet Leigh in* The Manchurian Candidate *(John Frankenheimer, M.C. Productions, 1962). Digital frame enlargement.*

Mel Gordon leads us to consider the historical phenomenon of the *lazzo*. For the Commedia dell'arte, this was a small, carefully prearranged subroutine structured with, as it were, open ends, so that it could be inserted artfully but arbitrarily, if necessary even suddenly, into any point in a performance, and seem to belong. Commedia troupes would create and rehearse a number of these *lazzi*, giving each a memorable, characteristic nickname every member could use—"The Fat Man," "Cooking with the Pig," "I Cannot Find a Place to Piss," and so on—so that, should any untoward event intrude upon the spontaneity of a show, such as a missed line, a hectoring, an accident, anyone onstage could call out the secret code name and everybody would transition instantly into the routine, a perfect way of stalling for time until the rupture could be stitched over. Even more than being defensive and remedial, the *lazzi* could work to spice and enliven a performance, to give it a generally unique and spontaneous character, since their usage was only in the here and now, not part of the performed routine.

While in stage work a troupe repeats performances several times a week, thus building a duplicable ongoing routine with one another's cooperation, in film work actors are contracted into a "cast" but labor on only parts of scenes at any one time—perhaps for a single day, or a single shot. The entire film is almost always not worked through start-to-finish on successive days, as in theater. To make matters more isolating, actors in film work find that they may not always—or not ever—meet the entire remaining cast, and crew. Some actors play only a scene or two with only one or two others and never meet some of the folk whose names will appear beside theirs in the credits. While the drawing of film workers together as a "family" constitutes both a solid rationale for managerial exploitation (see Clark) and a charming myth of solidarity (see Truffaut's *Day for Night* [1973] for a touching evocation) in truth most movie actors work as independent contractors—as some actors (like Cary Grant) did even when most were under studio contracts— bringing along a discreet bundle of talent and personality, commitment and interest to the working scene, there to integrate themselves as best they can with others, on a provisional, day-to-day basis. Each scene will seem in the end to have been acted once only (meat for slipping into the menu of the final cut). Acting "troupes" in cinema do not fashion *lazzi* so much as individual actors do. The individual actor's subroutines, picked up or invented, become actorial *shticks* available on command for helping out at a vital moment, should need be felt. Robert De Niro's attenuated stare. Gwyneth Paltrow's silent flashing smile somewhere between superciliousness and modesty. Jesse Eisenberg's thoughtful pause between sentences, while his eyebrows rise. Toshirô Mifune's coupling of squat stance and steely gaze. Ben Affleck's slacked jaw.

The *lazzo* in screen performance is typically tiny, both gesturally and temporally, because film time costs. It will occupy the space of an inhalation, lending the actorial presence a peculiar, identifiable quality that we can see repeated over and over if we look at a chain of the performer's works, but also giving the actor a half beat in which to gather his wits. Michael Caine has a little smile that he often gives before words come out of his mouth: the same shape of the same mouth, the same brevity, film after film: and a way of giving his eyes to the lens; John Gielgud a way of lifting his head, extending his noble chin, and gazing up and off-camera to indicate penetrating reflection; Bette Davis a bag of vocal tricks, a way of biting off her syllables; Barbara Stanwyck a style of asserting yet seeming interrogative (when she isn't). Any little routine can give the actor a flashing break while being completely in the audience's line of sight, a kind of "onstage backstage" in which it is possible to orient the self, recollect what comes next, muse upon something entirely unrelated while breathing, find a point of relaxation. Anthony Hopkins often inserts a pause after the first few words of a phrase: "Tobeornottobethat—is the question whether 'tis—nobler in the—mind to—suffertheslingsandarrowsofoutrageous—fortune or . . ."

Lazzi are neither unconscious nor, in truth, spontaneous, although spontaneity does mark one's experience of them. The actor knows what is being done, after all, and has tried variations and modulations, so there is no professional gamble as to what will or will not work. Sometimes a particular *lazzo* comes to be identified with a particular star personality, and sometimes a *lazzo* is configured to spring out of the dramatic moment. The classically trained actor will have mastered and stored a repository of gestures and tactics that can be "improvised": Ian McKellen fingering the tablecloth as he sits at Donald Sutherland and Stockard Channing's dinner table in *Six Degrees of Separation* (1993). A generally useful *lazzo* is the silent gaze, brief or long. Marilyn Monroe uses it, and permits it, before speaking, very notably in the train-car-whiskey-flask scene of *Some Like It Hot* (1959). Davis produces one, in her too-thick eyeglasses, as she hesitantly enters the salon as Charlotte Vane early in *Now, Voyager* (1942). Katharine Hepburn produces glaring gazes, but in turnout, taking care to look *away from* Spencer Tracy in *Adam's Rib* (1949) as they squabble. These tiny routines are useful doubly: for the actor, finding footing; and for the production, adding flair.

In *Psycho* (1960), Anthony Perkins masters a stammer that buys time both personally and dramatically, the latter because it telegraphs a kind of ingenuous innocence and a reclusive, nervous discomfort with social interaction. Playing as his scene partner in the chicken sandwich scene, Janet Leigh uses careful and perfectly mouthed speech partly to indicate the propriety of Marion Crane—at least here, at this moment—and partly, *sotto voce,* to assist Perkins in establishing Norman with the speech defect: his defect is all the more noticeable against her crispness. The stammer is a technical wizardry, because it works to heighten our eagerness to anticipate the word that is not yet quite coming out, in short to draw us closer to the character, by way of his mouth. His mouth, the opening of Ali Baba's cave.

Leigh is present again two years later, conversing gently with Frank Sinatra's Major Bennett Marco in the vestibule between two railway cars on a fast-moving train in John Frankenheimer's *The Manchurian Candidate.* She is trying to draw him out, but with both politeness and circumspection, because he seems a nervous wreck. Sinatra's trick here is to avert his eyes, again and again in the sequence, while her eyes are bright and open, taking him in. Because he cannot look at her we are drawn into his interior. *Why* can he not look? She is notably good-looking, pleasant, friendly, courteous, generous, considerate, and kind. Is he hiding something? Is he afraid? A magnetic force draws us toward Major Marco not because of what he says—although every phrase of George Axelrod's dialogue has eloquence—but because he keeps dropping his eyes as though somehow he has been defeated by life. Leigh of course makes a point of *not* looking down.

The acted *lazzo* can be a feature fully integrated into a sequence rather than a withdrawal for respite or separation for emphasis. It can become a character's personality. In *The Man Who Knew Too Much* (1956), Doris Day and James Stewart maintain a slightly abrasive marital relationship, Stewart doing his drawling hem-haw (a star *lazzo* if ever there was one) and Day chirping or wailing her lines, just like the emotional singer she (and her character) is. Day direct and forthright, somewhat melodic; Stewart hesitant and pensive, somewhat staccato. Virtually any scene prior to the conclusion will show this tension, perhaps none more explicitly or painfully than Ben's administering sedative to Jo before informing her that their son has been kidnapped. She is insistent, pushing questions at him almost lyrically. He is stalling, holding back. But these behaviors are utterly *characteristic*—that is, appropriate to, embedded in the character broadly seen. We may think of this pattern of action as a *lazzo of personality*, since the mannerisms, attitudes, and tactics involved are used consistently by each performer, seeming to found a basal personality structure. Indeed, actors know that one way to "create" a character's personality is to find a behavioral tic, a mini-routine that can be reiterated in many circumstances. One can be reminded of Bill Murray's gut-splitting wide-eyed stare in *What About Bob?* (1991) or, for a less distinctively human case, Kim Hunter's (Zira's) batting eyelashes in *Planet of the Apes* (1968).

Are characters recognizable by their *lazzi,* their eccentric turns, not only to viewers but also to other characters? How, indeed, do characters in film seem to know one another?

Excepting the demented or perceptually handicapped, the people we see onscreen retain what they—and through them, we—have experienced of one another already. That is, they do not have to be reintroduced. (Dorothy and chums having once met the gruff, bombastic Wizard are not surprised when at a second meeting he is gruff and bombastic.) This "character memory," as one may imagine, is really not as obvious as might seem, given that in everyday life people's memories are considerably more fleeting. But when a screen character is named for the first time she is known in all interactions for the remainder of the film: nobody says, "Sorry, what was your name again?" An exception to prove the rule is Rupert Pupkin's (Robert De Niro) scene with the receptionist (Margo Winkler) in *The King of Comedy* (1982): she simply *will not* remember his name, not, at least, without revising it! The figures we meet in film seem to know and fundamentally comprehend one another. This is, of course, a dramatic convention. No matter their moral or diegetic status, the characters recognize and read the others' motives, as though, somewhere sometime before the story began, they were all introduced. There seems something intrinsically social about character groupings, whether a team of criminal athletes committing a heist (George

Clooney and company in *Ocean's Twelve* [2004]) or a team of socialites attending an important dinner (William Powell, Myrna Loy, and friends in *The Thin Man* [1934]): the figures not only "fit" the narrative but also "fit together," attending to one another's gestures and foibles with familiarity and ease.

There is thus something disarming about the principal character arrangement in Armando Iannucci's *The Death of Stalin* (2017). Here, in Moscow of 1953, we have the kingpin and his major flunkies, obsequious ladder climbers all, willing to shed blood in the name of his august power and their own chances of living another day. Beria (Simon Russell Beale), Molotov (Michael Palin), Malenkov (Jeffrey Tambor), Khrushchev (Steve Buscemi). Stalin dies early, and the film is principally about the palace intrigues leading up to, and falling away from, his state funeral. Who will gain ascendancy? Which past plots and secrets will come back to haunt, and which will now be officially forgotten? It is a naked contest for brute power, between men who are each, evidently—too evidently, we might mistakenly think—incompatible, unfriendly, unlinked to his colleagues. In scene upon scene, encountering a still corpse upon a Persian carpet, finding Stalin still alive, attending his bedside, watching him gape in awe and confusion at a picture on the wall (Christ giving water to a lamb), watching soldiers clear out the furniture and paintings within minutes; dealing with the children, a neurotic daughter and an alcoholic son; squabbling and scrabbling for control of various police forces and the army, led by the gruff and down-to-earth Zhukov (Jason Isaacs) who led the defeat of the Germans; stepping on top of one another at each opportunity, plotting, cajoling, finally, in the case of Beria, having one's brains blown out and body incinerated immediately afterward. The point of the film is the disorganization, the madcap catastrophe that is high power, when seen on the inside. And the virtuosity of the performances, what chills and perdures, is inchoate fragmentation. Alex Clayton has offered me his speculation that the actors rehearsed separately—literally in separate locations—and didn't come together until the scenes were shot; whether or not this is fact they perform *as though* completely wrapped, each, in an impermeable envelope of self. Wrapped and carrying no traces of having met the others before.

This "fragmentary virtuosity" strikes superficially in telling of a social situation, fearful, chaotic, violent in which disorganization rules; and more deeply in depositing a disturbing impression, the film reverberating against more conventional stories where the characters relate in concert. Here the choreography does not seem to flow from a single artist. Having ringed himself with his boys, Stalin pays no attention to them. Malenkov does not listen to Khrushchev, Khrushchev does not listen to Molotov, nobody listens to the hysterical Beria. In fragmentation, the performances are wholly modern, even psychotic, leading to an explosion that was always, we should have realized, inevitably bound to happen. When the actors make use of *lazzi,* they do so each on his own tiny stage, surrounded by a pithy darkness, none, perhaps, more signally than Beale, whose Beria seems to look through people rather than at them as they address him, who again and again turns away into the fetid abysm of his private malevolence.

But give the screw one more turn. The narcissism of each man's selfish, disconnected performance, each man's coma, is but a narrative artifice. In the lighting, editing, and flow of the film the parts are seamlessly and perfectly interwoven by the filmmaker: the narcissisms gather to form a choir. The characters are solo acts, but the actors beneath are a team performing, in extension, the *lazzo* called "Me, Not You." If in some films idiosyncrasies and unfamiliarity are covered by the "convention of mutual knowledge" in this film, even though the characters as historical types did know one another, and even though, here, they can predict one another's actions to a degree, the convention of bonding is dropped, and we have the shocking sense of what is always in cinematic production true, always because in part this is what cinema is, a collection of strangers wearing the masks of friends.

18

Breathe

FIGURE 18 *Katharine Hepburn (l.) and Doris Nolan in* Holiday *(George Cukor, Columbia, 1938). Digital frame enlargement.*

George Cukor's *Holiday* (1938) is a family story. Rich and snotty Julia Seton (Doris Nolan) and her affable sister Linda (Katharine Hepburn) inhabit a fabulous mansion on 5th Avenue. The father (Henry Kolker) is a magnate of fine proportions, it matters little how much money he has because we can't count it. His son Ned (Lew Ayres) likes to drink, or drinks anyway, but is a nice fellow. Julia is engaged to be married to a charming if, in the father's view, irresponsible young man, Johnny Case (Cary Grant, a real case), who has rather Bohemian ideas of how, after marriage, he and she might fare together.

Working to convince his soon-to-be father-in-law that wishing to take time away from work to find out who one is in life does not make one un-American and irresponsible, Johnny found some distinct relief in Linda's friendship. These two irregulars bonded, shared stories, and learned to do somersaults together, Linda, of course, secretly falling in love with him. Planning to sail to Europe, Johnny has invited his fiancée to join him. Now he comes to the Seton residence to tell the father he will accept the offer of a job, but only on the proviso that he can quit in two years if he's not happy. The old man cannot dampen his enthusiasm to shape, control, and finally stage-manage his well-protected daughter's married life, boasting joyously that he will arrange the entire honeymoon—"You will land at Plymouth or Southampton and proceed straight to London. I shall cable my sister tomorrow"—and provide the newlyweds with a haven on, of course, the Upper East Side—"I'll arrange for you to have your house to go into March 1." For Johnny this last is the last straw—

JOHNNY: What house is that, Julia?
JULIA: Father's lending us the sweetest little place on 64th Street. . . .
    Would you also arrange for the servants, father?

—and he balks, proclaiming that even more important to him than his love for Julia is freedom.
    "Thank you, sir, very much! But I don't feel I can accept"—the epitome of grace and politeness. The epitome of couth and grace. As only Cary Grant can do it. "I'm going," says he. "Julia, will you come with me? Either way, I'm getting on that ship."
    And now, Hepburn's magical Linda:
    We may recollect that this actor never loses a sense of the dramatic moment as singular and unrepeatable, worthy of special attention, an opportunity for her to muster some apparently spontaneous gesture of vocality, movement, portage, or tone. She was trained on the stage, where at each performance reality is reborn. It is therefore not the typical and predictive, spunky and feisty, energetic and purposeful, direct and unreserved, clarion and confident Hepburn—of *Sylvia Scarlett* (1935), *Bringing Up Baby* (1938), *Woman of the Year* (1942), *Adam's Rib* (1949), *The African Queen* (1951), *The Lion in Winter* (1968), or *The Madwoman of Chaillot* (1969)—who calls for our consideration here, as she plays audience to Julia and Johnny—a desperately interested, wholly engaged audience—but someone different, even contradictory.
    While in the 1930s Katharine Hepburn had been one of those who displayed "clean, neat, and sleek hair, tailored clothing, the athletic body, the beauty of realism" (Ohmer 190), there was at the same time a growing feeling in Hepburn's audience, especially that part of the audience distant from the cultural mecca of the East, that her "Bryn Mawr patois" (McLean 6) and erudite elocution, her sophisticated wit and her snippy, even contentious bravura were distasteful, even loathsome. In 1938, an exhibitors

"revolution" culminated in the production of a full-page advertisement that explicitly trounced on Hepburn, among a group of other too-elevated types: "We dust-bowl dwellers do not appreciate English conversation" (6). Hepburn's pictures suffered at the box office.

As to her femininity—at the time, this conventionally meant a kind of radiant docility—films of the decade had mocked it "as a mere masquerade" (Mann 299). And the public response to Howard Hawks's thoroughly hilarious *Bringing Up Baby* (1938), in which as an excitable socialite Hepburn puppets Cary Grant's absent-minded professor like a master, had been sufficiently tepid to show that as far as her career prospects were concerned storm clouds were on the horizon. Audiences did not, perhaps, admire the scathing social critique that Hepburn's snippy brilliance implied. To make matters worse, George Cukor's "quite somber" *Holiday* (McLean 12) "was rejected" the same year by a movie audience "still reeling from the Depression" (Mann 300). At this time in her life Hepburn was suffering on the personal side, too. Her flighty love affair with the tycoon Howard Hughes was heading for land; her somewhat strained relation with Ginger Rogers—they had worked together in *Stage Door* (1937)—was becoming a lost cause: "Hepburn left RKO in 1938 just as Rogers's solo popularity and critical acclaim were cresting" (Lugowski 149–50). And soon, too, in late September of 1938, the Long Island Express, the worst hurricane to date to slam the east coast, would ravage the Hartford Connecticut area and flatten the Hepburn family home that was a bedrock of her emotional life.

In short, the Hepburn we meet in *Holiday* is not the shining star she would become in only a little more than a year, when *The Philadelphia Story* was released. She was neither high in the saddle nor a public darling, and she was working out of defensiveness and emotional stress. Yet something amazing happens. While in its gross plot *Holiday* is finally a love story and Hepburn "gets her man," a great deal more than heteronormative coupling is on the table. A "smaller" moment can loom large. And here in the Seton salon is one very, very small moment in *Holiday* in which Hepburn's special talent looms very large indeed.

To observe, she's been perched on a chair, along with sweet-tempered, ne'er-do-well Ned, their matched silent expressions registering embarrassment at and disapproval of the pushy father. Avid follower of this entertainment line by line she now looks up, a bright ray of hope piercing that paternal cloud cover to hit her face. "You've been extremely kind and generous, sir," Johnny wraps up, "but it's not for us. . . . I can see now it's got to be a clean break. It's simply got to." Won't Julia leave her father's riches behind? "I must decide now, must I?," says she, brusquely.

Cut to Linda's pronounced expectation on her sister's behalf: will Julia finally leave the stifling cocoon of this house and go out into the world with this splendid, this perfect man?

But for Julia, this is the absolute end of the road. She sends Johnny packing, and Linda's hopeful eyes darken, her head lowers, a cloud of sadness seems to form over her. In long shot, we see the entire family, Linda on the arm of the chair. Sadly, in a low monotone, "I'll miss that man."

Julia turns from the fireplace, stunned: "He's really gone!"

Mr. Seton, pompous in rejection: "Yes! And in my opinion—"

But now, now!—

NOW!

Sharply, very sharply, as sharply as only Hepburn could manage with that flinty, articulate voice; and with an expansion of volume for which our ears have been given no preparation, so that it hits like a punch: "Good riddance, eh?!"

As she turns a gaze pleadingly upon Julia we realize—it's like waking from a dream—that all the action until this point has been only a preamble, a slow warming of the blood. Some great beast is here awakening. "He loves you," Hepburn says, meaning to be helpful, "he'll be back." But proud Julia has collapsed into a cocoon of negativity: "Be back, did you say!" (The camera is dollying into the two women.) "What do you think I am! . . ." And swiveling to face her father: "I'll be all right. Even a little more than all right, I should say!"

A crystal clear two-shot. Hepburn at left, seizing Julia by the elbow and spinning her around so that their faces are glaring into one another. And *in one single breath*, only one breath, one huge breath, a breath that the actress knew all through this scene she would be needing to take and so waited for, prepared for, summoned: "You don't love him! You don't *love him*! *Answer me*, do you or do you *not*? You don't do you, I can see it, it's written all over you, you're *relieved* he's gone, *RELIEVED!*"

The way it comes out of Hepburn is like this: "You don't love him you don't *love him* ANSWER ME do you or do you not you don't do you I can see it it's written all over you you're relieved he's gone RELIEVED!" The punctuation on the tongue.

"Suppose I am!" Pouting, defensive, angry.

"She asks me 'Suppose she is.' Are you?, say it!" But this, too, *all in one breath*, without so much as a half-syllable in which to gasp, so that it's like this: "*She asks me suppose she is are you SAY IT!*" The poetic diction of Gertrude Stein.

With a huge decorative white flower blossoming on the chest of her dark dress, Julia now blossoms with arrogance. "I'm so relieved I could sing with it! Is that what you want?"

Linda is breathing deeply, gasping for footing, and the sound of the breathing is speech itself—a stage trick, in which the performer is aware that the intensity of the audience's engaged focus upon her will turn every bodily gesture into meaning. To breathe is to act. A huge change in the face, the eyes bright, the mouth open in unconstrained joy (a remarkable achievement, since we see the entire face-à-face in profile).

>LINDA: "<u>Yes</u>! <u>THANKS</u>!!! (Turning to her brother): Oh, Neddy Neddy, have I got a job now! (She is leading him toward the door, breathlessly.) Is your passport in order? Mine is! What do you say?"

Once again, Hepburn speaks the lines in one fluid breath, disregarding the punctuation. Her pallid but muscular right hand, lovingly seizing Ned's tuxedoed arm, is a potent sign of optimism, futurity, encouragement, love, and warmth.

>NED: Oh! When?
>LINDA: Now, tonight!
>NED: Oh, I don't think I could—(still under papa's foot).
>LINDA: Oh, of course you could, if I can you can. . . . Will you come?

Ned has gone gelid with fear, and his father has come up angrily behind him, like a dark shadow. "Where are you off to?"

>LINDA: On a trip, on a ride, oh what a big ride, do you mind?

But still one more time the breathing trick, the speech racing out in a smooth ascension, a roller coaster car heading up to its peak, and rounding it, and plummeting: "*On a trip on a RIDE OH what a BIG RIDE DO YOU MIND*???"

Ned can't. But Linda will come back for him. It's a swift but solemn promise. Then she turns to Julia off-camera, radiance and the energy of an unbridled pony racing in her. "You've got no faith in Johnny, have you, Julia. (And, never gasping, never taking breath, and without punctuational pauses.) His little dream may fall flat you think well so it may what if it should there'll be another. *Oh* I've got all the faith in the world in Johnny *whatever he does it's ALL RIGHT WITH ME.*"

Here is virtuosity in its cleanest, boldest, most radiant form, residing entirely in the actor's situated, idiosyncratic use of her body, particularly her lungs, as a vehicle. As to lungs, also the tongue, and the blossom of the voice: William Butler Yeats, a great phrase master: "An actor should understand how so to discriminate cadence from cadence, and so to cherish the musical lineaments of verse or prose that he delights the ear with a continually varied music" (387). And the director/impresario Peter Brook, describing a great actor: "His tongue, his vocal chords, his feeling for rhythm compose an instrument that he has consciously developed all through his career" (424).

Donald Ogden Stewart's script notwithstanding, Hepburn mobilizes Linda through her breathing power, which combines significant pulmonary strength with acute diction, even stellar diction, the sort of diction one is hard-pressed to find in actors today who are trained to pose and exert the body athletically, as though the set is a gym, but not to speak discernably. Hepburn can ramble swiftly over a chain of words without dropping a single syllable, making every word crisp even though she is in a verbal race with herself. Equally intelligible—finally dominant—is the heard quality of the racing itself, a quality that trumps the dialogue and sums to the character's building excitement and confidence.

Of particular note here, however, is this: that in watching *Holiday* any viewer could well take the performer's strengths entirely for granted—one can suppose that in 1938 and afterward many people did—and in this way fail to take special note of the diction, the enunciation, the phrasing, and the vocal power with which he or she is being confronted. Thus, Hepburn's strike is both fierce and subtle. Her ability to combine ferocity with subtlety is a hallmark of her talent.

And an index, too, of the elusive ways in which a performative moment can owe not to a brilliant script or sympathetic direction, or even actorly wisdom, but simply and bluntly the actor's physique. Because what is happening with Hepburn in this scene flows from her chest. In any scene an actor faces the problem, where and how to catch a breath? Because in speaking the actor expends the self, and in speaking is vitally present with the character.

"On a trip on a RIDE OH what a BIG RIDE DO YOU MIND???"

19

Director/Virtuoso

FIGURE 19 *Basil Rathbone (l.) and J. Edward Bromberg in* The Mark of Zorro *(Rouben Mamoulian, Twentieth Century Fox, 1940). Digital frame enlargement.*

Rouben Mamoulian's *The Mark of Zorro* (1940) contains a bizarre little scene:

Don Luis Quintero (J. Edward Bromberg) takes a moment from obsessively controlling the Los Angeles pueblo to meditate in his cozy study. He stands to the right of a large brass astrolabe, some antique version of the medieval device used to measure the position of the sun, moon, planets, and stars—in short, to help people know where in the universe they are. Into the scene strides Capt. Esteban Pasquale (Basil Rathbone), and positions himself on the left side of the device. "Esteban!," says Luis fretfully, "I've just been told a horrible tale about a madman in Madrid . . . Zorro. He thinks I'm running a great risk by staying here!"

Esteban has reached out and given the astrolabe a pungent twirl, all of the rings cycling in different orbits simultaneously: a glittery lure for the eye. "I have a plan . . ."

Don Luis looks at him, is distracted by the shining astrolabe, looks down and stops it with his hands. "What is it?"

Esteban begins to relate his scheme, *and once again fingers the astrolabe to make it spin.*

Don Luis, looking down again, reaches out with both hands to stop it.

"Doesn't it suggest to you that Zorro is the tool of Don Alejandro and the cabbaleros?"

Don Luis: "How would you prove it?"

Now the signature Rathbone tenor malevolence: "We can at least . . ." *he gives the astrolabe a third spin,* ". . . help the situation."

"How?!" (Spin, spin, spin, spin!)

"Form an alliance with Don Alejandro."

"That's impossible!" Both of Luis's hands come up and stop the device, as his face shows more and more perturbation.

Esteban sternly proposes a match between Luis's niece and Alejandro, *forcefully spinning the astrolabe again.*

Luis, slowly smiling. "Not bad! . . . Not bad at all!" Now he reaches out himself and pushes the astrolabe into an even more vigorous spin, as Esteban shows the camera a cruel profile. The scene dissolves.

The dialogue in this encounter is informative, but in a circumstantial way. Listening, we hear of Luis's troubles and Esteban's manipulative plan, yet at the same time the process of the film story will manifest all the significant elements of this. That Esteban is a malicious schemer we have learned already, and can in any event read directly from the casting of the evil villain Sir Guy Gisbourne from *The Adventures of Robin Hood* two years earlier. The character styling is patented Rathbone. Luis's bumbling nervousness appears elsewhere in the film, too, as part of his manner. The names of various other characters who are part of the plan are ultimately of little concern to us. And most importantly, the entire plane on which is set the relationship between these two men, their discourse, their attitudes, and their intentions finds itself overlaid with another plane that attracts our attention much more strongly: the astrolabe and the various hands coming up to activate or deactivate it.

Spin! Stop!

Why need Luis stand next to his astrolabe in the first place, and, for that matter, why need we even learn he possesses one, so that the thing can be invoked dramatically and become a toy in the scene? What is gained by this small but potent directorial trick, both in terms of the continuance of the story and in terms of our involvement? This "business"—something to do whilst delivering one's lines—is a virtuosity.

Mamoulian wishes to convey that although Esteban works for Luis, he does not particularly like him. And Luis, for his part, is afraid of Esteban and in withdrawal. Esteban gains some control here. The writer has come up with a discussion that will allow the furtherance of this motive through the dialogue, but we hardly notice the dialogue because that whirling device is an optical lure, and when the eyes are teased fully and intensively it can be difficult to hear the speech, especially if, as here, the actors are delivering their lines tersely. Esteban is on the rise, and the boss who would keep him in line fears for his life. A double perspective.

The use of the astrolabe convèys precisely this formation. When Esteban spins the thing he is casual, effortless, as though in presuming to play with Don Luis's toy he is occupying a status that ought properly be his, that, indeed, he thinks already *is* properly his. And reaching up over and over to stop the spinning, Luis makes it plain that Esteban is impertinent: the action must halt if not the impertinence itself. The distracting astrolabe waylays Luis from thinking straight (the old spinning-shiny-object-hypnosis trick), much in the way that Esteban the distractor is waylaying Luis in general. So, the astrolabe, an invention that sends signals, here signals in two contradictory ways, alternately:

Schematically:

a "I will play with your toy" . . . "No, stop it."

b "I will *definitely* play with your toy" . . . "No, *really*, stop it."

c "This toy is *mine* to use as I wish" . . . "No, it certainly *isn't.*"

d "MY toy!" . . . "No, actually *my toy, and now I'm getting the last laugh.*"

This little game of shuttlecock, slipped so glitteringly into the scene, is Mamoulian's. But there is a subterranean, special facet to the plan here, bringing the moment to the level of virtuosity. It operates through the invocation of the astrolabe; its precise placement; the design of the prop in terms of reflectivity; the cinematographer's key lighting; and the actors' masterful timing. The astrolabe divides the acoustic and visual aspects of the scene (already as Luis first approaches it we are wondering what this thing can be), and the constant movement of the two men to put it into action and still it, left, right, left, right, takes our attention entirely away from everything else. Whatever the (irrelevant) details of the conversation, Esteban is challenging Luis. And Mamoulian has contrived to show all this visually, purely through the spinning and abrupt cessation, so that even in our distracted trance, even as we think of movement and stillness and nothing else, the power alignment between the characters is plainly felt. In short, *the deep meaning of the scene is conveyed through mime.* As more than the facial expressions the astrolabe and the hands that drive it command us, the characters are guided and shown to perform a kind of magic. Colin Williamson notes how "sleights that are 'of the hand'" constitute "mechanics and materiality of so-called older forms of prestidigitation" (136). In our present case, the sleight does not constitute hiding or suddenly revealing an object, it constitutes a sudden manufacture of illusion and distraction, for both a character and the viewer. Williamson very helpfully quotes Georges Méliès:

> In prestidigitation, one operates in view of an attentive audience that will notice any false move. You are all alone, and their eyes never leave you. (54)

Recall how Don Luis never took his eyes away from Esteban's digital maneuvers in purloining his toy, how, noticing the spinning astrolabe and being aware of how it was affecting him, he reached up to make it stop. Note, too, how when he makes it spin at the end of the scene, the diligent, always scheming Esteban *turns his eyes away.*

To watch this scene with the sound turned off is a wondrous pleasure.

20

Heimlichkeit

FIGURE 20 *James Stewart in* The Spirit of St. Louis *(Billy Wilder, Leland Hayward Productions, 1957). Digital frame enlargement.*

I have noted that actors in a production tend to make their characters behave as though they are familiars to one another, citizens of a shared world. Another aspect of this dramatic coherence, at the deepest level, is a thoroughgoing scenic *heimlichkeit* that infects the fiction. Places, objects, persons, attitudes, vocal tones, performative tics—all aspects of the manifestation—become familiar to the audience in association with certain characters, so that if there is repetition after an (even surprising) introductory exposure the audience can react with open acknowledgment of the "naturalness" of the effect. In *Lord of the Rings*, when first we meet Gandalf (Ian McKellen) we discover that he has a tendency to *intone*. Later on he is the resident intoner, and those around him match his sonorous intonement with their rapture, their eager listening, and so on. Or, early in *Howards End* (1992), Anthony Hopkins turns his head away from his interlocutor when speaking (a not unfamiliar Hopkins device), thus in a way gaining amplification for his voice. When, as the film progresses, he continues to do this, we have come already to recognize and expect it, *and so have all the people he talks to.* To speech patterns, philosophies, gestures there is a continuity: to the way of carrying a shirt upon one's shoulders, to the flickering of one's fingers as one dons one's eyeglasses. In the story world, as would seem, no one, not even the stranger, is a stranger. (Even the monster in monster movies turns out to be precisely the sort of creation a monster would be.)

Homeliness is not decorum, harmony, appropriateness, intelligibility, or sweetness, all of which are desirable yet do not necessarily characterize our sense of home, the embracing haven. Here is Ken Blakemore's description of the post-prandial dinner table in Bunbury, Cheshire, midway through the 1950s:

> We all chat as Mum butters thin slices of bread and we all help ourselves to slivers of moist, red cheese. This is the food Mum likes best. The tea in my cup is strong and brown and has thick Jersey milk in it, with two teaspoonfuls of sugar. (qtd. in Kynaston 601)

Not converse or talk, but *chat.* Mum, not mother. She uses the still-not-ubiquitous staple, *butter,* not only on bread but on *thin slices of bread,* on which not just our young narrator but *everyone (equably)* is sharing a *very good cheese.* Cheese is one thing; good cheese something else; and *very good* cheese a prize indeed. This cheese is being taken up *in slivers;* and it is both *moist* and *red,* which is to say peculiar to an English district, probably locally made, and surely never packaged for mass distribution. Because *Mum likes this food best* there is a sense of her warm embrace, a sense that the diners are in the protective arms of the beloved *caregiver.* As to their tea, its being strong and brown nicely accompanies and contrasts the *thick Jersey milk,* which is the real telling point of the observation. Tea with milk is conventional, but not especially decorous; this, however, is not milk but *thick Jersey milk.* Not just thick milk, milk from *Jersey cows,* which is to imply, the best, richest, fattest, happiest, most nourishing and flavorful cows in England. And now the child's memory is capped with a pudding, *two teaspoonfuls* of sugar added in. Sweetness and light, as Matthew Arnold said.

Even in a film that is truly hideous, off-kilter, or utterly disturbing, ensemble acting can be *Heimlich* in that one feels settled "at home" with the straightforwardly identifiable characters (*Harry Potter and the Sorcerer's Stone* [2001]). A film may invoke tragedy, pathos, or murder yet be *Heimlich* (*Dinner at Eight* [1933]; *You Can't Take It With You* [1938]; *Death on the Nile* [1978]). We find comfort watching folk who find comfort, even if saddening things happen. However we prefer our tea, we can catch the special glimmer when Jersey milk goes in.

But one also finds occasional meaningful, even virtuosic disruptions of continuity, *unheimlich* moments. Imagine the difficulties that might beset performers when they are asked to portray socially problematic qualities, as with Matt Damon in two interesting films, quite different from each other. In Gus Van Sant's *Good Will Hunting* (1997), he is a consummate prodigy, so accomplished with numbers he can solve puzzles better than the university's supreme mathematician, and so deftly glib with language that, untutored himself, he can outtalk, out-argue, outperform a smarmy graduate student who takes himself as being naturally superior, or dazzle and confuse a panel of NSA interviewers, in whose company he does not wish to belong. In scene after scene we are led to recognize—with pleasure—Will's adroit intellectual alienness, his inability at simple social relations, his psychological wound matched by his innocence and his cool, calculating way of assessing situations—his sense of *unheimlichkeit*. Always our familiar, he is never really known to any of the other characters, so he is a dramatic cipher. In the office of his psychiatrist, Sean (Robin Williams), he has a breakthrough emotional moment in which Sean walks up and embraces him. Because Van Sant films this in profile and from a medium distance we sense Sean holding warmly to his breast a soul and a body he wishes to protect, relax, and nurture. Will is only going through the motion of an embrace, though, even as he sobs.

Doug Liman's *The Bourne Identity* (2003) adds a different note of complexity. Will Hunting may not be known by his chums, but they are with him, and we have a reassuring sense that he knows himself, when he does not. Jason Bourne, heroic protagonist, has a severe amnesia. We meet him being fished out of the sea unconscious with bullet holes in his back. We follow his healing, his landing, his adventures as he pieces them together from fragments of information as unclear to him as to us. Jason is thus both acting in, and audience of, this film story. Some of the other characters feel they know Jason and relate to him, such as Marie (Franka Potente), a girl who gives him a ride away from Geneva and becomes his lover. Yet, as we know, the Jason one might conceivably know is actually, deeply a cipher, a blank space in the formula. We can have some limited sense of *heimlichkeit* in watching only because the performances and settings are recognizable: the recognizable Damon; racing away from people with guns; austere, high-tech spaces of the CIA holding controllers who suck in and digest information in a comfy, routinized way. High security is warm protection, even if hypermodern, forbiddingly practical, and telecommunicational rather than speechly. In the center of this dramatic universe, Damon's Bourne moves as a blank, a neutral pronoun, as facts about him are filled in only slowly. Damon must wend his way through the scenes without apparent knowledge of where he is, without a sense of memory, without a way to identify the people he meets. Though his senses are acutely activated he does not find the treasure at the end of the rainbow.

He discovers without warning that he is extremely adept at mortal hand-to-hand combat, indeed trained to kill with remarkable efficiency.

Dispatching a pair of policemen in a park he wonders, How can I be doing this? Damon rapidly scans the situation and holds facial expression under control, giving us a powerful sense of him calculating and being blocked at once.

In both *Hunting* and *Bourne,* we have a familiar, *heimlich* feeling with the film as a whole while being forced to negotiate our way around a central character who *doesn't feel at home.* Our desire for coherence is openly provoked, reflected back upon ourselves. In numerous other films—not only the other Bourne pictures but Soderbergh's *Ocean's Eleven* (2001) and its sequels, as well as *The Informant!* (2009), *Green Zone* (2010), *Hereafter* (2010), *The Adjustment Bureau* (2011), *The Martian* (2015), *Suburbicon* (2017), and others—Damon is used as an unsocialized type, to some degree. But a sense of humor and intensive presence of mind allow him to survive interaction and race forward. He has become *the* actor to embody quirky people. This sense of the alien stepping into an already *gemütlich* environment in which everything is right, everything in its place, everything is organized, and producing, by his entrance, a thrilling disruptive wave, is a virtuosity through misfit.

With the figure we call the movie star a certain *heimlichkeit* inheres in the body's chain of appearances over time, quite beyond what may appear in any particular film, as if every character played by the star *knows* every other character, is in the same family. Any displacement of that order of the self is quickly recognized, potentially disruptive, both locally, as regards the present drama, and globally, as regards the studio's bank account, since the star's predictably being known and therefore constituting an attraction at the box office is fundamental to studio production. After his small turn as (SPOILER ALERT!) a villain in *After the Thin Man* (1936), James Stewart, or "Jimmy," as he came to be known with affection by his millions of followers around the globe, played almost exclusively lovable or admirable roles, characters of local or national honor yet at the same time, and markedly, men built of homespun stuff, the simple country-boy virtues of respectful deference, sweet kindness, and self-effacing devotion. For examples, in *Mr. Smith Goes to Washington* (1939), *The Shop Around the Corner, The Mortal Storm, The Philadelphia Story* (all 1940), *It's a Wonderful Life* (1946), *Call Northside 777, Rope* (both 1948), *The Greatest Show on Earth* (1952), to go only partly through his august career, he seemed onscreen a man of virtuosic *heimlichkeit,* thrown into circumstances beyond his control to shape or influence except by exceptional force of determination, hard labor, and perseverance. His selfless heroism is of a piece with our comfortable proximity; he is one of us; he belongs. The drawl, the wide-opened eyes, the winning smile, the hem-and-haw delivery that makes it seem he is struggling to be articulate—all these work together and in exquisite harmony to form the "Jimmy Stewart personality" film lovers know and love with such familiarity.

But in Anthony Mann's *The Naked Spur* (1953) we find something totally uncharacteristic, something brave and authentic in the diegesis—and for the actor to have achieved—but ugly. As a bounty hunter chasing, catching, and dragging back for sale to the justice system a hardened criminal (Robert Ryan), against the pleas of a young woman in their company (Janet Leigh), he has noble motives but also a hideous rage. To see "Jimmy's" gritted teeth, frenzied eyes, and perspiring face is to find the star image tarnished, but even here we feel at home in his anxious presence.

Various strategies are used in production to effect what will appear to be familiar relations between members of a cast. Make-up people will modulate skin intonations so that characters will seem sufficiently like one another onscreen: for example, in John Ford's *The Searchers* (1956) as Natalie Wood must appear late in the film to have spent long years in captivity by natives, her flesh is tanned; but in early scenes she is white. In the finale she must be rescued by a notably white John Wayne. She had to seem darker than him; but not so much darker that pictorial harmony was jeopardized, or, even worse, severe lighting headaches made for the cinematographer and his team. Her makeup showed that she had crossed an ethnic border yet at the same time remained a girl who had been lost. In science-fiction films, alien creatures are heavily made-up actors, but the makeup must render them, if alien to the earthling protagonists, still inhabitants of the same thoroughly-conceived dramatic universe: strangers yet not so very strange as to be unrecognizable. Even, as in *Arrival* (2016), when aliens are concocted to be unrecognizable, they are only "unrecognizable," that is, recognizably unrecognizable. The clothing in a film will appear, all of it, to have come from the same manufactory, whether it is a costume department or the studio of Edith Head. The lighting and film stock will be balanced in usage, allowing for radical discontinuities in setting while at the same time retaining a pleasing coherence in overall design. Scenes, like characters, "know" one another. In producing a quite atypical virtuosic turn, the actor will be sensitive to her having been made to look *not so very atypical at all*.

"A violent order is a disorder," Wallace Stevens wrote, "And a great disorder is an order. These two things are one."

21

Collapse

FIGURE 21 *Valentina Cortese in* La nuit américaine [Day for Night] *(François Truffaut, Les Films du Carrosse, 1973). Digital frame enlargement.*

Since it occurs in a real world the virtuosic turn is subject to collapse through a sort of eruption in which the unperformed physical self seeps uncontrollably through the envelope of the characterization, this with ultimately destructive results. A world-famous pianist on the concert stage, throwing himself into the *Allegro agitato* of Rachmaninoff's Sonata No. 2 Op. 36, without warning stops and falls forward onto the keyboard. Several long moments of abject silence. Then he stands and stumbles off the stage.[1]

---

[1]A typical after-effect of triple bypass surgery, which was undergone by this pianist, in fact, not long before.

Or: the famously loquacious Alexander Woollcott becomes silent, suddenly, during a radio broadcast on January 23, 1943, but listeners do not know he has suffered a fatal heart attack. Or: operatic divo Leonard Warren falls dead on the stage at the Metropolitan Opera just as he is about to sing Verdi's "To die, a momentous thing!" from *La forza del destino*. Or: performing a reconceived Shylock in a Broadway-bound production of Arnold Wesker's *The Merchant*, Zero Mostel dies in Philadelphia during a preview. Or: Dick Shawn, celebrated for his rendition of Conrad Birdie in *Bye Bye Birdie*, drops to the stage at the University of California San Diego in 1987, confounding the audience who think he is riffing. Or: famed conductor Giuseppe Sinopoli succumbs to a coronary while conducting *Aida* in Berlin, 20 April 2001. Such collapses, we expect, would not appear on film.

There are legion cases where at a climactic moment demanding special concentration and exertion, the performative bubble bursts (because of a bursting bubble in the person mobilizing it). William Hickey dies during production of the film *Better Than Ever* (1997). Nicholas Ray dies while filming *Lightning Over Water* (1980) for Wim Wenders. The human body shows through what is now become only a characterological veil, as human mortality trumps the immortal configuration of the performed presence. Often, however, virtuosic performance needn't go so far as to collapse, and any moment of severe disruption, whilst garnering appropriate attention and concern because of what it is and portends, deeply entrenches our conviction in the virtuosity more generally. In Truffaut's *Day for Night* (1973), the more that Séverine (Valentina Cortese), actor in the film-within-the-film, forgets her lines and must have a shot retaken, the more wholly do her coworkers accept her as a genuine, if fading, star. We expect from the brilliant performer not merely brilliant performance, with all that entails (Séverine is posed as an actor of unparalleled talent and a huge filmography), but a kind of immortality, a convicting sense that virtuosity of this kind can and will go on and on, without limit. Evidence to the contrary happily missing in almost every case, the performative body does not seem subject to conventional limits. Virtuosity impresses in part because it seems more than human.

And of course it is not.

So it is that when a virtuoso dies, that is, when a human dies who has been known as a virtuoso, disbelief spreads through the fan population. Associated with stunning virtuosic turns, death is inconceivable, impossible, out of nature. When Robin Williams dies, David Bowie, Mary Tyler Moore, Don Rickles, Chuck Berry, Jonathan Demme, Michael Jackson, Roger Moore, Adam West, Jerry Lewis, Aretha Franklin, Elvis Presley among an army of such figures: quivering disbelief; denial; enduring maintenance of the star self through repetition of the public image and rapt disattention to the human self beneath the virtuosic face.

But if screen virtuosity denies death, then it must somehow not be alive, not part of the mortal stream. It attaches or mirrors, reflects or imagines mortality but is not typically tied to the living body of the performer as stage virtuosity is (because onstage, actors, virtuosic and not, are alive). In film the body of the performer always existed *before*. As though the body of the film performer, *as it was when filmed,* is *already always no longer with us*. Virtuosic bodies in cinema may fail at mortal collapse because of technicalities: when Natalie Wood drowns during production of *Brainstorm* (1983) the script is adjusted and the company shoot around scenes she can no longer perform, yet she remains fully performative in the film. When Heath Ledger dies during production of *The Imaginarium of Dr. Parnassus* (2009), his role is cleverly altered and taken over in principal photography by three actor-friends who agree to step in, and whose incarnations and transformative substitution is now written into the script. When, having filmed *Strangers on a Train* (1951) for Hitchcock, Robert Walker perishes from an inadvertent injection[2] during filming of Leo McCarey's subsequent *My Son John* (1952), some of his scenes are literally cut out from *Strangers* and inserted into the new film in a new context.

Of course, to the degree that cinema is convincing about the presence of its characters, because they remain visible, challenging, and vivacious as time goes by, we can believe that the actors performing the characters remain as well, never die, live on always as present as the characters are; that for some of us, and in a special way for those who reach virtuosic heights, death does not exist. And of course, if there is no death, there is no life. While onstage the virtuosic moment is always a gamble with death (like any acted moment) on film the virtuosic moment is immortal, and the performer we consider virtuosic is beyond time.

---

[2]From medical personnel who refused to accept his claim of a drug allergy.

22

Bigger Than Life

FIGURE 22 *Michelle Williams in* My Week with Marilyn *(Simon Curtis, The Weinstein Company/BBC, 2011). Digital frame enlargement.*

A particular problem of compositional integrity is raised in the virtuosic moment, because it has the potential to dominate the audience's experience and thereby throw the surround out of balance. Orson Welles is the legendary exemplar, being physically (thanks in part to the lens) and narratively huger than huge, bolder than bold, and with the singer's voice: Falstaff; Long John Silver; Louis XVIII; Gen. Dreedle; Tireisias; Wolsey; Hank Quinlan; Arkadin; Othello; Harry Lime; Michael O'Hara; Charles Foster Kane. Consider, too, a less enunciated case, Humphrey Bogart's stunningly evocative performance of Queeg disintegrating on the witness stand in *The Caine Mutiny* (1954), which is so detailed, so finely wrought, so thoroughly expressive, and so powerfully rendered breath after breath that it is difficult for the viewer, thinking back to the film, to have memory of anything else. Bogart's other performances are considerably more balanced through their diegeses, especially Vincent Parry in *Dark Passage* (1947), interacting with

Lauren Bacall in her cozy apartment, sometimes beneath bandages; or Spade in the ensemble piece, *The Maltese Falcon* (1941).

From genre to genre expressive balance varies in quality and importance, with the melodrama supporting the greatest range of tonality, albeit sometimes to the detriment of characterizations, because the principal subject, the beleaguered woman, is not only the principal agent in a story but also the deep subject of the film as film. With science-fiction films alien presence has an almost natural virtuosity in itself, astonishing expressivity being carried and supported through character design. Canny filmmakers tend to hold off presentation of the alien figure—this "emotionless" figure, as Barry Keith Grant describes some aliens (7), this triumph of effects— until the table has been laid with a first few courses. In William Cameron Menzies's *Invaders from Mars* (1953) it is some considerable time before we see the Martians whose presence has caused such disturbance; almost twenty-five years later the aliens in Spielberg's *Close Encounters* (1977) appear only in the final scene of the film. Both diegetically and figuratively onscreen, aliens can make earthlings disappear.

Virtuosic performance in police procedurals, historical epics, and westerns offers particular challenges because these sorts of film depend strictly on tightly framed relationships—Kenneth Burke calls these "ratios"—between setting and character, between character and action, between action and agency, the particular weave cultivating the tapestry and the tapestry being the structure. To scream out in role, figuratively, is to elude the warp and woof of the form, to take up a placement disproportionate to other aspects of the work. The villain in the western, for instance, cannot be more villainous than the terrain is rugged, the hero is noble, the townspeople are eager (or afraid) to be civil. The sci-fi alien can be hideous to look at, but not more than the hero is handsome and dignified. The comedian is inherently virtuosic, and comedy films can be either displays of individual talent or artful cacophonies produced by many comedic sources working with, or against, one another: flip Jack Gilford, stodgy Michael Hordern, and irrepressible Zero Mostel in *A Funny Thing Happened on the Way to the Forum* (1966); but every comic moment leaps out from its surround.

With the biopic, however—especially the biography of a figure already well known to viewers—the problem of virtuosic performance is magnified and made more complex. Since in its formal claim the film *is* the persona at its center, an actor's hyperexpressiveness in the role will disrupt only if the bounds of the figure's known personality and record of acts are broken through: typically the central expression *is* the filmic unfolding. As long as the actor persists in "being" the central figure, properly; as long as the character receives suitable treatment from the other characters (a matter of actors' treatment of one another's work), the film can have the necessary balance and "make sense." The "biographical virtuosity" works through submission to real character, which means submitting the self to characterological shaping from an outside force: Gary Cooper as Lou Gehrig; Madonna as Eva Perón; Robert Hardy as Churchill; Ingrid Bergman as Golda Meir; James Stewart as Charles Lindbergh; Jessica Lange as Frances Farmer; Barbra Streisand as Fanny Brice. Virtuosity in such cases resides in the actor's willing engulfment by the putatively "accurate" personality of the principal, insofar as this personality takes shape as appearance and mannerism. With Frank Langella as Nixon we have a carefully studied commitment of the voice, the actor knowing full well that he is no physical match.

But it is possible to have a fictional biopic, the story of the life of a person "famous" in the movie but not famous in everyday life, because nonexistent. Judy Garland as "Vicki Lester" in *A Star Is Born* (1954). Here the external "dictates" are purely invented. There are structural limits. The shrinking violet Esther Blodgett before being transformed into the international celebrity cannot be so very shrunken that producers would fail to notice her in the first place. If she is nothing at all but ordinary, yet she is *not ordinarily ordinary*. And because the star born as Vicki—whilst at certain moments bearing acute resemblance to Judy Garland!—doesn't exist in fact, because the star subject is a deeply false one, audience expectation of the "accurate" backstage personality derives from only a generalized suspicion and curiosity about the lives of the famous, this suspicion, however widely shared, itself springing from fictive "biographies," other inflated constructions like this one. Without actual knowledge of the star-making process the viewer cannot judge the fidelity of the film, but can only see portrayed—completely portrayed, if the performance is what would be called "good"—what she expected in advance to see. We find only what we know how to find. Our sense of performative virtuosity—Garland's genius performances as Vicki—derives partly from the fulfillment of this expectation and partly from the chocolates coming in an unexpectedly beautiful box. A similar formulization, with a truly magnificent frame, works behind the production of Powell and Pressburger's *The Red Shoes* (1948), there in service of a fictional prima ballerina, Victoria Page (Moira Shearer), about whom we also have particular expectations the film must be careful to fulfill even if it doesn't trouble to touch upon anything else.

The very same must hold true for real subjects of biopics. If a person— Marie Curie (Greer Garson)—however actual, is so unknown no one has ever heard her name, if she is only a cipher, little is to be gained in producing a biography. And when one does produce a biography, it must glance upon, even dive into, the knowledge that is already out there. So, biographical treatments of Winston Churchill that play upon his bulldog determination during the Second World War tend to be successful (consider a recent one with Gary Oldman), while a different treatment (such as another recent film with Brian Cox), in which Churchill is shown to have doubts and fears, indeed to have argued against the D-Day plan, causes doubt in the audience about its strength. In *My Week with Marilyn* (2011), Michelle Williams puts on the guise of a depressed, harried, set-upon, and unconfident Marilyn Monroe visiting the United Kingdom and working with (and for) Olivier on his 1957 production *The Prince and the Showgirl.* Audiences in 2011 already in the know about Marilyn's apparent problems with depression, and her anxiety about acting, could find Williams more than adept at striking these chords firmly.

But one difficulty in achieving a virtuosic performance of a real person is that extremity of sensibility and expression will be attributed to the subject of the characterization, not the actor. In *My Week,* we tend to see the fascinating Monroe, not the fascinating Williams: terrific for the film and the coherence of the performance, but not so terrific for giving viewers room to find in Williams, here, the genius she is. Further, since the biographical subject must entirely dominate the biography the disproportionate domination rests as primary evidence that the figure merits biographical treatment. Other figures (other characters) must be shown to be nothing but adjunctive, however fascinating. A fine example of this artificial diminution is the case of Dr. G. H. Hardy (Jeremy Irons) in *The Man Who Knew Infinity* (2015). While he is shown as host and mentor to the young, foreign mathematical prodigy S. Ramanujan (Dev Patel), more than anyone the man responsible for Ramanujan's being able to achieve what he did at Oxford, nevertheless the characterization of Hardy is entirely appended to that of the biopic's focus, the light on Irons always dimmer than the light on Patel.

Once framed for narrative, the biographic subject constitutes an automatic flamboyance (not to be confused with virtuosity), since the screenplay will be a chain of meaningful, momentous, and magical moments involving this personage, else why would the story be interesting to tell? For an actor to land a lead role in a biopic is therefore both a coup—the fact of the casting is likely to be taken as proof that the performer has special talents in line with those of the subject—and a debility, since with acting however astute the subject will dominate. Actors may always want their characters to dominate, but if a character dominates relentlessly the actor disappears. In labor, one hopes one's workmanship is not blatant but also not invisible.

Knowing it, the actor may contrive to flip the domination formula, however.

Meryl Streep is commanding in the acting profession roughly as indubitably as Margaret Thatcher was commanding in the British Isles, so she is a suitable candidate for the role; yet not for a moment do we lose sight of Streep inside "Thatcher." Cate Blanchett can seriously be thought a paradigm of technique and personality, thus the logic of her casting as Katharine Hepburn in Scorsese's *The Aviator* (2006); yet, this is a Hepburn who is always magically Blanchett. Given that the biographic subject *stands out powerfully,* the actor might find it challenging to achieve a special moment of virtuosic virtuosity, a moment of *standing above the figure's outstanding moments,* hence the frequent inclusion of invented scenes of the "everyday," where the subject can triumph as a normal (surprisingly more like everybody else than anybody else could have expected). As Lindbergh, James Stewart glows beyond his character at the one desperate instant he suddenly fears his "Spirit of St. Louis" has run out of fuel over the ocean. Or, the biographic subject will suddenly die or be killed, violently, surprisingly, unbelievably to the onscreen multitude: Buddy Holly (Gary Busey), Franklin Roosevelt (Ralph Bellamy), Harry Houdini (Tony Curtis), Malcolm X (Will Smith), if unsurprisingly for the audience because, at least presumably, the audience already knows the story. The shocking absence of the signal figure leaves behind a memory trace and an emotional wake, which work together to elevate the now terminated performance retroactively to a chain of virtuosic moments, which are even sometimes recapitulated in a cinematic ballet at film's end (as in Wim Wenders's *Hammett* [1982], with Frederic Forrest zealously typing as his past flashes by [in his thoughts]; or James Marsh's *The Theory of Everything* [2014], where as Eddie Redmayne "remembers" Stephen Hawking's past we see a chain of scenes from the film all run backward, as if time is flying away from him). Whilst such work is done largely by the editor, not the performer, yet it is the performer in role—that is, the *subject*—upon whose frame the garment of virtuosity seems to sit.

The cinematic "death" of the biographic subject who is no longer alive when the biopic is released must be made sacrosanct and elaborate in order to vie in emotional tone with the death of fictional subjects in conventional dramas, who, adopted into the audience's zone of care, provoke suffering when they leave the scene: Don Corleone (Marlon Brando) in *The Godfather* series or Darth Vader, a villain we love to hate, in *Star Wars*. In less-than-biographical circumstances, entire films are devoted to establishing, growing, and celebrating the character who is terminated at the finale; whereas in the biopic, devotion is *a priori* to the film, and is taken for granted, assumed, and forgotten. Biopic drama unfolds through, and is somehow tied to, historical syntax, whereas conventional drama unfolds through character arcs and purely cinematic syntax. Dramatic unfolding wraps characters in a binding of the audience's commitment and strong feeling, positive or negative, the breaking of which causes a kind of rupture of engagement. Given that in watching film, engagement is all, a rupture of engagement is a serious rupture, to be sure. The problem with a biographic subject fading from the scene—Jimmy Cagney's splendid George M. Cohan in *Yankee Doodle Dandy* (1942); Vanessa Redgrave's Mary, Queen of Scots (1971)—is that the death is only real—that is, only, onscreen, a reflection of an actual event that occurred in the ordinary world, thus, a faithful documentary indication. Elaborate, profound, extraordinary, shocking as it may be played to be, finally it is a mere happening. As indication it has relevance in the screened "life chain" of the character, but as an emotional provocation for the viewer it is too factual, too much a thing of history, to incite grief. To mobilize the audience's sympathy, the biopic must stray from history, free itself from the everyday so that it can blossom on the screen.

In fictions, the "death" of a central character always happens "only now" and "only here," so that the viewer feels attached to the moment, exactly as she was attached to moments that came "before": Yuri Zhivago (Omar Sharif) collapsing of a heart attack in the street as he tries to run after the tram on which Lara (Julie Christie) is riding (1965). A death moment can therefore be a splendid opportunity for virtuosic performance in a fiction film, performance that is virtuosic because the evaporation in our sight of a characterological presence is explosive. In a biopic death becomes humdrum, merely a necessary stroke to round out the portrait, an item in the record of what already happened in the same world where the film is screening.

23

The Spectacle of Things
Falling Apart

FIGURE 23 *Colin Firth in* The King's Speech *(Tom Hooper, See-Saw/The Weinstein Company, 2010). Digital frame enlargement.*

On stage the virtuosic "cadenza" is vulnerable to collapse for notable physical reasons. The presence of actors in the same physical domain as their audience, notwithstanding that the fiction of a divided space is typically maintained in some way, leaves the normal perils of the body open to view: illness or general debility of some kind, a sudden fit of coughing, an inadvertent slip on a carpet, accidentally dropping an important prop, forgetting a line, or any form of extreme discomfiture (as when, in *The 39 Steps* [1935] we see the wound-up Mr. Memory's [Wylie Watson] anxiety lest he be asked the wrong kind of question by someone in his audience). The stage can be perilous, too, because of something going on with the actor just beyond the audience's sightline, whether direct (a good-luck piece suddenly missing from an easy-to-reach pocket) or indirect (backstage contortions and contestations when things go wrong). Actors working together onstage are living their lives in an ensemble, albeit with careful choreography; life easily intrudes on fiction because life is never far away.

In film, because what the viewer is intended not to see occurs in another space, and at another time, virtuosic actors can feel confident that in the final cut only moments of supreme accomplishment will appear, these framed and edited together in such a way as to show the performer in the best of form. (In fact the editor may be able to improve upon the actor's form through curtailment or extension of a dialogue or movement shot.) Since screen performance leans toward the virtuosic (because meticulously constructed) virtuosic collapse can be reframed as a commercial entity in itself, a special circumstance of heightened value carefully added into the cinematic mix for special effect: the blooper sequence. At the end of Hal Ashby's *Being There* (1979), for a celebrated example, the brilliant British comedian Peter Sellers is given special—in its context, peculiar—attention because the end credits are accompanied by a sequence of spit takes as over and over he fails in one crucial scene from the film, each time getting something else wrong and breaking up. This particular sequence is functional for a film every moment of which is chocked full of delicious irony, odd juxtaposition, double meaning, misunderstanding, and profound stupidity suggesting a massive comedy of errors. But Sellers's ironic actions are performed with such grace, suaveness, innocence, and aplomb as to seem natural *and only natural*, not cultivated for humorous effect (which all open comedy must show itself to be). The film plays as journalism, albeit a very strange and improbable sort, with characters drawn from everyday life. The blooper sequence allows audiences to let go of the comic suspense that has been restraining them, to openly acknowledge that yes, as they perhaps *suspected but could not claim they knew (since the clinching evidence was withheld)*, this whole thing, seen in retrospect, was altogether contrived, and properly the star of the show is now the guide pointing all this out for a laugh.

But the blooper sequence, with the offscreen voice calling "Cut!" again and again, is a recognized feature of film now: we avowedly take the picture to have been stitched by unseen tailors who can make mistakes and also edit them out. An actor can fall out of role, yet without becoming the person he would be off-camera if no extra camera-behind-the-camera were present filming him. Viewing, we are not all the way off-camera, but we are certainly outside one central frame, the script as filmed (unless, of course, the blooper sequence is scripted as well).

Self-conscious routines can be made entirely diegetic. In *The King's Speech* (2010), George VI (Colin Firth), who has a debilitating stutter, must give a radio speech to energize and encourage his countrymen during the Second

World War. How is he to manage? By taking lessons from the primary speech pathologist of the time (Geoffrey Rush). These lessons (for the King backstage) are revealed in detail, especially emphasizing the royal foibles with words most of the viewers say regularly without effort. Effectively this is a royal blooper sequence, valorized because (a) we can see that the pathologist is making progress of some kind patching it up (b) because in the final event the King comes through a true hero, and (c) because the King is the King. He is of course a man whose heroism triumphs over his own body, here, there, and everywhere.[1]

François Truffaut's *Day for Night* (*La nuit américaine,* 1973) includes a touching diegetic example of *collapse as virtuosity.* The film is about the making of a film, *Meet Pamela.* We spend a great deal of time with the production crew and the actors, noting especially the kinds of neurosis, fear, and incapacity that beleaguers actors at work, especially Séverine (Valentina Cortese) who must play a typical (and tedious) melodramatic scene where, overcome by anger and frustration, she turns and storms out of a room. Her problem is that there are one too many doors side by side in the set, and without fail she builds up the anger, swivels, and storms into the wrong door—which leads to a closet.[2] But Truffaut does not permit his scene (containing the film scene directed by the filmmaker Ferrand [François Truffaut]) to be played for humor. Séverine, we learn *sotto voce,* has a son who is gravely ill and her every moment is touched with anxiety and fear. Ferrand continually steps forward to comfort her, all the while fearing his actress will never be able to get this scene right, or anything else in the picture, for that matter, and that the producer's money is going down the drain. Working against time on one side and Séverine's personal situation on the other, he has to find a pathway to the correct door. But the more difficult things become for Séverine, the more brilliant seems Cortese.

More than merely a loss of performance, virtuosic collapse can be a performance of loss, an intentionally acted evaporation of an actor's ability to put up and sustain part of a fictional world. The audience's overriding concern is that fictional world, not any single performance, except that any performance is a pathway into that world, a stabilizing guyline. On whatever level it happens, a performer's disintegration drains our belief, faith, and trust, no matter momentarily or not. In recursive works, like *Day for Night,* with recursive moments, such as Séverine's catastrophe, our very attachment as watchers is juggled. When in a fictional film-within-a-film "actors"

---

[1]A similar kind of triumph over the imprisoning body centers *The Diving Bell and the Butterfly* (2007), *The Theory of Everything* (2014), and *Molly's Game* (2017).

[2]Truffaut may have been inspired to use this move because of a little gesture of Brian Donlevy's in *The Great McGinty* (1940).

spectacularly lose their footing it is only the fiction-within-the-fiction that is rent, all of this a lure for our attention. The film itself is reified if the inner fiction-within-the-fiction becomes weak, since weakness is drama. In recursive works generally, the innermost layer of presentation is very often characterized by some rupture, in which a played "player" falls apart, dies, is wounded, has a breakdown, loses a battle, and so on. For an actor like Cortese to act an "actor" who cannot quite sustain her identity can seem a supreme accomplishment, the interior performative collapse finally being realized by those who watch as an accomplishment of the real actor. The accomplishment seems brave and phenomenal if the collapse is brave and phenomenal, although technically acting collapse is hardly different than acting anybody or anything else.

The structure of Vincente Minnelli's *The Band Wagon* (1953) actually works out this complex formula step by step. Tony Hunter (Fred Astaire) was at one time the glowing star of Hollywood but his career has declined and he is a near has-been. Arriving in New York he is met by old friends (Oscar Levant, Nanette Fabray) who have written a musical for him to star in. The idea is that the costar will be the fabulous and internationally celebrated diva of ballet, Gabrielle Gifford (Cyd Charisse), for whom Tony has a crippling admiration and to whom he feels artistically inferior: what is a lowly hoofer, after all, against a prima ballerina? The problem is compounded when Gabrielle meets him for the first time and, due to her own shyness and egotism, puts him off as though she feels superior. Will these two ever manage to work together? (And parenthetically, will their two incompatible dance styles ever find a merger?)

In order to illustrate their emotional impasse, a number of rehearsal scenes in which Tony and Gabrielle try out tandem dancing *notably and crucially fail to work*. Thus we see, not once but several times, Tony unable to dance with Gabrielle, and she with him; nor can they behave politely to one another. Tony's steps seem awkward and misplaced, Gabrielle's elegance overdrawn. We sense it is the fictive "secret personalities" collapsing, since both are dance professionals who have signed contracts, but they look unprofessional, especially to the production team whose anxieties mount. Yet the film's reality status as a whole is strengthened by the failure of the play-within-the-play: the worse these two are at their routines the more we warm to them, and trust that things will work out to make this musical (and this film) a wonderful experience. In short, the cinematic "collapse" is promise of something positive waiting its turn. Our protagonists do manage to become fast friends, commit themselves each to the other's style, and energize the show. When the show has a colossal failure in out-of-town tryouts, the "performers" are not dismayed but band together to overcome the pitfall and bring the show to Broadway as a resounding success. The tryout disaster is only a "disaster," incontestably winking that Tony and Gabrielle have recovered from staged "collapse" into sufficient staged "health" to go on now and make a boffo hit (for more on the musical genre see Feuer).

As to falls—from power, from grace, from capacity, from hope, from triumph—one lethal opportunity not often invoked in cinema is provided by sex. For audiences who content themselves with simple pleasures of the everyday, what greater and more dizzying height from which to plummet, after all, than sexual achievement, indeed desire followed directly by satisfaction? In Alejandro González Iñárritu's *Birdman or (The Unexpected Virtue of Innocence)* (2014), Mike (Edward Norton) and Lesley (Naomi Watts), a pair of experienced actors, are scripted to have sex onstage in a play-within-the-film. Offstage, as it happens, they are married, and Lesley has been rejecting Mike. Now Mike sees an opportunity for a real action guised onstage as only a fake one: that is, as only a fake one that audiences will be willing to believe is real while supposing it is actually fake. He proceeds in front of the audience (notably signaling excitement) only to fail—spectacularly, and, as he takes it, *ultimately*. Not only is the virtuosic moment of stage performance collapsing, but Mike's virtuosic personal performance has collapsed as well, and in front of a judgmental crowd.

The clear lesson here is given by Shaw, in his pithy Prologue to *Caesar and Cleopatra*:

The high gods had a lesson to teach. . . . Therefore before they raised Caesar to be master of the world, they were minded to throw him down into the dust, even beneath the feet of Pompey, and blacken his face before the nations. And Pompey they raised higher than ever, he and his laws and his high mind that aped the gods, *so that his fall might be the more terrible.* (5; my emphasis)

24

Limping On

FIGURE 24 *Leonardo DiCaprio in* Django Unchained *(Quentin Tarantino, The Weinstein Company/Columbia, 2012). Digital frame enlargement.*

Mike's sexual peccadillo with Lesley in *Birdman* is especially disturbing in being visible to strangers. He has no hope of a virtuosic moment, but Edward Norton is virtuosic in showing us Mike's inability to recover, expressly by recovering. Had the wound been invisible, the heroic recovery would have been invisible, too.

Much fan scuttlebutt about *Django Unchained* (2012) centers on the tale of Leonardo DiCaprio cutting his hand during a take yet continuing on: the audience would assume his actual blood was makeup: the character simply suffered, the actor presumably did nothing. Making *The Manchurian Candidate* (1962), Frank Sinatra had to play a vicious fighting scene with Henry Silva, in which we see Sinatra slam his hand into a table. The mortal stakes of the drama make the fight seem powerful, but what isn't visible is that Sinatra actually seriously injured his hand, but carried on as though nothing had happened: invisible virtuosity. In Gore Verbinski's *Mousehunt* (1997) William Hickey performed while dying of cancer: virtuosity invisible.

In Minnelli's *Designing Woman* (1957), the ultra-glamorous, ultra-chic, and ultra-cool Lauren Bacall worked through late 1956 in full knowledge that her beloved husband, Humphrey Bogart, was dying. Harold Lloyd performed all his fabulous acrobatic comedy routines, many of which involved climbing or hanging, without the thumb and index finger of his right hand (lost in a bomb explosion). Natalie Wood had lost a finger and strove through posture and angle to hide her affected hand. Keanu Reeves tends to cover up a massive surgical scar on his belly, from a motorcycle accident. There are adjustments actors must routinely make that call for strength and talent in the extreme, but the effects are invisible to start with.

One rather extraordinary invisible virtuosity: the English comedian, director, raconteur, wit, medical practitioner, and scholar Jonathan Miller revealed on live television to Dick Cavett that he suffered from a "frightful stutter," and still worse: that until he awoke each morning and tried talking he would not know on which letter of the alphabet the stutter would be triggered today. Each day, then, he had to reinvent ways of speaking normally, carefully framing sentences in which no word beginning with "the offending letter" would be uttered. Cavett's jaw dropped. Here was a side-show of bizarre crippling, a man known far and wide for hyper-articulate volubility threatened with giving the impression of a mindless fool. Miller exercised a laborious daily act of camouflage polished to virtuosity, yet with such aplomb that he felt the transformations natural. So impetuous was Miller's affliction that it was entirely unperformable; Cavett begged for a little show of what it could be like, but, "Oh, I don't think I can."

What is more deeply involved in debilitated virtuosic performance is that while the audience is held away from perceiving the trouble yet the trouble is there. A facile approach to the issue assigns as motive for concealment the personal vanity of the actor, suspected because of rumors and publicity stories in which performers are described as neurotic egotists who spend their lives thinking of nothing beyond themselves. In practice, however, there are very sound systemic reasons for hiding conditions of debility and difficulty from viewers.

Most obviously, the actor's status as "capable" and "malleable" is a stock in trade of the performance business. "I can do many things, not just one thing," but more crucially, "I *can* do. And because I *can do,* I stand before your eyes *doing.*" Actors get work having shown that they can appear attractively and persuasively onscreen, and because producers and casting agents regard them as skilled, willing, and adept. Many actors do regular gymnasium work to help maintain this impression. Getting hired means for actors appearing hireable, which is to say, promising success in the role that is up for grabs. Performers who require special considerations when they work, especially if they are not yet well established in the movie business, are likely to be more expensive to work with, only because some of the accommodations they need take up time and on a film shoot, time is literally money.

So, a performer may fear other people's perception that he or she has limitations, even when he or she doesn't. The Nanette Fabray case is notable here. Watching her perform, in film or on television, audiences had an impression of only energetic, even vivacious capability. Her hearing problem was not just invisible, it was also unthinkable, except, of course, to her closest friends (who wouldn't be in the paying audience). What, however, might directors, producers, and casting agents have thought about the likelihood of her doing musicals or comedy had they been briefed in advance about her trouble? Preventing discovery could have been career-saving. There are numerous conditions physical, emotional, and social that actors might wish to hide, the case of Rock Hudson's sexual orientation being important. Hudson was not outed until his illness in 1985, a time when homosexual identity was still very widely deplored if not condemned in American society. The actor went to trouble to keep secret what might very well have been labeled a debility by producers.

But the charm of film, a business issue, may be affected, too. When the actor is seen working hard to bring a role to life, harder than viewers might think ideal, she is also, more than apparently, *working*. The acting is visible as work; and the more any performer struggles in the audience's view to make the character come alive the more the *work* can be seen; and in being seen as what it is the more work begins to resemble *work generally,* any kind of work, such as the work audience members do every day themselves and paid good money for an opportunity to forget. If acting is work, and if the working actor is like other workers, the commodified, transactable glamour of the presentation evaporates, along with the aura of actors being *special* types who commit themselves more fully or undergo greater strain than other people. Actors know acting is work, but maintain the fiction that it isn't.

The viewer's romantic belief that what he is seeing has merely sprung into existence before his eyes (the camera, remember, is never not ideally placed to see all of, and see into, the performance; and also does not exist) is compromised and dismantled when work is made visible, because in order for such work to be efficient planning and arrangement must have come before. The very structuring of the dramatic moment is opened to examination. But film narratives work because we do not examine them. We may wonder about the story without requiring light on the performance itself as a construct. Therefore, to cover the actor's troubles—for the actor to do so or for the film production to lay a cover for him—is also to cover *the very idea of troubles*, the gravity against which the performance is lifted. That our fantasy world exists only because laborers cause it to, gives a demoralizing and, from the point of view of the producer, who strives for audience engagement, false view. To go on fruitfully, the struggle must be concealed.

It is audience engagement that is up for grabs. When we are absorbed in the theatrical moment, live or filmed, the fictional world really is as real as real can be. But it is simplistic to think engagement and entrancement merely bogus attachments. They are also real: one is really entranced, really engaged: and the labor that winds on beneath, the labor of production, being itself real, too, is, in being real, in being of the physical world, *not "more real*,*"* only real in another way. To deprive the audience of engagement and entrancement by emphasizing, in a *politique* of deconstruction, that the struggle of the worker is more important, more fundamental, is a deplorable falsehood, since while that worker really is struggling, struggling not giving an imitation of struggling, his or her struggle is not empty in itself, not mere muscular and nervous strain, measurable and alienable, but a devotion undertaken in the name of something greater than itself, that an audience of strangers (who are also brethren) should be touched.

In this light even more than the actor's characterization meriting belief, the actor's presence does. I mean the actor's presence before us, at the moment of action, when the existence of the performer and the existence of the role coincide, mesh, merge, marry, even unify, because the presentation is here, now, and seen as it is here and now given to be seen. Any distraction from this marvel of simplicity, any slight reverberation of consciousness either in the actor or in the caught viewer brings down the gossamer presence, reduces affective belief to suspicion and doubt. This doubt, a true macula, is the residue left to us when we see the actor's debility showing through a character's able body. That a character might have a debility (that a characterological debility might be scripted) is something else altogether: Ronald Reagan amputated in *Kings Row* (1942); Jane Wyman blind in *Johnny Belinda* (1948); Susan Hayward on crutches in *With a Song in My Heart* (1952); Derek Jacobi limping in *I, Claudius* (1976); Richard Dreyfuss hospitalized in *Whose Life Is It Anyway?* (1981); Tom Cruise wartorn in *Born on the Fourth of July* (1989); Mathieu Amalric paralyzed in *The Diving Bell and the Butterfly* (2007); Andrew Garfield with polio in *Breathe* (2017), even in cases when the character's wound is shared by the actor, too, so that a wholly different unity is made, such as with extremely overweight Darlene Cates in *What's Eating Gilbert Grape* (1993). As long as it resides in a character we will watch both ability and debility eagerly and without disturbance to our mode of attention. Indeed, a character's debility is a *form of characterological action.* Debility in and of itself is no obstruction to engagement with drama. What deflects us from the heat of the moment is a foreign weight on the character's shoulders luring attention to its source: the actor that the character must bear upon her back.

Publicity is a key influence in this matter, since press and media about an actor's private condition can make the character permeable, in a way the performer might not have chosen. Garland, for example, becomes "famous" for being off the set, calling in sick, coming to work late, being hard to get along with; and we are told afterward of various addictive medications in her diet. John Barrymore becomes legendary as a drinker—his Larry Renault in *Dinner at Eight* (1933) is seen as something of a self-parody. Charlton Heston becomes a major figure in the NRA, and we see militarism in his characterizations. Reagan becomes President of the United States and when people watch his films in retrospect they see a politician in waiting (on "biographical reconstruction" see Goffman, *Asylums*). Yet actors know that getting one's name in front of the crowd is a good thing generally. Now with media virtually omnipresent where actors live, more and more of the people we watch performing characters are made known in other venues, both augmenting their work and conflicting with it. Given the vast multiplication of interviews, profiles, revelations, probings, and speculations it becomes increasingly difficult to watch a virtuoso performance without thinking one knows something private—and confusing—about the actor, something, perhaps, that accounts for, explains, dissects the virtuosity as nothing but a symptom.

25

The Eternal Return

FIGURE 25 *Robin Williams in* Hook *(Steven Spielberg, Amblin/TriStar, 1991). Digital frame enlargement.*

Every takeoff must have a landing. What goes up must come down.

The problem in finishing off a virtuosic moment—without a finish it is not an entity—is that the flow of the drama subtending it must now be rejoined, and in such a way that the virtuosic performer appears virtuosic no longer, merely present in the same way that all the other parties are. You cannot step into the same river twice: Heraclitus.

The virtuosity evaporates, goes into the air. The virtuoso endures.

It is often helpful that the magical moment should conclude with an unambiguous signal, a telltale flourish or cadence. No one—least of all the compadres in on the act—should be left wondering whether the "show" is over.

The operatic aria tends toward an extravagant finish, a loud, sustained, high note difficult to reach and to keep holding as the breath runs out, thus definitively stretching the voice "as far as the voice can go": "the end" (*Nessun dorma*). Or else a finish that fades to almost nothing, again extended through a regulated expulsion of air as it gently heads toward oblivion (the last of Mahler's *Songs of a Wayfarer*).

A cunning virtuosity riddling any deep understanding of acting and theatricality is Anthony Hopkins's Hannibal Lecter in *The Silence of the Lambs* (1991), a film full of disturbing moments and visions. The Hopkins/ Lecter combination remains with viewers at film's end; indeed *after* film's end. Images from this performance squat untamed in one's thought. Once sprung out of the flow of activity in the film that held and supported him, the figure of Lecter refuses to return to ground, even comedically toying with our expectation of pacific stabilization by strolling away from the camera genially in the final shot. "I go. Watch, you can see. But I am never gone." Thus Hopkins's stunning extended riff in this film is an uncompleted, unterminated virtuosity, one that becomes detached from its structural position in a single drama and seems to extend into the being of the performer himself. After Lecter, can Hopkins ever give a performance that does not seem virtuosic—that does not, indeed, smart of Lecter (a structural, not a biographical question)?

A more conventional reduction of virtuosity, or virtuosic cadence, shapes the final moment of *The Nutty Professor* (1963) when Jerry Lewis, who has transcended the day-to-day reality of the diegesis in two contradictory but equally outstanding ways, one klutzy and one suave, seems to find his power to exceed suddenly dissolved. He becomes, like all the others around him, just a flickering screen presence. This is the moment when, his Buddy Love vanquished forever, his Kelp goes happily down the school corridor with Stella Stevens wrapped in his arms, still in possession of the elixir that transformed the hyper-nerd into the lounge lizard but no longer thinking to use it. This final Julius Kelp is brand new, still tortured in movement yet far more normalized than the man we met at film's beginning. While the original Julius was a beneficent monster, this one is a mere eccentric, not unlike Jerry Lewis himself, as we may think. The extremity of performance style by Lewis, as either of these two characters, lifted us out of the commonplace "reality" of the college setting, its students and classrooms, always visible in emphatic commonplaceness. But in the final shot the setting seems no more than neutral, the story's foundation crumbles, the brazen characterizations are routinized.

There is a demonstrative reduction, too, in the final transformation of Buddy Love. He has swaggered onto the stage during the big dance, his gaze supercilious and his pose self-consciously slick. But at the microphone, as he speaks, the voice that comes out of the streamlined body is suddenly fractured (simulating what used to be known as a "broken record," a vinyl disc with a scratch on it: for Love, a normal voice inadvertently marred by "something caught in the throat"). Soon more cracking interrupts, and still more, until the melodic Love voice has morphed into disjointed, tonally incoherent Kelp, now strangely inhabiting Love's body, which has suddenly become suitably deflated in posture and, miraculously, less colorful.

One virtuosic moment can be erased by another. In *Now, Voyager* (1942) Bette Davis makes her entrance as a mousy, tasteless little girl whose clothes are too old-fashioned, eyeglasses too huge, manner too timid. Descending a long staircase, she emerges into our fixed visual field piece by piece, heading into a salon where her imperious mother (Gladys Cooper) introduces her to Dr. Jaquith (Claude Rains). Jaquith is extraordinarily kind to her— as, apparently, no human being has ever been. Slowly, a breath at a time, Charlotte comes out of her shell. It would be good for her to take a cruise somewhere, he says, and we next see her walking down the gangway of a ship, this time elegant beyond elegant. (Orry Kelly designed her costumes in both parts of this transform, improbably, since he is widely known to have beautified Davis and the early costume is truly mundane.) Charlotte's posture has become dignified rather than imploded, her clothing swanker than swank, her face artfully made up, and her hair covered by a spectacular, black, broad-brimmed hat that swoops around that face drawing our eye with it. As she moves leftward and down the gangplank in the shot, the camera seems to hover around her like a curious gull. Frowzy Charlotte was indubitably a virtuosic construction of Davis's, now evaporated by the virtuosic, glamorous Charlotte.[1] A topping of a topping.

Musicals provide some of the clearest examples of virtuosity receding into (landing upon the surface of) normality, exceptional performance—"The Performance"—transmogrified as only routine. A notable trope that makes the movement possible is the show-within-a-show, a calculated figuration in which characters become "characters" in a "production" that is the central business of the film as a whole, an entertainment archetype ostensibly "put on" by the characters we have been following. The theme of "kids putting on the show" has been much repeated. But more subtly fascinating is the normal, single musical number itself, a piece of action typically lasting around five or six screen minutes, in which everything we see and hear, seamlessly emerging from the fabric of the film, is grammatically disconnected except that we earlier recognized the central figures as performing types who could lapse into numbers like this. And that they *could* sing and dance seems the only reason why they now *do*. The musical number is elaborate, distinctively colorful and harmonic, and "out of this world."[2]

---

[1] A modulation in many ways recapitulated in *The Nutty Professor*, yet that film is typically compared only to versions of the Jekyll-Hyde story. As an adept of Hollywood cinema, Lewis would have known Irving Rapper's film well.

[2] It was not only the much-celebrated Arthur Freed Unit at MGM that created and produced such virtuosic numbers ("Ding-Dong! The Witch Is Dead," and so on). Beyond what can be seen in the Freed catalogue, one finds pleasing extremity of construction (virtuosity) in such numbers as "The Gold Diggers' Song (We're in the Money)" and other Busby Berkeley items in *Gold Diggers of 1933* (1933) and in the choreography of Jack Cole (see *Three for the Show* [1955] and *Let's Make Love* [1960]).

The musical number is *de facto* emphatic, because much attention is devoted to scenarizing in a stimulating, colorful way, sometimes on a special set-within-the-set, sometimes through newly utilized conventions of cinematography providing for different kinds of views, and always, inevitably, through extremes of vocalization and bodily movement that come affectionately to be known as "song and dance." The phenomenon called song-and-dance is always an elevation. And the performance of song-and-dance routines is manifestly difficult. Try it: even if you can dance as Mickey Rooney, Eleanor Powell, Vera-Ellen, Gene Kelly do, singing on key and to the beat at the same time is a real kicker, and keep smiling, even if you're planning to pre-record and lip sync the whole thing. The musical number addresses one of two diegetic domains. It is sometimes a private and intimate, deeply revealing, confessional of love or some other emotion in a situation where expression has previously been impossible, but contiguous with other settings in the same fictional domain: Gene Kelly and Debbie Reynolds in "You Were Meant for Me," from *Singin' in the Rain* [1952]; Johnnie Ray singing "If You Believe" in front of a small audience in the family living room, but clearly speaking to God, in *There's No Business Like Show Business* [1954]; Fred Astaire and Ginger Rogers doing "Cheek to Cheek" in *Top Hat* [1935] or, to show antipathy on the intense personal level, yet playfully, "Isn't This a Lovely Day (to Be Caught in the Rain)?" in the same film. In Barbra Streisand's legendary "People" from *Funny Girl* (1968), Fanny Brice's privacy is invaded by us as she confesses to herself that she is in love. Richard Beymer and Natalie Wood perform a "wedding" in *West Side Story's* "One Heart" (1961), simulating a private moment in a church (by their manner and the environment their manner seems to invoke).

And sometimes, by comparison, the musical number is a representational ceremonial, where figures sing and dance their way through a mock-up of some very familiar everyday situation, cultural formation, social grouping, or event: in the song-and-dance ceremonial an inherently uninteresting routine, borrowed from the everyday, perhaps, and emphatically copied, is made especially noteworthy. The extensive setting, the bright costumes and makeup, the vivacious style of singing and dancing can all show quotidian reality—the reality of the surrounding story—left behind and now played up with a distanced eye and a loving heart: the "Who Will Buy?" depiction of early morning life in Covent Garden, from *Oliver!* (1968); "Get Me to the Church on Time" from *My Fair Lady* (1964), showing a bachelor's final moments before his wedding; "Something Wonderful" at the funeral of the King of Siam in *The King and I* (1956). These numbers have a quality of existing in and for themselves, rather than expressing a vital plot point more strongly. In *Oliver!*, for instance, Covent Garden fruit, vegetable, and flower vendors may go to work at first light and cry their trades but the continuity of this story does not require that we watch them do so. The King of Siam does die, but his deathbed need not occasion a special song. Whereas in *Singin'*, Kelly's Don Lockwood intends to confess his love for Reynolds's Kathy Selden anyway, and the song and dance elevate the moment, otherwise normal, into something memorable. A list of ceremonial numbers could stretch almost indefinitely, but one textbook show-stopper is the "Heavenly Music" number of *Summer Stock* (1950), with Kelly and Phil Silvers performing a "hillbilly" song in dress rehearsal for a summer stock play. Garbed and made up as a caricatured pair of ignorant yokels, with trousers too big, they strut left and right warbling an infectious little ditty, at one point shifting to the side and finding themselves backed by a trio of adorable dogs who, at the chorus, start barking accompaniment on cue. It's something of a mock-up of typical song-and-dance numbers where principal singers are backed by a chorus, in this case the chorus being notably, and lovably, non-human. Obviously, the dogs outshine the human performers here, who now slide leftward again and do a relatively tame second verse. As this nears conclusion they slide back rightward and now there are about nine dogs, a happier, more cacophonous chorus. One imagines the first group of dogs went off and called in their friends. Leftward slide the men for the third verse, and when they return there is a pack of some twenty-five dogs howling and yelping like a zany imitation of the Mormon Tabernacle Choir. To spice the broth, the producers include a plentiful array of breeds here, no two pups alike, so it's a song-and-dance puppy party with a pair of stray humans. A number like this manages an *emergence* from the flow of the film (the dogs appearing "out of nowhere"), sustains itself on an elevated plane, then, on the musically definitive final beat, wraps up. "Wraps up" and is placed "on the shelf." We are transported back to the everyday of the show preparation, perhaps through a dissolve to a new scene, perhaps by the inflow of other characters commenting (not in song) on the number we, and they, have just seen.

Another frequently employed trope is to have a stage manager, director, or producer rise out of the audience, step onstage, and break up the (utterly entertaining) rehearsal by the film's stars (also stars of the "show"-within-the-film), because it "isn't working" or because "it's fine but we're late." The tone of the number, elevated as we take it, is broken for good, replaced by the working tone of the "everyday," where people crab at one another, arrangements don't quite get made correctly, people bump into things, and so on.[3]

The song-and-dance number is a special and definitive case of the more general elevation-declension movement by which virtuosity extends beyond the limits of the supporting drama, outpours at some height, and then fades

---

[3]The ascension of normal working reality into hyperreal art and the declension back into the everyday are alternated several times, with increasingly rich dramatic effect, in *The Red Shoes* (1948).

off as the performer re-enters the fold. Appertaining to an "everyday" self, a working character in the story, the performer's transformation seems "magically" powered: we are never given a full and clear explanation of how such a transform could be effected. It merely *is,* and our gratitude is presumed to stand in for critical attention. Shifting upward, the performer plays out in a signal, utterly singular, emphatic way, compared with the baseline of the "everyday": demonstrates *especially* harmoniously, *especially* colorfully, *especially* poignantly, *especially* humorously, *especially* extremely, *especially* movingly: the virtuosity, in short, is special. And then (the song finishing its last verse), the players morph again, now in reverse, becoming only the "ordinaries" we are to believe they were to begin with. As we look at the process in this analytical way, we can see a version of the classical 1886 story recounted by Robert Louis Stevenson as "The Strange Case of Dr. Jekyll and Mr. Hyde." Mr. Jekyll the quotidian; Hyde the virtuoso.

"Jekyll and Hyde" is a recipe for the elevation-declension transform, an originary case that foregoes all the smaller transforms that came later. In Dr. Jekyll we have a dignified, well-known, and respected gentleman of the medical profession (equipped with a laboratory) who occasions no particular interest from neutral observers, being, in every palpable way, normal. He works, he continues, albeit in a way that builds and falls with the dramatic phrasing of everyday life, but always in himself, of himself, and through himself as he has come into our knowledge. In this way he is not unlike the "Tony Hunter" of *The Band Wagon,* "merely" an old hoofer now working in a new show, or any of the characters we see in films whose lives, though altered through transformation, begin in almost tedious routine. In Jekyll's laboratory a preparation is concocted—in cinema's nineteenth century, laboratories, like hospitals, were all about preparations, concoctions, and spectacular effects—and once he has administered it to himself our friend seems to disappear from view and a certain Mr. Hyde roams the streets instead, diminutive in stature, queer in aspect, more than naturally alarming to those who meet him in the shadows. Who is this Hyde, the narrative asks, and what relation does he bear to the dear Dr. Jekyll who cannot at present be found at home? Where has Jekyll gone, and where has Hyde come from?

Notable in this story, this first case of the two-way morph, is that the rhythmic return of Dr. Jekyll is accompanied by a certain weariness, or at least a presentation that distinguishes him vitally from Hyde; just as Hyde is distinguished vitally from Jekyll. One can imagine Hyde as a song-and-dance man after a big number, changed back into his everyday self and flopping on a couch in pure exhaustion (although the people who sing and dance in cinema must always have the energy in reserve for another take). In the "report" of a Dr. Lanyon we are given revelation of Jekyll's return:

"Lanyon, you must remember your vows: what follows is under the seal of our profession. And now, you who have so long been bound to the most narrow and material views, you who have denied the virtue of transcendental medicine, you who have derided your superiors—behold!"

He put the glass to his lips and drank at one gulp. A cry followed; he reeled, staggered, clutched at the table and held on, staring with injected eyes, gasping with open mouth; and as I looked there came, I thought, a change—he seemed to swell—his face became suddenly black and the features seemed to melt and alter—and the next moment, I had sprung to my feet and leaped back against the wall, my arms raised to shield me from that prodigy, my mind submerged in terror.

"O God!" I screamed, and "O God!" again and again; for there before my eyes—pale and shaken, and half fainting, and groping before him with his hands, like a man restored from death—there stood Henry Jekyll! (n.p.)

In contemporary musical and dramatic productions of the twentieth century, the abject horrors of the chemical ingestion and its workings are elided by the mysterious application of "talent" and "drive," which have beset the individual at some earlier moment and now render him capable of springing into extremes of performance. When he is done, however, we find ourselves confronted with someone who seems, relatively speaking, "pale and shaken, and half fainting, and groping before him with his hands." The performer has gone through the pressure chamber of renormalization, has been made into an everyday civilian again.

This is no claim that unparalleled talent and exceptional energy are diabolical, criminal, or malevolent, in the way that Stevenson's narrator believes this Mr. Hyde to be. The performer is transformed upward into a noble sphere where talk is sung, gesture is danced, even if there is no song and dance. Sung, the word gains benefit of a harmonic tone which exists in a tonal range (or key); so it has a distinctive, "special" power to affect. In declarative performance (the Greek theater, the nineteenth-century Shakespearean production) actors used the voice principally, modulated through emphatic alterations in pitch and rhythm to bring stress and repose; but putting the words into actual music allows for leaping well above declaration. When, in the first line of that famous song Kelly croons, "I'm siiiiingin' in the rain, just siiiiingin' in the rain . . .," that word "singing," now notably transformed as "singin'," and then stretched through the high note and the extension of the first vowel as "siiiingin'" becomes far more than a declarative statement, "I Am Singing." The word-sound explodes the singer's joy into a momentarily unbounded, unboundable efflorescence, a Roman rocket going up into the sky (forever), and it also contradicts the downpour in which the singing occurs, helping us to understand what about Don Lockwood at this moment makes him invulnerable to the weather: it is his pure reservoir of desire and feeling. He is unaffected by the everyday universe: the sidewalk is no longer itself, and when we see him rhythmically shifting along we witness the metamorphosis directly. The lamp post is a magical device to help him fly. And, giving the number a punch that is possible only in cinema, when he hops into the street and twists around, the camera flies upward and swoops around him to exaggerate his sense of delirium, and ours, to make us understand how, thanks to his evocation, we are rendered invulnerable to the weather as well. Without that camera move, we might come to sense a difference in experience between the highly transformed Lockwood and our own safely protected selves in the dry theater seats. But with it, the theater seats disappear, because we are flying over a man whose spirits are flying.

In this context, let me turn briefly to a powerful, even vertiginous, virtuosic moment that has gained too little recognition, principally because the performer is known for being out of control in an especially entertaining way and because the filmmaker has long been thought too brash and too popular to be taken seriously. This is Robin Williams as Peter Pan in Steven Spielberg's *Hook* (1991), the moment when first he flies.

This Pan is turgid and earthbound, so caught up with his cell phone he cannot attend to his children. Visiting his Aunt Wendy in London, with family, he finds himself whisked away by magic and deposited in Neverland, where the Lost Boys, deflated with disappointment, refuse to admit that he is the Pan. Will he be able to lose his mundane identity and ascend to a higher plane? As to performance, can our boring businessman actually become a creature very like the actor Robin Williams (whom he has all along deeply been)? Tinker Bell (Julia Roberts, miniaturized photographically) comes to his aid, throws fairy dust on him, and he soars into the air. Let us not decline to properly merit the swelling, breathless music of John Williams as Peter hits the stratosphere. But Spielberg has the clever idea, originating in *Singin' in the Rain,* I think, of placing his camera not just near Peter in the sky but in fact above him, so that *we are flying even higher than he is at this transformative moment.* He sails forward at great speed: with clouds scudding past and a royal turquoise sky, flipping over at one point to lie on his back with hands cupped behind his head (a characteristic iconization of Williams's effortless ebullience) and then flipping again to look below where, far off and glimmering like a jewel, the sacred island floats in the sea, a glowing emerald of romance.

26

Borders

FIGURE 26 *Ethel Waters in* The Member of the Wedding, *with Julie Harris (l.) and Brandon De Wilde (Fred Zinnemann, Stanley Kramer Productions, 1952). Digital frame enlargement.*

Thinking of virtuosity, one is eventually confronted with the boundary problem (about which, more theoretically, see Douglas). Where exactly can we think a spate of virtuosity begins and where does it end? How much virtuosity can there be, how ongoingly continuous, before it becomes the main event itself? How intense can a highlight be before it is overwhelming? And could a virtuosic moment be unintelligible as such?

Intelligibility

Intelligibility is a technical matter, not a state of will. One has to comprehend the challenge in order to see the triumph, else one is merely responding to increases in amplitude: louder singing, faster running, blunter dialogue, more facial twitching. (The distinctly memorable is different from the virtuosic.) What is the performer faced with, and how is a solution found and expressed so as to keep the overall fictional process continuous whilst the instant is exceptional? When film actors work, they are not typically in control of either the length of a screen appearance at any instant (the extent of a shot) or the placement of a moment in the continuity of the film: these are in the editor's domain. They are almost never in control of their exact appearance—how much of the body will be in the frame, from what exact angle will the body be shown? How will the voice be recorded, and what other sounds might be heard at the same time? All these features of the moment are indeterminate for the actor. Strangers shape the final product.

In David Lean's *The Bridge on the River Kwai* (1957), Alec Guinness has two striking moments, one showing every evidence of virtuosity while not actually being virtuosic; the other giving only scant appearance, while being a consummately brave address to a complex problem. In the first, his Colonel Nicholson has shown antagonism to Colonel Saito (Sessue Hayakawa), commandant of a prisoner-of-war camp in Burma. Head of the British contingent, Nicholson has categorically refused, on several occasions, to hand over vital military information. He is now to be punished, partly as a way for Saito to assert dominance, partly as a signal to the prisoners that cooperation with their captors is the desirable path. Nicholson is locked into a small bamboo box in which he will bake all day in the sun. At one point, we see the guards hammer the bolting sticks aside, open the door, grab him, and drag him back to Saito, and Guinness plays this moment by letting himself go entirely limp so that the guards must both navigate and support him. (The actor would have quietly informed the extras playing the guards that he intended to do this; might even have rehearsed a few steps with them, to give them the feel of his "dead" weight.) What the performance shows is Nicholson's deprivation, his physical frailty, and through it the limitations of the fragile human body under torture (in war). The body is always weak, the leader's body is as weak as any man's, and the commandant is hale and hearty as he stares at his physically and mentally deflated victim.

The scene is acted in such a way that a clear picture juxtaposing Saito's unrepressed sadism against Nicholson's degrading disintegration is offered (to us and to the assembled congregation of prisoners), without ellipsis, without contrivance, without "polite" indirectness. Nicholson is being "done to" and we are watching the doers doing him. But are there particular acting challenges that make this moment summative? Does Guinness here triumph by meeting a notable challenge in bravura fashion? The cameraman (Jack Hildyard) is mostly employing a long lens, so there are few instances of Guinness's face getting close inspection. He can easily collapse and let himself be carried and dragged and the make-up man will see to it that there is profuse perspiration on him (perspiration, visually speaking, being no more than beads of liquid which can be sprayed on as easily as they seep from within). The strength of the moment is in Lean's direction and Donald Ashton's design, and into the frame of both the actor calmly fits himself. This looks and feels like an especially intense moment, and *for the character* it is: the invocation of torture, the blazing sun, the cage, the sweat—all these independent of what the actor is (however professionally, but also without particular challenge) doing.

Near the end of the film, however, we have a moment demanding a different kind of registration altogether. Under Nicholson's direction, and partly as a morale-boosting activity for them, the British prisoners have been put to work building a wooden railway bridge over the River Kwai. When we finally see the thing, there is little to do but marvel at its glorious construction. Nicholson is filled with pride: the pride of accomplishment in creating an exceedingly beautiful, functional thing; the pride of satisfaction knowing that by giving Saito this gift he has purchased a modicum of liberty for his men; and the simple human pride at being able to assess his accomplishment with the commandant, his military equal and opposite number, his great antagonist, with whom he can now share a glass of liquor and an amicable toast. Unbeknownst to the Colonel, a team of British, American, and Canadian commandos, backed by native insurgents, have headed through the jungle with the express purpose of destroying the bridge as the first train is midway across it. By night they have waded into the water and laid explosives, keyed to a detonator set downstream and hidden behind rocks.

The sequence that follows is one of the great testimonies to camera placement and film editing in American film, bar none, but although it involves the imperiled recognition by daylight that *the river has gone down, and the wires are probably visible*; and the celebratory ceremony before the train comes, with Nicholson formally giving Saito the bridge and examining it with him, I shall forbear to go into any further precise description in fear of distracting from Guinness's great moment. This comes after Nicholson has seen the wires *and anxiously pointed them out to Saito*, with the two of them walking down the river bank to find the detonator. Saito is knifed. Nicholson finds the prize detonator, with a young Canadian soldier (Geoffrey Horne) guarding it, but on his back, already mortally wounded. "We're here to blow up the bridge, sir," this one dutifully explains.

NICHOLSON (entirely uncomprehending): Blow up the bridge?!!!

And what we see in Guinness at this signal instant, the camera at waist level looking up into his face, is a whole melody of emotions moving forward note by note:

First, oblivious stupidity—what can this man possibly be saying to me? My bridge is a magnificent coherent unity, and fragmenting it is unthinkable: literally.

Then, disbelief at (rejection of) the words, because this bridge being obviously fabulous who in his right mind would want to blow it up (blowing up has become thinkable)? Both of these registers—confusion and denial—make for a Nicholson gone over to the enemy, a man who thinks of the bridge not only as his accomplishment as leader but as Saito's due. The bridge must hold (good British workmanship to be shown). The train must pass. One stands behind one's work.

But then we catch a third note: anger, real inflammation from within (as distinct from his high temperature earlier, in the oven): *keep your bloody hands off that detonator.*

This followed by a fourth: so very dim, but soon growing. Recognition. A progressively crystalline recognition of a truth—"What have I done!"—that has so far eluded him: that he and Saito are enemies (having laid this fact aside, he forgot it), that he and his country are at war with the Japanese, and that he is committing an act of treason.

A fifth note, shame, accompanies the recognition.

And then, to cap it off, a sixth term, astonishment, crossing the actor's face and lifting him entirely out of the film into a kind of astral aura. (The character, severely wounded, is still somewhat dazed.) The ironic folly of war. The entropy that follows all design. Now, head turning upwards, eyes lifting to the heavens as he falls, Nicholson's is a body virtually without consciousness as it drops upon the detonator handle, sending the bridge up.

The triumph for the actor here is in mounting all of these reactions in serial order, oblivion—denial—anger—recognition—shameful regret—surrender, fluidly transitioning one to the next, so that the entire political structure of the film passes firmly before us by way of Nicholson's face. Only now, and in retrospect, is he seeing this story the way we have been enabled to do. One reads Guinness's work with unmistakable clarity because in this long development his face is the only thing in the frame that changes. And the actor knows, mobilizing all this, that the setup will be this way.

Intensity

Sometimes virtuosity inflects a tiny moment with big implications. In *Psycho,* while giving her a chicken sandwich for lunch in his salon, Norman Bates (Anthony Perkins) is caught with difficulty speaking to Marion Crane (Janet Leigh), and he stammers. She has asked if he does things (around the motel) for his mother and he says, "The ones she—she—she thinks I'm ca—capable of doing." Norman has a stammer that comes out when he's especially nervous. Maybe he's shy around women (this one is nothing if not a robust woman). Maybe he's just self-conscious being asked about Mother. Maybe the stammer just takes him without warning or explanation. Perkins produces his line quietly and with only a slight groping pause. He has very long fingers and he is folding them together as he talks, smiling in a friendly, sweet way although talking to a complete stranger.

Two significant pathways are opened to our suspicion here. First, since we saw Norman before (and will see him later) speaking without the stammer, perhaps he is faking, putting on a "debility" to put his guest at her ease. A civil thing to do, but not only civil. There are good reasons, pleasant and scheming, for such behavior. But the stammer shows imperfection, with undeniable emphasis, so we could come to a position of distrust. We all have our imperfections, but . . . . .

But worse, Norman's vocalization gives patent proof that at least sometimes he is not in full control of his body. There are many people in the world who speak without form—using malapropisms, interrupting with "um," putting words in the wrong order, and so on—but there are not many such folk in cinema. If Norman seems odd in his parlor, he is generally odd in cinema, too. The language in cinema (foul or fair) is raised to a high level of articulation by virtue of trained performers who control what they are doing. So here is Perkins controlling the cultivation of uncontrolled speech, shaping a defect. If the mouth is uncontrolled, how about the rest of the body?

Might Norman's body, not fully in control, fall under the control of someone else?

Without spelling out the story of *Psycho*, I believe I have signaled to readers who know the film (without ruining it for readers who don't) that this little stammer is a tiny key to a very great puzzle indeed, yet at the moment Perkins produces it the thing seems like a trivium. Indeed, our cultural predisposition to favor fluid, grammatically correct speech (whatever the situation; whatever the situational grammar) makes the stammer officially *unimportant* by its very nature, the sort of expression we do not think of as *achieved* or *accomplished*, both of which, in this film, it is.

A fascinating contrast would be Meryl Streep in *Florence Foster Jenkins* (2016). Jenkins was a wealthy woman who fancied herself an opera singer, although she could neither produce the breath to sing nor keep a melody on key. Taking lessons (hopelessly) but possessing unlimited funds, she purchases for herself the opportunity to give a concert *at Carnegie Hall*, no less, with an accompanist she has paid but who is terrified of ruining his future chances by appearing in public with this atrocity (Simon Helberg). What Streep must do, both at the concert and throughout the film, is sing in such a way that we believe she cannot sing. In *A Prairie Home Companion*

(2006) and *Mamma Mia!* (2008), she made it plain that she can. Here, then, producing a failed operatic diva, we have a performing diva singing out—*precisely on its proper key*—a scripted "off-key performance" by a "hopeless wannabe." Every failed attempt at a high note, every missed beat, every missed vocal placement is rehearsed, prepared, accomplished, and polished, *and bold*. The character with no skill at all is performed by an actor with all the skill in the world.

Extension

How much film time might a virtuosic performance take up? How expansive and elaborately developed can it be?

If we look at Ridley Scott's *Alien* (1979), we find at the moment of Ash's destruction a virtuosic performance from only the cephalic *part of* Ian Holm. Since he is playing a robot, the control of his facial features needs to seem somewhat mechanical; and since he has been sorely wounded (by crew members, to defend themselves against him) the rest of him—what rest of him we can see—flails and gesticulates madly, and notably beyond the entity's control. The work is very precise and very crafty, never showing off but always detailing some particular malfunction, the building sum of the malfunctions being our only signal that the machine has been successfully disabled (the idea of structuring disintegration this way having emerged from the "death of HAL" sequence in Kubrick's *2001: A Space Odyssey* [1968]). Each malfunction must be visible in itself and visible as an accretion upon what came before. The work could easily be overdrawn, and, optically rich as it is, go on and on and on, yet if Ash is not drawn with bold, swift strokes he will not seem sufficiently desperate to inspire us with the sense of urgency required by the drama. What is special about Holm's performance here is the range of intonation and feeling he achieves with tightly limited facial movement and in a short time. The frame is tight on his head. The actor has limited expressive tools available.

Since the face fills the screen, the disintegration expands as far as the screen will permit. The eyes, mouth, nose, and facial muscles are all magnified and made terrible, terrible and increasingly so, but as ultimately Ash will expire the virtuosity comes to an end.

Parentheses

The actor may take care to avoid using discreet signals to indicate the beginning and ending of any acted moment, since part of the fiction onscreen is that all eventuality flows evenly through time. The actor may avoid parenthesizing, or may see no need for it. Further, each event began before the scene in which we see it and will continue afterward. If the drama takes the liberty of selecting out only precise depictions from the larger pre-diegetic flow; if it makes fragments in any one of which the actor will physically *begin action,* nevertheless he will appear to be *simply doing* an action commenced already ("This is the shot where you react to seeing the monster"): virtuosity builds within the action. Or, a virtuosic moment can be signaled with a splashy beginning and a carefully curtailed conclusion. In *The King of Comedy* (1982), for example, Sandra Bernhard is wacky and frightening every moment we see her, but there is virtuosity when she performs "Come Rain or Come Shine" for a tied-up Jerry Langford (Jerry Lewis) in her East Side townhouse. She has gilded the table for him, fancy china, crystal goblets, silver cutlery, candles aflame. She is going to give him something special, make him love her, make him pay attention to her. Changed into a black peignoir she decides spontaneously to sweep the dinner settings onto the floor in a crash, after first tossing one of the crystal goblets over her shoulder. And now, *a capella,* she swings into an imitation of Tina Turner and moves into a rendition of the song. The throwing of the self into song performance, the wholesale investment of talent and desire into channeling another performer out of dutiful affection—this is virtuosic. The difficulty for the viewer comes in linking the virtuosity to Bernhard's Masha, since she is such an unrelenting flake and has never shown talent like this before. Thus, here, we see the performer inside the character. Yet there is no doubt that the moment begins when we see the dinner settings destroyed, and ends as Jerry interrupts Masha when she has done a verse or two. The song routine is parenthetical to the broader performance of character, and it is openly declared as such.

But Ethel Waters gives a different turn to virtuosity in *The Member of the Wedding* (1952). Berenice Sadie Brown is the maternal figure in a southern home, tending to a teenaged girl, Frankie Addams (Julie Harris) and her ten-year-old cousin John Henry, a fulsomely precocious, endlessly curious neighbor boy (Brandon De Wilde). All through the film Waters's Berenice is warm and giving, sincere and humble, truthful, wise, generous, diligent, observant, caring, and real—as contrasted with, say, the unreal, wholly narcissistic Masha. But at a supreme moment, a retreat into a religious and vibrant virtuosity, she merely gathers the two children to her sides and sings the spiritual, "His Eye Is on the Sparrow." This is not an imitation of soulful performance, it is soulful performance at its most authentic. And it is not an amateur's rendition, it is a wholly committed, deeply moving, almost earth-shaking performance of faith and art. We see the light gleaming from Berenice's face, and the way she regards her two charges with unconstrained bounteous love. When the hymn is done, the virtuosity clicks off and the moment slides back into regularity, a spiritual retreat into chores of the everyday.

27

Facing

FIGURE 27 *James Stewart in* The Man Who Knew Too Much, *with Daniel Gélin (Alfred Hitchcock, Paramount, 1956). Digital frame enlargement.*

The face is a central resource in acting, especially for cinema given the prevalence of dramatically important facial close-ups of recognizable celebrities and the care devoted to producing profit from these. And indeed the face alone, as though a being in itself, could be virtuosic or even a virtuosity. But the face is not always important in the virtuosic moment, and it can be misleading to think that, because actors' faces are so prevalent and so well known, in virtuosity the face must play a controlling role. The facial expression as a conveyor of emotional state, alignment, and attitude works handily where faces can be discerned, but as it is in routine life, facial expression in acting is variable. The knowable face identifies the presence and typical comportment of the star beneath this and the actor's other characters. When we try to think of a performer we have seen onscreen we

find a broadly identifiable version of the face, the kind of picture that fits
into a publicity shot or fan spread more than an instant of expression from
the film. It is infrequently that one recalls a face of the moment—a specific
moment. Facial expression is short-lived.

Consider, for instance, Roy Scheider, who has a sculptured face and has
filmed many iconic moments. What most people remember is an expression
in *Jaws* (1975) when, witnessing the Great White shark up close for the first
time he swivels in panic and says to Quint (behind the camera), "You're
gonna need a bigger boat." We can hear the voice, but can we recollect the
precise wide-eyed frozen-cheeked panic in his face? In Roy Scheider's very
specific face: long, gaunt, hollow-cheeked, bright-eyed: sincere, *at this very
specific moment*. We conceive it out of reason, not memory. To what extent
were his eyes squinting?

If we think of Marlon Brando's much-celebrated characterization of Don
Corleone in *The Godfather* (1972) we may note that there are no precise
facial expressions that come to mind, beyond a general turning down of
the mouth (a kind of background). Bette Davis in *What Ever Happened to
Baby Jane?* (1962) presents the same problem for memory—a monster, but
precisely how? It is hardly easier to conjure a vision of Marilyn Monroe's
wide-eyed and innocent look at Daphne and Josephine in *Some Like It Hot*
(1959): strangely for those who think of Monroe as a body type, her ability
to put on a memorable face in this film was elemental. Judy Garland in *The
Wizard of Oz* (1939) has the memorable singing voice (frequently recorded),
the memorable blue gingham dress, the memorable cooing affection for
Toto, the memorable caring attentiveness to her traveling companions, but
what were the expressions of her face? Or Margaret Hamilton's Wicked
Witch: "You and your little doggie, too!"—-grim, forbidding, hideous: but
what does she do with her lips?

The actor's *famous face* is not the virtuosic face. Some comedians
work facially. Jonathan Winters; Stan Laurel; Charlie Chaplin; Phyllis
Diller; Jerry Lewis. Robin Williams did not use the face principally,
notwithstanding the extreme plasticity of his expression; his routines
involved a rapid shifting of language, invention, and evaporation: he
was a singer. Lewis's open mouth has become iconic, but onscreen does
he use it a lot? The same for Buster Keaton's closed mouth and opened
eyes: do we see them in detail or in caricature? When we say that we
recognize an actor by her face, we do not mean by her facial expression.
To recall a physiognomy, and put it on record, is not to remember a
precise expressive moment. A veritable prodigy of facial manipulation for
expressive purposes—the movement under strict and precise control of
specific muscles or muscle groups—is Bill Nighy, but he does not tend
to work in such a way as to iconize any particular expression except,
perhaps, the relaxed expressionless face he takes up in moments between
facings while he shrugs his shoulders. Like Lewis, he flutters facially from

expression to expression, a raised eyebrow, a turned down lower lip, a half smile, a pair of widely drawn eyes, all moving ahead at a clip, every one leading musically to the next: a concerto for the face. For Nighy as for so many actors in cinema, the face and its capacities are absolutely essential to the production of the image, and yet very little if any of the very precise work of facially expressing is retained by viewers and experienced as a facial virtuosity. "The still waters are made swift," as Ortega wrote about the history of painting in the West, but in an observation that one may apply as well to cinematic face work. It is rare to possess a stilled image not of an actor's facial structure but of any particular facial expression: a gasp, a grin, a sheepish pout, an anxious contortion. In everyday life, we do not retain expressions or freeze them, but offer and move on; in that way cinema reflects everyday life.

The close-up insert, a cinematic feature no other medium can offer, might seem to offer special opportunity for facial gesturing. Yet for the most part, while in close-ups we are given formalized views of a subject, especially lit and sculpted for the lens, characters do not facially gesture there, as we will see. Two features of the close-up are developed instead, its capacity for branding and its invitation to affiliation.

Branding, the indelible attachment of a name to a face, a crucial basis of film marketing, permits a range of poses resulting in a limited range of views, almost never face-on directly and almost always with dramatic shadow that is shaped in some way, that drapes with aesthetic panache across part of the face. Paradigmatic are William Daniels's portrait shots of Garbo. The performer becomes associated in the public mind with close-up views of her, produced for dramatic or publicity purposes. Indeed, the very successful performer reaches a point where she *is* the person represented in one of these head-and-shoulder shots. The star brand is thus not only a name but an appearance, of which the studio can take ownership contractually. When an actor held a studio contract, his employers were entitled to "exploit in connection with [a] photoplay any and all of the artist's acts, poses, plays and appearances of any and all kinds. In addition, the studio had exclusive right to determine who else might use the actor's image" (Clark 23–4). Genre films and ancillary merchandise could be tagged with an actor's brand, increasing the paying audience, not to mention the asking price, for both the performance and any saleable objects related to it. Branding is a production activity and ultimately a producer's value. But branding is not given support by extreme and notable momentary expressions, poignant virtuosities that stand out from a scene, from a film, and from the established *face* of the actor. We could take as example Brando's expression of disappointed nauseation, with the head turning away in rejection, as he is made aware in the back seat of a car that his brother has set him up for possible execution, in *On the Waterfront* (1954)—wan not swarthy; defeated not aggressive or triumphant; pensive not active. Or in the finale moment of *Personal Shopper*

(2016) Kristen Stewart's trembling, wide-eyed uncertainty, her apparently seeing something on another plane of existence.

Affiliation is something different. It is a property of the audience's relation to figures of the screen, a feeling of heightened familiarity, thus recognition and memory, an invocation and retrieval of feeling, at the close-up moment, related to earlier experiences of the same actor in different contexts; since regardless of dramatic context the facial close-up could isolate the performer as an object worthy of special attention. If the viewer could place a name to the face, she could also mount a feeling of familial proximity, a sense of friendship and companionship, a valuable commemoration, even a kind of love.[1] If we sometimes wish to be close in order to see someone better—to identify her or to examine her features out of interest; or for navigation; or because our affection causes us to lean in for proximity—there is a socially constrained limit to how near we might come before violating what Edward T. Hall recognized as "personal space." This means the camera close-up, past a certain point, becomes informational, diagnostic, but not dramatic. Beyond mere identification one can feel the desire for a transfer of "contagious magic," to use a term coined by J. G. Frazer: the desire to "catch" whatever special qualities the preferred performer exhibits, and that one already accepts and adores, through a virtual *frottage*. Although the screen forbids touch, automatically and inherently, it does not preclude either the will for touch or calculated approximation (the zoom-in), the building up of desire, and possibly even the fantasy of such desire being fulfilled. "I was close enough to touch her."

Yet again: do we inevitably recall the precise face we are close enough to touch?

The close-up in film has another effect more problematic for the actor who needs to express a sentiment at some particular instant in a scene: Melvyn Douglas peering into Garbo's eyes with his own eyes bulging, as he coos, "Your corneas are magnificent!" in *Ninotchka* (1939), or smiling with beguiling mischief in *Theodora Goes Wild* (1936) when he convinces Irene Dunne's aunt to give him a job and let him sleep on the property. The close-up seriously magnifies. Thus, the actual face that it shares with the audience is literally a gigantic one, the face of a living giant, often enough taking over the bulk of not only screen space but also the screened moment and the viewer's world. It is a "face" bigger than faces. We never anywhere else see a face this large, except in infancy, looking up at the parent.[2] It is not difficult to imagine the challenges facing make-up artists and gaffers

---

[1] In commercial marketing, the consumer's ability to recognize the object for sale is separate from the consumer's devoted affection for it, a habitual attitude expressly cultivated through the design of publicity.

[2] One's parent or, for that matter, any object in the world looming gigantic in relation to the self. Claes Oldenberg's giant sculptures and designs for monuments (hamburger; ice-cream bar;

in covering blemishes or birthmarks, toning the face, lighting it or bounce-lighting it, backlighting it, and so on, to get a specific effect, when any and every technical step taken will result in a vision that is spectacularly large, when every crease and every cover-up will be as magnified as everything else. In the case of heavily made-up performers, such as those playing sci-fi aliens, care must be taken for close-ups to use makeup in a different way than for medium- or long shots, since in close-up everything will automatically stand out more. Indeed, by virtue of its presence alone the alien can seem virtuosic in a shot, standing out and obliterating or masking the presence of other characters. As one cuts from a medium shot into a close-up one jumps to a prodigious face from which every muscular movement, signification, tic, or gesture is magnified. For an actor there is no way to prevent the facial gesture in close-up shots from overwhelming the tonality of gesture present in the film as a whole, other than through minimizing one's muscular movement.

This kind of minimalization requires intense concentration and deep relaxation, in the context of an actor's sharp sense that any and every flicker on the face will be huge when seen. Yet at the same time, a smile is a smile, and a half smile is a half smile; one cannot reduce expression so much that it falls out of the required register altogether. This is one salient reason why in close-ups we don't find ourselves confronted very often by the dance—even the slow dance—of facial gesture. The still face is stunning enough, a monument and a gesture in itself. (A monument to stardom. A monument to this performer. A monument to this monumental moment.)

It is difficult in acting to quiet the natural response to undertake facial business when one is aware of that abnormal condition of being watched; that is, the knowledge of being watched may intrude upon the pose, and part of actors' response to this problem is adaptation to the condition, getting comfortable being in front of the eye, which might appear as vanity. The dictum to calm expression gets particular application in the close-up, because it is not *what the face does there* but the *nature of the face itself* that constitutes the meat of the shot. When I look in the mirror, seeing a being who is present for only myself and not the being observed by those who watch me, I flinch at the knowledge of being looked at, that knowledge being especially pungent because I recognize myself not only as the object but also as the subject of the moment: I know my own knowing, I am verifier, checker of that face, subject of critical gazing as much as object of a critical gaze (yours and my own). The actor must contain or erase or dispel that flinching, that worry before the camera, must be gazed at without remembering what it is to gaze. In the close-up even the smallest tremor of self-consciousness could swell into an unwanted facial gesture, a misplaced

scissors, and so on) spring, he claimed, from memories of his infantile gazes at a gigantic world (*Proposals*).

or grammatically inappropriate sign, indeed a sign given when the character is doing nothing.

How problematic it can be to discover oneself relentlessly giving off signs, with no specific intent, signing without meaning. For the actor in close-up, the only desirable sign is the entire face. The face signs itself, signs presence, and signs the attentiveness of those who watch. Watch again the macro-close-up (shown originally in 70mm VistaVision!) of James Stewart's face as Louis Bernard whispers to him in *The Man Who Knew Too Much* (1956), and note the stillness of the mouth and head, but the rapid racing of the blue eyes across the desert of the screen. The VistaVision projection, at least on some screens in suitably equipped theaters, was some forty feet tall, and the print virtually grain free, so that Stewart is vitally and painfully present here, with a telltale modulation of the eye placement at each whispered phrase. To allow for something like this to happen, an actor must be very secure, or train himself to be oblivious of the circumstances (as though that were possible), or learn over a long period how to be at ease with the camera—to treat it as one would treat one's closest friend.

Is the actor's concern about stillness, and eliminating signs that he is aware of others' awareness, merely a personal matter, a desire to be in command, a fear of seeming awkward? It is a manifest professional commitment, because any indication on the part of an actor that he knows he is being watched will transfer to the character (the actor and the character sharing, as they do, a single face), and when the character behaves as though he or she is being looked at the audience, present to do this looking, is invoked. But the overriding fiction of cinema is that the looking audience is not there. The actor and character's self-consciousness pops the bubble of the cinematic fiction, unless that fiction is specifically elaborating a characterological moment in which someone is being seen by someone else in the drama. Yet there are times when even here, in the "clinch" moment, the natural self-consciousness of a character will be diminished or eradicated in the name of overriding dramatic purpose. Bogie in fedora on the tarmac at the end of *Casablanca,* when, gazing into Bergman's face he can never not be aware she is also gazing into his, yet that awareness is evaporated in the name of his loving concentration: and vice versa.[3] We accept characters apparently looking for a dramatic purpose; but in cinema, the audience looks without letup.

In *The Disorderly Orderly* (1964), Jerry Lewis's Jerome K. Jerome not only works as an orderly in a hospital for rich, sick people (who lounge out on the lawn enduring their agonies) but himself suffers, from "empathy

---

[3]As to Bogart and Bergman: here, as with other actors in such emotionally culminating two-shots, they help the cinematographer by actually *not* looking directly at each other: the picture will show that they did.

disorder." To an unbearable degree he feels the pains of anyone with him, most especially if the patient points to the problem through complaint. Learning of the symptoms, Jerome acquires and suffers them, moving his facial muscles (and, to a somewhat lesser extent, his body) in simulation of the agony. Thus, a sequence of tiny gestural sonatas is produced. Pretty much all the work is done by Lewis in silence, as the momentary victim loudly whines discomfort. What the Lewis character produces is precisely the "pantomime of complaint" that, in *The Body in Question,* Jonathan Miller (in his medical guise) tells us patients will typically perform in front of the doctor as they describe their symptoms. Miller wisely indicates that by noting the precise spot of a problem but also, through hand gesture, what kind of pain it is described as, the doctor can usefully diagnose. A kidney stone, for example, would be indicated by a patient pointing sharply with one finger to the kidney area, in imitation of a sword or lance being jabbed into him.

All of Jerome K. Jerome's "painful," "excruciating," "debilitating" facial twists are accomplished with Jerry Lewis apparently not realizing, so completely is he invested in a hyperfeelingful Jerome. The character's state of consciousness is rationalized in the script. And, at least in these interactional scenes with patients, that state of consciousness is almost always transferred to an agonized face: mouth pulled far down, eyes crossed, cheeks sucked in, body contorted. Lewis's performance in the film seems virtuosic altogether, but there is no one particular moment in which the virtuosity shines indelibly until late on, when he is caught in the middle of a road with a moving van rushing toward him. The wide eyes accompanied by a desperate extension of the arms (hopeless to stop oncoming reality), the mouth open but without something to say.

It is interesting to note that while in classical cinema close-ups were used to indicate the face, its direction of gaze, its fullness or hollowness, in short the quality of the characterological *persona,* they have latterly become the locus of important dialogue spoken in low voice, not gestural expression. Secrets are told, solutions to problems found, mysteries resolved in close-up: only for the audience, who, because of the camera's magnification, lean in closely to catch the jewel.

28

Magnitude

FIGURE 28 *Ralph Richardson in* Greystoke: The Legend of Tarzan, Lord of the Apes *(Hugh Hudson, Warner Bros., 1984). Digital frame enlargement.*

Virtuosity will have the effect of seeming tonally amplified to one extreme or the other, notwithstanding its actual measurable sound. The virtuosic moment is more pronounced than its surround. It may be necessary for the actor to produce an expression turned up very loud indeed: Marlon Brando in *A Streetcar Named Desire* (1951) calling out, "Stel*la!*" or, almost spitting in Vivien Leigh's face as she lies abed, "Ha! . . . ha! . . . . . Ha! Ha! HA!"; Dustin Hoffman crumbling in the dentist's chair in *Marathon Man* (1976) as repeatedly he is asked, "Is it safe?"; Michael Pitt's urgent plea, "We don't do this! We make love!" as the students raid the barricades in 1968 Paris in *The Dreamers* (2003); Ralph Richardson stentoriously slurping his soup from its bowl, to humor his naif grandson, in *Greystoke: The Legend of Tarzan, Lord of the Apes* (1984); little Bobby Clark screaming, "She's *not* my mother!" at the top of his lungs early in *Invasion of the Body Snatchers* (1956) (early enough that it ought to come as a warning) or Ronnie Howard screaming uncontrollably in his bedroom in *The Courtship of Eddie's Father*

(1962). The placement and technical capacity of the microphone on set, or in the dubbing studio, will have much to do with how much strain the actor must endure to give the ultimate impression of being strained.

Such ventings are kept under control. Controlled they must be if they are to be repeatable (for more than one take) and effected in such a way as not to damage the performer's voice. The voice must be warmed, the lungs rehearsed. Damaging the voice, however much authenticity it might promise to afford, jeopardizes future work, and the work of acting is importantly about continuing itself. It is also structurally crucial that the magnitude of the virtuosity, while hovering above the tonal levels that surround, must not exceed those levels by such a degree that it makes the moment seem a bad fit with the overall arrangement. Dramatic performance is always an ensemble affair. Brando is surrounded by emphatic and tailoring silence; Hoffman is playing against Olivier's sickeningly calm voice; Pitt is surrounded by chaos; Richardson's dinner companions (a large number) are oohing and aahing; little Bobby is posed against far too comforting Kevin McCarthy, and frantic Ronnie is soothed as he screams—unrelentingly—by Shirley Jones and Glenn Ford.

The "amplitude" of a moment can be purely visual. A superficial example:

In the ballet of *An American in Paris* (1951), Gene Kelly tap dances with four "buddies." (In a little homage to Eugène Atget they disappear in military uniform into a haberdashery[1] and emerge two beats later in bowler hats and fancy blazers.) He must outshine them, mostly through pedal complexity and bodily grace, in order that he remain persistently visible as the star Gene Kelly; yet he must also take pains not to outshine his partners by so much that it looks as though they have no business dancing with him. If his moves are too much "louder" than theirs, the routine itself comes under the wrong kind of inspection. This problem is raised more punctually in the "I Got Rhythm" number, where he is accompanied by an eager audience of becharmed children. Clearly they do not move as he moves—it would be alarming if they did—but he cannot move in a way that won't fit the scene and legitimize their constant adoring presence. In the *Greystoke* dinner scene where Richardson slurps his soup, he is seated at the head of a long table larded with elegant food and arrayed with a large company dressed in tuxedoes and long gowns: people whose stiff manners prevent them from taking the kind of ease that Johnny (that is, Tarzan), now heir to the estate, shows and that the grandfather wishes openly to approve of. The old man must be careful to slurp, to slurp as he has never slurped before, muttering sweetly, "Yes, quite right," in a way that makes him stand out powerfully as an aging delinquent himself, yet not so powerfully as to make the uptight diners around him seem not to merit places at his table. If they

---

[1]Such as we see in his "Boulevard de Strasbourg, Corsets" (1912).

don't merit places here, they are mere decoration; if they are decoration, this is a decorated scene, someone has decorated it; the fiction dissolves.

Conscious of the problem of maintaining scenic balance, the actor works with his scene partners to produce the right kind of (artful) discontinuity. The director is conscious as well, and must see to it that space (physical and narrative) is cleared for this kind of move, desirable and sufficient emphasis achieved, and balance carefully maintained. "You could do a little more on this line . . . . On that line, it's a little heavy." Gently, perhaps understating: actors know how to read directors, and appreciate the guidance if it is polite.

As we noted earlier with James Cagney in *White Heat* (1949), the explosiveness in a scene must be prepared for technically, so as to be possible and effective before the camera. The action is a dance in rectangular space, after all. What may be less evident is that the actor must examine the script to see what levels of expressivity will be required of his character in every scene he will have to play, so that he can plan and prepare a reasonable arrangement of amplifications, with the work in various scenes gradually efflorescing until a climactic moment of explosive power arrives. One way to build a character arc is to work backward, first choosing the single "loudest" moment and then ratcheting up the performance "volume," shot by shot, in preceding scenes; as well as ratcheting it down in moments that follow, so as to create the impression of having reached a solitary (and suitably magnificent) peak. The size of this peak, objectively, is bounded by the actor's physicality, will, and sense of professional propriety. Actors come to know their physical limits, much as any working person would need to know the limits of the tools in use and of one's skill in using them. For the actor at work, the self *is* a principal tool.

Nicholas Ray's *Bigger Than Life* (1956) demands that three actors, working somewhat independently, produce expressive arcs that build from a very low point (a "daily reality") early in the film, increasing in expressive volume until a climax where a very tall peak is reached. Relatively quickly afterward the tonality may decrease until, at film's end, we have a scene balanced with what we saw at the beginning. The actors are James Mason, playing Ed Avery, a friendly school teacher suddenly beset by a crippling and possibly fatal disease and put on cortisone treatment; Barbara Rush as his loving but increasingly fearful wife, more and more anxious as she watches her husband's personality disintegrate on overdoses of the drug; and Christopher Olsen as their ten-year-old son, initially Dad's best friend but, scene by scene, withdrawn, alienated, and afraid of his father until he screams "I hate him!" In the film's climactic scene—not its resolution but the scene at the top of the performers' arcs, all three—the father catches the son attempting to purloin and hide the offending cortisone pills, calls him a thief, tells his wife that there is no point in them going on with life because their son is headed for doom, takes a pair of scissors with which to slay the child, and locks her into a cabinet in order to be free to act. The son's peak comes as a moment of abject silence and terror, as he waits in the bedroom at the top of the stairs having been able to hear everything being said below. The wife is pleading with her husband incoherently, screaming, crying, begging, cajoling. Mason plays the apex moment standing on the stairs with a bible in one hand and the opened scissors in the other (lest we forget for an instant what he is thinking of doing). He is talking about the passage where Abraham is commanded by God to lay his son on an altar and take his life. "But," says the wife, "God sent a ram instead, and saved the child."

"*God was wrong!*" bellows Ed, with a sharp, loud, harsh voice that may call up memories of Hitler giving a speech. He has become a dictator in his own home.

To watch the film is to marvel at the way the three actors work as a unified ensemble in succeeding scenes, striking tones that elegantly balance with each other's, and raising the pitch, scene by scene, until we come to a point where a child is standing on the edge of death because his father believes it is morally correct to slay him and the mother has been prevented from prevention. What is even more remarkable about these performances in *Bigger Than Life* is that the film was shot out of sequence.

29

Virtuosity Classical

FIGURE 29 *Delphine Seyrig and Jean-Pierre Léaud in* Stolen Kisses [Baisers volés] *(François Truffaut, Les Films du Carrosse, 1968). Digital frame enlargement.*

I have given several examples of moments in which a single actor in character transcends the territory of the drama, rises up, flies off to a contextually relevant virtuosic Neverland, then lands again. A *single* actor, or a Roman candle sent off by itself. There is a Renaissance strain to this formulation, the heroic singularity highlit and standing away from the ground of reality; a principal form surrounded by minions; especially in a moment where exceptional strength or capacity is called for in order that, diegetically, the "world be saved." In films of the classical Hollywood style—screwball comedy, for instance—we find more balance between characterizations, ensemble work more meticulous, a chamber performance rather than a concerto. But regardless of the variably accented imbalances as a story twists, a moment comes in which all harmony and order is restored, in which every soul receives a just reward. A beautiful composition of esteemed virtuosities together. A classical cadence. A virtuosity by ensemble performance.

Take the final moment of Ang Lee's *Sense and Sensibility* (1995), where we are outside a tiny rural church with children's streamers fluttering against the rolling green. British countryside, unspoiled. A sunny day. Greener than green, an atmosphere fresher than fresh. As Patrick Doyle's music swells to its climactic phrases, handsome Alan Rickman's Colonel Brandon, in scarlet tunic, and Kate Winslet's Marianne Dashwood, lace bonnet upon her head, emerge into the sunshine, newly wedded and beaming with joy, with, just behind them, Hugh Grant's Edward Ferrars and Emma Thompson's Elinor Dashwood, betrothed, too, and catapulted into bliss. Then march old Robert Hardy's Sir John Middleton and Elizabeth Spriggs's Mrs. Jennings, two very good, very honest people, grinning approvingly of goodness and honesty. After all the mistaken fears of missed opportunity for love and marriage, the Dashwood sisters are in the end, and here before our very eyes, rewarded with the futures they desire (and, in Jane Austen, deserve). Off at a distance, a very long distance, upon his white steed, the denied lover, Greg Wise's Willoughby, watches so as not to break the thread of his feeling. His dark eyes are sad. Then as the music resolves into a final chord he turns the horse and rides up the greensward into history, and Brandon, all smiles in the wedding carriage far below, throws a shower of golden coins into the air.

What is here for us but the extraordinary dignity and vitality of Rickman and modest ebullience of Winslet, the bashful gentility of Grant and final certainty of Thompson, the good natures of Hardy and Spriggs, and Wise's delicate melancholy—all these conjurings played in such a way that editing will bring them together on the screen, together in a most beautiful array, all the questions and tensions of the story now drawn quietly and assuredly to a close. It is perhaps for a sense of assurance (ideally captured here) that fans read Jane Austen. The scene is a virtuosity in itself, but to fashion it the very discreet, only swiftly flickering virtuosic turns of all seven actors are required: not only expression but expression with precision; not only precision but echo; not only echo but harmonic balance. When actors in a group such as this one rehearse together, they work on voices and line readings. Postures, faces, gestures—all these tend to come only in front of the lens.

Here a trio of ensemble moments, each displaying classical virtuosity, the containment, enrichment, and illumination by form:

Brief Encounter (David Lean, 1945)

Laura Jesson (Celia Johnson), our sweet heroine, middle-class, well-behaved, not very presuming, not quite young, and not yet old, has been to the local town for a day's shopping and is now, on the train platform, ready to go home. She stands near the platform edge, the door to the station's tea room behind her. An express train roars through and we see the lights of the racing windows flickering in staccato upon her torso as she watches. Suddenly, with a start, she backs away and raises her hand to her face. Turns. Walks swiftly into the tea room.

At the counter are two regulars, the manageress of the place Myrtle Bagot (Joyce Carey), a type whose speech pattern shows her incessantly reaching above her class yet whose rather shrill voice signals uncorrectable indelicacy, and Albert Godby (Stanley Holloway), the stalwart Cockney station guard, helpful, dutiful, unpresuming if a jocular tease. Laura steps up, speaking as she steps, "Oh please, could you give me a glass of water?, I've got something in my eye and I want to bathe it." (Removing her gloves.) Myrtle, notably shrill: "Would you like me to have a look?" (Mother, Auntie: trustworthy and no-nonsense.) Laura is still in discomfort, speaking fluidly but swiftly: "No, no, don't trouble, I expect the water will do. Thank you." Myrtle stands back watching; Albert, standing beside Laura, has turned his head with concern to look at her, too: "Bit o' coal dust, I expect," looking to see Myrtle's reaction as Laura raises the glass to her face. Myrtle is not content: "A man I knew lost the sight of one eye from getting a bit of grit in it." Albert has been leaning toward Myrtle to participate in the interaction actively. Laura has been tilting her head back, applying the water directly from the glass. Myrtle's line is delivered with meticulous attention to pronouncing all the t's. (And "grit" somehow seems an appropriate word for Myrtle to speak, a word Laura would never let pass her lips.)

> ALBERT, bluntly: "Nasty. Very nasty." (Is he talking about the poor unfortunate man's experience, or Myrtle's delivery of this terrifying comment?)

"Better?" says Myrtle loudly—apparently the distraction to Laura's sight has also reduced her hearing.

"Not really," says Laura in close shot now, lowering her head, reaching up for the eye.

A male voice gently from behind. "Can I help you?"

Laura spins around, still touching the eye, as, suddenly at screen right, Dr. Alec Harvey (Trevor Howard) approaches in mackintosh and hat. "Oh, no, please, it's only something in my eye."

Cut to Myrtle, watching keenly, and, with indomitable working-class perseverance, not to say authority: "Try pulling yer eyelid down as far as it'll go."

Alfred, head tilted back a little as he watches Laura offscreen, and trying honestly to be helpful: "—And then blowing yer nose." (His serious face shows he's offering folk wisdom, not mocking.)

ALEC: "Please let me look, I happen to be a doctor." His smile is warm
   as she looks into his face. He is completely compassionate, amicable,
   direct.
LAURA (yielding): "It's very kind of you."
ALEC, taking her arms by his hands: "Look . . . turn 'round to the
   light, please. . . . Now, look up . . ." His left hand comes up to bring
   her lower lid down. "Now look down." He lifts the upper lid. "Keep
   still—I see it." With his right hand he has reached inside his coat and
   is withdrawing a folded handkerchief. Holding the lid up he reaches
   forward very gently but competently and gives the tiniest wipe.
   "There."
LAURA, expressively: "Oh! What a relief, it was agonizing!" She
   touches the eye again.
ALEC: "Looks like a bit of grit," examining the item (and giving
   distinctly professional authentication to that word [so that we may
   conclude in retrospect that Myrtle, who spends her life near these
   railway tracks, was being distinctly professional, too]), then using
   his thumb to flick it off the handkerchief (demonstrating the proper
   place for "grit" in this world).
LAURA, somehow feeling the need to explain: "It was when the
   express went through, thank you *very* much, indeed." Very briefly,
   they smile at each other. We hear a bell ringing on the platform
   outside. Albert, off camera: "Here we go. I must run." We see him
   scoot behind the pair and exit through the door. "How lucky you
   happened to be here!" Laura adds, as in pouring a little triple cream
   upon a crumble.
ALEC (smiling): Anybody could have done it.
LAURA: Never mind, you did, and I'm most grateful.
He looks a little to his right, off. "There's my train," politely touching
   the top of his hat, "I must go. Goodbye."
LAURA, still with hand to face: "Good bye."

A pathway must be found whereby Alec and Laura can meet, acknowledge
one another's presence, fall into a feeling of ease each with the other. The
writers (Noël Coward, Anthony Havelock-Allan, David Lean, and Ronald
Neame) have conceived a slight optical problem in a public arena small
enough to be warm and comforting—indeed, a traditional location in Britain,
the station tearoom—and have carried the action forward speedily and
entirely without decoration, so that point by point, and with a discernable
rhythm, the relationship commences and develops: but only to a point (since
we must be led to wish for a reprise).

But the script notwithstanding, what are the performers doing, all four,
in this tightly defined space and in their respective social roles—all the
dramatic roles in this film are, importantly, social roles—to bring balance,

form, and appeal to the discourse, the four discrete voices constructing a coherent sense of line and a graciously rounded scene?

First, a trick of the casting, since actors can bring their magic only when they have been contracted to a piece of work. There are differing voice types, and this is part of the casting design here. Myrtle Bagot is a soprano (indeed a soprano with pretensions to being a coloratura), played by "one of [Lean's] favorite actresses" (Brownlow 153). Albert Godby is a baritone,[1] most of whose intrusions in this scene take an "oom-pah," grounding form. Both Laura and Alec are altos: their voices are pleasantly situated in a middle range, and neither of them, in extremely expressive phrases, goes very high or very low. This is a woodwind quartet for flute, bassoon, and an oboe and clarinet in conversation. As long as the speech of these creatures shifts around in a reasonable way, continually making logical sense, as long as all four can be sounded to some extent, yet not necessarily to an equal extent, we can sense unity.

Next, the event. A discomfort is produced; addressed; treated; and resolved. Irritation; pain; relaxation; comfort. This tiny scene is like a miniature epic in itself, with extravagant movements now neatly reduced to brief, sequential momentary gestures. One could argue that all of the connections between characters in *Brief Encounter* are brief encounters. The grit will make possible the crystal, functioning in this way both as itself diegetically (a piece of grit from the passing train) and as structural metaphor (the grit around which the action—the molecular atoms— becomes arranged). As we need Laura afflicted, something must wound her, yet not so severely as to inspire, so near the beginning of the film, anxiety. The piece of grit is perfect in size—as a plot prop. And anyone on earth could have grit in the eye, so it's a common enough experience for which no detailed explanation is required. In short, a very simple structuring device neatly put in place by the roaring express train. She must, of course, be on a train platform, but as she is headed home, and as in Britain people typically travel by train, the platform is automatic. Again, nothing explanatory, nothing elaborate, nothing out of the ordinary: so that whatever happens here now, and whatever eventuates from it later, is born in the commonplaceness of normal life. That is: this story could happen "anywhere."

Four distinctive attitudes toward the problem yield a melody in four voices. Laura in pain and frightened, with short breath and continual reaching toward her face. Myrtle slightly pompous pretending to expertise, owning plenty of received opinion. This positions her on the social ladder, because received opinion, expressed with so little reservation, belongs to the

---

[1]The resonant depth of that voice helped him as from March 15, 1956 he initiated the role of Alfred P. Doolittle in *My Fair Lady*.

working classes. "Manageress" of the tearoom does not mean high status, it means one is a worker saddled with additional responsibilities and who advertises a title as a way of self-aggrandizing. Albert sees his place in the world as subservient to Myrtle, perhaps, as we will learn later, so that he can have a tiny coo with her at night when the tearoom is closed. He echoes, he adds his two bob, and in the end shows that before everything comes duty to the job—shepherding the train into and out of the station, not tending to passengers' personal needs. *That* job has been allocated to no one, but in her presumptive rule Myrtle has taken it upon herself. Alec is full of knowledge (none of it received opinion), and his awareness is directed in service of his professionalism, but he is secure enough in his position that he can afford to be genial, gracious, and friendly in a modest and kind way. All four of these lines of presentation circle smoothly around the speck of grit, allowing the scene to move along.

To some degree the lighting favors Celia Johnson and Trevor Howard, because they are billed above the title, whilst the vocal presentations of Carey and Holloway sound more loudly than the others do, so that aesthetically as well as scripturally a balance is struck among the four characters.

Finally, all this happens not in neutral space but in a railway station, with four characters differently involved in train travel. One guarding the platform (all day and all night, for any train and all trains: the uniform, the bluff manner of speaking directly to the point). Another catering refreshment (people become peckish and tired when they travel, so here is a generosity out of which one can profit). Two others are mere travelers who need to embark from this particular station, not at the same time or on the same train (a fact that will later become devilishly important) but in the same general way (this is life in a British railway station). One, briefly incapacitated, is in danger of missing her train, but she is quickly saved. The other must cut off his genteel interaction so as not to miss his. What this complex circumstance provides is a sense of pacing and rhythm, since in the realism of the film's setting we must find trains entering and exiting the station with precisely scheduled regularity (see Schivelbusch). Thus, given that each character is timing gestures to the schedule the scene moves on, and with expedition. Train time is controlling this dramatic universe, and since these four are in the same station it is the same train time for all of them: as though a conductor (a train conductor?) were counting out the beats. No single performance stands out forcefully, and the scene collapses if all of these actors are not present exactly in this way, together. An ensemble virtuosity.[2]

---

[2]And as such one of the trademarks of David Lean's filmmaking.

Stolen Kisses [Baisers volés]
(François Truffaut, 1968)

A disarmingly simple scene about a young person being disarmed by simplicity.

The players: Antoine Doinel (Jean-Pierre Léaud), roughly twenty-four, something of a goof, entirely well-meaning and innocent of social practices; also quite lovable. Fabienne Tabard (Delphine Seyrig), the extraordinarily svelte wife of Monsieur Tabard (Michel Lonsdale), owner of the shoe store where Antoine has a job stacking boxes in the storeroom. Fabienne drops down occasionally to nab a pair, drops down, because the Tabards live in a posh apartment above. Connecting their place to the store is a long winding stair (*de rigueur* for Paris). Tabard himself is an uptight poop of the first order, pedantic, terribly boring, yet at the same time nothing but polite and hospitable. All three mean good. However! This particular trio is playing some dissonant music, perhaps Debussy or Berg.

First, Antoine isn't actually working for M. Tabard, he is only "working." In truth he is an employee of the Blady Detective Agency, and Tabard, thinking somebody in his store is filching the profit, has asked for an agent to be put in place: hapless Antoine.

Next, Fabienne Tabard is the absolute epitome of bourgeois French sophistication and allure. Blonde hair, striped brown and cream skirt dropping just below the knee, gracious movement as though trained in a boarding school in Switzerland, and a diplomatic manner. Watch out!

Antoine is in the apartment for a technical reason involving the shoes, and Fabienne invites him to table. Linen tablecloth, glasses of nice red wine, a meal, some fruit shared around. Antoine is awfully nervous. Tabard is slicing fruit. Fabienne is listening. Polite chatter with voices climbing up and falling down tiny hillocks of possibility. Sweetness and light enough.

Tabard must go back downstairs.

She invites the kid into the salon for coffee there, collecting a tray from a houseboy in a spotless white jacket. She brings the tray to the low coffee table adjacent the apricot yellow-upholstered sofa. She sits in her chair, smoothing out her skirt. Antoine walks in from the dining room, a tie, a herringbone sport coat. Sits not far from her, accepts a cup and saucer. In silence she takes the pot and pours into his cup. She looks carefully at what she is doing, he glances up at her sheepishly. The pot goes back onto the tray, she extends the sugar pot. He selects one cube, but as she is about to move the pot back he signals with his index finger and selects one more. Take the little spoon and stir that cup while you watch her pouring her own coffee. With slightly emphatic movements the pot clinks back, she leans over and takes one lump. Sits back and stirs, while, still busy stirring he watches. Stirring, stirring. (How much stirring is required to dissolve some sugar cubes?!) Fabienne is a magnet, he cannot move his eyes. Eyes on her, fingers moving the spoon.

She looks at him and looks down again modestly. Several seconds with the sound of spoons tinkling in cups and nary a word. They are both looking down. She sips, clinks the spoon back onto the saucer. Puts her cup and saucer down. Stands up, glides back to the high windows next to which a record player sits. Removes the plastic lid, searches through some LPs. He is still holding his cup and saucer, still stirring. All of the foregoing *in one single shot.*

Now we cut to a close portrait shot of Antoine, looking up-left at her off-camera, his eyes very open, still holding the infernal cup and saucer and slowly moving the spoon in a circle through the dark liquid.

Back to the long shot, with Fabienne at the window now turned to look his way. A black disk is in her hands, she puts it on the turntable, bending a little, and speaks as she bends. "Tu aimes la musique, Antoine?"

Back to the portrait shot. He looks up, still like a robot stirring that coffee, eyes wide open, and says obediently, "Oui, Monsieur."

JUMP! to tight portrait shot of Fabienne, looking up his way in shock.

Jump to macro-close shot of his spoon going onto the saucer.

Jump to macro-close shot of her disappointed face, all the energy of certainty and desire quickly dissipated, and there is a very fast zoom-in accompanied by a harsh musical tone on the soundtrack.

Cut to close shot of Antoine's hands putting the cup and saucer down sloppily, there is a clashing noise and a coffee spill on the tray, his body is moving off-left. Zoom-out to show him racing out of the room, a quick turn to look back in case she is following, racing and racing, and then a fast grouping of shots in the stairwell, with the iron elevator cage in the middle, as he races down the marble stairs, and around and around, level after level, out the lobby door, across the alley, into the shoe store stock room, around a ladder where one of the salesgirls is perched, grabs his coat, says he is sick, races through the store and away.

What could this be? Youth, initiation, impatience, blunt fear, invocation, seeing the future, reacting to scathing improbability, a case of bridled desire, intimidation, hopelessness, panicky decorum, experienced smoothness of movement and calculation, trembling uncertainty?

Bright light flooding the room. The coffee black and steaming. Antoine responding to all of Fabienne's tiniest movements with the polite silence broken by the stirring sound in the coffee cup. Yet how polite can one be when confronted with a woman like this, whose smile undresses you and whose voice, even in a tiny question, is a siren's?

A trio this time, and for dance, not voice. Lonsdale, tall, bear-like, a sagging and depressed face, wistful eyes, but a very articulate voice, a lecturer's voice, so that even speaking of daily trivia he sounds profound, but he doesn't move a muscle, which is why he strikes us as pedantic. Seyrig, sleek, beautifully dressed, who moves like a model and shows reticence with the young man, holding back her gaze when she wants to look, playing out the formula of modesty. And Léaud, at one and the same time utterly clumsy and utterly polished, his movement graceful, poised, but his attitude nervous and indecorous. When Antoine says, "Oui, Monsieur," it is not because he is convinced Madame Tabard is not a woman, it is because while he is with Madame Tabard all he can think about is punishment from her husband. In his mind he is transgressing, and Tabard is there to watch over him with an eagle's eye. Discovering that for the boy the husband can never disappear, she is deflated with disappointment, since she thought he might be excitable enough to be adventurous (and at any rate the husband disappeared for her a long time ago).

Lonsdale sitting slumped and then upright, turning his head but little. Seyrig making only necessary movements, each one polished and perfectly precise, so that we must wonder if the precision, the restriction she is imposing on herself, is her way of guarding against terrifying the kid by too much casualness, too much forwardness. Léaud looking up, looking down, stirring, stirring, looking up, looking down, stirring, stirring, stirring, stirring. Then stirring. And stirring. Looking up. Looking up eagerly, while stirring. (Is the stirred coffee his stomach?)

Lonsdale has very little to say, just enough to establish himself as the anchor of the proceedings before slipping away for business. Seyrig has nothing to say until she has ascertained that the fear can be broken. Léaud speaks only inappropriately, only makes a horrible gaffe, and then, clumsy, awkward, afraid for his life makes a run for freedom. No single performance stands out forcefully in this scene, and the scene collapses if all of these actors are not present exactly in this way, together. An ensemble virtuosity.

Bringing Up Baby (Howard Hawks, 1938)

The characters in the quintet: trumpet, Katharine Hepburn, a flibberdigibbet who knows what she wants and tolerates no nonsense getting it. Saxophone, Cary Grant in glasses, a paleontologist who thinks dinosaur bones are the most important thing in the universe, and who believes he is being stalked by Katharine Hepburn. Double bass, Billy Bevan as a bartender with a trick up his sleeve. Kazoo, Fritz Feld as an exceedingly neurotic psychiatrist. Drums, Tala Birell as the psychiatrist's socialite wife, bada-boom.

The scene: a characteristic 1930s nightclub, with a bar where people get martinis and tables where, drinking them, people say delicious, scandalous things.

The time: One night.

Susan (Hepburn) enters wearing what is probably the most preposterous outfit in the history of Hollywood film (designed by Howard Greer to give this effect): shimmering, most likely gold (the film is in black and white), with a kooky headgear involving a veil and an undulating veil support dropping nearly over her face. She heads directly for the bar, but when she orders a martini she and Joe the bartender get into a conversation about his special trick, which he's shown her before but now proceeds to teach her again (so that we may learn at her side). "Watch very carefully . . ."

"I'm watching."

"I take an olive. I throw it in that glass . . ." Then he puts another olive on the back of the hand, and with his other hand gives the olive-hand's wrist a smart smack and the olive goes flying up through the air right into Joe's mouth. Susan now tries it, because she will absolutely not be mastered. But her olive falls on the floor, precisely at the moment David (Grant) is stepping in. He slips on it, hits the floor, and gets up with the back of his suit entirely ripped. Having met him earlier and ruined his day, she is clearly his Nemesis.

She sidles over to a table where Dr. Lehman (Feld) is sitting alone and introduces herself before helping herself to some of his tidbits. "You may have heard me lecture. I lecture about nervous disorders. I am a psychiatrist," he says, boldly (too boldly) blinking his eyes. She says something to the effect of how it must be interesting treating all those crazy people. "Not everybody who is neurotic is crazy," says he, twitching his eyes again. He speaks with a Viennese accent. She has now helped herself to the black purse sitting on his table, which she lost. She asks him what he would say about a man who continually thinks a woman is chasing him, and we get a fulsome analysis boiling down to, "The love impulse in man very frequently reveals itself in terms of conflict."

David comes up. "Say," says she, eyeing the tear in his garment, "you've got ...."

"I have no such thing," he says, indignant (as only Cary Grant can be).

The two of them sidle off, while Mrs. Lehman returns from the ladies' room and takes her seat at the table. Looks at her husband, boom. Looks at the table, ka-boom. "Where's my purse?"—boom chaka boom chaka boom!

There is so much going on here, in what feels, until the very end, like a rhythm-free downhill ski, that it is hard to keep up. Chunky Joe, the martini, the olive trick, the olive in his mouth, Susan slapping her hand as she repeats his mantra, her olive hitting the floor, David slipping, David getting up with his rip, Susan confronting Lehman, Lehman's obvious lunacy, the diagnosis of David, David squawking away after they argue about it while she, purse in hand, strides behind for a second, to help him cover his (bared) ass, the wife whose only function in the scene is realizing she's lost her purse. Grant erect and stilted, like a paleontologist on holiday. Susan having a splendid time, she always has a splendid time—even with total strangers. Joe like an automaton, doing his trick once, twice, any number of times, exactly the same way; he's like a machine at an arcade. The psychiatrist who could use a psychiatrist, and his improbable diagnosis.

A pervasive feeling hints that there are no two of these characters—not even (perhaps especially not even) the psychiatrist and his wife—who belong in this one place at the same time. Mismatch is a word that comes to mind, but random assortment is better, except that there are relationships between them that make their conjunctions believable. David apparently being "followed" by Susan; Susan knowing the bartender from before; Susan fascinated by the psychiatrist. No single performance stands out forcefully, and the scene collapses if all of these actors are not present exactly in this way, creating their sparkling stereotypes, together not being together. An ensemble virtuosity.

In ensemble acting, the performer need not regard her character as intending to be emphatic as an individual, or for that matter even touting an individual existence, but may think of her character instead as part of a carefully selected and carefully framed group. Any eccentricity of the character is intentional only in relation to the greater design of the group, and such an eccentricity is balanced by the eccentricity of another. It is the ongoing challenge and duty of each performer to give the moment to his colleagues, and in this way we have a sense of mutual support and smoothly arranged ornamentation in the performing. Any instance of the drama will interconnect characters' distinctiveness centripetally, toward a hub, rather than leading characterizations to fly apart centrifugally, toward idiosyncrasy.

As to the "melody" of the moment, the thread that binds elements of the action chain one to another, it will be carried now by one character, now by another, now by still another, and character performance will have as a key feature the ability to hand off the themic baton after a phrase, contributing to the relay. For Truffaut, Lonsdale sets up Seyrig to entertain Léaud, Seyrig's fascination with Léaud plays against the missing Lonsdale, Léaud's panic appears to be caused by Seyrig until we learn at the finale—the spectacular finale vortex on the stairs—that it was caused by his consciousness of Lonsdale. Hepburn watches, then bounces off Bevan; bounces off Bevan a second time dropping the marker; causes Grant to collide with the marker; bounces off Grant; enjambs Feld who enjambs Grant bouncing off Hepburn, who paves the way for the finale by Birell. Johnson, alone, is put to suffering, implores Carey for help, receives Carey's solicitude along with that of Holloway, turns away Carey's intrusive helpfulness, hears Carey's warning, then Holloway's, is met by Howard, interplays with Howard, is touched helpfully by Howard while Holloway moves past to vanish physically the same way Carey has already vanished from the frame, has a touching moment with Howard, who follows Holloway out to the trains. Lonely Rickman's glow spreads over to winsome Winslet, then noble

Grant's glow spreads to self-effacing Thompson in echo, then jovial Hardy and buoyant Spriggs glow together in still a further, more mature echo, as solitary Wise, the one who has not joined the party, the Man Without a Glow, counterpoints stalwartly in a great green space and we swing full circle with now-ebullient Rickman celebrating his moment of joy in a shower of gold.

No single action or character takes precedence in these routines, yet each of the routines as a composite works with compound action and immense dramatic force, whether comedic or melodramatic. Virtuosity is in the collaboration. While collaboration may be central in many individually glowing virtuosic moments—their depending for success upon the support of an acting team—only in ensemble work are the parts formed to belong in the arrangement.

30

Near Misses

FIGURE 30 *Darryl Hickman in* Leave Her to Heaven *(John M. Stahl, Twentieth Century Fox, 1945).*
Digital frame enlargement.

Emphasis—through dramatic unconventionality; outlandish gesture; magnified presence—can help performance gain attention, perhaps so much attention it is mistaken for virtuosity. Virtuosity involves either action by the performer, or the perception of same by the audience, as *outstanding,* that is, as *standing out.* Here follow some types of case in which performers much noted for personality or talent (that is, *big*) appear—but *only* appear—to eclipse a scene virtuosically. The bravura apotheosis is not reached, albeit the performer is considered the sort who will predictably shine; or the sort who is distinctively, automatically attractive. In cases of these types, though the act is beyond wonderful, one has a near miss.

The Case of the Residual Diva

The viewer may read virtuosity in, based on a lingering residue of a performer's accomplishments in another sphere altogether. The performer is "here already" established, even if not exceeding the territory of the work at this actual moment. The plinth frames the statue. Thus, a figure very well known—perhaps for something beyond cinema—plays out the very act that made her famous earlier, elsewhere, but presently under the cover of a diegetic character rather than as her received performative self. The character seems to inherit the qualities of the performer, who is as visible as the character is precisely because of that inheritance.

Take Sugar Kane Kowalczyk in Billy Wilder's *Some Like It Hot* (1959), who bears a disarming resemblance, through and through, to Marilyn Monroe (greatest sex symbol of her time if also an actor of unheralded strength). Late in the film, Monroe is perched on a tiny nightclub stage singing Herbert Stothart and Harry Ruby's "I Wanna Be Loved by You" with band accompaniment: an unquestionably cultivated "night-club stage performance" (Sugar Kane is a pro), wherein bodily gestures appeal to the audience and the character is played as cute, talented, musical enough to be traveling with an all-female band, and attractive in the way that Marilyn Monroe is widely understood to be. Monroe's allure is a matter of star construction patterning, not a function of any cinemagoer's putatively independent taste. Sugar Kane's allure imitates (so closely that it becomes) Monroe's.

While Monroe's fans will find themselves swept away because she has the camera to herself for a relatively long time, her routine here is not virtuosic. Though as a visual figure she rises, as a singer she cannot: not as Billie Holiday does with seeming effortlessness, or Ella Fitzgerald, or Judy Garland; not even as do June Allyson or Doris Day. In this scene neither Monroe nor Sugar Kane work to transcend what they "otherwise, normally" are in the space behind, or outside the story, and Sugar Kane's qualities never transcend Monroe's offscreen "self." The song number drives the plot forward, but only in the way that other scenes in the film do, including ones that do not contain Monroe's work. She fits nicely into the design of a machine in motion. The spotlight on her is a diegetic spotlight-within-the-story, not the spotlight being used to tell the story. Sugar Kane stands out, but only as much as Monroe does (here and everywhere), too.

An earlier case historically is Marlene Dietrich using her already-well-known cabaret style to reprise, for Alfred Hitchcock's *Stage Fright* (1950), the much performed (and, for her, trademark) number, Cole Porter's "Laziest Gal in Town."

It's not 'cause I wouldn't
It's not 'cause I shouldn't

And you know that it's not 'cause I couldn't
It's simply because I'm the laziest gal in town.

Here, from both the stalls out front and backstage, we are given views of
the routine, no more captivating than any other Dietrich routine on film.
We may indeed have slipped into another Dietrich film, waiting just behind
Hitchcock's film, as in its "dressing room." Dietrich has virtuosic moments
in *Stage Fright*, just as Monroe has them in *Some Like It Hot*, but this
Dietrich number, like Monroe's, does not achieve that elevation.

A distinct rationalization is available as Dietrich and Monroe sing. Both
actors play performers, not ordinary citizens who pay to see performances
(such as audience members usually are). Dietrich's Charlotte Inwood is a
major stage star before she walks onto that stage, Sugar Kane is a qualified
lounge singer. Thus, when each character is on a stage giving a performance
of the sort she is already known for, that performance, bold and alluring as
it may be, is accountable to the contrivance of the story and through that
accountability diminished in flamboyance. Instead of directly experiencing
the singing as such, we directly experience being informed about the singing.
But the glamour of our being informed is itself a reference to what we
already knew about the performer, from outside this film. The wings shot
of Inwood helps, too, giving note from a decidedly professional standpoint
(just offstage) that she is in performance. Virtuosity, by contrast, always
springs and unfolds without, or beyond, our expectation.[1] It is supremely
difficult for an actor playing a performer character, especially a virtuosic-
performer-character, to be virtuosic in the playing. Judy Garland seems to
have moments in *A Star Is Born* (1954), especially "Happiness Is A Thing
Called Joe," but the membrane between her Esther as virtuosic and Garland
herself as virtuosic doing Esther's virtuosity is very permeable.

In these scenes of "received" virtuosity (virtuosity by default), we are
offered a (pleasing) residue of pre-diegetic fame, a fame established for
Dietrich on the stage; Monroe by way of magazine publicity, but for both
not in the present film. In *Some Like It Hot*, we have the (already) famous
Marilyn Monroe doing a character who is inherently not famous at all in
the same way but who picks up a special glow because of Monroe. For *Stage
Fright*, the famous Marlene Dietrich degenerates into the merely "famous"
Charlotte Inwood whose "fame" inhabits another (purely diegetic) territory
altogether, less universal and more European, less provocative and more
proper than the world we expect she lives in, yet here, too, the performer
shines through the veil of the character. Clearly, there is benefit to be gained

---

[1]There is a stunning virtuoso moment in the "Dramatist" episode of *Jack Taylor* (2010), when as
the bedraggled hero Iain Glen slips without the least warning into a powerful, even entrancing
dramatic reading of several lines from John Millington Synge's *Deirdre of the Sorrows*.

at the box office by casting a major star whose fame is already established, because a crossover audience is pre-built. As the real-world fame of the performer *in performance* in the film helps elevate the producer's profit, it also depreciates the status of the performer *as performer* by repositioning its source outside the work.

Those who are already famous need not always sink below the level of virtuosity when they put their acts on film. As Jakie Rabinowitz in *The Jazz Singer* (1927), for example, Al Jolson sings Irving Berlin's "Blue Skies" to his mother (Eugenie Besserer), she seated on a low ottoman adjacent the treble end of the piano and the camera positioned between them, watching him. He plays the song tenderly, over and over turning his head to smile at mother while his fingers knowingly find the keys. A kind of musical pietà.

Then, with several bars of left-hand vamping, he says, "Now I'm gonna play really jazzy, like I perform it," and he launches into a razzmatazz version of the kind Al Jolson audiences already know and love (and which, presumably, they hoped they would encounter in this, his and everybody's first talking picture). But somehow when that jazzy Jolson emerges it is not as a pre-diegetic Jolson, nothing but a premonition of the character Jakie. Profile to the camera, he is the ambitious Jakie, the young jazz singer in full flourish. Jakie is infected by Jolson, not the other way around. When he announces that he is going to "do it" the way he would on the stage, he clues us that as Jolson he is "doing" the song "as Jakie will do it, simulating how he will do it," rather than as he, Jolson, would do it if this were only his stage act.

The Animal Case

Animals onscreen easily take attention away from human performers, and actors know this and are aware that trying to upstage an animal will result only in the diminution or destruction of their own work. With the fascinating or adorable cinematic animal, the character almost entirely disappears because of the nature of the creature. Whether cinematic animals are virtuosic or not, generally, is a tender question, one that applies more forcefully to some species than to others. Insects, for example, while they may be intensely horrific, monstrous, or chilling, do not generally tend to seem virtuosic, in that they are taken to behave naturally rather than to "work out" performance (even if, to some degree, they do). I think of the spider photographed in such a way as to seem gigantic and menacing onscreen, in Jack Arnold's *The Incredible Shrinking Man* (1957); the creature was guided by puffed air, and the photography blown up. The monstrosity is thus created not through the spider's movement but through cinematographic trickery. But the power of the characterization (if I may call it that) is rooted in the spider's spideriness, an essential, natural quality that outshines any one move. In the same film we meet a cat whose nature generates another powerful, for most people more affecting "performance." This pointedly catlike cat seems at one instant very powerful, violating the boundaries of household petdom; it transcends its day-to-day identity as pet resident in this house: but a cat does not become virtuosic baring his teeth. If the moment seems virtuosic, as this beast tries hard (but unsuccessfully) to eat the hero, it is more Arnold's clever design at play than the matted-in cat's behavior. Very often an animal's untutored and unsculpted behavior can seem dramatically vital, even heroic, especially because no sculpting, no tutoring is brought to view; consider the dramatic effect when, in westerns where a hero is shot and falls to the ground his horse "nobly" returns to the ranch without him and leads helpers to the rescue. But when we watch this kind of behavior, there is little call to think of it as virtuosic, the explanations called "training" and "trainability" and our preconception of "equine nobility" sufficient for making account.

Animals who speak—Aslan the lion (Liam Neeson) in *The Lion, the Witch, & the Wardrobe* (2005); Frank the pug (Danny DeVito) in *Men in Black* (1997); Francis the Talking Mule (Chill Wills) (1950); the cast, generally, of *Planet of the Apes* (1968–2017); or any of the legion animals artfully animated, from Donald Duck (Clarence Nash) to the Tasmanian Devil (Jim Cummings) to the dogs in *Isle of Dogs* (2018)—may seem especially phantasmal and engaging but will also strike viewers as palpably unreal, or at least "real" only in the phantasmal domain, not in the everyday. We take it as read that animals cannot speak, in the conventional human sense of "speech" demonstrated by able-voiced human characters, so that any tiger, giraffe, pig, or pussycat producing "speech" as a character becomes unbelievable in its own terms. In order to "receive" such speaking, we must either reconceive our assumptions about the animal world or regard the speech as fake. It is interesting that most people choose the latter approach, but the philosophical implications of limits to animal life go beyond this discussion. Suffice it to say, the talking animal in film tends to point instantly to contrivance of one kind or another. We sense the pre-diegetic, real, everyday, non-speaking character of the creature always along with the animation.

Nevertheless it is possible to train and photograph an animal in such a way that a performance takes form, makes a contribution to a dramatic moment that is spectacularly out of proportion with everyday expectation and that evidences very precise behavior executed with perfect grace—this in such a way as to steal the scene or motor its central action. Since dramatic disproportion, surprise, and formal perfection are pretty much what is involved in virtuosic performance—the showing of some specially honed ability carried to a level of derring-do—the animal can be thought a virtuoso, at least (like humans) a virtuosic exemplar of its kind. The construction might be choreographic, as with the "Heavenly Music" number of *Summer Stock* that I discussed above, which offers exceptional canine participation principally through the positioning of the dogs, the camera's relation to them, and the (for audiences virtuosically splendid) timing of their contributions manipulated offscreen. I think of the exceptional training, and hilarious schticks, of Mr. Smith in *The Awful Truth* (1937), leading to his apparently brilliant mischief in Irene Dunne's apartment, or of the black poodle in Minnelli's *Designing Woman* (1957) who makes a spectacularly mistimed entrance with the wrong shoe in its mouth. While it is evident that dog wrangling is being used to produce moments like these, some combination of the wrangler's invisible skill and the audience's tendency to anthropomorphize puppies works to convert trained animals into animal performers exhibiting wondrous capacity. Both of the situations above are comedic, and perhaps it is the comedic form that lends the exceptional authenticity and sharpness to the dog's performance in each case, though in *Lassie Come Home* (1943) the heroic collie performs amazing life-saving actions, including struggling across a turbulent stream.

The virtuosic performance for a memorable moment brings the show to a halt, ascends above the action. Lassie, Mr. Smith, and Lauren Bacall's poodle are show *slowers* but not necessarily ascenders above the action, albeit the spectator's eye is momentarily focused upon them. They are shot and edited to seemingly "produce" a moment so gut-splittingly stunning (heroic, funny) we lose all orientation to the scene, but such a loss, in these cases, is fleeting and recouped instantly. The drama re-establishes itself and moves on, does not discount at all the splendid power of the doggy act to toggle our mood, toggle but not stun. As the behavior is not conspecific we tend not to value it as virtuosity: people tend to give the highest rating to other people.

Animals are choreographed for the screen, yes, and with the camera's collaboration the choreography can look spectacular. This happens with humans, too.

The Case of the Child

While children are scene stealers through their (always already available) guilelessness and charm, if not precocity, still child virtuosity is rare. We take the child by default as being unprepared for full social participation, which means, bluntly, not yet capable of a complete round of activities undertaken maturely and responsibly. Children behave clumsily by adult standards. They are perhaps undeveloped, raw, inarticulate, unformed. Whilst by standards broader than adult standards—human standards—children are by no means raw and unformed, but are very much, and wholly, themselves, still it is adult standards, not human standards, that tend to background our judgment of cinematic action as meaningful. (Not our valuation of popularity, or calculation of praiseworthiness, but our treating films as intelligible.) The child (often considered a "mere child") is not likely to have mastered grace and form, an articulate spontaneity of expression and sense of timing fitting to what audiences expect of virtuosity. Always the child seems to be imitating; striving for; struggling against confines. When Bojangles Robinson danced on the staircase with tiny Shirley Temple, to whatever extent the routine had virtuosity that virtuosity belong to him because of his kindness, his attentiveness, and his dancerly grace. He was certainly the better dancer, she was the one almost keeping up; and it was not difficult to see how the routine had been choreographed to make it possible for her to keep up this almost keeping up, without having Robinson's experience.

(Gene Kelly dances with Jerry the Mouse [whom we take to be younger!] in *Invitation to the Dance* [1956]. But the mouse's steps are not only simplistic, they are nonexistent except as cell drawings. Jerry is animated. Gene animates.)

What looks like child virtuosity often stems from a younger person successfully imitating the simplified movements of an older one. The very little Ronnie Howard in *The Courtship of Eddie's Father* (1962), in a scene played in the kitchen breakfast nook, coaches his very tall dad (Glenn Ford) on how to pick up a girl; the dialogue, Howard's terrific timing and phrasing, and the fine chemistry between the two actors all contribute to what may seem a virtuosic moment, surely one that sticks in memory because it has erupted from the rather conventional surface of the film. Howard's Eddie is written as a precocious little boy (in a neat behavior split he can look like a child but talk like an adult, a standard trope with cinema and television children) and his principal working contribution (for him the cuteness is not work) lies in getting the timing right, that is, dropping emphasis onto the right syllables. He does this quite as flawlessly as other actors typically do, but we are amazed because we expect him to be as imprecise as he is young. Does his apparent virtuosity lie in our depreciated expectation? (Ford does not seem virtuosic dropping emphasis onto *his* syllables correctly.)

Virtuosity characterizes Darryl Hickman's drowning scene in *Leave Her to Heaven* (1945). With Gene Tierney watching coldly from her rowboat he complains of a cramp, begs for help, then sinks, but he has earlier set up this moment (a boy with a crippling disease) rolling himself out of the rowboat and into the water with great effort, and again soon afterward by imploring Tierney to help him swim across the lake so that he can impress his big brother (imploring in a notably cloying, far too eager way that makes her cringe). The eagerness, the desperation in his voice, the slight pudginess (read, innocence) of the young body, the difficulty with movement, and the labor of the swimming leading up to the moment the cramp hits all draw us into the precariousness, as does Tierney's splendid supporting gestures of staring through sunglasses and withholding expression as she eggs him on. While the film is generally about a family infected with violence, told in a highly decorative melodramatic style, this little scene seems to stand out and away, to be etched permanently, to persist in the background of everything else that happens. Cold virtuosity, for both performers.

Virtuosic, too, is a single moment in *Bigger Than Life* (1956) where Christopher Olsen, trying to catch football passes from his father in the backyard, continually misses the ball. (He cannot catch? The father cannot throw?) After two devoted but failed efforts—the camera's position and Olsen's expression bluntly announce how crucially this tyke wants to please his dad—the father pronounces that they'll do one more and if this is a flub there'll be no lunch. The kid runs toward the camera and the ball sails over him, his expression of defeat showing that he doesn't think he had a chance. He's fallen onto the grass, stretched out, head to the right, sobbing. It's a medium shot, containing, thanks to CinemaScope, an entire body, trembling with tears, resting exhausted in, yet also distinguished from, the lush green grass underneath. The resignation in that body, the sense of having lost all opportunity for a father's love (forewarning of what's coming ahead) is accomplished entirely without self-reference by the child. No self-awareness; no consciousness of place (on a set); no miniscule sign that for him this moment is not real.

31

Discounts

FIGURE 31 *Jean-Louis Barrault in* Les enfants du paradis [Children of Paradise] *(Marcel Carné, Pathé, 1945). Digital frame enlargement.*

Here is philosopher of art Denis Dutton on the special skill required for, and displayed in, virtuosic performance:

> Where a skill is acquired by virtually everybody in the culture, such as with communal singing or dancing in some tribes, there still tend to be individuals who stand out by virtue of special talent or mastery. Technical artistic skills are noticed in small-scale societies as well as developed civilizations, and where they are noticed they are universally admired. The admiration of skill is not just intellectual; skill exercised by writers, carvers, dancers, potters, composers, painters, pianists, singers, etc. can

cause jaws to drop, hair to stand up on the back of the neck, and eyes to flood with tears. The demonstration of skill is one of the most deeply moving and pleasurable aspects of art. (53)

With the proviso, of course, that any demonstration of the artist's skill is at least slightly self-reflective, pointing attention at the working of the moment rather than the greater Working that a moment reveals. And also with the proviso that viewers must know enough to recognize a skill when they are shown it. Part of what the virtuoso accomplishes is a kind of self-effacement, in which whilst skill is being demonstrated the fact of a demonstration of skill is not.

But what if virtuosic skill is entirely taken for granted, subjected to a discount?

Surely one of the most virtuosic moments in cinema, a case of pure invisibility, is found in Marcel Carné's *Les enfants du paradis* (*Children of Paradise,* 1945) as, around 1825, the "celebrated mime" Baptiste Debureau gives a public show upon a little stage erected in a village marketplace swarming with citizens and gawkers. Debureau is none other than the internationally famous mime artist, Jean-Louis Barrault (1910–1994), colleague of, among many others, Albert Camus. In his little routine in *Children,* Debureau cleverly mocks a bourgeois fatcat in his audience by miming a bourgeois fatcat paying bloated attention to the stage while simultaneously being pickpocketed unaware—the pickpocket mime is also Debureau. While it is impossible to use language for accurately describing what a mime does without language, suffice it to say we are given the treat of watching an artist whose gestural moves are refined and polished in the extreme, whose sense of posture and movement is wholly and uncompromisingly expressive and this often in multiple ways at once, whose face is an uncountable number of masks in vivid array, and whose inner manner as he works all these tricks is, as appears, completely absent, completely silent, completely outside the perimeter of the stage (and the screen).

Yet through it all, this exceedingly competent Debureau, this dancer among dancers and maker of fluid movement, this displayer of consummate paradigms of emotional expression, cleverly watching his audience watching him, is Barrault, and not only Barrault but *the famous* Barrault. Barrault is not merely an actor at work. He is both *performing a man exhibiting a virtuosic style* (Debureau) and *displaying elegant virtuosity of his own.* This is a virtuosic performance of a virtuosic performance. Should we play it down, because, after all, playing Debureau so skillfully must have been no particular challenge for Barrault? Or should we marvel? (Debureau seems stunning. But since, presumably, the movie audience doesn't know the challenges confronting a mime artist, since the audience is wowed but uninformed, can it recognize Debureau's virtuosic triumphs? And Barrault's?)

We can find the same kind of recursive virtuosity in George Cukor's *A Double Life* (1947) when as the virtuosic Shakespearean actor Anthony John performing *Othello* on a stage-within-the-frame, the virtuosic actor Ronald Colman uses his own virtuosity to create the virtuosity of his character; Colman had a notable (non-Shakespearean) stage career before coming to pictures. Albert Finney, performing a Shakespearean actor doing Lear in *The Dresser* (1983) had been in the Royal Shakespeare Company, performing *Coriolanus* in 1959. Doing a Iagoesque Francis Urquhart in *House of Cards* (1990–1995), Ian Richardson tapped his own long experience (much of it at the RSC). These characterizations all contain virtuosic virtuosities.

When we watch Barrault in *Les enfants*, the question must arise, "Is Barrault's virtuosic talent fabricating the virtuosic mimicry of Debureau?" Or, "Is Barrault showing us his *own* mimic virtuosity (albeit in another costume and context)?" Is Barrault ideally cast as Debureau because he can always already produce routines such as Debureau is producing? Are we being given a special treat as viewers, an open access to a performance by Barrault made available as long as we agree to think of him as Debureau? Again, we are always getting a performance from the actor, but the actor need not be playing a character who has his selfsame virtuosic skill. Since Barrault/Debureau is shown in full medium shot, entire body, without any cinematic fabrication, his marketplace performance is as real as any Barrault performance would be.

Most screen actors who have a signal virtuosic talent shown onscreen in the name of a character are not generally engaged making the same display under another name outside the frame. Giving an astonishing performance in *Personal Shopper* (2016), Kristen Stewart shows a virtuosity she is not called upon to show outside the diegesis. But Barrault the mime is alive as such behind the screen, even as he is filmed being Debureau. There are other filmic moments when Barrault acts without miming, transposes himself into an un-Barrauldian character: as Restif de la Bretonne in Ettore Scola's *La nuit de Varennes* (1982), for example, striding down a cobblestone street at night, with the camera backing up ahead of him, and his shoes, with metallic plates for preservation, scraping against the stones with each footstep, producing a display of flying sparks. Arresting, and wonderful in Barrault's handling, but even if he did have to be *the famous* Barrault to do it, that is, an actor of supreme talent who could make the effect, still there is no mirroring of the *famous* Barrault in Restif, who is neither a mime nor an actor.

Barrault's use of his own mimic capacity to enliven Debureau's mimic capacity could induce viewers in the know to discount the virtuosity of the routine, to say in effect, "Utterly brilliant, *but of course it would be,* since the mime is being played by the utterly brilliant Barrault!" Or, more bluntly: "We're not even watching a character, we're watching Barrault, and the character is non-existent." This would be something like saying, after watching the athletic star Burt Lancaster doing his own high-flying work in *Trapeze* (1956), "Terrific, galvanizing, *but of course it would be, since he is an athlete!*" (Lancaster had a background as an acrobat.) Or watching the concert pianist Oscar Levant, one of whose trademarks was the Gershwin Concerto in F, brilliantly performing the Gershwin Concerto in F in *An American in Paris* (1951; where he is magically every player in the orchestra as well as the pianist!), and demurring, "Well, this is heavenly, *but of course it would be, because Oscar Levant plays the piano!*" Or watching the Olympic swimming champion Johnny Weissmuller swimming away from crocodiles in *Tarzan the Ape Man* (1932) and demurring, "Exciting, terrifying, *but of course it would be!*"; or Moira Shearer dancing Victoria Page dancing "The Red Shoes" and concluding, "*But of course, what else!*" Cyd Charisse's astounding disrobing-rerobing ballet in *Silk Stockings* (1957) is to be discounted, *of course,* because, after all, before coming to cinema what was she but a ballet dancer! Even the witticism of Woody Allen's early films, especially ones in which he performs directly before the camera, such as *Annie Hall* (1977), is far from virtuosic because, after all, what was he before making films but a stand-up comic! One may sense glory, but esteem it as not acting, not a triumph of performance: or not a triumphant performance before the camera. It is an enactment, even an excitement, but the idea of triumph is imported. *One could take that view.*

Yet one would be self-depriving to do so. These *are* acting virtuosities, because given *to the lens* no matter where else. *Because here for us,* no matter what. The "near miss" should be, but isn't, virtuosic. "Discounts" only obviously are.

Any attempt to discount cinematic virtuosity will fail, because regardless of where the vision of performance originates—in the street or in the cinema—it is exactly what we see it to be while we are seeing it. And if it causes "jaws to drop, hair to stand up on the back of the neck, and eyes to flood with tears" this is due to strengths made palpable before a lens no matter through what manner of work, calculation, contrivance.

Many examples could be adduced of virtuosic talent clearly shown onscreen yet produced by actors who are not claimed to possess it off-camera. No knowledgeable viewer could discount these as *virtuosity, of course, but —!*

- In *What's Eating Gilbert Grape* (1993) when Leonardo DiCaprio (at the time a virtual unknown in cinema) embodies a youth with developmental disorder, no one says "*But of course, he is actually developmentally disordered in real life!*," and discounts the performance.
- When in *Now, Voyager* (1942) Bette Davis embraces the young Janis Wilson to give her courage and comfort no one says, "*But of course!*

Bette Davis is always encouraging and comforting, just like this," and discounts the performance.

- When in *Deathtrap* (1982) Christopher Reeve connives with Michael Caine to kill Dyan Cannon, with really chilling malevolence, no one says, *"But of course! Reeve and Caine are always killing people,"* and discounts the performances.
- When in *Some Like It Hot* (1959) Tony Curtis does an astonishing imitation of Cary Grant while seducing Marilyn Monroe on the yacht, nobody says, *"Of course! But that Tony Curtis is always going around imitating people!"* and discounts his serious work here.

(Yet somehow—because his art is inestimably great?—that Barrault doing Debureau is *just* Barrault, *of course* Barrault, from whom we *would expect nothing less!*)

A fascinating variant on discounted virtuosities is to be found in film scenes depicting auditions or tryouts, where a performer well known to us as virtuosically brilliant must show what he or she can do, in front of some (usually exceedingly) judgmental producer, theater owner, or the like. Barbra Streisand's Fanny singing for Florenz Ziegfeld (Walter Pidgeon) in *Funny Girl* (1968). Judy Garland in *A Star Is Born* (1954) putting it all out there to impress Charles Bickford. Dustin Hoffman in *Tootsie* (1982), with his Michael Dorsey bragging to his powerful agent (Sydney Pollack) that he plays a great tomato. In the audition scene our discounting maneuver operates as we watch secure in the knowledge that the "striving talent" (now incarnated by a famous performer whose auditions are long in the past) will surely succeed, the guarantee so airtight that we can sit back in only half-engagement watching the performance-within-the-performance. One hopes, in fact, watching these scenes, that the onscreen judge will be astute enough to see in this "unfound presence" what we learned a long time ago to see, the blazing talent shining forth.

A crucial aspect of discounting is the audience's foreknowledge. Those who come to Woody Allen for the first time decades after his stand-up career may well know nothing of it and thus not discount his screen stand-ups as the work of a "star already." Seeing Charisse in *Silk Stockings* (or any other film), does the viewer watch on the basis of knowing about her previous balletic career? The more a performance comes from an actor contemporaneous with the audience, the more likely is the possibility of discounting, the more likely the audience to know the performer's roots. Ironically, in cases where the audience comes to the screen decades after a film was made the performances seem "authentic" and less discountable, as well, this because little or nothing is known about stars of yesteryear. A figure like Katharine Hepburn is attributed a highly expressive, even emphatic screen personality by viewers unfamiliar with the fact that she came to film from the New York stage (as did John Barrymore and so many other actors); she had a stage voice, knew how to make herself heard in an auditorium (the stage performer was not microphoned until after the late 1980s).

If watching performative virtuosos we downgrade or discount what they are doing as "natural" or "obvious," we are rejecting a gift.

32

Virtuosic Silence

FIGURE 32 *Jerry Lewis with cigar in* The Errand Boy *(Jerry Lewis, Paramount, 1961). Digital frame enlargement.*

In *Stage Fright,* the diegetic Charlotte Inwood is one fine performer yet she cannot hold a candle to the great Marlene Dietrich—the Marlene Dietrich we see in the other parts of this film, and in such films as *The Blue Angel* (1930), *Blonde Venus* (1932), *Shanghai Express* (1932), and *Destry Rides Again* (1939). In *Some Like It Hot,* Sugar Kane Kowalczyk is a sexy and hypnotic presence as she sings, and in every other manifestation, but regardless, she doesn't hold a candle to Marilyn Monroe, the Marilyn Monroe we see in this film, especially in a seduction scene with Tony Curtis, and in her other work from *The Asphalt Jungle* (1950) to *The Misfits* (1961).[1] But a brilliant performer might be contracted to play a brilliant performer— Laurence Olivier as Archie Rice (in *The Entertainer* [1960])—in a rendering made visible to us as *beyond spectacular*, in short where the character is everything the actor is known to be and more. A problem for the actor trying to mobilize a character who has some real strengths is that to the extent that audiences play upon their knowledge of the actor's famous abilities, the character's abilities erode, since what is being visibly done is attributed to the actor first, and the character is only his shadow.

Silence can twist "discounts" and "near misses." Some examples:

Sammy Davis, Jr. does remarkable work as Sportin' Life in Otto Preminger's *Porgy and Bess* (1959), although Sportin' Life is a pusher, not a performer, thus moved to extremity of rhythmic gesture and movement (in the Davis style) by hot desperation. Davis needs merely to inhabit this role, with his typical electricity. Watching his "It Ain't Necessarily So," one feels contact with Davis, not Sportin' Life. In Lewis Milestone's *Ocean's 11* (1960), by contrast, he plays Josh Howard, a member of Danny Ocean's pack and party to a multi-casino heist, as well as a singer. At one moment, in a kind of aside (and also over the closing credits), Davis sings the title song with unforgettable panache, momentarily transcending the film, certainly transcending Josh. Or, in Powell and Pressburger's *The Red Shoes* (1948), the Sadlers Wells dancer Moira Shearer cast as the ingénue ballerina Victoria Page dances a chain of splendid onstage performances, then gives a heartbreakingly beautiful star turn in Robert Helpmann's "The Ballet of *the Red Shoes*." Vicki merges with Moira, but is also relatively diminished, since what viewers tend to see onscreen is Shearer dancing, not Page— although Shearer is persistently called "Miss Page." Or, the blues singer Johnnie Ray playing Steve, the only "non-performing" child in the Donahue family in *There's No Business Like Show Business* (1954), at two critical instants breaks into galvanizing song performances, "If You Believe," and "Alexander's Ragtime Band." Steve does manage to emerge, but behind the electrifying façade of Johnnie Ray.

There is thus a peculiar silence associated with some virtuosic work: the silence that is diegetic, lingering behind the pronounced vocality that is performative.

With Debureau in *Paradise,* for instance, we have two pleasures at once. First, an exposure to Barrault at the peak of his form, and the knowledge that this performance is preserved on film! Then, a dramatic moment inside the film, where Debureau manages to sail away from the bounds of the overall

---

[1]Very notably in *How to Marry a Millionaire* (1953), where in one scene her svelte Pola Debevoise, desperately short-sighted but trying to fix herself in a ladies' room without the aid of her eyeglasses, bumps into walls with brilliant comic aplomb.

story with his tiny act, sail away and enter our affection. (In the world of
silent film, because everything is silent, silence itself does not signify. In a film
with much gabbing, silence is profound.) Is the mime's artistic withdrawal
from sound made especially dramatic only because it is a withdrawal from
sound, regardless of the quality of the performance? Can we say that mime
is virtuosic in itself, regardless of its being free from the gravity of daily
movement? Certainly Debureau's routine is a virtuosity. The costume
and make-up work assist viewers in disconnecting themselves from the
(dominating) thought that performing his mime—miming his mime—is the
very classic Barrault. Barrault does not quite become invisible, and Debureau
does not quite come alive.

A remarkable mime is played as interlude in *The Errand Boy* (1961).
Here is a virtuosity of physical gesture, musical sensibility, comic timing,
and graphic representation. Beleaguered and nerdy Morty S. Tashman (Jerry
Lewis) stumbles into the boardroom of Paramutual Pictures, sees the long
oval table, and sits down at the head. He takes a cigar, and begins to lecture
to the (invisible) assembled board members, using for "words" the various
sounds of jazz band instruments playing in his head (and on the soundtrack,
for us to enjoy). This is a carefully orchestrated variation of Count Basie
and Frank Foster's "Blues in Hoss' Flat." Through miming speech by way
of the music, Lewis "becomes" each instrument in turn, but simultaneously
each instrument becomes a vocal attitude: a naughty flunkie is excoriated
by way of a wailing trumpet, and so on. It is an entirely masterful display of
mimic talent, made emphatic because the situation, the actor's posture and
gestures, and the pointed, explosive instrumentation give us conviction that
Morty is "saying" or "using words" when no speech is present. Is Morty
perceived as Jerry Lewis in this sequence? Does Morty disappear silently
into the (actually silent but) loudly declamatory Jerry? Yes, surely. But all of
Jerry Lewis's characters are perceived as Jerry Lewis, even as, unintelligible
in himself, he turns invisible and vanishes into his characters. What Morty
does here only Jerry can do: but *one of the things Jerry is doing, that only
Jerry can do, is becoming a Morty who is <u>doing what only Jerry can do</u>*.

33

Virtuosic Support

FIGURE 33 *Louise Latham in* Marnie *(Alfred Hitchcock, Universal, 1964). Digital frame enlargement.*

A special precariousness is created by small, elegant, pithy, and tightly contained moments of virtuosity from supporting players, those workers who make their living performing bits or extended character parts. One could go so far as to say the character role is a virtuosity in itself, standing out and away from the flow of action and flowering with quality.

Many actors specialize in "character work," being required to move with fluidity from production to production, studio to studio, production base to production base, and to take what might amount to but a few days' booking on each film. The filming of scenes is typically scheduled (by the assistant director or production manager) so as to make maximal use of acting talent and sets while salary and other expenses are kept as low as possible (expenses such as set construction and breakdown, cast and crew travel, electricity and lighting setup, costuming and makeup), so that a character player in the studio era may have found all of his or her scenes being shot in the same location (one or two sound stages in a studio; an outside location, quite unusually outside the Hollywood area), and this within a few concurrent calendar days. It is a regular feature of character acting that one meets other actors in the film either briefly or not at all, since one is on the shoot for only the scenes one is in, and as they are organized in the shooting schedule. The actor's talent and work history being well known and taken as read, she can function as a technical specialist, coming in to make a very precisely defined contribution and executing the work calmly, swiftly, professionally, and with minimal need for rehearsal.

While the star is present for all, or most, of the principal photography the character actor drops in and drops out.

In Hollywood filmmaking culture there is a hierarchy that structures relationships between principal players and character actors, between name stars ("above the title," "big box office") and support players who may or may not, after significant work, come to be known; and whose fame, if they attain any, may or may not outlive them. For the most part, the celebrity of such performers as Helen Broderick, Thomas Mitchell, Alice Brady, Flora Robson, Daniel Gélin, Guy Kibbee, and Florence Bates faded over time, without publicity agents on the payroll after their deaths or without production contracts keeping them in action. Further, character parts are always smaller and less dominating than star parts *as dramatic elements*. Yet, as character work pays off through its visibility and distinction the character actor has real promise of a secure career if work in any one picture is sufficiently visible, distinct, and notable as to gain producers' and directors' attention. The character player lives in a world of contradiction, needing to at once gain and not gain attention: be seen forcefully enough to inspire future working arrangements but refrain from soliciting so much attention that the balance of the film is warped; don't showboat, but give a good show. How, then, does a character performer manage virtuosity? He is decorating, rather than centering, the scene, and every element of the décor generally falls beneath the notice accorded the principal characters and the plot.

Quirkiness and marked visibility, both physical and behavioral, tend to feature in "character" performance: the pudgy body and honking voice of Eugene Pallette (1889–1954), almost always curtly out of breath (as in *My Man Godfrey* [1936]; *The Adventures of Robin Hood* [1938]; *The Lady Eve* [1941]); the sleek, dark, ethereal tranquility of Gale Sondergaard (1899–1985) (as in *The Letter* [1940]; *Anna and the King of Siam* [1946]). A character turn is both emergent and reclusive, breaking through the skin of the narrative but shaped, controlled, and restrained so that it does not mar, color, or reconstitute the space in which, for what producers consider the best economic reasons, the star is intended to shine. Ian Wolfe (1896–

1992), say: a crooked butler with eyes askance in *Saboteur* (1942), then a cheap roadside hustler stodgily marrying Farley Granger and Cathy O'Donnell in *They Live By Night* (1948), then a pedantic planetarium keeper creepily invoking the end of the universe in *Rebel Without a Cause* (1955), finally a sly forger in *Dick Tracy* (1990). Or Martin Landau (1928–2017), lanky, unctuous, and shifty-eyed as the nefarious Leonard in *North by Northwest* (1959), mysterious and bizarre as Béla Lugosi in *Ed Wood* (1994), and trapped with emphysema in a wheelchair as frail Max Rosenbaum in *Remember* (2015). In Douglas Sirk's *Magnificent Obsession* (1954) Agnes Moorehead (1900–1974), fierce and red-headed, was Nancy Ashford, Jane Wyman's confidant/nurse, but in the same director's *All That Heaven Allows* the following year she was the snoopy gossiping neighbor Sara Warren; for Orson Welles in 1942's *The Magnificent Ambersons* she had been the wise, sad, plain-looking Aunt Fanny, who could reprimand too brash young George Minafer but always stood by him, faithfully and to the end. In *Dark Passage* (1947) she was a sharp-tongued, ambitious intruder. Benny Rubin (1899–1986) recurs in Jerry Lewis vehicles, in *The Errand Boy* (1961) as the fastidious bureaucrat Mr. Wabenlotny and in *The Disorderly Orderly* (1964) as the singing, multi-accented waiter at the Italian restaurant; in *The Family Jewels* (1965) he is a recognizable but uncredited sign-painter. Several performers had constant work supporting John Wayne and other western heroes: Harry Carey Jr., Walter Brennan, Ward Bond, John Qualen, Hank Worden, and weaselly, timid, cunning, shifty-eyed, or modest Elisha Cook, Jr., who made more than two hundred appearances in film and television, including in *The Maltese Falcon* (1941), *The Big Sleep* (1946), *Shane* (1953), *The Killing* (1956), and *Rosemary's Baby* (1968).

To see the power and merit of character performance, briefly consider three exemplary avatars: Norma Varden (1898–1989) as the toffee-nosed waitress in *Waterloo Bridge* (1940); the toffee-nosed Mrs. Osborne in *The Major and the Minor* (1942); the toffee-nosed wife of a blithering pickpocketed Englishman at the start of *Casablanca* (1942); the toffee-nosed Mrs. Bland in *The White Cliffs of Dover* (1944); a toffee-nosed wealthy-looking woman in *The Amazing Mr. X* (1948); toffee-nosed, curious, and ineffably stupid Mrs. Cunningham, offering her throat to Bruno for a lesson in *Strangers on a Train* (1951), as well as dozens upon dozens of other performances: Madame Courbet in *Les Misérables* (1952), Lady Beekman in *Gentlemen Prefer Blondes* (1953), a woman at a cocktail party in *Three Coins in the Fountain* (1954), and a Roman matron in *The Silver Chalice* (1954). Miss Varden specialized in toffee noses, as we can see. Always the same nasal and twirpily high-pitched alto tone, the same high cheekbones and wide eyes far too innocent for a personage of her age, the same not-so-subtly couched snobbery. The wide eyes, failing to quite grasp just as they gape, are the centerpiece of the strangling in *Strangers*, and in choosing this particular character player for that part Hitchcock was showing his very typical astuteness about populating scenes with precise types.

Joseph Schildkraut (1896–1964) was sniveling and arrogant in *Marie Antoinette* (1938) or *The Man in the Iron Mask* (1939), and obsequious as Batouch in *The Garden of Allah* (1936) or the oily Mr. Vadas in *The Shop Around the Corner* (1940), where his spectacular, spluttering ouster from the scene is a notable thrill for the audience. In DeMille's *The King of Kings* (1927) he was a brazenly pouting Judas. Part of Schildkraut's technique was to make his personality disappear beneath the always slightly garish mask of the character, and to play the character for a dangerous kind of submission. Bowing when bowing is not called for or when, according to only atavistic rules of social propriety it is, so that for him, relaxation and casualness are blotted out of the social landscape. His fawning crooked smile, his raising his eyes up to others under a too carefully arched brow, his too speedy or too hesitant way of entering a scene—all of these combine to fascinate and repel, at once. He is the intimidated Otto Frank in *The Diary of Anne Frank* (1959).

And Conrad Veidt (1893–1943), tall, darkly handsome, unforgettably imperious, even stiff, gracile while brittle and unfeeling in *Casablanca* (1942), duplicitously heroic in *Nazi Agent* (1942), hypnotically evil in *The Thief of Bagdad* (1940) yet fully sympathetic in *The Wandering Jew* (1933) even as he was unforgettably piteous, in his early days as a star of German Expressionist film, in *The Man Who Laughs* (1928). Veidt's particular power lay in his eyes, which produced what the camera saw as an extraordinarily penetrating, even magical gaze, whether commanding or pleading or calculating. He possessed a trained baritone voice, so that his lines resonated when he spoke them. His dancerly poise made it possible for him to brilliantly effect characters whose surface could be thought to belie an underlying motive, or characters who led a double life, as in *Nazi Agent*. He always dominated the frame, and the sculpted nature of his face made lighting him a rich achievement. While some of Veidt's roles were higher ranked than character parts, his extreme nobility of pose, his height, his operatic voice, and those eyes always made him so exceedingly characteristic that he played onscreen as other character actors did.

The flavor and tone of a motion picture can rely on clusters of character performances to give a sense of variety, complexity, and texture. Without strong character actors, films are bold-faced but ultimately tedious vitrines for advertising and marketing only the stars—a situation which is ultimately exhausting for the star performer and limiting as to prospects for an expansive career, since a vital aspect of the star image, as it is sold, is a rhythmic alternation between moments when the figure is offered to us and moments when it is artfully withdrawn. In *Red River* (1948), the almost ubiquitous John Wayne chortles to Walter Brennan that it might be fun to watch Montgomery Clift and John Ireland "going at it" with their guns in a shooting match, but then the camera features Clift and Ireland only, and we sense that Wayne, with the loyal Brennan behind, is out of the scene gazing on just as we are. Thelma Ritter (1902–1969) brings a sad desperation to Samuel Fuller's *Pickup on South Street* (1953) but a year later an outspoken, wise, staunchly working-class, bluntly no-nonsense groundedness to Hitchcock's *Rear Window*, and then, a quiet tranquility to *Birdman of Alcatraz* (1962) as the modest, self-demeaning mother of Burt Lancaster. Dub Taylor (1907–1994) made a career of eager spluttering (a local citizen in *The Fastest Gun Alive* [1956], a poker dealer in *The Cincinatti Kid* [1965], Michael Pollard's disingenuous father in *Bonnie and Clyde* [1967]). Gladys Cooper (1888–1971) brought a sharp-gazing clarity of diction as Bette Davis's harridan mother in *Now, Voyager* [1942], frail Clarissa Scott in *The Valley of Decision* [1945], Rex Harrison's blessedly practical mother in *My Fair Lady* (1964]). The character actor's labor contract on any one picture demanding relatively little time, it is not strange to see character players doing a lot of work. Dub Taylor made two hundred and fifty-six appearances, for example, Ian Wolfe three hundred and three!: not only is the player much in demand, the exact nature of the demand is such that it doesn't limit work elsewhere.

Especially in classical Hollywood—but not only there—the character role tends to be written for extremity of personality, odd responsiveness, sometimes expressive amplification (the booming or shrieking voice; the ghoulish or mawkishly innocent expression). Consider whiny Edward Everett Horton (1886–1970) alongside Fred Astaire in *Top Hat* (1935) or Cary Grant in *Holiday* (1938); and quietly acerbic Herbert Marshall (1890–1966) in *Trouble in Paradise* (1932): strangely personable but also types as effete as ever inhabited the screen. Or any of the numerous, usually comic appearances by Eric Blore (1887–1959), whose figures never say what one expects them to or cease to provoke, say in *Sullivan's Travels* or *The Shanghai Gesture* (both 1941); in *Top Hat* (1935) he is the valet who saves the day with his own collar. And Alice Brady (1892–1939), hysterically squeaking in *Joy of Living* (1938) or *My Man Godfrey* (1936), as high strung as a violin string about to snap, neurotic, even idiotic, yet at the same time winningly out of touch with the mundane. The character role is brief and attention-grabbing, intended to spice the proceedings with an odd angularity, a neurotic personality, an especially evocative physical appearance or demeanor, an eccentric style of expression, all of which can work alone or in combination to provide a brief, and typically entertaining break from the nexus of the plot, a frothy cocktail to uplift the imagination away from the press of business. For the character actor, if virtuosic moments are almost guaranteed they are sharply defined, rigidly contained, and relatively brief; what must be accomplished to reach the heights of performance is often not expressive personality (since expressivity is scripted for the character) but expressive idiosyncrasy, a performative "face" instantly recognizable yet never banal.

Character players are hired to a film on a partial-participation basis, typically for a period of time specific in the agreement: one day, two days, three days, a week, perhaps two weeks, with compensation on a time basis. Three days, opening date – closing date, at $250.00 per day, plus traveling expense, as a typical example from contracts of the late 1940s and 1950s. To survive, the character performer must pile up substantial opportunities for work, must become typical. Character acting is scenic, in that the nature of the scenic frame shapes the performance. Stars, by contrast, outplay, outlast, and dominate over scenes.

The character is likely to be remembered more for scenes than for pictures, indeed; scenes recalled even when the contexting film itself is forgotten: a strange laugh, a tender look, a brave climb. While the virtuosity of a star will necessarily eclipse a scene, leap out and swell, even go so far as to negate a scene in the display of personal strength—the suaveness of Cary Grant and of Grace Kelly in the nocturnal hotel sitting room in *To Catch a Thief* (1955) as (much-celebrated) fireworks go off behind them;[1] their passion is indelible, but who remembers why there are fireworks?—the character actor's virtuosity is embedded in place, even part of the scene, pictured or scripted, rather than a performance inside it.

Because character roles attach to scenic design players are intrinsically generic, linked by personality and trade to genre form at its purest. Many players who made copious films in one particular genre refrained from, or had trouble, crossing over to another: Gladys Cooper is never far from the class melodrama, Walter Brennan from the western. If a scene can share fundamental structural attributes with a different type of scene in a different type of movie, if the scenic tone and sense of propriety could seem to match, crossover will work. C. Aubrey Smith (1863–1948), for example: he was a colonel in *The Prisoner of Zenda* and an island priest in *The Hurricane* (both 1937), then another colonel in *Four Men and a Prayer* (1938), then a duke in *Kidnapped* (1938), and a duke again in *Queen of Destiny* (1938), and a general in *The Four Feathers* (1939), a professor in *Five Came Back* (1939), a colonel again in *Another Thin Man* (1939), a stiff-lipped lawyer in *Trouble in Paradise* (1932), another general in *Balalaika* (1939), a judge in *City of Chance* (1940), and a colonel in *Rebecca* (1940). Colonels, generals, judges, professors, lawyers: all of them demonstrably positions of dignity, poise, command, even nobility. In *The Garden of Allah* (1936), Smith had been a priest. In *Romeo and Juliet* (1936), Lord Capulet. In *Little Lord Fauntleroy* (1936) the Earl of Dorincourt. In *The Lives of a Bengal Lancer* (1935) Major Hamilton. In *The Scarlet Empress* (1934) Prince August.

---

[1] A moment reprised by Steven Spielberg as Jamie (Christian Bale) watches Mr. and Mrs. Victor's lovemaking in *Empire of the Sun* (1987) with the *feux d'artifice* of aerial bombardment lighting up the sky outside his window.

And winsome Jane's beleaguered father in *Tarzan the Ape Man* (1932). These among numerous other cross-genre but similarly dignified military or professional roles. By contrast, Edward Everett Horton made mostly romantic comedies or musicals in which he was the eccentric sidekick.

Its scenic quality qualifies the character actor's work by boundary as no other film work does. The "character" is more likely to be notable in reference to scenic elements and functions than in reference to the motives of other characters; and this notability is borne only as far as the edge of the scene, regardless of the number of scenes involved: clumsy, gangly Mischa Auer striding along with Alice Brady on his arm in *My Man Godfrey*, his opera cape hopelessly fluttering; or, in another disconnected scene, bouncing around a sitting room in imitation of a great ape. The character personality seems to radiate to the boundary and reflect back on the actor at work.

Regardless of the general vivacity, extremity, and notable oddity of character-part virtuosities, and their significant derivation from a basis in the script, it is possible for an actor in a subsidiary role to generate a truly outstanding, wholly virtuosic performance that becomes magnified and indelible. This notwithstanding the fact that character performances are structurally so distinctive, so boldly drawn, and so dramatically curtailed that viewers are prone to esteeming them virtuosic. An actor's genius can make for moments of genuinely undeniable and unforgettable touch. Consider Louise Latham's (1922–2018) performance as Bernice Edgar in Hitchcock's *Marnie* (1964). As the protagonist's mother, Latham works with only a small number of other performers, including 'Tippi' Hedren and Kimberly Beck for one scene, Hedren and Sean Connery for another, Bruce Dern for another, Hedren alone for yet another, these adding to one very short scene, two long ones, and a brief flashback. And for a film that was photographed over seventy-eight days in total, she accomplished her work in nine working days from the 11th through the 21st of February 1964, then six further days in March for retakes of the same scenes,[2] working principally on Universal's Stage 21 (at the east side of the lot), except for the short "Marnie's bedroom" scene which was filmed on Stage 28. The dramatic content of this actor's appearance, its final relevance to the story, even some of the personality quirks embedded in Bernice's action are all embedded in Jay Presson Allen's script, so that the actor (who got the part instead of Patricia Neal, having been recommended by Allen [Unsigned note]) had some background ideas and suggestions for coloration that she could work with. "Latham was surprised that so much of Hitchcock's interpretation of Bernice Edgar seemed to be left to her choice," Tony Lee Moral reports (63).

---

[2]Retakes were often necessitated for technical reasons having little or nothing to do with actors' work.

The glow of Latham's work here stems from three quite idiosyncratic contributions, all of which resonate powerfully through the film and seem always to be present in Marnie's consciousness as generator of her anxieties. First, Latham gives Bernice a debilitating limp, which harmonizes with lines in the script about her pained leg. Limps build sympathy. Especially in the bedroom scene, where we hear her on the stairs, the imbalance of the limp as she descends becomes a vital undertone, a percussive motif. But the limp also affects the speed with which the character can move across space, thus giving her an intrinsic meditative, reflective, tortured quality. Marnie walks with business-like aplomb. Little Jessie Cotton skitters around.

Secondly, Latham brings some of her natural Texan background into the character by having Bernice drawl, almost lasciviously (for an analysis, see Pomerance, *Marnie*). The drawl in itself is a negation of, a resistance to, Northern crispness and functionality of speech. It is emotive, it feels its way through time.

Finally, and most emphatically, she is able to cry on cue. At a key moment tears spontaneously well up in Bernice's eyes, seen in medium close-up. The character can thus believably become an overwhelmingly sensitive, passionately religious, physically injured creature, struggling through life without support and bearing secret memories of her maternal love and the childhood events that led to Marnie's birth and Marnie's trauma, both.

34

Control

FIGURE 34 *Johnny Depp in* Pirates of the Caribbean: On Stranger Tides *(Rob Marshall, Walt Disney Pictures, 2011). Digital frame enlargement.*

Actors working on the stage tend to do their own makeup, and there is a venerable tradition in its application. Film actors are made up by the producer's agent, the make-up artist. Some make-up artists are legendary, one of the most notable among them being Dick Smith (1922–2014) who aged Dustin Hoffman for *Little Big Man* (1970), made Linda Blair's head spin around and bare chest show writing in *The Exorcist* (1973), gave wrinkles to David Bowie and Catherine Deneuve for *The Hunger* (1983), aged F. Murray Abraham for *Amadeus* (1984), blew up Michael Ironside's head for *Scanners* (1981), made Meryl Streep's head rotate in *Death Becomes Her* (1992), turned a bubble into a childish, then an adolescent, then a young adult, then a fully adult Jeff Bridges in *Starman* (1984), uglified Hoffman as Ratso Rizzo in *Midnight Cowboy* (1969), created Don Corleone out of Marlon Brando in *The Godfather* (1972), turned Hal Holbrook into Mark Twain, and much more. In the hands of someone like Smith, the actor relaxes with confidence, no matter the excruciating length of the transformation (and some of these transformations take a very long time, indeed; day after day). A make-up team was effectively part of studio infrastructure, while typically being independent contractors; for instance, among the Hollywood production facilities one was bound to find one or another member of the Westmore family at work as principal. When considerable production began to focus on effects makeup, Smith was a leader, followed by such talents as Rick Baker, Del Armstrong, Christopher Walas, and more recently Ve Neill. The proliferation of sci-fi movies involving "alien" creatures has been a heyday for cinematic makeup, and at Paramount, where from 1987 to 1999 production was centered for the *Star Trek: The Next Generation* and *Star Trek: Deep Space Nine* television series simultaneously, latex prosthetic appliances manufactured in-house to cover the faces of the many actors who played Klingons, Cardassians, and other alien types were destroyed after production *each day* and remade for the next day's shooting (the process of latex masking made this an easy task) in order that "black market" sales of such valuable tokens could be prevented.

Since it is central and vital, especially in virtuosic moments, the question of who controls the actor's appearance is exceptionally pertinent. As has been well-rehearsed, the image of the performer (star or character player indiscriminately, as long as a studio contract was in place; and later, to a large degree with independent contracts) rested in the producer's hands, obviously in close consultation with the director, the designer, and the cinematographer, all of whom would have good professional reasons for caring about looks. The actor's investment was, and is, the preservation of self in line with optimized future employment: to be sufficiently recognizable that in a demo reel an identifiable presence can be found and evaluated.[1] Not all performers require to be identifiable always onscreen, and certainly not in every dramatic circumstance. The actor can succeed by disappearing beneath the makeup sometimes, as in John Huston's *The List of Adrian Messenger* (1963), where stars such as Frank Sinatra, Kirk Douglas, and Robert Mitchum (some of the biggest names in Hollywood at the time) vanished under masks made by Bud Westmore and his team. For this film, audiences were lured to pay at the box office by blatant advertisements touting these celebrated *names*, but seeing the movie were put to the chase because the famous personalities—that is, the famous faces—were simply not there to be found. Not until the final moments, in fact the closing credits, are the masks dramatically undone in "curtain calls."

What does the actor experience and endure in performance in regard to the image of the self recognized again each day? However real, this self is

---

[1] In studio filmmaking publicity photographs and/or star portraits were managed by the studio and accomplished in the studio's own photography studio by studio employees.

certainly the off-camera, away-from-production person, felt and touched by the actor intimately, through memory, sensation, aspiration, and breathing. This self has will, which is to say the performer may think it advisable, or desirable, to take a certain path or to avoid one, and the director and his creative team may have conflicting thoughts in the matter. Numerous tales have circulated about the gang of producers walking onto Gore Verbinski's set on the first day Johnny Depp was to appear as Cap'n Jack Sparrow. When they saw him, they loudly balked (golden teeth, ringlets, kohl under the eyes!). He said he'd be happy to resign, and they instantaneously relented. The actor wants to be happy with the look, to know that viewers see onscreen—and, if he watches, to see onscreen himself—a being who relates to the figure he feels, knows, hopes, and remembers himself to be; the figure he would ideally wish seen. This is the case even if the actor would be thrilled to lose the self under the mask (Geoffrey Rush in the same *Pirates* films, for instance): if looking in the mirror actors could find themselves the makeup may have been insufficient.

At the heart of the makeup issue is self-consciousness, a quality that can hinder more than assist the actor's work. The self-conscious person carries about an image of the self; indeed, as the social psychologist Theodore Newcomb taught, what we call the "self" is exactly a picture of an organism held by that same organism. This "self" is both an idealization and a compensation for deficiency. It sets me as I dream myself ideally to be, shifting some valued aspect of myself to the center of any presumed viewer's attention, casting my pimples aside. My self, as I hope to know it, "beautifies" me, highlighting ways in which my physique conforms to culturally accepted standards. And it works to cover problems, or "fills in" what I believe others, looking at me, would regard as such: ears too big?, hairline receding?, shoulders too small?, lips too thick? Nothing is beyond the make-up man's surgery, nowhere is there a performative face that cannot be turned into another face.

In performance, the role will be a mask itself, and a mask also laid on from without. The writer does some of the work, the director some. The set designer, costumer, and make-up artist are heavily involved. The cinematographer does quite a lot. What my head and face look like onscreen will be a function of the lens, the lighting design, the distance and movement of the camera (or my own movement in front of it). A wide-angle lens will squash my features, a little at 44 mm., more at 38, even more at 24, and grotesquely below that. Monstrosities look monstrous, often, because they are photographed in wide angle. The performer's characterological mask is arranged by those who require a certain look, and part of acting work is accession to demand, relaxing into someone else's design, allowing oneself to be seen *without imposing a personal view.* One very good reason for trusting one's director is the opportunity to lose anxiety about one's looks by allowing that one *appears for* someone else; yet at the same time, when a director wishes makeup to radically change an actor's look onscreen, possibilities and eventualities will usually be discussed. (In the Depp case cited above, the actor controlled his look.) Sometimes, for technical reasons involving photography, make-up tests must be done, allowing the actor to catch a glimpse of what the finally realized character will look like.

The made-up *look* is a principal tool the film actor must use in climbing to a virtuosic moment, because ultimately the virtuosic moment has to center on an action of the sort that would believably be committed by the sort of person who looks the way makeup has made the actor look (makeup, as resolved through lighting, film choice, and film processing).

These delicacies are horrendously confounded, muddled, and entangled for both actors and their audience when in off-camera interviews the performer is asked to talk about a characterization, because in most cases the characterization belonged most vitally to other people, who are not being interviewed. Giving oneself to the camera, one is not fully conscious of the outside view of the giving self. It is the internal reality that dominates in acting, for the actor: the clearing, the emptying, the purifying, the simplifying, the diminishing of a "self" to the point where the character can be born (and borne), but the performer must, to achieve any heights at all, relinquish the need to control what it all looks like. Anthony Hopkins, for one case, can speculate, guess, or surmise, afterward, what he may have been doing as he created Hannibal Lecter, may even suspect he tried this or that particular trick. But in the moment he had to somehow become the vile conniver Jonathan Demme needed him to be. Demme was part of that characterization; and Demme was the one who had control of the working environment, the one whose satisfaction concluded a day's work. For making his limp in *I, Claudius* (1976) Derek Jacobi put a stone in his shoe, and so he didn't need to reimagine himself a limper, conceive the form of a limp as an image and imitate it, or think to take on the constricting skin of a man who had spent his life limping, because the stone itself produced the discomfort. What he needed to know was that some bodily adjustment was occurring "already," and that it would have a certain appearance, to which he could play.

It being a matter of team knowledge what the performer can and cannot reasonably do before the camera, the frame within which guidance and requests can be offered him is a carefully limited one: performers must not be subjected to unwarranted "influences" from the surround, so working spaces are guarded. I was on set many years ago whilst the very great actor Glenn Ford shot scenes as the President of the United States. When I got to the soundstage, production assistants in great number approached me smilingly with a warning: "Do not speak to Mr. Ford!" And, "Whatever you do, *don't speak to Mr. Ford!*" And also, "You can roam as you like, but stay away from Mr. Ford!" Having received the message, I was roaming down a slim corridor where through an opened door I saw a very bright room, in a chair at the center of which sat Glenn Ford being made up. His eyes shifted to gaze at me. Blankly. I felt a chill, because I was doing an eye-to-eye contact with the "Mr. Ford" I was to stay away from. Was this "staying away"? Dutifully I kept moving. Soon he came onto the set and in only a few successive takes did his lines with aplomb. The crew were delighted. He stepped into the darkness behind the camera, where I was also standing. He was standing next to me, so tall I had to look up. "What you're doing," said I, softly, "is absolutely incredible." (He was, it seemed to me, channeling Richard M. Nixon. His performance as I had just seen it was, indeed, virtuosic, although he was working in a film with almost no circulation so the performance wasn't much seen.) He looked into my face, broke into a huge smile, and thanked me casually and chummily. A tiny moment, but a moment that revealed something interesting. This President was intended to be terrifying, dominating, imposing, even frightening in his manner. And it wasn't only Glenn Ford effecting these qualities that day. It was the production team, carefully briefed and carefully striving to spread through the set, long before the camera turned, a certain fear of the actor who would be embodying the fearsome character. "Glenn Ford is very, very hard to work with . . ." "Glenn Ford is difficult . . ." "Glenn Ford has everybody in the production on the point of freaking." They laid the dominating power onto him, and when he was on set he permitted this to happen in a graceful, professional, quiet, responsive, helpful way. Another actor who worked with Ford in a very different context much later reported to me that Ford was nothing but friendly and helpful.

I noted earlier that a "self" and "self-concept" can be idealizing and compensatory. But for an actor it can be obstructive and confusing. For an actor at work every moment of attending to flaws that the ego wants to cover over is a moment where the character ceases to be. The possibility of deep engagement with one's character and one's moment, deep engagement that can become virtuosic, lies in leaving the self aside. Because of the power of the lens, even the tiniest flickers of facial expression will be magnified to take over the screen. Earlier, I noted an actor saying that "doing nothing" can be a prophylactic to these disruptive, tangential, awkward flickers of conceit, by which the person strives to move through or step over suddenly remembered flaws. The actor has to know that if there are bodily flaws the production team knows them, and either they will be covered—skillfully— or left to show, for all the best dramatic reasons.

In the virtuosic moment, there is no actor's "self" intruding between the performing energy and the character façade: the energy is entirely channeled into the building up and maintenance of that surface. Lest this seem a precious arrangement, let me stress that all of us, when we are working, have virtuosic moments, moments in which some exceptional and uncanny challenge is met and survived with brilliance, and in any of these moments, for a writer working with words, a carpenter working with wood, an app designer working with codes, a costumer working with fabric, a chef working with tofu, . . . there is no obtrusion of a "self" this side of the work. It is the work that is all-absorbing, the font and repository of all conviction and concentration, the ground of belief, the atmosphere in which projection is possible in whatever light the métier favors. Although the actor has spent rehearsal time looking in the mirror and discerning the face that goes with the name, yet it is already a face not so familiar.

35

Virtuosic Play-Within-Play

FIGURE 35 *Rosamund Pike in* Gone Girl *(David Fincher, Twentieth Century Fox/Regency, 2014). Digital frame enlargement.*

A performer is sometimes called upon to present a virtuosic fakery, that is, a characterological falseness that boldly, spectacularly does *not* pretend to be anything else. A virtuosic lie:

James Stewart, 1952

In mid-career, James Stewart performs in clownface more or less all through Cecil B. DeMille's *The Greatest Show on Earth* (1952). Buttons is a fixture in John North's Ringling Bros. Barnum & Bailey Circus, centerpiece of the film. He wanders the circus "backyard" from friend to friend for casual, helpful, genial, reflective, and generally Jimmy-Stewartesque conversations. With his gangly form, his gentle, extremely recognizable voice, and his delicacy of manner our feeling of ease in identifying him beneath the makeup seems entirely natural. While it may seem incongruous that a major Hollywood star would take on an incognito performance like this, the situation perfectly suited the taste of Stewart, who never ceased being an actor before an icon:

> He heard that Cecil B. DeMille was planning a circus picture in which there was a clown part. He called DeMille up and asked for the role. "It's a very small part," DeMille told him, "and the clown never takes off his makeup." "Is the role essential to the plot?" Jim asked. When DeMille said, "Yes," Jim said, "It's a deal." He was so eager, he even took a 75 percent reduction in his usual asking price. But $50,000 was what the other stars—[Betty] Hutton, [Cornel] Wilde, and so forth—were getting as well. He also agreed, for the first time, to last billing: "And James Stewart as Buttons, a Clown." He made these concessions because, as he put it, "Wal, it's a good part, even if it is short. And I've wanted to work for this man." (Fishgall 226)

The makeup includes a thorough coating of white-face, covered with a pronounced over-mouth painted in red around red lipstick, and a red button nose. He sports a very tiny blue-and-silver striped top hat, of the sort one might imagine proper for a trained monkey laboring for an organ grinder. His hair is of a red somewhere between beet borscht and grated fresh carrots, and it splashes out over his ears in wild shocks meant to give him the air of being goofy, forgetful, and eccentric. There is black around the eyes only to give them accent. The clown figure, speaking generally, is a paradigm of the theatrical type designed for optical perception at a distance, and our Buttons emerges partly from the Commedia's Pierrot in his mask of expressivity laid over a white ground.

We are never far out of touch with "Buttons," and we never have for him anything but the feeling of sweet affection that, in almost all of his film work, Stewart motivates in his audience. But Buttons also has and shows dignity, even nobility, since the "silly" clown's behavior when he is not in front of an audience shows far more couth, far more propriety, and far more attentiveness than one might expect from the hilarious, spontaneous, fun-loving, puppy-toting figure in the ring.

As the film begins, and for some duration, our response to Buttons is just this warm admiration and acceptance, with no crack in the façade. Further, he mobilizes the audience to sympathy in the context of a strange and ironic fact: that as a performer, the clown is improbably *attached to* his clownface, since, oddly, Buttons does not, in fact, take off that mask. (It seems to have become a face; not just makeup *on* a face.) Backstage in everyday clothing, he has the face still fully made up, morning, noon, and night. The effect produced is, at least initially, immense commitment to performativity, true diligence and belief in the role he has adopted in this business concern.

To shed the face in the dressing room, we might feel watching "Buttons," would show cynical detachment, a craven admission that the performed face was only an overlay, easy to doff as one returns to the real (and really treasured) actual self. As Buttons does not effect this return we take him as a committed clown far more than we ever take Stewart as a committed performer: Stewart, after all, goes home, becomes a quiet married man. Buttons has gone beyond only "performing" the clown, and has allowed himself to be wholly transformed: transformed at least in his face, which, for the clown, is pretty much the whole. To conclude: we sense that we are meeting Buttons in whole. The whole person, the whole personality, front stage and back.

But:

We come to learn that Buttons has reason, in fact the best of reasons, for wearing this face all the time. He is a man in hiding, and the clownface is an easy, conventional, and fully effective screen. We may intuit this aspect of his being because the circus manager, Brad Braden (Charlton Heston), a man whose acumen and directness has been fully established (and with which we engage) begins to wonder about, and query him. It is enough without knowing details to be invited into Brad's wondering confidence. If we started by believing that underneath Buttons's greasepaint there was *nothing*; that this man, whoever he once was, somehow changed his nature—alchemy, surrender, intensive conversion—and has become *completely a clown*, we now wonder if instead the greasepaint is being worn by a real man with a real identity, a being as yet unnamed, one without a known past, without a discernable motive for making himself up. Buttons the clown now becomes a mere cover character being worn—being performed—by this unknown man. The unknown man, whoever he is, is the actual character in the story.

The circus parade. Something truly magnificent in the history of cinematic color, on the diegetic surface a display to the paying crowd inside the Big Top, all the performers tricked out in fabulous—although, as we saw in the preparatory moments outside the tent earlier, entirely mocked up—costumes. The women in particular are far beyond stunning, some in shimmering, spangly avocado green gowns, others in midnight jacaranda purple, the horses in matching green, the elephants with jewels, the cowboy horsemen in spanking red and white, and everybody moving past the camera—George Barnes's cumbersome three-strip Technicolor camera—inside the actual circus tent, in front of a predominantly real audience. Buttons is leaping up onto a float and down to the ground again, clutching his pup, gesturing expansively. The parade glides by, to the sound of Dorothy Lamour singing "Lovely Luawana Lady" and Betty Hutton doing Rudolf Friml's "Only a Rose." All is twinkle, saturated color sufficient to cause fainting, the promise of light, the exoticism of pure theatricality.

And old woman seated in the crowd (Lillian Albertson) makes a signal with her folded parasol, and Buttons runs up her way.

Some artful distractions, easy for him, perfectly in tune with his normal act: popping colored paper toward some young kids, letting a little girl open a tin canister from which a set of colored paper balls springs out, tossing the pup up in the air and catching him, then handing him to a little boy for safekeeping. And now he comes to the lady and leans over to her ear.

"Hello, mom!" The Stewart trademarked good-boy voice, in stage whisper.

She is worried. "They have been around asking about you again!"

He soothes her gently, but without delay, because this can be nothing more than a brief pause, the show must go on. As he withdraws he says, "See you again next year," a line that, in this exact context, is heavily fraught with sadness. "Buttons," whoever he really is, has a mother who loves him, and whom he loves, but they can see one another only this way, only through the limiting, teasing veil of the circus.

Inside this little vignette—which is a moment inside the scene—is a particularly sharp moment-within-the-moment, lasting only a few seconds, in which Barnes has framed a portrait two-shot of Stewart and Albertson as he leans her way. He is at screen left, looking up with adoration, and at right, her head very near his, she is canted a little his way and her eyes are in partial turn. He fixes her in his attention, but she, attending to him, is constantly also on the lookout for trouble: his protector, his nurturing womb. The adoration in his eyes is conveyed to the viewer by way of the unshifting direction of his attention, this over and above the fixation onscreen of the eye makeup. But we see that the grinning painted mouth belies his serious attentiveness, and the second mouth, his actual (reddened) mouth within the painted mouth, is determined, hard, resolved, just as the painted mouth is gaudy, displaced, soft, and brazen. From a distance it would look as though the clown were happily grinning at an old lady. But the camera position does not place us at a distance. We are just at the limit of the zone of closeness, able to detect details of "Buttons's" facial gesturing that would be unavailable to the circus audience farther off (DeMille in this way placing us both in the circus tent and in the movie theater at once).

The dual portrait is effected by makeup as well as by the camera. Mother's lips are painted with lipstick, to balance her son's. Her gray hair puffs out from the side of her prim blue hat, roughly the way his red hair sprouts from beneath his tiny blue hat. She is focused on him just as he is focused on her, parties to a clandestine meeting no other circus worker will expect or recognize. He leans angularly her way, she leans angularly his. His adoring masque is balanced by her mask of anxiety, itself balanced by her own struggle to maintain the façade of an entertained customer.

The clown's wearing makeup *backstage* has clued us forcefully to the fact that he is not preserving the clown face because it is in his work contract, since the backstage is the place where work terminates and workers talk with one another about it. The circus management has painted him for performance, but he has painted himself for life. It turns out that the man inside Buttons is far from gay, playful, charming, and stalwart, indeed a fugitive in flight whose protective masquerade is a matter of the greatest seriousness to him. In the moment with Mother, it is this deeper man who is in conversation, not the clown, his alter ego. While he is in the clown identity, and while the clown makeup is particularly stressed onscreen with the sharp contrast between the red mouth, the white face, and the blue hat, that identity in this virtuosic moment is a double fakery. Fake, because clowns are merely characters worn by performers, evanescent, flimsy. Fake, because if Buttons is mounted by a makeup-wearer to entertain the audience he is simultaneously mounted by an unknown, someone unaffiliated with the spirit of Buttons, perhaps an evil unknown. Clowns, like other characters, do always seem at least briefly to be mounted by unknowns underneath, to be puppeted, but the puppeteers are taken to be conventional folk, such as the ones we meet backstage here. The man behind Buttons is only pretending to be one of these. Because he is not the circus performer he has been pretending to be, his creation Buttons is not the clown we take him for.

Does all performance—certainly all screen performance—perhaps work this way, with the puppeteer more unrelated in everyday life than we take him to be? Is Buttons the Clown different in kind from any other performative mask, worn by some actor we suspect we can imagine but who is actually a total stranger?

In the vignette with his mother, Buttons gives us a hardy clue to the misfit between mask and wearer, opening a crack in our blissful acceptance of his "happy" face. The James Stewart underneath the man underneath Buttons may have been even more unrecognizable, just as he was even more untouchable.

Rosamund Pike, 2014

A more explicit case of faked virtuosity, a virtuosic accomplishment that is only a tool, comes in a late scene of David Fincher's *Gone Girl* (2014). SPOILER ALERT! Our thoroughly domesticated protagonist Amy (Rosamund Pike) is seen in a painful, traumatized moment:

241. INT. LAKEHOUSE DINING AREA—DAY

A new camera shoots from PATIO through the glass into the DINING AREA. Amy stumbles into frame past a new Stairmaster and Bowflex. She's in a ripped T-shirt and panties. A length of BINDING trails from one arm and leg: she's been TETHERED to something off camera, unable to reach the door. She looks at the camera and screams silently. Pounds on the glass. Tumbles to the floor, crying. (Flynn, "Yellow Revisions, 9/27/13," 142)

Pike's slender body emphasizes the scantiness of her ripped T and panties, thus helping drive home the acumen and violence with which she was captured and tied up, and the agony she experienced in that condition. Her "look at the camera" is unmistakably given in desperate hope that the video feed is being transmitted somehow—and since we are not informed about the details of the in-house camera setup here, we share her hope—transmitted to some saving agent who will rush to her side. The "silent scream" reads somewhat perfunctorily in the script, but is performed by Pike with unparalleled skill: in an elongated, horrified, trembling, entirely uncontrolled manner, as though the violation to her person has been of the most intimate kind and she feels herself now metaphorized by the torn clothing. Her wail is that of a trapped or sorely wounded wild beast, multidirectional, apparently loud, spasmodic, out of control. Her "pounding on the glass" is a gestural doubling of the scream, a scream of the body. And her "tumbling to the floor, crying" very clearly indicates her sense of destitution, forsakenness, abject humiliation, throbbing pain, and helplessness.

Watching Pike here we are fixed with sharp indication of Amy's victimization, and of her heroism in escaping and making this cry. To call the actor's work here virtuosic is to understate, because the character's body seems even to emerge from the scream to implore the viewer from a close distance. Although in the shot she is relatively small and seen from afar, as though from the in-house television camera, we feel close. With no sound being "recorded" inside the house, her "scream" is entirely mute, and manifestly augmented for being this way.

Here is the succeeding scene:

242. INT. LAKEHOUSE BATHROOM—DAY

In the mirror above the sink, Amy examines her weight, tanline. Pale, thin, beautiful. Aside from the shorter hair, she is back to being AMY. She pulls off some DUCT TAPE, cuts it with a BOX CUTTER. Tests the tape. Then she picks up a BOTTLE of WINE. She uncorks it, pours it out in the sink, peels away the foil. In the mirror we see her lower it and . . . reach beneath her skirt with it. (Flynn, "Blue Draft, 8/29/13," 143)

Here are multiple clues, enchained:

1 That Amy has moved from the dining area where she was destitute on the floor. So, she is no longer so demeaned or wounded as to be immobile, and, perhaps, also no longer destitute. A quick signal.

2   Examines her weight. The way a healthy young woman might do
    at any time. Concerned about herself. But also, perhaps, checking
    on the way she would appear to others: indication that she may at
    this instant be backstage of a performance; thus, that doubt might
    reasonably creep into our reading of the previous scene. We saw: but
    perhaps in error. Error not accidental.

3   Among the things she examines is her tanline. Tan as an indicator of
    physical health and vigor. The tanline was not revealed in Scene 241.
    Is this a woman who had a tanline in the first place, who has been
    indulging herself, not a woman who has been mistreated? "Pale,
    thin, beautiful" has the power of augmenting our suspicions. Thin,
    as in emaciated and conniving? Pale, as in drained of spirit?

4   Pulling off the duct tape shows that the bindings were both (a) not
    so difficult for her to handle, and thus (b) very possibly self-imposed
    in the first place. A confirmation that notwithstanding the look of
    241, Amy was not the victim of a seizure.

5   Using the box cutter, rather than a cruder implement, indicates (a)
    that she is completely prepared for the moment we are watching,
    has arranged to have a sensible tool at hand; box cutters are semi-
    professional; and (b) that she is in a very awake and adept state,
    self-guided, since of all sharp implements box cutters are notoriously
    dangerous when mishandled. Just as the box cutter *could* seriously
    injure her were she actually not in control, it *will not* injure her since
    she is in excellent health.

6   Testing the tape: Now that one use is terminated there's another
    need for strong tape (not that strong tape would be needed in
    any event; she has been giving a performance to camera, we now
    suspect, and the strength of the tape would not read). She tests
    because someone else, someone entirely alien to this scene—such as
    a police officer or judge of some kind—may well examine and test
    the tape to see if it is the *kind of thing* that could have bound and
    disempowered her, as she might well be intending to claim. It will be
    a prop in a later performance, and like all performance props it will
    work best if it is real.

7   The bottle of wine. "Ahhh," we are led to think, "She is going to
    have a moment of delight," but quickly we are disenchanted here,
    too, as she pours the wine into the sink. A direct gesture of dismissal:
    regardless of how expensive this wine was, she has no use for it *as
    wine* at all. The foil peeling might be a little mysterious for some
    viewers, but we will grasp her purpose when

8   she makes to use the "cleaned-up" wine bottle to masturbate. To be
    so in control, and for such a commitment of pleasure, she must be

(a) feeling just fine; and (b) strongly, uninterruptedly self-involved. Thus, Amy is about Amy. In 241, Amy was the helpless passive victim of some stranger, not herself at all. But in 242, "she is back to being AMY," active, in control, directing her movement and, beyond that, directing movement toward ultimate pleasure and fulfillment. But then:

9   we must think, wait!: perhaps it is not for masturbation at all that Amy wants the wine bottle. She is working it vaginally in order to prepare, for readers later on, a proper diagnostic sign of violation. A vaginal exam will be done at a hospital. She is an actor committed to every aspect of the role.

Scene 242 is the complete undoing of Scene 241 in terms of a viewer's reception of information and capacity for interpretation. It is the announcement that the authentic Amy of 241, performed with such virtuosic expressiveness by the talented Rosamund Pike, was in fact only a virtuosic "Amy" being performed by a character; so that Pike is giving us a virtuosity upon a virtuosity, performing a performer (who at first doesn't look like one). Our reading of the first Amy as a character who is genuine (and as a genuine character) of course establishes and facilitates our labelling the second Amy a real being, quite congruent with the formula about plays-within-a-play adduced by Erving Goffman:

The performers-to-be of the inner play are seen going through last-minute preparations before the curtain within a curtain goes up. The paying audience thus gets to see both sides of a stage line. In consequence, they are hardly carried away by the play within the play . . . But again, they find that in being eased out of belief in the play within the play, they are automatically eased into belief concerning the play that contains the play within the play. The more clearly they see that the play within the play merely involves performed characters, the more fully they accept that it is performers who are putting on these characters. But, of course, it is not performers who are putting on these characters; it is characters who are putting on these characters. (*Frame Analysis* 475)

Here, "Amy" and Amy are both played by the brilliant Pike.

In the cases of Buttons and Amy, the character's self-concealment spreads across the entire narrative, but it does not make explicit address to the world at large, notwithstanding that one may choose to detect in these performances a direct address to people's "performance" of everyday life, some indication that behind the polite social façades public "characters" all wear there are working actors of quite another disposition. My point in drawing out these examples is to show that a special kind of virtuosic performativity is at play in them, and that the little shows-within-a-show the characters give by playing "characters" are structurally important in specific, localized, bounded ways, not broadly. "Buttons's" conversation with his mom is a warning to him. Amy's performance is a clue about her. And in both cases, the most powerful virtuosic moment contains elements of sham, disguise, fakery, and artifice.

Sean Connery, 1963

A play-within-a-play can be struck in which a character is kept entirely oblivious to his own "theatrical" participation: that is, in which the paid actor—in the case I will point to, Sean Connery—plays the role of someone who will be "cast in a role" without knowing it. "Buttons" knows he has cast himself in a role; Amy knows she has done so, too. Here now is a scene in *From Russia With Love* (1963) where James Bond, arriving at his hotel room one night and about to run himself a nice hot bath, hears something rustling in the bedroom. He wraps a towel around his waist, picks up his Walther PPK and creeps by way of the balcony through the French doors in order to surprise the intruder. But the intruder is a beautiful woman, naked in his bed. They coo at one another for a few minutes, Tatiana Romanova (Daniela Bianchi) making it plain that she knows all about "Bond, James Bond," and it becomes obvious that they will spend the night there. As he settles in with her, the camera through which we are watching all this pulls upward and back so that we find ourselves in a room behind the headboard of the bed, where two shadowy men with a (different) camera on a tripod are making a movie of the whole scene. Tatiana clearly knew she was helping with a setup, and that James is soon going to be blackmailed. What is virtuosic about Connery in this scene is the smooth, but swift modulations he effects in Bond's tone: tired in the bathroom, turning on the water; lazily wrapped into himself as the steam rises up; suddenly alert, perking his ears; stealthy and catlike as he gets the gun and creeps away; bashful and innocent as he sees who the intruder is; suavely coy, even hilarious, as he banters about a secret coding machine and the perfection of her lips—"You're the most beautiful girl I've ever seen" (quite sincerely, as if in a pickup routine); "I think my mouth . . . is too big" (macro-close shot of the mouth partially open); "No, it's the right size"—and then artfully oblivious as he fades into sexuality. These modulations are not easy to make with pointed exactness as Connery manages, and much of his action occurs in lengthy shots that will be edited to seem fluid and continuous. But through the entire scene, the man who turns the tap on, the man who takes his clothes off, the man who creeps with his gun, even the Lothario—all of them must soon be seen as a self-dupe, and only a self-dupe. He thinks he knows what is going on, but he is wrong. Connery must manage to convince us of Bond's earnestness, but also of his blithe ignorance, his failure to look around more carefully. The spy who feels too much.

What all of these, and other, cases show is that virtuosic moments of performance need not be staged as genuine: indeed, that in working to stage such moments as patently false, actors work out a special kind of virtuosity, that firmly engages not absorption but spectacular disbelief.

36

Upstairs Downstairs

FIGURE 36 *Joan Fontaine in* Rebecca *(Alfred Hitchcock, Selznick International, 1940). Digital frame enlargement.*

The movie screen is both flat and intensely reflective, the latter a product of decades of material research dedicated to producing brightness. The light from the projector hits the screen most strongly in the center, and in earlier decades, especially the 1930s and 1940s, hotspots in the middle of the screen were frequent bugaboos that aroused the passionate concern of filmmakers and engineers. Today there is very high lateral diffusion in cinema screens—a property of the chemistry of the material—so that light will spread evenly across the entire surface. By a convention of cinematography, it happens regularly that when we look at the screen's "deep" picture we forget that we are faced with an immense two-dimensional space that has neither depth nor direction (beyond the fact that one could direct the gaze from the center to the corners, hardly a frequent tack). The screen is spatially uniform.

"Up," "down," "left," "right," "in," and "out" are narrative illusions, codes translated as we work to configure a familiar space.

These much-esteemed "directions" are less characteristic of what we are looking at when we watch a film than reflective of our narrative interests and the graphic codes we prefer for furthering them, graphic codes understood in advance by those who make films. An object placed close to the camera will seem to be nearer to the viewer than an object placed far away (the celebrated nearby coffee cup in Mrs. Sebastian's salon in *Notorious* [1946]; far-off Lars Thorwald smoking his cigarette in the dark, across the courtyard, in *Rear Window* [1954]) whilst actually both types of object, being on the screen as light reflections, are at the same distance from the viewer's eye. "Near" and "far" are formulaic interpretations, not physical facts. In animation, computer-generated just as much as early cel-painted, the formulaic quality is given emphasis. *Spider-Man: Homecoming* (2017) has a striking sequence in which through CGI the Staten Island Ferry splits lengthwise in two, and we see the rip proceeding along the craft from an emplacement at one end, so that it *seems* to come toward us.

Staircase moments inspire a particular interest. A staircase will seem to run up and down, very often in a more than splendid way: broadly, sweepingly, draped with curtains, studded with ornament (see Busby Berkeley's paradigmatic electrified violin number in *Gold Diggers of 1933* [1933]). Whereas it is so regular a feature of film as to pass notice to show characters moving laterally in space, to no particular effect beyond populating a scenic space that is being established—passersby on a sidewalk, for instance, or, as in *The Bourne Ultimatum* [2007], commuters bustling through Waterloo Station)—movement on a staircase tends to imply diegetic meaning. People go up and down stairs choreographically, dramatically, pointedly, and are allocated purpose by us as we view their transit.

Bobby Henrey in *The Fallen Idol* (1948). Claude Rains in *Deception* (1946). Agnes Moorehead in *The Magnificent Ambersons* (1942). Abraham Sofaer in *Stairway to Heaven* (1946). Moira Shearer in *The Red Shoes* (1948). Martin Balsam in *Psycho* (1960).

Regardless of the use of the stairs at any instant—Shearer's Vicki Page "going to lunch" with Anton Walbrook's Lermontov mounts a most splendid stone stair laced with flowering weeds that tickle the hem of her azure cape, in the hills above Monte Carlo—the narrative will always be prepared to define the "up" space as being distinct from, even culturally separated from, the "down" one. "Upstairs" tends to mean (a) situated in a discrete, private zone (such as that of the family bedrooms [Plato retreating to his mother's pink room in *Rebel Without a Cause* (1955)]), a zone strangers do not normally penetrate—hence the abject terror that can be inspired in viewers by a marauding outsider penetrating a home and moving to the upstairs (see, for example, Andreas Katsulas in *The Fugitive* [1993]). Or (b) a zone of "upper-stratum" power, sophistication, and control, as when in a sci-fi film we find the cockpit of a spacecraft "up" (the moon shuttle of *2001: A Space Odyssey* [1968]) or when in an urban thriller the malevolent head honcho of a nefarious corporation inhabits a swank office suite on the top floor of a skyscraper looking out through plate glass at the city, often by night (Michael Douglas's lair in *Wall Street* [1987] or Ronny Cox's in *Total Recall* [1990] or Matthew Goode's gleamy hypermodernist aerie in *Watchmen* [2009]). Or (c) a territory of phantasmal or spiritual elevation and ethereal experience, as when a high priest or lama inhabits a zone that must be reached by climbing upward through dangerous (gravity-defying) mountain passes on rocky "steps" (*Lost Horizon* [1938]) or when the afterlife is posited as being situated "on high" (*Stairway to Heaven*, *Heaven Can Wait* [1978]) or when supernatural power is shown to drop or shoot down from a high position (*Phenomenon* [1996]) or when so-called extraterrestrial experiences are made possible when one transcends earth's gravity and ascends to a high planet or station by means of the "stairway of technology" (*The Space Between Us* [2017]). Or (d) a haven of superior mental power achieved by somehow "climbing the rungs" of learning into an "ivory tower" (*I.Q.* [1994], *A Beautiful Mind* [2001]). Up is not only a nexus in elevation but also a case and a feeling---a proposition---of being elevated.

As "up" is made emphatic already by virtue of elevation, virtuosic moments seem almost normal there. Roy Neary (Richard Dreyfuss) near the top of the Devil's Tower in *Close Encounters of the Third Kind* (1977).

"Down," contrastingly, is earthly, mundane, pedantic, quotidian, routine, laborious, grueling, more physical than conceptual, dirty, vulgar (of the street), and lower (of the body). Godfrey (William Powell) is discovered in *My Man Godfrey* (1936) literally "down in the dumps" (at a City dump site beside the East River, well below the elevated townhouses and apartments that "look down" on all this). The satanic underworld with all it connotes is "down there" (*Legend* [1985], *The Time Machine* [1960]; *Lord of the Rings: The Two Towers* [2002]; *First Men on the Moon* [1964]), the place where an abysmal figure delights in ruling ugly denizens of a fiery darkness.

Virtuosity "down there" is typically hideous, grossly malevolent, out of control. Ernst Stavro Blofeld in his lair, plotting control of the world, in the James Bond movies. Saruman's horrifying Orc-world in *Lord of the Rings* (2001–2003), Tolkien's representation, many claim, of the horrors of the Industrial Revolution.

When a character descends from on high toward camera level, she is approaching a stratum closer to what the viewer occupies as viewer. The act of viewing is taken generally, in itself, to be a mundane and practical act, regardless of how uplifting, how ethereal, how magical the screen fantasy might be. The story as entity could be "elevated" above us only because we take ourselves, watching, to be earthbound and the story to float in an untouchable "higher" zone, even if the setting is characterized as the *boue*

(*Boudu sauvé des eaux* [1932]). We think of our watching selves as being on a neutral surface and the story "lifting" or "lowering" us. As Buckminster Fuller had it, "vertical is to live." When a character ascends or digs down, she moves "away" from us, but also toward some other diegetic zone: a more tranquil, more powerful, more ethereal, more unreal, more abnormal, more remarkable place; or a hell.

Nicholas Ray structures a stunning moment in *Rebel*. Jim has come home from the chickie run, emotionally shaken. It is very late at night. He gulps some milk, and, seeing his father dozing before the television, stretches himself on the sofa, upside-down, his head dangling toward the floor. We cut now to *his upside-down perspective*, that is, a perspective in which everything visible of the domestic space is spread evenly before us (in CinemaScope), with the floor on the ceiling and the ceiling on the floor (one could recall Fred Astaire's "You're All the World to Me"). But now we see (that is, Jim sees) the mother (Ann Doran) flying up a staircase decisively and purposefully, almost as though spiritually, a sprite or ghost; but as the camera revolves through one hundred and eighty degrees to pick up a normal viewpoint (ours but not Jim's) we can see that she has been descending, has left the upstairs sanctum where she had privacy of self and is now situating herself in the public living space, indeed, a space that in other parts of the film she has shown to be beneath her dignity (because of all things she is a pretender to class). It's a "come-down" down there, and she is "coming down" to Jim's level (and to her husband's: he has now awakened). This flight "up" that we saw, but really a dropping down the stairs is a virtuosic moment for Doran, yet it might seem the creation of only the camera. As a worker, she does what virtually anybody would do on a staircase. Indeed, Ernest Haller's rotating camera is vital in making the strange vision possible. But if we look closely we see more: Doran is moving with two styles of gait. In the first shot, as she races "up" the stairs, she is fluid, almost balletic, almost in flight: the movement has the swift urgency but also the perfect grace of Victoria Page's flight away from Lermontov in the brutal finale of *The Red Shoes* (1948) so that, ringing the bell of that earlier flight, Doran very subtly suggests the presence of a mortal moment, if not precisely here then soon to come. When subsequently the camera is turned and, landing, she comes off the bottom step to rush across the living room toward us (toward Jim) she is bent over, anxious, nervous, somewhat stilted. This slight shift in her use of the body gives Doran a distinct quality of being two women: a woman of one kind on the stairs (ascending/descending) and another kind being "down." Before her dialogue cues us, her body has given away the emotional shift.

This virtuosic shot is memorable—aficionados of the film never forget it—but we can easily think to displace it by claiming that it is intended to represent the boy's consciousness more than to appeal to the viewer's, a postulate that actually does nothing to neutralize the aesthetic effect. It will be clear to anyone who sees the moment in a relaxed and open way that Jim's consciousness actually *becomes* our consciousness here, and this exactly because of the emotionally striking, initially confusing, and dramatic nature of the movement in the shot, all produced by Doran working with the camera. She is magically powerful at first, and then a gross threat—especially since it is in a vulnerable, upside-down position that Jim is watching her approach.

Doran's moves are emphatic but not ornamental. The French cabaret performer Georges Guétary does a staircase ascent with great flourish in *An American in Paris* (1951), strapped into a most elegant tuxedo, and with top hat and gleaming cane, chanting "I'll Build a Stairway to Paradise." The particular polish of his smooth (much practiced) technique shows it off as a virtuosic accomplishment. More than a man "doing a song number," he seems to embody the living quintessence of song and staging.

But the situation is heavily designed, and much of the sense of virtuosity is attributable, quite beyond Guétary, to the optical world in which he moves. As he goes up, beat by beat, the song wafting out of him, he is in relative darkness with a single follow spot haloing him. Suddenly more light floods in and we see the stairs lighting up as he touches them, beat, beat, beat, beat, and then a small army of bizarrely dressed elegant female bodies, white drapery hanging on them, a lacy white Eiffel Tower perched on every head. As we catch the background, a sea of scarlet, the camera pulls back to show the whole staircase with immense human candelabras at either side, each one half a dozen girls entwined with candle torches. As he sings in this "chaos," stretching out his arms flamboyantly to display his prowess, his kingdom, and his obedient subjects, Guétary sports a billboard smile. The choreography makes him a god of sorts, climbing from earth past his angelic minions in order to have discourse in the summits: the stage performer with all his art, that is, raising himself to interact with the muses. But invoked, too, is the *monde* of high Parisian fashion, in short, elevation to chic status, a tasty gift to the viewer's imagination, especially in immediately postwar America where many who had heard about the *magnifique Paris* could be thrilled at this guyed-up sample. What is virtuosic about Guétary here is his way of using the voice to extend himself outward from the (massive) staircase, beyond the sphere of the women, beyond even the stage set, for this is all very clearly a stage set being used during a performance before an onscreen paying audience as well as the paying audience watching from without. "I'll build a stairway to paradise . . ./With a new step every day!"

Is Minnelli and Kelly's choreographic idea here, and the Freed unit's use of this particular song, a reference to Powell and Pressburger's *Stairway to Heaven*, in which yet another massive staircase—with its chain of decorative sculptural figures on each side, and moving itself like an unearthly escalator—has a built-in danger: the hero must tread with care lest he be kidnapped into the "other" zone. Just as in *Stairway* the use of the staircase by the sumptuously bewigged Heavenly Judge (Abraham Sofaer) and important members of the court, who are delivered vertically into the sphere of human action below, is arbitrary, theatrical, and delightfully artificial so is the song routine by Guétary artificial, because of the (too) emphatic debonair flair with which he graciously extends his arms, twirls his body, takes up angles pointing upwards and keeps his eyes gazing down at his audience.

Marnie ('Tippi' Hedren) makes a momentary virtuosic climb up the curling staircase in the Rutland mansion near the end of *Marnie* (1964), after having shot her horse Forio. She is in a (catatonic) trance, and her steps are mechanical and chillingly metrical. The camera ascends beside her (on a crane), so that we can concentrate on the muscular action of her body and its rote quality, her blank stare almost purposeless, almost unconscious. A complex array of eye movements, head cantings, and bodily posturings is undertaken by Joan Fontaine descending the De Winter staircase to start the ball in *Rebecca* (1940). Again a tracking camera. Here is a woman who is descending into hell, but doesn't know it. Another fully implicit Joan Fontaine moment has Cary Grant making his way up the staircase in *Suspicion* (1941), with that (very famous) glass of milk for her, a purposive, fixed look in his eyes, as though he has a plan, as though he is in process of executing that plan, as though the execution is an execution: thus the look that feeds her dark suspicion and ours. Yet another case of emergence upward out of a dark nether region is the case of the little ragamuffin Andrew Ray, covered in soot, climbing the stairs from the basement coal room into which he accidentally tumbled into the upper precincts of Queen Victoria's Windsor Castle in *The Mudlark* (1950). Again the camera at the top of the stairs, beckoning, welcoming him. But the camera can also be a cold witness: Tommy Udo (Richard Widmark) pushes wheelchair-bound Mrs. Rizzo (Mildred Dunnock) down a staircase in *Kiss of Death* (1947), the agony of the moment being made predictable and definitive by his placing her first at the lip of the upper landing where the camera waits, too, so that she can see her awful future and we can see her seeing it. This moment more or less established Widmark's screen career, not minimally because of his raucous giggle as she falls.

An especially precarious and emotionally brilliant virtuosity is achieved by James Cagney in the finale shot from *Yankee Doodle Dandy* (1942) where, having concluded his long session with President Roosevelt (an extended flashback from which the entire body of the film flows), George M. Cohan is descending a staircase in the White House. We watch him from the bottom as an extra-diegetic orchestra strikes up "Over There," Cohan's signature tune, and the composer on the steps "hears" it at the same time. He spontaneously dances his way down, ostensibly an old man and yet catching every step perfectly, his rhythmic bouncy steps perfectly synchronized with the downbeats of the tune. This is pride, jubilation, purposiveness, and also compactness, since in this number Cagney's George does not use extreme arm or leg gestures but moves functionally, if also sportily and decoratively.

The functionality of the movement aids the actor in keeping himself precisely positioned on the set, because to shoot this was a dangerous move on his part; he could very easily have lost his step and gone tumbling down the whole flight of stairs. The self-protection should not have been visible to the audience, however, so Cagney covers it with a look of having had a spontaneous thought to kick his legs. It seems something of a natural twitch, albeit in rhythm, that turns into the dance step down the stairs (improvised on the spot by the performer).

In *I Am Love* (2009), Emma, the mistress of a great house in Florence (Tilda Swinton), has come to the door to meet a handsome young man who has just defeated his chum, her son, in a race. Believing the son should have won, he wishes to bring as tribute a beautiful cake he has baked. She shakes hands, admires the cake, and turns to leave. Up the stairs to bed, quickly glancing off-camera to be sure a party of which she is hostess is proceeding nicely. Up, up, all the way up. The young man takes his leave, walks out into the snow. But then:

From outside we glance up to see her draw the curtain and peek at him through her window. This is a perfectly perfunctory, normal, even unnoticeable little gesture that gains force only because walking up the stairs she made no effort to turn and look back. She is stealing a glance. Watching what no one but the audience can see her watch. This is as though to make the open claim, "I wished to look back but I prevented myself." The constraints of her place at her husband's side, and as her son's mother, hold her in thrall. Thus, on the staircase, we feel the tickle of desire for her to pause and give a smile again, but she refuses to do this; and gazing from outside, we are a little disappointed, perhaps, that she exercises her curiosity in such secrecy. If this moment is supremely frustrating for the young man, or for Emma, and for the viewer, it will be resolved later in the film.

If Cagney's was essentially a virtuosity of the physique, the body in emphatic display, Swinton's, also embodied, is more cerebral. If Cagney's Cohan had an idea—celebration!—his body instantly and thoughtlessly conveyed it. Swinton's idea is gossamer delicate, a mere whiff of sentimentality inflecting it. We are seeing a signal of her attention, her reflection, her self-discipline, her desire, all swiftly enjambed and given, each, the smallest conceivable articulation, so that we notice only if we are already swept up in desire. It is worth adding that the act of moving up or down a staircase in distinctive and often complicated clothing, and with a perfectly calibrated sense of ongoing poise in the ascent or descent, a complete lack of jitteriness, off-balance stumbling, or jerkiness in the flow is not an easy one to master, so that even doing a straight climb (Hedren as Marnie; Grant as Johnny Aysgarth; Fontaine as the new Mrs DeWinter) one must work the muscles to move continuously and evenly through vertical space, as though in flotation.

37

Lost in the Stars

FIGURE 37 *Christopher Plummer in* All the Money in the World, *with Mark Wahlberg (Ridley Scott, Imperative Entertainment/Scott Free, 2017). Digital frame enlargement.*

How in today's image culture can it be possible, even normative, for audiences to be blind to virtuosic performance, to be eluded by exceptionally masterful acting under the most difficult circumstances? I will consider some such moments of "lost brilliance," but ask first about the cultural setting in which they are *not* received.

As image and typification, the movie-première crowds pictured in *Singin' in the Rain* (1952) and *The Day of the Locust* (1975)—raving throngs near red carpets, klieg lights, limousines, and stars in mink—while still entertaining, are an anachronism in our Culture of the Image. Those who flocked to such premières (of the 1920s and 1930s) had not spent their youth learning to watch images on television, or raided the Internet, or watched five films a day at festivals. For this earlier, more innocent audience the film image was hardly ubiquitous, was always already an expansive treasure bringing spectacular thrill, and to give viewers today even a hint of the thrill people had in watching, filmmakers must spend millions upon millions of dollars to produce incredible, virtually incomprehensible special effects, such as vast destructions (Krypton in *Man of Steel* [2013]), explosive battle scenes (in *District 9* [2009]), or eerie and complicated transpositions of the human body by way of enormous and visually glowing laboratories full of sparkling equipment (Kevin Bacon in *Hollow Man* [2000]). Such imagery is calculated to render audiences speechless. And by spending formative time in front of imagery about which no comment can successfully be made, viewers have learned to keep their mouths shut in eager, but essentially silent, hunger for more. They do not respond to the images they see.[1]

Consequently, although it is widely known that motion picture images result from the concentrated work of particularly skilled individuals, viewers do not laud these makers, do not extol the richness of the vision. The virtuoso moment tends to go unremarked.

Unremarked not because it is taken for granted, but because the viewer takes unresponsiveness, in general and her own in particular, for granted as normal and expected. Passive reception and digestion of imagery, and constant readiness for ever more of the same, replaces a consciously feelingful participation.

Critical language, serious and popular, has "evolved" with this new, silent viewer in mind, and seeks to address only the most salient, egregious aspects of film, thus furthering the tacit idea that there is no point attempting to dialogue with the screen's complexity. Nor in trying to express how inexpressible the vision is. Speaking back does not, I think, even occur to most film watchers: writing a letter, openly declaring a view, weighing in. Virtuosity now is weightless as air.

To some degree, that virtuosic acting might elude attention is attributable to conventions of the acting profession itself, which endeavor, like medicine or architecture, like the dance, like so many finely developed human creativities, rests on arcane practices and knowledge not widely shared with the uninvolved. Fans have no trouble ogling fantastic accomplishments by sports figures, whose labors seem so transparent; and invoking sports openly because it partakes of the ritual of competition, what Roger Caillois calls *agon*, central in our culture. But the actor's magic is inherently invisible because long tradition has kept it out of public discussion. Many actors who make public appearances in what is guised as a "casual" setting pointedly avoid talking about how they do what they do.

Here are a dozen recent examples of "unrecognized" virtuosic performance—performance that is stunning and special, that lifts itself

---

[1]The few exceptions to this rule are often cited as extraordinary cases: the audience responding to *The Rocky Horror Picture Show* (1975); the singalong *Sound of Music* (1965); the screening of *The Wizard of Oz* (1939) to Pink Floyd's "Dark Side of the Rainbow" after 1973.

out of the plateau of the story, but that has been regarded, if at all, only superficially or only as a way of furthering the publicization of a star image:

- Eddie Redmayne as a sensitive effete with a far too complicated bond to his mother in *Savage Grace* (2007). Sensuous in every imaginable way, and in every scene. Soft spoken and agile—indeed gracile; poetic, bearer of a disturbed personality, finally spasmodically and horrifically violent. When he smokes he contrives to make the cigarette seem a floral, a phallic fingerling, a direct extension of his soft core. The actor's challenge here: making indecisiveness, fragility, lassitude, and an air of privilege all seem attractive in a viewer's tough, aggressive, competitive world. When he holds the cigarette, Redmayne performs a tiny dance gesture with the free fingers of his hand, always in pose, always tasting a pleasure.

- Jessica Chastain in *Molly's Game* (2017): believably an Olympic-level skier at first, then suddenly gravely injured and subjected to a wholesale spinal reconstruction, then unemployed and depressed, then abused by a cheap crook who uses her as an assistant, then, progressively, his helper in running a secret poker game, and then an entrepreneuse who steals the business and goes big time until she is arrested by the FBI on dubious charges and undergoes the legal process. There is hardly a moment in the film when she does not maintain balance precariously on a knife edge, testing situations without really understanding their deep mechanisms, putting herself at risk, dangling a cluster of nervous men like talismans. Chastain's challenge: knowingly performing action in the face of a constant lack of knowledge.

- Kevin Costner (hugely famous for *Bull Durham* [1988], *Field of Dreams* [1989], *Dances with Wolves* [1990], *JFK* [1991], *The Bodyguard* [1992], and the unhappily received *Waterworld* [1995]) appearing somewhat briefly as the psychologist-father of Chastain's Molly in the above film. Wracked with guilt, yet gelidly professional and unctuously controlling, with abusive emotional restraint and intellectual prowess. An intelligent, if not too intelligent, sharply analytical diagnostician who misses no clues, but offers not a jot of warmth. The challenge for him: erasing the famous "Kevin Costner."

- Michelle Williams, as is said "channeling" Marilyn Monroe in *My Week with Marilyn* (2011) to reveal how, in 1956, and trapped with Laurence Olivier in a strange country as they film *The Prince and the Showgirl,* the actress is entirely divorced from control of her own body and feelings. Terrified lest her talent be compared to Olivier's—he has been proclaimed worldwide as a major acting force—unsure of herself in the extreme, yet at the same time magnetic in her

innocent demeanor, especially in a scene where she is brought to
Eton and swamped by a gang of twelve-year-olds in top hats who
think she's the bee's knees. Her challenge: mental and emotional
disintegration and fragility on camera, without ever compromising
charm.

- Christopher Plummer as an Alzheimer's sufferer searching for a Nazi
  war criminal in *Remember* (2015) and again as J. Paul Getty in *All
  the Money in the World* (2018). A character dignified to the point
  of rigid absurdity in the latter, yet never allowed by the actor to
  verge into the absurd: a man terrified of his money, terrified of losing
  his money, and unable to recognize people for what they are. And
  groping desperately for any shred of memory in *Remember*, frail
  because his immediate past has been swallowed in a cloud, slow-
  moving because he does not know the ground on which he steps,
  vitally purposeful, and variably benevolent and evil. In both these
  films Plummer offers a view of aging as linked to power, but power
  not handsomely controlled. Plummer's challenges in both films:
  finely modeled debility, since although he is old enough himself (b.
  1929) he remains energetic, hardy, adventurous and his characters
  are far removed from that.

- Timothée Chalamet in *Call Me by Your Name* (2017), a seventeen-
  year-old boy coming into awareness of his sexual feeling and
  emotional capability through a chance encounter. Chalamet
  was seriously lauded in popular and professional circles for this
  performance, but attention was not paid to the delicacy and
  accomplishment of the work, his tiny moments of uncertain
  modesty, his excitement sheathed by his painful anxiety, and
  his loneliness as expressed through the piano. The challenge to
  the performer here is conveying a distinct, acute sense of thrill,
  something specific enough that any viewer could be brought to a
  memory.

- Tilda Swinton in *I Am Love* (2009), as a poised but terrified woman,
  firmly ensconced in great wealth that only too late is recognized
  by us as hers by falsity. She has been holding her own against the
  amassed force of a great family, and her heart has been purloined
  (see also Pomerance, "Swinton"). This is a character created by
  Swinton to suffer a thousand pains, but incapable of recrimination,
  abuse, revilement, pathetic sadness. For Swinton, the need was to
  eclipse her stunning appearance and noble talent, to convey both
  domestication and domestic imprisonment, helplessness at the same
  time as graceful privilege.

- Charlotte Rampling in *London Spy* (2015): mother of a murdered
  young man who had a secret past. Cold and calculating, withdrawn

into a coil of heavily protected fearful anger. Graceful in the way
that a porcelain vase in a museum is graceful: to be looked at,
but not touched. Her mansion is a museum, the murdered son its
ghost. The challenge for Rampling: to convey attitude, thought,
and sensibility in utter silence (since she has very few lines but
considerable screen time).

- Jim Broadbent in *Le Week-End* (2013) and *The Sense of an Ending*
  (2017), first a sweet and well-intentioned retired professor brought
  face to face with his past in an encounter with a prized student
  who has soared, perhaps too high; then as a gentleman haunted by
  the return of a relationship from his past that is incongruent with
  his present circumstance, especially in a scene where he lunches
  helplessly with his irritated ex-wife. The challenges to Broadbent,
  who is known for extreme articulateness: to maintain a sense of
  vivacity in hesitation, black doubt in reconsideration. Once he was
  sure of things; now he cannot be.

- Saoirse Ronan in *Atonement* (2007), as an ineffably charming
  thirteen-year-old girl in the post-Victorian English upper class. In a
  shocking scene, uncomprehending, stunned, frozen in wonder and
  trepidation she witnesses her older sister having sex with a beau in
  the estate library. The challenge: to convey, visibly, both recognition
  and innocence, both culpability and amazement at once. Very sweet
  and beautiful, she must figure as the cause of a great tragedy.

None of these performative moments received pronounced attention as
virtuosities, largely, one must suspect, because they are all delicate, ornately
formed, precise, and principally momentary, and our culture favors
the gross, the outlandish, and the brutal. Redmayne in *The Danish Girl*
(2015) got far more public attention, for obvious reasons; and as Stephen
Hawking in *The Theory of Everything* (2014) he was both praised and
criticized. Ronan got immense publicity, and an Oscar nomination, for
Lady Bird (2017), while with *Atonement* she was doubtless too young
to solicit consideration. Costner is too firmly established as a major star
(sometimes of films thought dubious) to be taken seriously as a serious and
accomplished actor, so his touching work in *Molly's Game* is obliterated by
the footprint of his reputation. Plummer is so very skillful he is easily taken
for granted.

The contemporary audience may have been silenced by its fascination
with the profusion of screens, platforms, and elaborate applications of
technology, so that virtuosic acting isn't enough to stir emotion. This is a
profound pity, because the artistry and labor involved in acting is far more
complicated to achieve than effects, and far subtler in power. Exceptional as
they may be in brilliance, special effects are essentially a cerebral challenge:
how to do something efficiently and believably for the camera through

careful, but ultimately mechanically calculated work; effects are caught through recognition and identification, not feeling. Virtuosic performance is much more than cerebral. It involves music, movement, spontaneity, honesty, and a display of responsiveness that come only from the fully human and fully engaged spirit directed to the fully human and fully engaged witness.

38

Virtuosity Pianissimo
Virtuosity Forte

FIGURE 38 *Peter Lorre in* Hotel Berlin *(Peter Godfrey, Warner Bros., 1945). Digital frame enlargement.*

It is one thing to say that virtuosity might fully escape notice. But that it might require special, even delicate, attention because it is constructed to be very quiet, is something else. "Pianissimo virtuosity" involves gestures of great but quiet pith: subtleties, hints, undertones, resonances, whispers, often physical smallness. Two notably quiet virtuosities deserve mention in this respect. They seduce and expand our consciousness and feeling, yet each favors modesty, simplicity, brevity, and extraordinary sweetness.

One is Elliott Gould's repeated match-striking gesture in Robert Altman's *The Long Goodbye* (1973), where his Philip Marlowe never seems to lack a cigarette between the lips and is forever, regardless of the location of action, finding a local surface on which to make a flame. The match striking comes to seem analogous to the ritual action of an orthodox Jew touching the *mezuzah* when he enters a house; a way of introducing self to place, of accepting the boundaries and qualities of a locale and finding ground there, and a way of placing the moment in a rhythmic sequence, which, overall, constitutes the "jamming" of the character in the "combo" of the other performances. As Gould is rather tall, there are instances when he must bend a long way over to find the surface appropriate for this action, sometimes all the way to the floor; a move he makes with a dancer's grace and, of course, without losing a beat.[1]

To appreciate a second case we must examine a series of three scenes in George Cukor's *Let's Make Love* (1960). A charming but wholly untalented rich man (Yves Montand) must learn—in order to impress the girl he loves (Marilyn Monroe)—(a) to be funny, (b) to sing, and (c) to dance. Montand's Jean-Marc is inept even when his unlimited monies are being used to pay the best teachers that can be found: Milton Berle, Bing Crosby, and Gene Kelly. Walking around on his ankles, chanting, "Doh, doh, doh," in hopeless imitation of Berle; trying to phrase a song line the way Crosby effortlessly does; and dancing with Gene Kelly, Montand's multiple incapabilities are hilarious, virtuosically on show. The character's being a klutz while rolling in money adds ironic spice. The combination of his desperation and sincere devotion makes his failures all the more spectacular. But on a level barely whispered about, Montand is doing eloquent and difficult work. Viewers of the film would have known in 1960 that Yves Montand was one of the world's great entertainers, a comedian and actor (star of numerous films), a chanteur (in fact a recording artist of merit), and a dancer of real accomplishment. The virtuosity in play here, then, is not just a commitment to humility and self-abasement; it is a devoted but invisible labor against strength, in order to produce fallibilities that are not the performer's at all. In final effect, Jean-Marc's incompetent stumbling is funnier than Berle's; his "singing" has more charm than Crosby's; and his "dance" puts Kelly in the shadow.

In "forte virtuosity," the scene is typically lavish and the performer lavish within it; the act bombastic, emphatic, and unmissable. Yet what makes for difficulty remains beyond the audience's ken. The "Don't Rain on My Parade" number from *Funny Girl* (1968) is a clear example. Barbra Streisand sings a syncopated and fast-paced song while progressing from a train station to a moving train to a dock on New York's west side to a ferry waiting to shuttle her to an ocean liner that has already sailed, ending with the proud (but also bombastic) words, "Mr. Arnstein, here I am!" Notwithstanding that

---

[1]Before being a film actor Gould was a dancer on Broadway.

the sequence, directed by Herbert Ross, is fully lip-synched—the performer is relieved from having to produce long-breathed phrases (characteristic of Streisand's vocal style) while energetically mobilizing a forward stride—two noteworthy challenges arise because the sequence includes many close-ups of the singer's face—that is, especially her mouth—intercalated among long establishing shots of her body in the landscape. The synchronizing of lip movements to the soundtrack must be more precise than we see in other routines of this general type, because jumping in to see the mouth "actually" making the song—in all of these different locales, with all of this motile energy—is one of the thrills of the routine. When the camera swoops very close to the performative body the singing must seem absolutely real. And through facial expressivity, Streisand's Fanny must always be conveying grit and forward-looking drive. So, beyond her lip-synching Streisand must be fully expressive in close-up, whilst never for an instant losing the beat of the song. When a singer is on a stage before an audience, emotional transition can be effected by vocal modulation alone.

So triumphant is the singing in this sequence that the viewer's critical point of view ebbs, casting aside the sort of doubts that could easily flood in because of the fortuitous—far too fortuitous!—camera positions (possible only in artifice), such as moving backward in the air just ahead of the prow of an approaching tugboat. Because we wish to see Fanny arrive on time to catch Nicky, the forward movement of the sequence, its editing, responds to our felt impulse; and the rhythm of the music emulates a chugging motor, pushing us forward.

Another kind of *forte* virtuosity is shown by Matt Damon at a critical moment in *Good Will Hunting* (1997). Will is being interviewed by agents of the NSA for a high-level intelligence job—a real job, that is, that will bring him off the streets and into the high echelons; that will be attached to a real paycheck; that will afford prestige and dignity, exactly the dignity his genius appears to merit. However: Will is politically liberal-Left, incalculably far from the NSA. Seated in front of a huge picture window that opens out upon nothingness, the interviewer confronts him bluntly: "The way I see it, the question isn't, Why *should* you work for the NSA. The question is, Why *shouldn't* you?" Here is Will's reply, delivered by Damon (who also wrote it) in one long matter-of-fact, informative rant, with hardly a breath, and with sentences run together for emphasis:

Why shouldn't I work for the NSA?. . .(laughs) It's a tough one! —But I'll take a shot. (Brief pause.)
    Say I'm workin' at the NSA and somebody puts a code on my desk, somethin' no one else can break. Maybe I take a shot at it and maybe I break it, an' I'm real happy with myself because I did my job well. But maybe that code was the location of some rebel army in North Africa or

the Middle East and once they have that location they bomb the village where the rebels are hidin' and fifteen hundred people I never met, never had no problem with get killed. Now the politicians are sayin', "Oh, send in the marines to secure the area," 'cause they don't give a shit. Won't be their kid over there getting' shot just like it wasn't them when their number got called 'cause they were up pullin' a tour in the National Guard. It'll be some kid from Southie over there takin' shrapnel in the ass. He comes back to find that the plant he used to work at got exported to the country he just got back from, and the guy who put the shrapnel in his ass has got his old job, 'cause he'll work for fifteen cents a day and no bathroom breaks. Meanwhile, he realizes the only reason he was over there in the first place was so that we could install a government that would sell us oil at a good price, and of course the oil companies used the little skirmish over there to scare up domestic oil prices—a cute little ancillary benefit for them, but it ain't helpin' my buddy at two-fifty a gallon. They're taking their sweet time bringin' the oil back, of course, maybe they even took the liberty of hirin' an alcoholic skipper who likes to drink martinis and fuckin' play slalom with the icebergs. It ain't too long 'til he hits one, spills the oil, and kills all the sea life in the North Atlantic. So now my buddy's out of work, he can't afford to drive so he's *walkin'* t'the fuckin' job interviews, which sucks, because the shrapnel in his ass is givin' him chronic hemorrhoids. And meanwhile he's starvin' 'cause every time he tries to get a bite to eat the only blue-plate special they're servin' is North Atlantic scrod with Quaker State. So what did I think? I'm holdin' out for somethin' better. I figure fuck it, while I'm at it why not just shoot my buddy, take his job, give it to a sworn enemy, hike up gas prices, bomb a village, club a baby seal, hit the hash pipe and join the National Guard. I could be elected President.

The effect here is a verbal slide *up* a mountainside, a thrilling escalation and expandingly articulate description of negative effect, murder, exploitation, fraud, and finally political triumph, by implication an accusation of the NSA and a description of a world gone morally, ecologically, economically, and interpersonally amok. What makes the moment virtuosic, beyond the exquisitely sharp, unrepetitive, and pointed text is the thoughtful but essentially unexpressive face Damon presents as he speaks (with the camera moving slowly in to magnify his face onscreen as the monologue proceeds), this neutrality giving thrust to the import of his words. Further thrust is provided by his casual speech mode, cutting off the ends of words, slurring sentences together, employing the rich Boston Southie speech pattern by throwing in an expletive but in a fully casual, merely informative way, as in the buddy "walkin' t'the fuckin' job interviews." It sounds like a real person speaking through a real voice about a real condition, in short, it is a social diagnosis: but abbreviated to its most salient points, spelled out almost mathematically on the blackboard of the interviewer's—and the watcher's—mind.

To ice the cake, Damon keeps his blue eyes focused forward, unaccusing, innocent, matter of fact; and his open mouth never for a second fails to emit a syllable, so that as an expressive face it is entirely absorbing. The tousled hair drops over his forehead boyishly—-genius in the body of someone so young!: so young, that is, so incapable of tactic and malevolence, so earnest in commitment to merely saying what he thinks, describing what he sees. It is a voice to which we should be listening. Only a fool (for instance, the NSA interviewer) could fail to see the world this way.

With Damon here, the curtain of emotion is held back to reveal the magician of rhetoric. But great virtuosity can also be achieved through fidelity to emotion in unguarded display. While the tone of the voice may remain moderate, the modulations of facial expression and body posture can telegraph profound (magnified) meaning. Such is the case with a scene played by Peter Lorre (with Helmut Dantine) in Peter Godfrey's *Hotel Berlin* (1945). Dr. Martin Richter (Dantine) has escaped from Dachau and hidden himself in the guise of a waiter at a large hotel. There he finds another escapee, the "drunken and disillusioned" Professor Johannes Koenig (Lorre), winner of a Nobel Prize, "who acts as the film's conscience" (Youngkin 225). The writer of this bravura material is Jo Pagano, but the material springs to life in the mouth and through the expressive powers of Peter Lorre:

RICHTER: Good morning, Professor Koenig.
KOENIG: Richter! Hmph (*a casual laugh*), Martin Richter. Aren't you happy to see me?
RICHTER: No. What has happened to you since you left Dachau.
KOENIG: (*dreamily*) Dachau. Since then I have been in another place for two months. Not really a place. . . . They don't beat you up like in Dachau, no. They're wonderful specialists there. They put you through what they call a "softening up process." (*Puts on his spectacles, stares at a small wire cage*)
RICHTER: (*eagerly*) I see you're working on your experiments again. That's wonderful, professor!
KOENIG: Oh no no. Ahhh. (*Thinking to self while speaking*) I wouldn't touch them. I wouldn't touch these poor little things. Just let them die a natural death. (*Raising up his posture*) Why, one should think everybody has the right to die a natural death. (*He stands face to face with Richter, then turns sadly away*)
RICHTER: (*pacing up to Koenig from behind, touching his shoulder*) Professor, please get out of this mood. Someday we will be back in Leipzig again. Do you remember our laboratory there? (*At the mention of Leipzig, Koenig has his head in his hand*)

KOENIG: (*purposively*) I do not want to remember anything, do you hear? (*Agonized*) Richter, I do remember. Beautiful laboratories, yes. *Fascinating* experiments. It's not important. (*Throwing himself down onto a divan, arms folded across his chest*)

RICHTER: (*standing over him*) But it *is* important, Professor.

KOENIG: (*softly, cajoling*) Why? Can you tell me why? (*We are looking down at him, his arms behind his head in feigned relaxation*) I only have a right to torture these ... poor little animals if it's for the good of mankind. (*Wry smile*) Mankind, hah. (*Sour face*) Oh, incurable. (*Sitting up, leaning his heavy head on his hand in depression*)

RICHTER: (*with energy*) It was you, Professor. It was you who taught us that nothing, nothing on earth, is more important than science and the integrity of science.

KOENIG: (*he has placed his arm on Richter's shoulder*) But didn't I also teach you that as a scientist you have to have an open mind (*his eyes are wide open*). Science progresses (*with a mocking wave of the hand*)! And in the light of new discoveries we have to discard the old ones (*a hand wave again*), no matter how painful. And they've done it, yes! We Germans. We no longer have to work on animals. We work directly on the human body. (*A new angle shows his wide-eyed, wholly serious face*) Why, in our gas chambers in Birkenau alone, we can exterminate six thousand people in twenty-four hours! We have achieved the complete utilization, even of the corpses (*standing beside Richter, his arm genially on Richter's shoulder*). Aren't you proud of our modern scientists, Martin? (*Shakes his head*)

RICHTER: (*seizing him*) Professor, I came here because I need you! (*Koenig is shaking his head, his brows furrowed, and twisting his mouth as though tasting something bitter*). You told me to come to you when we were in Dachau.

KOENIG: (*pushing him away, turning in disgust*) I do not remember what I said when I was in Dachau. Leave me alone, Martin. Ciao. Go away.

RICHTER: Professor, don't you realize this is the hour we planned and waited for! Now we can fight! (*Koenig has been drinking, now holds his glass with both hands, in close-up*)

KOENIG: (*unbelieving*) Fight .... fight for what? (*Ironic smile*) Maybe for the rebirth of Germany. Maybe you still believe there are some good Germans left.

RICHTER: (*seriously*) Yes.

KOENIG: Amazing! Have you seen them??? Where are they? Maybe here, yes? (*Looking behind him*) ... maybe in the closet (*leads Richter over left, to a standing cupboard*). See? Good Germans! Yes, find them. The good Germans. (*He has opened the closet and sits in it, laughing*) The good German, huh? (*Breaks into uncontrollable laughter, then coughing. In close-up we see his head in his hand, his tortured face*) Have you not read the Bible, Martin Richter? (*A pinky finger in the mouth, reflectively*) God will have forgiven Gomorrah if He could have found *ten* righteous men there. *Ten!* Only ten! But He did not find them, and He destroyed Gomorrah. (*Grave*) There are not ten good Germans left, and He shall destroy Germany. (*He stands, as though to state a scientific fact*) We shall be wiped off the face of the earth. Serves us right. Absolutely right.

Notwithstanding that the subject matter of the dialogue contributes some of its seriousness, import, and specialty—Warner Bros. pressed hard for March 1945 release of the film (an updating of *Grand Hotel* [1932] in World War II terms) before the Russians could invade Berlin (Youngkin 226)—and notwithstanding the brutal truth contained in Koenig's noble comments, watching the scene is an electrifying experience. To see this broken man losing breath, losing hope and the will to continue, but then suddenly finding it again and speaking out; then, fallen back into the shadows of isolating depression, losing that hope and deflating once more, then finding strength again, and offering his concluding proclamation. Lorre continually makes the Professor's head so heavy with care he must hold it up by hand. Lorre's biographer Stephen Youngkin reflects, "On the cutting room floor lay remnants of a larger role, now inexplicably disconnected" (226), this no doubt because three teams of cutters were slaving to slash 50,000 feet of film by 80 percent in five days. Nevertheless, Lorre's arc of emotion in this one scene and his wavering between disillusion and commitment to history are a virtuosic triumph. It is a wonder to see the astoundingly broad range of expression, most particularly with delicate hand gestures, so copious and mutually incomparable, ornamentations of the exquisitely varied facework: "Peter Lorre's mind was like a puppeteer, controlling the strings that pulled each of his facial muscles individually, setting the perfect expression for his role" (Corinne Calvet, qtd. in Youngkin 129).

He had, further, a way of attracting attention with his wide open eyes:

Lorre's eyes told most of the story. Wide-eyed glances, minatory gazes, and baleful looks gave him, in one writer's words, "the appearance of a Buddha contemplating the mysteries and miseries of the human soul." Writers described them as bulging, protruding, globular, and poached. Writer and producer Hal Kanter said they were "very far apart, like a hammerhead shark." (Youngkin 129)

Lorre knew the position of his eyes and used it with calculation. "I defy you to look into both of my eyes at once. You can't do it. Now when I worked with actors that I liked—Bogie was a prime example—I taught him how to act with me: 'Just pick one eye and look at it. The camera will never know the difference'" (Lorre, qtd. in Youngkin 130). In this scene in *Hotel Berlin*, the open-eyed gesture is used minimally and for precise emphasis on particular wordings: "You have to have an open mind"; "We work directly on the human body." And with his voice always in medium amplitude there persists a stunning variation in the range of his vocalizations—imploring, querying, defying, questioning, challenging, informing, venting—and the extraordinary face work that accompanies them.

39

Virtuosity as Event

FIGURE 39 *Joan Crawford in* Mildred Pierce, *with Ann Blyth (Michael Curtiz, Warner Bros., 1945). Digital frame enlargement.*

In cinema, virtuosity stands out from its surround, de-contexts itself almost ceremonially, letting the arc of the plot, the overriding thematic concerns, the interplay of characterizations, even production features all pale and fade as it expands to gain the viewer's complete (however brief) focus. Virtuosity becomes an event. But the marked quality, the standing out, might easily suggest language or meaning but nothing about color, texture, pungency. And color, texture, and pungency make each discreet virtuosity what it is.

Take the prodigious Danny Kaye, working in R. Bruce Humberstone's *Wonder Man* (1945) to incarnate a Russian operatic divo trying to sing into a microphone but stymied by his allergy to flowers. This little routine takes up more than five minutes of screen time, and shows Kaye's typically zany, articulate vocalization at its zaniest and most articulate: the comedy of the Russian singer using Russian words will work only if every syllable is as clear as crystal but the too-clear sneezing obfuscates. Watching the diegetic "act," we forget who the character deeply is; we are heedless of the dramatic circumstances in the story arc. At the end of his routine Kaye will make sure his character drops neatly back into the film structure, but whilst he carries on he soars.

Any moment of virtuosity will work texturally to a degree, touching and "chemically" altering the nature of a scene. When he steps forward in the shadows to gun down Lee Marvin in *The Man Who Shot Liberty Valance* (1962), John Wayne's is a silent and astonishingly swift figuration. Jack Palance gunning down Elisha Cook Jr. in *Shane* (1953) grins lasciviously before pulling the trigger. After dancing "Singin' in the Rain," Kelly *ceremonially* hands his umbrella to a passing cop. In completion these moments completely evanesce: Wayne disappears; Palance goes silent; Kelly strides away.

While narrative and performance must both be structured to make a return possible after a virtuosity, the melody and rhythm of the recaptured ongoingness can be so captivating as to block us from noting an earlier structural necessity: that the film be expressly designed in such a way that a performer in character might temporarily, *and believably,* "leave" through elevation and enlightenment, that is, relinquish normality. That the normality of the story be such as can be simply *set aside.* A temporary normality, as it were; an evadable normality.

A film will depend not only on continuity, careful etching of scene (whether fabular or realistic), and intensive characterization, but also on openings for spasmodic, interrupting eventfulness. Certain actions may be paramount to the plot—in *Wonder Man* Kaye stepping into the body of his twin; in *Liberty Valance* Wayne setting fire to his homestead, built for the woman James Stewart took away from him; in *Shane* Alan Ladd's teaching young Brandon De Wilde what a gun is for—and other moments will be much less so: Vera-Ellen's long dance solo (*Wonder Man* was her debut), Stewart and Vera Miles riding the train, Jean Arthur's beautiful apple pies. Because in the structure of these classical films not every moment is powerful and eventful, the plot contains space from which the performer can take off, space in which the story can be abated. Kaye does so much toggling between the twin brothers he deserves a little rest, and the Russian song moment is a delirious rest. Wayne is so observant and diligently honest in his relations, but there comes a time for pure action. Ladd is unremittingly heroic, even golden, but where will his heroism go in the future if he does not take a moment out of the action for pedagogy? In *Mildred Pierce* (1945) there comes a wholly disturbing moment for Joan Crawford when, as Ann Blyth makes it patently clear she does not really care for her mother one way or the other but wants only to be pampered, the mother, visible only to us, must stifle an emotional response and kiss the daughter goodnight. It's not a major plot moment; in fact, it could be elided from the story as story material. Mildred's self-stifling is brief, but as Crawford manages it utterly spectacular; and made possible because Blyth's Veda is on the cusp of sleep, the light is about to be turned out on the bedside table, the moment between mother and daughter, however sad, is about to fade into history. The story zone is opened as a kind of "empty stage" on which, briefly, an actor may step forward to get the full attention of the viewers for something quite other than the continuing story. Other: not unrelated in shape or color to what has been going on, but shaped and colored in a special way. The virtuosic performance, an event of notable magnitude, is made possible, then, against a background of only partial eventfulness; a partiality that indicates the appropriateness of the viewer's attention safely wavering, of sensible movement in and out of the narrative.

What happens, however, in films that move forward with inexorable eventfulness, films in which each instant is charged with what Justin Wyatt has called "high concept," a condition of intense salability: an emotional outburst, a linguistic eruption, an athletic feat, an act of wanton destruction, an extended torture, a swift-moving display, a concentrated and self-revealing use of artificially generated effects, a powerful sound, a warping or modulation of the image, a character's fictive bodily transformation, a psychological black hole, all enchained in a throbbing and unbroken line? When in blockbuster features a film races through such events—sophisticated surveillings, computer data displays, racing vehicles, gunfire, rooftop chases—all spinning forward with apparently ceaseless impetus, there is no pause for reflection, no uneventful breather. Our reflection would be the (undesirable) antidote to consumption. In action films, even the ostensible "pause" contains a psychological or dramatic revelation about one or more characters, spelled out archly or cryptically so as not to immobilize the racing action of the viewer's thought. The action of the action film takes place *in the viewer's consciousness* much more fully than on the screen. And the churning machine is never escaped.[1]

In contemporary action film, we often see instances of expressive extremity: emotional bombast, megalomaniac pretension, do-or-die gallantry. These riffs are not typically virtuosic: they arise from a pungent line in the script, a telling camera angle, or a facial close-up (often in wide angle), any of which may be dramatically accompanied by a shocking musical

---

[1] In *Modern Times* (1936), Charlie Chaplin produces an unforgettable virtuosic moment by literally falling into a churning machine, a system of conveyors and gears by means of which he has been earning his living, and getting out alive. Here we see stunning athleticism, brilliant conception, ingenious design, and withdrawal from the action of a story that has paused to permit withdrawal. The special design helps us elevate this routine to a level of virtuosity we can consider special (since Chaplin is an unstoppable Fountain of Virtuosity more generally).

beat reverberating through the Dolby sound system. Such instances are definitely emphases, markers of narrative territory, informational as regards character, and signposts to narrative progress. But in these "magnifications," the actor's main contribution is to submit passively to the exigencies of makeup, lighting, lens, angle, costume, dialogue, and direction. Emphasis can be accomplished equally with performers strong and weak, craftsmen skilled and amateur. Contemporary cinema is full of exciting, shocking, emphatic moments featuring unvirtuosic performers: Clive Owen in *Inside Man* (2006); Kate Winslet in *Titanic* (1997); Rooney Mara in *Carol* (2015); Mark Wahlberg in *Patriots Day* (2016). While these actors and countless others in action cinema are talented, inventive, alluring, and convicted in their work, the form does not allow the breathing space in which to achieve virtuosity, a moment when the character is free so that the performer can be free.

40

Indelibles

FIGURE 40 *Burt Lancaster in* The Swimmer *(Frank Perry, Columbia, 1968). Digital frame enlargement.*

Memory fuels perception. We often say a performance or performative moment is unforgettable, that it has made an indelible impact or has had an indelible effect on the way we see film. It would be difficult to watch *Citizen Kane* (1941) without coming away convinced one had seen a number of indelible performances, but especially Orson Welles's. Anthony Hopkins's work in *The Silence of the Lambs* (1991) is widely regarded as indelible— certainly by watchers who are for years afterward unable to eat fava beans. Gloria Swanson in *Sunset Blvd.* (1950), waiting for her close-up. Marilyn Monroe in *Some Like It Hot* (1959), getting the fuzzy end of the lollipop. These performances are certainly virtuosic, but they seem even more: virtuosic forever. Etched upon the surface of time.

Surely the persistence of a performance is related to the viewer's interest in acting, in the fabular, in the stage or screen. Welles's Charles Foster Kane takes his girth and density from the story of which he is the center: he is indelible in a fabular way; and Welles never escapes the story. Hannibal Lecter is clearly an achieved surface, a textbook on performativity—in terms of both the actor's self-guising and the character's propensity for putting on faces: this is indelible in a thespian way. Monroe's Sugar Kane is indelible for the way she occupies space—she is almost unthinkable outside of the dramatic space, and so her lingering performance includes the setting: this is indelible in a staged way. And Norma Desmond is incarnated by an actor legendary from early movies because of her attentiveness to the lens: this performance is indelible cinematically.

Revealing indelibly virtuosic moments can be a way of opening richer, deeper appreciation of the cinema. One particular such moment was watched, originally, by only tiny audiences. Frank Perry's *The Swimmer,* released May 15, 1968, does not rank anywhere among the top box-office hits for that year, and indeed, its box office was notably weak. This was an eccentric vehicle for its star, Burt Lancaster. It was based on an eccentric story by John Cheever, published in the somewhat esoteric *New Yorker*. But Lancaster's Ned Merrill is interesting for anyone interested in the challenges of film acting.

An executive on Park Avenue, Ned has made the "executive" decision to swim all the way home today, that is, crawl through Westchester County quite literally, by using the elegant pools of his neighbors, one after another in a more or less unbroken necklace. At each stop he finds time for a polite, sometimes awkward, sometimes strained, sometimes utterly mysterious conversation that reveals something about his history, something about why he is the man he is today. Reveals and also hides, so that not until the final shot of the film does the puzzle come whole. Each of Ned's conversations—conversational scenes—is laid aside so that he can keep on his way, plunging into the water, swimming beautifully ahead, climbing out, giving a wave, disappearing. What deserves attention here is the one feature of *The Swimmer* least likely to be noticed by filmgoers searching for the story in this existentialist nightmare, namely, Burt Lancaster actually swimming the length of these various pools. Again and again, as the drama of what is unknown and what is gradually coming to be known mounts, we find Neddy stretched full-length onscreen, doing his crawl. Four features of these swimming shots are striking. Working together they build our image of Ned's power, his condition, and his fate: the power of a virtuosity.

- Burt Lancaster would be required to wear a tank suit through the entire film, save a small section of one scene where, to show proper manners to a pair of nudist friends, he takes the suit off. The film will be a display of his body, in other words; not only so that, diegetically, Ned can be seen to be exhibiting his muscles (attracting admiring comment from some of his friends) but so that, supradiegetically, Perry's camera can record the body in motion. The body, its health, its exertion, its laboring, its radiance giving implication of its decline, its passage through time: principal aspects because the film needs to make us reflect on mortality and experience, on our own bodies. The body must be seen again and again not as a support of some social role but as the fundamental structure of our lives. Lancaster is in very good shape here (as per normal). Tall, tanned, muscular, lean, and with what anyone who has seen his work knows is the largest, friendliest smile in show business. All of this embodiment rises to the surface to be seen in fluid motion. Grace, motility, strength, self-control, discipline, aesthetic form—expressed in synthesis as Neddy's embodied self.

- This healthy swarthy body is principally seen in water, however. Lush, seductive, turquoise water, sloshing around the muscles, providing a blanket out of which the head protrudes to breathe. Water illuminated by sunlight is always magically attractive to the eye,[1] but here the very idea of the film is a body subjected to sunlit water continually, in a sequence of additive moments: additive because Ned is going somewhere, and each pause for visitation adds to our speculation about what his terminus might be. The body bejeweled by water and sun, scintillating, but only for a breath, here, now.

- The swimming movements have inherent virtuosity, too, because of Lancaster's perfectly elegant form. He is doing a textbook illustration of a "proper crawl," and his long arms, long body, and barely moving head indicate not only that he is a good swimmer— which he certainly was—but more vitally that Ned is a stickler for formalities. If you're going to do a crawl, do it right. Thus the relationship between the quality of the swimming and the simple elegance of Ned's discourse, his polished manners, his acute sense of passing through other people's territory and yet, at the same time, being their convivial (that is, entitled) neighbor.

- Depth provides a fourth tone in Lancaster's virtuoso act. Shot for shot the water suggests both surface (which Neddy negotiates and breaks to breathe) and incalculable profundity. Depth of memory? He is traveling through the present but also through recollections. Depth of feeling? He discovers his deep longings, accentuated by the passage of time. Depth of confusion? His displacement temporally

---

[1]See David Hockney's *Sun on the Pool, Los Angeles* (1982) and his many other pool paintings.

makes strangers of people he thinks familiar, a problem drawn to a climax near the film's end when he must pass through a public pool, first obliging the guard by washing his feet, then wading past more than a hundred screaming children and adults crammed into a too-confining space. One has the distinct sense of Neddy not quite grasping how this public facility has come to being; nor who he truly is, whether socially above this forced experience or belonging fully to it; nor where he is in time, since he seems surprised by the existence of the pool, and by the argument of a workman and his wife, who want to be paid for a job done long ago that Neddy seems not at all to remember.[2]

The Swimmer is something of a paradox, then. An extended, deeply moving virtuosity executed with liquidity and virtually unknown, uncheered, unremembered for all that it is indelible.

---

[2]The swimming pool as setting for the play of social class, privilege, and loss is eloquently discussed by Iain Sinclair in "Two Swimming Pools or, *Schard*enfreude," in *The Last London: True Fictions from an Unreal City*, London: Oneworld, 2018, 139–63.

41

Virtuosity and "the Virtuoso"

FIGURE 41 *Christopher Reeve in* Deathtrap *(Sidney Lumet, Warner Bros., 1982). Digital frame enlargement.*

Writing in 1976 about the proxemics of advertising, especially about the signaling role of the body in its many constructed poses in advertising photography, Erving Goffman meditates on sign-giving in general:

It is, of course, hardly possible to imagine a society whose members do not routinely read from what is available to the senses something larger, distal, or hidden. Survival is unthinkable without it. Correspondingly, there is a very deep belief in our society, as presumably there is in others, that an object produces signs that are informing about it. Objects are thought to structure the environment immediately around themselves; they cast a shadow, heat up the surround, strew indications, leave an imprint; they impress a part picture of themselves, a portrait that is unintended and not dependent on being attended, yet informing nonetheless whoever is properly placed, trained, and inclined. (6)

This delicious and vital passage needs patient examination.

Consider the claim that "objects are thought to structure the environment immediately around themselves," a statement in which the transitive verbs, here in what I have quoted and in what immediately follows, are not highlighted by the author so as to draw our attention to the arbitrariness of their transitive nature itself. "Objects *structure* the environment," for example, instead of "objects are used in conjunction with extraneous matter by those who would form a structural picture of the environment." To elaborate further: "[objects] cast a shadow" instead of "objects can be subjected to sunlight in such a way that the light casts shadows of them." Or, "[they] heat up the surround" instead of "they are considered the source of a heating up." Goffman is speaking to a widespread *belief* in the "animate" quality of objects, that they *do* things, not that they are involved by us as *we* do things. While we may take signs to be informing about an object, we also seem to consider that those signs are *produced by* that object, in short, that objects self-identify, that objects speak. In the penetrating "read," we take it as routine to move, in interpretation and speculation, *from* the visible surface *to* something "distal," as Goffman writes, "hidden," and by virtue of being in itself invisible something presumably "larger": a moving force, a spirit, a personality, an identity, a perduring state of being.

The alternative to this attributive way of reading, it seems to me, is an ongoingly confused reception of a vast array of signals taken only as themselves (and some people do interpret the world in this way). We should remember that the specific ways in which we attribute motive and character to objects based on their signals can be both limiting and biased. We can be prone to engage in some particular kinds of reading-beneath-the-surface, but not others.

I mention this broad theoretical position in order to make clearer a stubborn diagnosis of performers and their virtuosic work, one made manifest in casual conversation, professional reviewing, even critical studies of performance, perhaps especially for screen acting. One is led to read *from* a moment of virtuosic performance situated in—pinioned to—a filmic exposition *to* the idea of an always-virtuosic, always-especially-talented, prodigious, special, even, in the extreme, sanctified or monstrous personality rendered by nature especially liable to concocting and delivering virtuosity to the willing viewer. The virtuosity, then, is *in* the performer and, barring cataclysmic life changes, remains in residence there "naturally" and "perpetually" as the performative career wends on. This reading of character is one of the roots of the star system. More than in what he or she does, virtuosity is in the virtuoso to the heart.

We examine Bogart being eloquent in *Casablanca* (1942), for instance, and extract a personage named "Bogie," always in some way like Rick, always leaving *some* trace of his continuing self in every act he achieves like a residue for the forensics folk. The styling of the self, a "Bogie," the attachment of it to an action—"Bogie" behavior—depends upon our making extractions of this sort, on our passing from the splendid moment confronting us to something "distal" or "hidden" that we give a name. ("When you name something, it belongs to you," Stephen Paul told me more than fifty years ago. Also: to affix a label is to commodify.) So, in this case, the Bogart of one film moment becomes the enduring "Bogie" of numerous filmic moments by virtue of this presumable if not ostensible underlying, gifted, characteristic, identifiable, lovable self, the "star persona" upon the frame of which successive characters are tacked. Searching, we find Bogie's eloquence everywhere; and finding instances of it, we proceed to detect in them some continuing and repeating characteristic that we can call "the essence." I recall once ages ago being told by a Bogart fanatic, "If you see an image of him, and first cover the eyes and then cover the mouth you will see that he is always smiling and weeping at the same time." Well. Keyword: *always*.

I am actually less interested at the moment in the problem that confronts a virtuosic performer who wishes, or even manages, to change performative style film by film (Jack Palance, Meryl Streep)—or the problem confronting one who wants to embed the self wholly in a present character, thus defying audience expectations to show similarity to earlier characterological selves (Marlon Brando)—than I am with the very different problem a performer encounters when, having been able to show virtuosity at some point before, she or he is not in a position to do so now (for any number of reasons). If this is a case of some quality wearing off, the quality is not star identity per se, it is virtuosic talent, which we take to be inside, always inside, and therefore withering if it does not appear.

I addressed a stunning case at some length in *Johnny Depp Starts Here*. We had been exposed to a magical transformer in *Edward Scissorhands* (1990), then *Arizona Dream* (1993), then *Donnie Brasco* (1997), and numerous other films, but then he jumped into Cap'n Jack Sparrow in the *Pirates of the Caribbean* films. Now he had to be considered a pathetic sell-out, a surrenderer to big-money forces, an actor who was nothing more than a show-off unable or unwilling to disappear inside fictive beings in spectacular moments: because Cap'n Jack was, after all, only a mockery of a fictive character. Edward was desperately lonely in his broken aerie. Axel desperately wanted love in watching home movies with his sad uncle. Donnie lived in desperation on a knife edge with the buoyant Lefty. In *Pirates* there was only superficial clowning, child's play. "What happened to Johnny Depp!!??" as though it was the inherent Deppness producing the work and it had been damaged, quite possibly by Depp himself.

But the history of American film has been filled with cases of virtuosity apparently gone stale, virtuosity lost. Sometimes the performer has aged (the vivacious, tragic Bette Davis of *Dark Victory* [1939] become the sadly weakened but spunky one of *The Whales of August* [1987]; energetic hoofer Fred Astaire in *Top Hat* [1935] later the slow, hardly motile Finian of *Finian's Rainbow* [1968]). Sometimes life circumstances have engulfed him (Richard Burton's acidic emptiness in *The Spy Who Came In from the Cold* [1965] and his rather tepid, almost mailed-in performance in *Where Eagles Dare* [1968]). While, of course, virtuosic power may endure: the sunny charm of Montgomery Clift in *Red River* (1948) and his galvanizing silences in *Judgment at Nuremberg* (1961; performed years after the devastating car accident).

In acting, one's very successful moments may occur out of happenstance, or because conditions happen to be rich, because of a scene partner's work, because of almost anything that could infect or inflect what's in the viewer's field of view but that, kept away from access to it as we are, we do not notice or credit. But there are structural considerations as well. It might not serve as well to seem, at any given point, too egocentric, too much a diva. Often the casual label "diva" is affixed to a performer by workmates when they see personal desire overtaking professional commitment. The continuous expression of virtuosic talent scene after scene in a film could ruin continuity, story development, and performer morale generally, since everyone who works onscreen wishes to be seen, and seen with approbation. This is even more the case today, with the studio system gone and actors with no seven-year contract to protect them. When he made *Kindergarten Cop* in 1990, Arnold Schwarzenegger, formerly an overmuscular tough-guy action hero, was given opportunity to display marvelous comic flair— partly because he was working with children and there was something innately childlike about him as well, partly because he knew timing and had the skill to carry off the humor. When he did *Jingle All the Way* (1996) there are many moments when the same flair returned—once again, the affiliation of the "giant" Arnold with childhood—but in numerous films between those two the virtuosity of his comedic persona waned. In *True Lies* (1994) there are plenty of wry, even ironic moments, but it's not taken as a Schwarzenegger comedy. In *Prelude to a Kiss* (1992) Meg Ryan showed innocence, radiance, and a fully-fleshed presence that never quite returned to the screen afterward. Julia Roberts had the same kind of vivacity in *Pretty Woman* (1990) but not thereafter, although her range and intensity were frequently visible. Is something "inside" these performers degrading through an uncanny radioactive decay? Or are their talents meeting with little situational support?

In order to respect scene partners and show that respect, as well as to preserve the treasury of tricks, actors marshal their talents, display only so much as will make a scene work properly. Opening for a moment of virtuosic display will be consensually agreed upon in production, formally or informally, as it becomes clear that a particular scene is appropriate. In *The Silence of the Lambs* (1991), for example, Anthony Hopkins's flair in the scene where he stares at Jodie Foster through his bars and sniffs her achieves virtuosity in its precision, its timing, its overall punctuality; but it also assists Foster in producing the impression of fearful but courageous presence, a sense that her Clarice Starling is trembling inside as she stands there with her chin up. The two virtuosities work together, and each actor knew what the other was doing and had planned to do.

A different problem is created for the actor when, having produced an intensified virtuosity with which audiences identify and accordingly being identified and lauded, she or he fails to amaze audiences by a wholly different kind of work, also virtuosic but not in the same way. Very shortly after the release of *Silence* (1991), Hopkins played the stiff, formal, self-restrained, yet inherently tender Henry Wilcox in *Howards End* (1992), this time to no special critical acclaim, surely not the sort of acclaim that had attended his Hannibal. He showed virtuosity again, consummately so, but not the flavor audiences had learned to taste, recognize, and then desire.

Do viewers perhaps appreciate virtuosic moments by attaching their feeling not to the magnitude of an expression but to its quality and form (not the portion size but the flavor)? They could in this way become "fans of" a certain style of motion picture or a certain style of characterization, and could look for it again and again: the pablum that guarantees satisfaction. An appeal and demand of this sort accompanied the late 1930s and 1940s career of Bette Davis, who purportedly needed a dominant, steely, articulate, and brave character who could also show some (often limited) capacity for sensuality and sensitivity. The evil, manipulative, inconsiderate twin she played in *A Stolen Life* (1946) didn't fit the formula, and the film had a tepid reception compared with *Now, Voyager* (1942) and her other films of the time. After he had made *Superman* (1978), showing off a goofy gallantry and unselfconscious daring, Christopher Reeve confounded viewer expectations as romantic and imaginative Chicago writer Richard Collier in *Somewhere in Time* (1980), viciously conniving Clifford Anderson in *Deathtrap* (1982), then the dignified but culturally alienated foreigner Lewis in *The Remains of the Day* (1993). In each one of these Christopher Reeve performances, there are moments of stunning virtuosity, but no two are comparable and the Reeve of Clark Kent and Superman is completely missing. In *Remains of the Day* there is a powerful moment when his athletic, tall, beautifully proportioned body is placed inside a larger, even more beautifully proportioned estate chamber, so that he is dwarfed by his circumstances, political, social, and historical, and he conveys a sense of that self-reduction by the way he pauses before speaking to search out the right words.

Perhaps in appreciating any one virtuosic moment onscreen the audience feels entitled to others, that is, to deserve other virtuosic moments similarly to appreciate. "Please, sir, I want some more!" In this sense, every shining virtuosic moment is the harbinger of its own demise, the exciting whisper that if it fails to find its echo leaves us slack in disappointment.

42

Negative Virtuosity

FIGURE 42 *Marlon Brando in* The Godfather *(Francis Ford Coppola, Paramount, 1972). Digital frame enlargement.*

An attractive performance carrying immaculate pedigree can be overdone and only negatively virtuosic, audiences being afforded opportunity to see behavior *as a performance* (a fakery that is an intrinsic, while unscripted, part of a greater fakery, the filmic production itself), worthy of no commitment whatever. The actor has lost touch with the magnitude of his or her own amplification, or is falling off key.

The "mentally ill" character is often a trap for acting of this sort, there sometimes being felt a distinct need to exteriorize, dramatize, make visual some state of being that is essentially invisible. In the much-celebrated *The Three Faces of Eve* (1957), for example, much down-to-earth, realistic detail is summoned in the performative work of the psychiatrist (Lee J. Cobb) and his colleague (Edwin Jerome); in the design of their psychiatric offices; and in the generally mundane tone of the film story outside its central ring, in order that the hyperdramatic work of Joanne Woodward will be modulated from without to seem less caricatured than it is. She is mocking up, and virtually mocking, multiple personality disorder through extreme and intensely contrasting personifications of an uptight housewife and a morally loose type, and it is only when we meet a third version, simple, direct, intelligent, and seemingly "unperformed," that the film seems grounded. The challenge with performing mental disturbance lies in a problematic feature of "mental" film, that the mind does not openly "perform" to camera, this leading audiences and performers alike to the conviction in, and emphatic display of, symptoms. The symptom is not only visible but inherently fascinating. And the performance is often a concatenation of credible symptoms, to the detriment of personality. Thus we find twitching, screaming, extremity of muscular exertion, paralyzed stillness, preposterous claiming, shadowy withdrawal, and so on.

There exist conventions for performing the mentally ill as though they are feature acts in a circus. See the charming (because overperformed) *The King of Hearts* (1966), where a large number of normally careful actors intentionally go "over the top" when their characters escape an asylum: Michel Serrault becoming a spasmodic hairdresser, Jean-Claude Brialy an exceptionally oily courtly gentleman. Or the provocative, challenging, yet often overperformed *Awakenings* (1990) where Robin Williams must encounter symptoms (from Robert De Niro and others) that audiences can credit. Or the chilling but also overperformed *One Flew Over the Cuckoo's Nest* (1975), with its dramatic caricatures. In these films one sees personifications that are unforgettable, but less because they result from virtuosic performance than because performers style them "unforgettably," that is to say, out of harmony. In *Remember* (2015), by contrast, Christopher Plummer performs the grueling effects of a mental condition without spotlighting it, and so the viewer has to keep reminding herself of his condition, just as the character does.

Another potential pitfall, for actors and filmmakers alike, is the death scene. Death having a great social and philosophical weight, *always already*, the only way to make it seem trivial is to attach it to a minor character or extra; when principal characters "die," the moment is automatically spotlit. In *Throne of Blood* (1957), Toshirô Mifune is struck by dozens of arrows, in a carefully framed medium close shot where each arrow flies in from a new angle to strike him in a new spot. This is a neat demonstration of "overkill," diegetically rationalized; and one can feel a directorial gesture, expansive, dramatic, high-pitched. This gesture carries us away from the characterological moment to some degree, distances and softens the death blows by accentuating the presentation: creative virtuosity without question, whilst the actor is entirely passive. Most depictions of violence use some approach to achieve such a commodious distancing and softening. In

Commando (1985) we see dozens of evil henchmen slaughtered by machine-gun fire, each of them dying in a spectacular way that can be achieved only by a trained stuntman doing acrobatics or flying away from (or toward) the camera on cables or from a springboard. The artificiality of the deaths removes us from them. The same happens in the battle scene of John Sturges's *The Magnificent Seven* (1960), with Robert Vaughn accorded an extended, almost balletic collapse in which the ballet supersedes the death; Brad Dexter given a tender pietà; and Charles Bronson administered the attendance of two innocent young boys who have idolized him: all profoundly religious, yet also stagey.

Frodo's death in *Lord of the Rings: The Return of the King* (2003) is hyper-ceremonialized as a mystic voyage to the West (an old mythical theme), replete with decorative barge, dirgeful parade, serious music. The same happened some years earlier, with Johnny Depp's William Blake sent off in a funeral canoe in *Dead Man* (1995), to die peacefully of his bullet wound on a great empty lake. "Great empty lake" as analogy to "curtain slowly falling." In scenes like these, the possibility of virtuosic allure in the death itself is contradicted by grounding conditions. If in truth there are no special, notably talented, flamboyantly expressive but at the same time real and authentic ways to die; if death is death; yet mise-en-scène can usefully aggravate the situation, drawing attention, finally, to itself. In *Pandora and the Flying Dutchman* (1951), Marius Goring becomes a spectacular whirling Dervish of death, playing out for Ava Gardner. This is a bit of choreographic nonsense that emphasizes a moment the film does not wish (cannot afford) to dwell upon otherwise.

The death of Kong is of course a signal dramatic climax in the history of cinema, and at the same time a negative virtuosity, even for the animators. It is the fall, not the falling creature, that captures our attention. This is a structural problem, not easily overcome, since the architectural tower from which the beast tumbles is central to the motif and any visual formation of the tower *as tower* negates a formation of the beast *as beast*. (To see the tower, one must stand at a distance.) In *Saboteur*, just before careening from the Statue of Liberty, Norman Lloyd whimpers how he'll "cling" to Robert Cummings's hand, and this little vocalization is a virtuosic preparation. But the fall that follows is more (and less) than just a fall, because we are given to see that eager, desperate face all the way down, given not a virtuosically desperate man but an optically virtuosic moment. The falling trick is thoroughly undone in *Watchmen* (2009), with Jeffrey Dean Morgan merely an object subject to gravity as he falls from his apartment picture window to the pavement; or early in *Wormwood* (2017), with Peter Sarsgaard dropping from the tenth floor of the Statler Hilton in New York as a mere corpse before we come to know much about him.

The more spectacular the manner of death the less any actorial virtuosity will be seen in the depiction. In *Gone Girl* (2014), Neil Patrick Harris is turned into a bloodbath—visually astonishing, but his performance disappears. Yet what may appear as an unachieved passivity can be something very different indeed. Marlon Brando is virtuosic dying at the conclusion of *The Godfather* (1972), with his Don Corleone in the backyard, playing happily in the sunshine with his little grandson as he teaches him how to use an insecticide sprayer on the plants. He has an orange segment in his mouth, so that he can look like a monster (Brando's improvisation), and he has raised his hands as claws to give the full effect. The kid is squealing with delight. The old man gets up and chases him, over the grass, among some fruit trees, and suddenly, off-beat, *merely* drops to the ground. Here the "mereness" of *merely* is the quintessence of brilliant acting, because it is fully committed investment in the truth of a moment—not the artifice of simulating one. The heart merely gives out, the body merely collapses, there is no display. There is no evocation. And for Brando to produce an action with *no* evocation is a masterful accomplishment. There is no "statement." The death is the end of all evocation, all statement. What was, ceases, and other things—here, the grandson—continue. Here, of course, was Brando's great contribution to screen acting: his ability to perform reality, to be real in the moment, fully, wholly, innocently.

Innocently, without reservation.

In *Don Juan DeMarco* (1994) he is a psychiatrist lounging in bed with his wife (Faye Dunaway). They are playing a private little game, tossing pieces of popcorn up in the air and catching them in their opened mouths. (An homage to the Katharine Hepburn martini-olive gag from *Bringing Up Baby* [1938].) There is something quintessentially beautiful about this scene, because it has the same innocent actuality, now with Brando having infected Dunaway. These two could be nothing other than a couple married for forty years, playing a bedtime game they have played dozens of times before, and being entirely involved in it. When Don Corleone dies, he dies as though playing a game in exactly this way: the body subservient to the laws of nature commanded by the form.

If madness and death are challenges to virtuosity so, and perhaps ultimately, is something I have mentioned briefly, virtuosic "virtuosity," that is, playing a character who, in the context of the filmic tale, is taken by other characters to be, and treated by them as, a "virtuoso." Claude Rains as Alexander Hollenius the virtuoso conductor in *Deception* (1946). Wilhelmenia Wiggins-Fernandez as the diva in *Diva* (1981). Cary Grant as Cole Porter in *Night and Day* (1946). To simulate in some scene a "virtuoso's" performance of "virtuosity," Rains conducting, Wiggins-Fernandez singing, Grant composing at the piano—if the virtuosity on film of Rains, Wiggins-Fernandez, and Grant is virtual virtuosity, this particular form is "virtual" virtual virtuosity—is of course impossible if the actor is not already a virtuoso, and prepared, even at a merely passing narrative moment, to seem so. The character's performed "virtuosity" does not overshadow the actor's virtuosity in performing it, a principal example being Jimmy Cagney's performance of "Yankee Doodle Dandy" in Michael Curtiz's 1942 film of that name. Half spoken, half sung; half danced, half pranced; aware of the audience, blithely wrapped into George M. Cohan's own sense of delight; instructive and definitive, and also dreamy and playful; bounded by the confines of a Broadway stage yet at the same time entirely free from gravity. Cagney escapes gravity not only as Cohan climbing up the proscenium of his stage, but also as himself, climbing the mountain of our imagination.

"I'm . . . a Yankee Doodle Dan- . . . dy," he says at the beginning. We have been hearing the orchestra striking the key, and as he does this line in a kind of augmented whisper, smiling at himself for being what he is saying he is, we hear singing. Not Cagney's singing—he is at present speaking. Our singing. The singing he is invoking as a wizard, inside his viewer's head.

43

Virtuosic Slippage

FIGURE 43 *Ingrid Bergman in* Gaslight, *with Charles Boyer (George Cukor, MGM, 1944). Digital frame enlargement.*

If it is to show extraordinary work, a virtuosic moment must first show work at all, which means, one must be able to observe labor, even highly skilled labor, in extremis. The performer as personality must stand slightly aside from the effort of the performance. Work visible but covert.

While the separation between characters and performers is part of our general understanding, in virtuosity the separation is of a special kind. Goffman refers in *Forms of Talk* to "animation" of speech, this being one of the activities at hand as we watch the actor. An animator is the resource—intellectual, physical, emotional—being employed for the construction of a moment: the lungs being used to power the speaking breath. Goffman also refers to the "author," the actual composer of the enunciation that constitutes the performance; and to the "principal": that entity in the name of which a speech is made. He makes it clear that when talk is produced, there is no need for the animator, the author, and the principal to inhabit the same body and, indeed, we can find in cinema that in many circumstances they do not. Watching performed characters, we take some persons beneath to be animating, and we know that each character is a kind of curtain dressing the animator. This animative separation notwithstanding, however, in the virtuosic moment a different separation is in play.

That is slippage, in which the character is momentarily, and knowingly, set aside so that the actor can make a display of making a display: of picking up the virtuosity, trying it on. Because it is, after all, finally an actor's display, not a character's display, that we admire as virtuosic, even if the display is handled "in character" and even if the character in question seems a virtuoso of sorts already. Watching Kenneth Branagh virtuosically play the virtuoso detective Hercule Poirot, for example, or virtuosic Eddie Redmayne playing the virtuoso physical theorist Stephen Hawking, we do not think or say, "What a marvel is this Poirot!" or "What a marvel is this Hawking!" We know and accept the marvelousness of Poirot, a fiction, because of his commercial history in both publishing, television, and filmmaking. Hawking we know for his eminent, world renowned theorizations, quite independent of the way he is portrayed onscreen. With Branagh and Redmayne here, we focus attention on the worker's working. I have discussed already a way in which virtuosity can go awry, how, for instance, an actor can flail at it so uncontrolledly as to be incapable of getting back into character; or how virtuosity can continue untempered so long that the characterological springboard from which it was generated is completely forgotten. In effective slippage, motion in two directions must be possible at once, the actor leaving the character to the side for a moment and later the character returning and leaving the actor aside. (Leaving, in a "whisper.")

The implicit contract: having come to believe in a fabular construction the viewer is now urged to suspend it for a little while, to neglect it, overcome it, transcend it, take the character entirely for granted in order to see the brave characterization as a thing in itself. It is quite as though a magician were to cry, "Lay aside the thrill of my wonderful trick for a moment and watch carefully as I show you myself doing it." With flamboyant gestures, smiles, courtly bows, and devious twists onstage, magicians do this "crying out" all the time, showing the tricking, not the method.

Regarding performance slippage, several points:

a   During the virtuosic moment suspending the character's existence does not endanger it. The character out of sight is one thing, the character dismantled or dissolved quite another. The performer's style and manner work to convey a continuous delicate touch upon the character who is presently absent, a fond pivotal regard, a sensitive contact, quite as though the character is a favorite of the performer, someone the performer would always wish to have close by but one who could, for the sweetest moment, leave the party. Consider Barbra Streisand's solo numbers in *Funny Girl* (1968) and the way, say with "People," she morphs into the famous singer Barbra Streisand (singing to show herself singing) but away from the famous comedienne Fanny Brice (who never sang the way Streisand does). The lyrics might have intentional meaning at the moment for the fictional Fanny; but it is unmistakably Streisand singing them, Streisand who at other moments entirely *became* Fanny but who now, just for a breath here and there, steps aside to say, "Pssst, it's me."

b   The virtuosic actor can resume the characterization entirely at will, on a breath; that is, the virtuosity can be stopped, is not itself rigidly emplaced in the script or tightly bounded by any features of dramatic organization, such as actors' need to interplay with one another in scenes or the scripted opening for a particular moment. "Entirely at will" means both that the actor can choose the instant to terminate the virtuosity, to bring down the curtain on it, and also a moment to let the character step gently aside to reveal the performative self: to make commentary, as it were, on the performative self in terms of the just-interrupted performance (Robin Williams was expert at this). It is the actor's power alone, through the force of will, because once one is in full swing nothing can stop the virtuosic phrase. In the virtuosic moment the actor works *ad lib*, which means both that he or she can extend the self in any direction as the feeling arises (jazz) and also that like its beginning and ending the duration of the moment is under actorial guidance and the movement back "down" into the regular action thus happens after a duration that is shaped by the performer.

c   Yet notwithstanding the *ad lib* quality of the work, the actor's transition first out of and then back into character, implicit in performance slippage, cannot occur in such a way as to disrupt other actors' work or the dramatic tone of the moment, any more than, say, the cadenza played by a pianist near the end of the first movement of a concerto with orchestra—played and very often actually composed by the pianist—can fruitfully expand and intensify with such complete absence of limitation that one loses a sense of the movement in which the cadenza appears, loses a sense of the orchestra, loses a sense of the concerto, even loses a sense of the concert, too, albeit that only by climbing away from the frame boundary to some calculated height can a cadenza, musical or prosaic, be effected at all. The virtuosity is *by definition* other

than, higher than, more ethereal than the regular material of the
performance, but when as actor one journeys to that precinct one
must be visible as the same being who was embedded in the drama
before (and who will be embedded again later). There is a sense in
which we might expect a virtuosity, being *ad lib,* to be eccentric,
idiosyncratic, one of a kind, but there is a hilariously ironic play
upon these exact performative circumstances in an early sequence
of Armando Iannucci's *The Death of Stalin* (2017) when an entire
(putatively virtuosic) concert must be reprised, audience intact, in
order to satisfy the whim of a dictator.

d   The manifest strengths displayed by the actor in virtuosity—say,
a quality of voice; a physical stature; athletic prowess; dictional
power—are not taken to read onto the character that has slipped
away in more than a tangential way: Hamlet, in "To be or not to
be," has morbid feeling, but the performer is the one with the breath.
The words apply to Hamlet; the speaking does not. Hamlet has the
actor's face, but only the actor has the actor's lungs. Meanwhile the
character, even without virtuosic strengths read in, is not weakened
by the actor's stretch but remains fully intact while being fully on
hold, retrievable with all qualities on display. In *The Thin Man*
(1934), William Powell pours a martini with professional acumen,
a real ballet of virtuosity, and no nonsense; but quickly descends
again into the apparently blithering, charmingly goofy Nick who is
waiting patiently to be re-inhabited. The character need not swell
as the actor swells; in fact the swelling of the actor is designed
to cover the character. We pay not to see characters but to see
actors playing them. Owing to this aspect of virtuosity, that the
character is stable while the actor sings, in performing Shakespeare's
soliloquies, which are like dramaturgical cadenzas, and which are
part of every Shakespeare play, the actor can stretch into virtuosity
without being trapped there and rendered powerless to bring the
character's "everyday" self back into the light. Were the soliloquy
to soliloquize the character to the same degree that it does the actor
on display, there might be no way to "return" the character to the
flow of the drama without making the feelings of the soliloquy seem
false, or at least overwrought. The dialogue alone does not make
for extremity: one can sit calmly and read one of these soliloquies
and it scans quite plainly, like all other text in the play: what makes
for the "dramatic" moment is the *performance of* the soliloquy, not
the thing itself. Doing Hamlet in front of a camera, say, you cannot
possibly seem virtuosic if you activate "To be or not to be" in an
unmarked, unadorned, only everyday tone, that is, a perfunctory and
unnoticeable tone that blends the words into all the

other words Hamlet utters. The tone can surely be constructed as "everyday," but it must be openly, virtuosically constructed as such: dramatized, exaggerated so that it will blatantly seem intentional, the blatantness being the telltale giveaway that this particular Hamlet is so involved in his moment, so tired and bored, he cannot even bring himself to feel emotion when conjuring an image of death. We experience a spectacularly spectacular "everyday." Of course, an actor playing the speech this way must take great pains to avoid a particular pitfall: being seen by the audience as a tired or lazy worker who does not muster the energy to mobilize the script, a performer well *beneath* virtuosity, who finds the play and the character tedious. However it is styled, audiences must *notice* the exceptionality of the "To be or not to be" soliloquy, pick it out as a divergence from the text, treat it as a special moment. This applies generally to soliloquies, and to virtuosities (of which soliloquies are iconic types). Every actor who plays a soliloquy must rise; anyone playing Hamlet is confronted at some point with the daunting challenge of doing "To be or not to be" in his or her own idiosyncratic, special, memorable, and *admirable* way, that is, in his or her own virtuosity, without copying others in an untoward manner or failing to rise to the occasion. Watching a chain of actors onscreen doing this speech, a necklace of virtuosities one after the other—watching how each moves or springs into it from the lines of dialogue that come before, and then moves back out of it when the soliloquy is done, one can appreciate what is stunning about a stunning display. Each Hamlet would be his own being in his own little world; each performer would shape every syllable, every turn of tone, every aspect of the stretch of the glorious moment.

e   And what the above feature—the character remaining at a distance from the performer's virtuosic strengths—really implies, too, is that in any performative setup a character might conceivably be designed and/or performed as a virtuoso without the actor being *seen* as one, since the actor's virtuosity and the character's are distinguishable. Whilst it takes an actor with virtuosic talent to play a virtuosic character, the issue is whether or not the actor puts his peculiar talent on show beside the character or does not. I would put Albert Finney doing Danny in *Night Must Fall* (1964) as a clear virtuoso being virtuosic. Yet when Edith Evans performs Lady Bracknell in *The Importance of Being Earnest* (1952), while the Lady is surely a virtuoso of haughty decorum Evans does not need to seem so at the same moment, so adeptly are the expressions woven into an integrated image of the character's self: this weaving is, of course, Evans's particular virtuosity!, but she hides it.

f In the virtuosic performance, the character becomes a toy (a doll)
   of the actor's, since the actor, now apart, is recognized as activating
   and manipulating it. The character is transformed into a little
   creature reduced in proportion for the moment and capable of being
   referenced tonally or gesturally at will, quite as though being picked
   up and played with as a model simulacrum. A word or phrase can
   be uttered in the character voice while other words or phrases
   are uttered in a voice slightly removed, slightly more decorous, or
   illustrative, or emphatic.

g But at the same time, no matter the exact form of the slippage, the
   actor must without letup remain bonded to the character through
   some umbilicus. The character cannot be cut off, abandoned,
   tossed off into space, like woeful Frank in *2001: A Space Odyssey*
   (1968) once HAL has had the pod sever his oxygen line. The actor
   cannot fly away from the character, but must twist or slide to a
   new position adjacent, or certainly nearby. Actors flying away from
   their characters (who also happen to be actors) extensively populate
   Alejandro Gonzales Iñárritu's *Birdman* (2014), one reason for the
   film's dramatic flatness and its need for spectacles (Edward Norton
   conversing backstage in the nude; Michael Keaton marching in his
   underwear through Times Square in the rain).

h For a spate of time, perhaps very brief, the character is entirely
   forgotten, while never being lost or made nonexistent. Entirely
   forgotten, so that the actor's talent shines forth naked and formed.
   It is this talent that we must be in a position to admire, not the
   character's life effected by means of it. Of course, actors may
   show virtuosity in their manner of mounting characters or having
   characters move through a scene, but when we watch the virtuosity
   we lose sight of the character in order to gain sight of the actor. The
   character Hamlet becomes authorial, and the actor stands out as the
   brave mechanism animating his words.

i If the character is a kind of skin or garment the actor puts on
   for the show and takes off afterward—in filmmaking, dressing
   and undressing daily, or even shot by shot—the actor makes no
   reference to that fact. So, the elaborateness or simplicity, the texture
   or flatness, the comfort or discomfort, the gaudiness or plainness,
   the coloration or discoloration, the ornamentation or the simplicity
   of the characterological form, *in itself,* gets no attention from the
   actor, although, plainly, the actor is making do with all of it, even
   more than making do. Stripping away the grand covering, the
   actor shows no difficulty, broaches no troubles. In slippage the
   same is true in microcosm: the actor slips out of the character with
   no feeling of embarrassment, no sense of being unclothed before

viewers, no self-consciousness as an evaluative being. Watch the extremely complex and brilliant scene in *Silk Stockings* (1957) when Cyd Charisse pulls off one character and becomes another, all the while dancing, and, notably, never showing the least concern or strain in such actions as yanking off stockings and shoes *to the beat* or slipping on a fancy negligee, *to the beat again*. This is all performance (virtuoso performance), yet also a clear model for the slippage that must go on to make such performance possible. In this musical number, Charisse does the slippage at the beginning, by the way she dully marches into the hotel suite, a person incapable of dance or romantic visions, the sort of person who would regard the dancing Ninotchka with some objective skepticism and from a chilly objective distance.

j   During virtuosic moments the actor's style dominates over the character's style—it must—but *entirely without disparagement*, because if the actor showing a performative self were to behave as though the character were beneath consideration, we would lose our capacity to believe in that character. We would lose that capacity because:

k   Once we are confronted with virtuosity our commitment and sense of belief are pinioned to a view of the virtuosic actor. The slightest twinge of expression from the actor will be magnified by the virtuosity, and our sensibility made vulnerable to derangement or at least disturbance. While we are in a position to trust the author, or to trust the principal, it is the animator who gains our trust most fully. Thus, for instance, in the very popular *The Odd Couple* (1968), we pin our belief to Jack Lemmon and Walter Matthau, not to Neil Simon, who stands behind both of them. Regardless of what they say (the lines they utter), it is their way of saying it that counts.

l   Since, when the actor steps out of it, the skin of the character has no value at all, it begins to seem a little like the molted skin of a reptile. If we think of it this way, we must envision that in becoming the character again the actor brings into play some power of revivification, some capacity to make a new skin; and we must hope that the "newness" of the new skin is not so pronounced as to notably differentiate that skin from the old one. Centrally, however, when the character is put aside for a moment, it is a kind of empty balloon, a mannequin. This movement between fleshly living souls and empty shells is the crux of Don Siegel's *Invasion of the Body Snatchers* (1956).

m   In being virtuosic, the actor may make claim to strengths that do not derive specifically from the challenge of doing the particular character presently left aside. One might be playing a vile murderer, yet suddenly speak with a magnificent voice (Orson Welles in *The Stranger* [1946]).

Let us take as an interesting negative case that of Charles Laughton (1899–1962). Here is a much esteemed, if sometimes cantankerous, performer of very great accomplishment and a fetish for disappearing utterly inside his characters. If we look at Javert in *Les Misérables* (1935), Rembrandt van Rijn in *Rembrandt* (1936), Sir Humphrey Pengallan in *Jamaica Inn* (1939), Quasimodo in *The Hunchback of Notre Dame* (1939), Capt. Bligh in *Mutiny on the Bounty* (1935), Earl Janoth in *The Big Clock* (1948), Judge Lord Thomas Horfield in *The Paradine Case* (1949), Henry Hobson in *Hobson's Choice* (1954), Sir Wilfrid Roberts in *Witness for the Prosecution* (1957), Sen. Seabright Cooley in *Advise and Consent* (1962) we find, in every case, characterization out of Hogarth or Reynolds, exquisitely formed, astonishingly detailed, yet no virtuosity at all, while at the same time acting that is generally unsurpassed. Why no virtuosity? Because Laughton is entirely invisible, always, what many call a "consummate professional." He never lets his character slip, he never peeks out. So we never find him at work, never see him excelling in craft, in technique, or in commitment. All we see is the character, and the character cannot itself perform an extradiegetic virtuosity. In *Rembrandt,* our Rembrandt is a master painter, but so wholly that there is no room for a Charles Laughton to squeeze in. Quasimodo is the paragon of hunchbacks, but to find Laughton we must read backstage material: his difficulty with the prosthetics, the unpleasant working conditions. In *Bounty* Bligh is despicable, to the very bone, his corporeality is entirely taken up with it, and Javert in an equal, yet variant, way. In *Witness* there is no room for Laughton because he is forever carried away being the adorably irascible barrister who is going to win the case, fiddling with his window blinds and monocle, riding his escalating device up the stairs, pilfering cigars.

When we stand back from these performances, and others of Laughton's, we can see an actor of culminating virtuosity at work with consistency, articulateness, and panache. But *in* the performances themselves he never takes liberty to show himself in a virtuosic moment.

This is not to claim that virtuosity need be immodest, merely that the virtuosic performer must, even swiftly, reveal the performative self to some degree in order to *be there to be recognized*. There must be an incision in the corpus of the character, through which the actor can escape for a quick breath in front of the audience, making himself visible as the operator.

For a counter-example, in the Townsend study scene of *North by Northwest* (1959), we find James Mason's Vandamm merely counting a beat or two while he maintains his circular movement around the room and his forward gaze. It is as though he is pondering, yet we also know he has made up his mind and is jibing, prodding, provoking, teasing Roger Thornhill: thinking will avail him nothing. Each pause by Mason, between words, after sentences, allows his previous barb, the one just leading into the silence, to evaporate, but also allows the actor to *show that he is letting his lines evaporate this way*, to claim space both in the room and in the corpus of the character. I am prodding this man. I know you are watching me prodding him. I am considering the fact that you are watching me, and also the fact that I am apparently a figure you deem it appropriate to watch. But more: I am letting my comments sink in. The weight of Vandamm's aggressive comments sinks into Thornhill, and into us, comment by comment. As a character Vandamm has found a way to be emphatic, but as an actor Mason is showing that *he believes in creating such a character.*

When we come away from *Mutiny on the Bounty* we think Laughton's Bligh was horrendous; Bligh was something to watch; Bligh was the nadir of the human experience. In short, we come away with Bligh. When we have watched *North by Northwest*, we come away with James Mason.

An especially intoxicating moment is given by Ingrid Bergman in *Gaslight* (1944). We are at Lady Dalroy's soirée, amid a crowd of dignified, richly dressed guests who are assembled to watch a pianist (Jakob Gimpel) perform Beethoven's Waldstein. Paula Alquist and her husband Gregory Anton (Charles Boyer), who has secretly been plotting to drive her mad, make a hasty entrance just before the music, having changed their minds about coming because Paula feels up to it after all, and wishes to honor her old patron Lady Dalroy (Gladys Cooper). When they sit before the piano, Gregory suddenly and demonstratively notices that his pocket watch has gone missing. Here is yet another in a series of disappearing objects, which he has been accusing Paula of pilfering and hiding away; and Paula has of course been in denial. But she is becoming more and more distraught, feeling that indeed she is slowly losing her mind and thus lacking an accurate memory of her own actions. For appreciating the delicate virtuosity about to be on display, it is crucial to understand that through the film so far, step by step and scene by scene, Anton has managed to remove the cognitive and emotional support from his wife, so that she is sensing herself progressively to be unbalanced, and because unbalanced, debilitated. But at the same time, while her distress mounts she has been holding in her fear and her anxiety; the camera has probed enough to discover it, but she has made a point of giving no display, especially to Anton or their presumptuous housemaid Nancy (Angela Lansbury). No display, yet a crumbling self. We are given to expect that Paula is going to implode, literally collapse inward as a result of her ungirded fears and her habit of directing anxiety inward, only inward.

Now at the concert she is of course immediately terrorized by Gregory's discovery, but the music has begun. As the Beethoven wends on, Gregory slowly reaches across Paula's lap and retrieves her reticule, which, now back with him, he proceeds to finger deftly as, out of the sharp corner of her eye, she timorously watches. And yes!, there it is, the pocket watch!

He gives her a reproachful stare and she shrinks into herself again, deeply mortified, perhaps feeling that this is the last straw for her. And suddenly she cannot stifle sobs, which leak out and grow, provoking other listeners to turn and stare. As the music builds her sobs become more and more hysterical (we have the feeling that she is moved by the Beethoven as well as by her fear), shame mixing with guilt mixing with horrified recognition of a darker self mixing with insufferable embarrassment for having insisted on coming to Lady Dalroy's only to ruin the good lady's evening. Paula and Anton of course duck out. But Paula is fragmented, and *the fragmentation is outwardly shown*.

I take this explosion—it is not huge, but the very outpouring of emotion is itself explosive with this woman, given the history of her openly shown self-repression—as indication of two things at once. Reading it in character, we see that Paula has reached and exceeded the limits of her tolerance for pain and distress, her ability to believe in any shred of a sane self. But given that Bergman has been enacting the self-repressions, and with consummate clarity and grace, this moment is also evidence of the actor's letting go, making the decision not to have Paula draw in her feeling at Lady Dalroy's. Especially because it interrupts the music, and at concerts the music is sacrosanct, and *this* music is, of all musics, Beethoven, indeed not only Beethoven but the Waldstein Sonata. The actor cannot possibly be unaware that her character is flooding away here, that she is causing the flood, causing it now, over *this* music.

After all, Paula could now shrink to a silent point, could come as close as possible to ceasing her existence. Yet instead the actor makes the decision to let the impossible emotion fly out, her sobs being not only tearful but also sharp and declarative. Paula has lost her ability to be sociably restrained, but Bergman has decided to let this loss of power come into forceful, visible, audible, embarrassing, discomfiting declaration, for Paula, certainly, but for the audience even more. And to the extent that the address is made to the audience, to the extent that the address screams out, "O, can you not see how mortifying it is for me to ruin the concert this way, yet I cannot stop myself!," it is an address from the actor, since the character does not know of the audience's presence and can make no address in that direction. We feel shaken by this moment not only because, through the transport of fiction, we are associating and identifying with poor Paula but also because brave Ingrid has given us a direct signal: "I am changing my performance style here." That is, "I am making open declaration of Paula's state by making emphasis to the camera. I am doing this. No one else. *And I am doing it for you.*"

This emphasis—magnificent because so very perturbing—is performed with both aplomb and actorial silence, with both gravity and simplicity. Paula merely starts whimpering as she hasn't done before, and in such a way that we can sense Bergman whimpering, too. The actor slips away from the character, just in the way that Paula and her husband slip away from Mrs. Dalroy's ruined soirée.

44

The End or "End" of Virtuosic Performance

FIGURE 44 *Albert Finney in* Night Must Fall, *with Mona Washbourne (Karel Reisz, Lawrence P. Bachmann Productions/MGM British, 1964). Digital frame enlargement.*

There are several ways in which one can speak of an "end" of virtuosity. Who is it for, for example? To whom is it addressed? And for what purpose? The virtuosic moment having inherent excitement and grandeur, it will gain esteem for those qualities if for nothing else. It will seem to exist as a paradigm of splendor. Because virtuosity holds the audience's attention keenly it gives highlight to the display of a performer's ability, helping build a specially accomplished professional identity: identity for the performer through pleasure for the audience. It sells tickets and makes futures.

But more crucially, I think, because acting is an art, not only a technique, the virtuosic moment is finally a garden in which the artist's soul fruits.

Virtuosity makes possible not only expression but ultimate expression, a search for borders and expanses and heights. The performer sometimes feels the need to find satisfaction in such a search.

But there exists a different kind of "end": a terminus, a finale, a completion and dispensation. In considering any virtuosic performance, for example, one can look to the way it climaxes, resolves, and "dissolves" back into the regular plane of performance, the way in which performance ceases to stick out and becomes only as visible, as attractive, as anything else inside the frame: the way the virtuosity ends. With stage acting, when the performer remains in the audience's view the transformation out of virtuosity can require a shift in posture, a re-placement on the stage or in relation to other performers, as well as a shift in enunciatory tone. But cinema does not require that the performer remain "in view." Often a long declamatory speech, given with extreme musical articulation, rising feeling, and expressive embellishment will be followed by a cross-cut to either another (attending) character or some object of reference or an entirely new scene.

A brilliant example of performative declension in climax is a lengthy and calculated harangue by the Fire Chief (Cyril Cusack) in François Truffaut's *Fahrenheit 451* (1966). This pompous toady and his loyal team, including his pet, the secretly rebellious Montag (Oskar Werner), have invaded an old house in which a woman (Bee Duffell) has been housing a clandestine library:

> CHIEF (*gazing around with awe*): Ah, Montag!! I knew it! I knew it . . . Of course, all this—the existence of a secret library—was known in high places. But there was no way of getting at it. (*Coming close to camera, reflecting*) Only once before have I seen . . . so many books, in one place. (*As he reminisces the camera dollies past bookshelves filled to the brim. He gives a nostalgic smile.*) I was just an ordinary fireman at the time—wasn't even qualified to use the flame thrower. IT'S ALL OURS, MONTAG!!

Cinematographer Nicolas Roeg uses bounce light coming up diabolically onto the Chief's face, while Montag, beside him, is lit conventionally. The chief strides around, gazing, touching, fondling, instructing—

> CHIEF: Take my word for it, Montag: there's *nothing* there. (*Montag, beside him, shifts his eyes to his right*) The books have nothing to say. (*He swats at some bookshelves, emptying two of them onto the floor. In extreme close-up we see his face, his eyes narrowing to read.*) Look, these are all novels! (*We see* Othello, Vanity Fair) All about people that never existed! The people that read them, it makes them unhappy with their own lives, makes them want to live in other ways (*we see* Madame Bovary) that can never really be (*we see* Le monde à côté *and* Alice in Wonderland and Alice Through the Looking Glass).

—but also openly thinking:

CHIEF: (*relentlessly pacing, gawking, touching the books*): All this philosophy, let's get rid of it. It's even worse than the novels. Thinkers, philosophers: all of them saying exactly the same thing, "*Only I am right*. The others are all . . . *idiots*."

One tells you that man's destiny is predetermined, the next one says that he has freedom of choice. No, it's just a matter of *fashion*, that's all, philosophy. It's just like Short Dresses This Year, Long Dresses Next Year.

During this long lecture, Cusack is relentlessly in motion, either prowling the library or shifting his facial expression to catch Montag's attention and fixate it on the destruction to come. He is not just a book burner, he is a fanatic, ablaze himself with the thought of the blaze he will cause. The voice is exceedingly eloquent, not forced—Cusack always used such a voice—moving up and down in register to produce musical emphases (of which I give only slight indication with italics) and bolstering the "naturalness" of his argument by dropping his voice, often, to the merely casual, merely quotidian, as though it stands to reason that all of what he is saying is already understood. The scene, already configured to be visually gripping because of the books flying off the shelves, the amount of material in the crammed space, the various colors of the covers, and the prospect of all this going up in flames, is made especially stunning by virtue of this frenzied ramble, delivered with sanctimony but also the greatest ease, a moral lesson, a persuasion. Any viewer could be shocked, as the scene wound on, to find the Chief's appeal somewhat winning: he has an engaging smile, however ironic he intends it to be, and his voice is a cajoling lullaby rather than a haranguing call to arms.

Yet he becomes resentful (in pose, as sophists will do), imitating the resentment of some vast populace, winning them over to the project of eradicating the object of their disaffection: "*Robinson Crusoe*: the negroes didn't like that, because of his man, Friday. And Nietzsche—ahh Nietzsche. The Jews didn't like Nietzsche. Now, here's a book about lung cancer: you see, all the cigarette smokers got into a panic so for everybody's peace of mind—we burn it! (*Picking up another book*) Ahhh, now this one must be *very* profound, *The Ethics of Aristotle*. Now, anybody that read that *must* believe he's a cut above anybody that hadn't. See, it's . . . it's *no good*, Montag. *We've all got to be alike. The only way to be happy is for everyone to be made equal.*"[1]

---

[1] In his journal of the filming, Truffaut expressed personal satisfaction that here and in the other book-burning scenes there are as many books cited as in the eleven films of Jean-Luc Godard all together (126).

A medium-shot portrait closes the act. He stands at screen left, holding out in his hand (toward screen right) a copy of *Mein Kampf*. There is a fully equivocal smile on his face, a shocking gleam of cold pride in his eyes. "We must burn the books, Montag. *All* the books." But now, as a reduction, a remarkable (and remarkably swift) change of key, of tone, of manner: "Sir!" comes an abrupt military voice from off-camera. And with utter peremptoriness, business-like, irked to be drawn from his pleasing reverie back to the task of the morning, "Yes, what's the matter?" The virtuosic moment is wrapped away with the library. The Chief has become only a public servant again. Only a dull man doing his tiring job.

In that final line, Cusack puts on a completely new voice. A commanding, not persuading, voice. A voice of vertically organized routine, exactly the routine from which his oratory has been liberating us.

A similar conclusion to virtuosity through vocal tone occurs in a film I have already mentioned briefly. The signal moment in Fred Zinnemann's *The Member of the Wedding* (1952) has Ethel Waters singing the hymn, "His Eye Is on the Sparrow," along with Julie Harris and Brandon De Wilde. Harris is at screen left, huddled against Waters's right shoulder with her head buried in Waters's neck. De Wilde is on the other side, clutching the other shoulder (and singing with great enthusiasm, if having a little trouble—adorable trouble—hitting some of the notes). The camera provides rich close-ups of each, but especially of Waters (a much-recognized singer, as well as actor), perspiration drizzling down her face, light radiating from her brow, her eyes turned up as though to heaven (but also, therefore, catching key light and becoming the brightest points in the picture). A transport of spirituality is wholly conveyed to the viewer as all three invest themselves in the concluding words of the hymn:

I sing because I'm happy, I sing because I'm free,
For His eye is on the sparrow, and I know He watches me—

—a transport that both results from and metonymizes the intensity of the virtuosic moment altogether. But this elevation cannot be extended past a certain point. When the hymn is over, the spell must be broken.

This is handled by Waters herself, in a beautiful but very tiny little turn, itself a virtuosity. The last word of the hymn, "me," is sung by the little boy alone, upon which Waters instantly says to Harris, rapidly, unmusically, mundanely, and even a little pedagogically, "Frankie you got th'sharpest set o'human bones I ever felt." The trance is over. We are back to "everyday life." Another change of vocal tone here, a voice, as it were, from "off."

Part of the difficulty with virtuosic climax is that the more intense the performance leading up to it, and consequently the higher the key in which the concluding apotheosis must be expressed in order to *seem an apotheosis*, the harder it is to sustain that elevated key for a long time without sounding out of control or insensitive to the inherently musical nature of the moment. The finale must occur either triumphantly (*Star Wars* [1977]), or explosively (*The Long Goodbye* [1973]), or with profound sadness (*West Side Story* [1961]), or comedically (as in *The Errand Boy* [1961], where hopeless Morty has become an executive type himself) but having occurred, it must be done. Done, done, and unmistakably done. At the end of *The Third Man* (1949) a woman strides past a man who has been waiting for her on a road, and without so much as glancing at him keeps going, into the distance. Alida Valli and Joseph Cotten. But what magnitude of distance? How unbearable would be this moment and the virtuosic, stolid grace with which Valli moves, her cold, cold dignity, if we were to see her walking away, walking away, walking away, walking away, walking away, walking away, still walking away, walking even further away, and walking away. And continuing to walk. And walking. And still walking. And walking. . . . We need to see her moving down the road, and then she needs to be gone. Gone for an end. Here the "end" of virtuosity is done through editing, through an editor's decision as to how long the shot should run after it is made clear that Cotten is being left behind, because in filming the camera would simply have turned and turned to give the editor plenty of leeway.

Sometimes a virtuosic performance is terminated through reflection, as when, at the conclusion of a spectacular scene, the audience having been left with a distinct memory trace that perdures long forward into the film, a later moment can offer a *modulated reprise*, that is, a calling back to the earlier scene but in terms radically different, terms that close the door. Typically, a rendition in a major key is reprised in a minor key, and abruptly. A signal example is given in Luca Guadagnino's *A Bigger Splash* (2015) by the actor Ralph Fiennes working in harmony with the cameraman's framing. This is the story of an internationally celebrated rock star (Tilda Swinton) who is having a serious vocal cord problem and cannot speak or sing. Her visiting manager (Fiennes) is a man full of plans, tactics, desires, and spontaneity. One bright afternoon at poolside he is carried away by feeling—by happiness?—and begins to do an imitation of Mick Jagger. He is shown jiggling toward the camera, shoulders raised up, hands tight by his side, and jerking away, all this in definite rhythm as he lip-synchs and sings to a Stones recording of "Worried About You." The camera makes some shots from below gazing up at him in adulation, and this with a slight wide-angle lens that spreads the space and the shape of his approaching form, exaggerating the rhythmic quality of his movement, its delirious spasms, its preposterous (but astoundingly accurate) mimicry. Neither the particular song, nor Jagger's association with it, nor Jagger himself, nor the idea of imitating Jagger or any other singer, nor the abstract idea of imitation have the least connection with the turn of the story at this moment: we are being offered a purely gratuitous song-and-dance gift, coming to us from an actor we had not previously associated with song and dance. Not only is Harry wrapped up in figuring himself as Jagger; Fiennes is, too. And part of our delight lies in the thought, now revealed, that an actor of this stature would be a Jagger fan. But of course he would. Anybody on earth would. And *that* idea of the vastly popular is connected to the "stardom" of Marianne Lane (Swinton), the magnitude of her audience, the myth that surrounds her stage presence. At any rate, the scene is sufficiently remarkable, and also sufficiently surprising (coming out of nowhere, and with such pleasurable intensity and real duration) that after it is done and the film moves on, we remember Harry this way every time we see him. He is a former lover of Marianne's, perhaps a man who loves her now, but also the man who did that song and dance.

Much later in the film, in the half-light of early morn before the sun is fully up, and seen in a long 50-mm shot that makes for a picture of reality, sharpness, and definition, we see that vivacious Harry is dead, seated in yoga position at the very bottom of the pool. The new setup—posture, placement, coloration because of time of day, lighting, the actor's rigid stillness—by contrast with our memory of the old one brings a curtain down boldly, ends if not Harry's dance then the trace of that dance still alive in our memory. Harry is dead because we are dismissing the memory of him.

Looking at ways of terminating virtuosic moments fluidly and coherently, so that they do not "break off" from the flow of a film's continuity, one is quickly brought to a larger, fascinating question: "Can there be too much virtuosity? Endless? Unstoppable?" Could a virtuosic performance be both so intense and so expansive that it covered the entire surface of a film, leaving very little space for the conventional to re-emerge?

Consider a principle of comedic space and time, invoked by Vivian Sobchack in a discussion of Jim Carrey. First, the ability of some performers to "seize the 'tiny' or brief instant chance proffers"—a matter of concern to Laleen Jayamanne writing about Chaplin; and to any improviser (Robin Williams as a paramount case) discovering a flashing doorway opened to (linguistic) opportunity—this ability possibly producing tactical "violations and transformations of conventionally circumscribed ritual time" that might bring on, as well as laughter, terror (203–4); there is a kind of "endless" division of time (204), or again, if we think of the improvised moment, a springing out of a springout from a springout. And then, according to an "argument of unlimited development," proposed in Perelman and Obrechts-Tyteca's *The New Rhetoric*, and invoked as well by Sobchack, a possibility "of always going further in a certain direction without being able to foresee a limit" (204), which is to say, I think, a radical approach to boundary. Might not virtuosity work as comedy does, any one virtuosic moment at once opening itself not only to closure and regression to normality but also to continuity through the accretion of further and further, perhaps "unlimited" virtuosic moments. Virtuosity begetting virtuosity, virtuosity dividing time.

This virtuosic self-expansion seems evident in the remarkable performance given by Albert Finney as Danny in Karel Reisz's *Night Must Fall* (1964 MGM British; a remake of the 1937 Richard Thorpe MGM film starring Robert Montgomery, Dame May Whitty, Rosalind Russell, and Merle Tottenham). A fun-loving, monkeyshines playboy in an English village, Danny shows himself very soon to be a vivacious (and powerful) young man somewhat out of control—we will perhaps conclude later that he is psychotic—taking up his duties as the caregiver of the ailing, aged Mrs Bramson (Mona Washbourne) a little too carelessly, finally diabolically, and attempting to rape her daughter Olivia (Susan Hampshire), as well as getting the housekeeper Dora (Sheila Hancock) pregnant and then coldly abandoning her. Very early on we (but only we) saw him commit a brutal murder, hatcheting a body in the forest and dispensing with it in the local pond. To say Danny is "flippy," a conventional euphemism for manic-depressive or even schizophrenic, is an understatement, and one that might lead to a much shorter development of the virtuosity in performance. This fellow can flip in any number of directions, evil personified, and since the film works largely with facial close-ups we see him in surgical detail, constantly changing his muscularity, constantly modulating his expressions, working up smiles, grimaces, squints, tooth-barings, anxious pensivities, frightened ricti of abject terror, broadly farcical playfulness, and a seemingly limitless chain of other emotive states.

Are any of Danny's faces real, or are they all just miniature performances, miniature expressive virtuosities flaring like rockets and then as swiftly erased as any scene in any film after an editor's brutal cut? He is notably, even oddly conscious of his audience always and we see him switch his face off directly when his body is turned away. There is no instant in the film where one is not conscious of Danny, whether he is onscreen or temporarily off-. No moment when one does not anticipate his deep motives with foreboding, nor any moment when Danny's grip on the viewer's consciousness relaxes. Albeit benefitting from the expert work of Hampshire, Washbourne, and Hancock, the film is a tour de force for Finney, athletic as a beast, passionate with an icy falseness, uncommitted to every gesture he makes.

Of Finney in this film, and of other virtuosities, one has to pose an obvious question: is the performer, incarnating a character who is a show-off, showing off? In the extraordinary display of ability and passion can we see extraordinary fondness for making extraordinary display? Or is such a fondness for making oneself visible exactly countermanded by the scripting of the character, who suffers an unbounded fondness for making himself visible?

Guided and framed by Reisz, Finney is always the central feature of a shot without ever seeming fully conscious: Danny is not conscious of himself; Finney is not conscious of being behind Danny; in short, Danny seems and feels alive. One could contrast, strikingly, the limitlessly capable

Laurence Olivier in *Hamlet* (1948), *Henry V* (1944), or *Richard III* (1955), all glorious productions in which he is himself the director: Olivier always seems aware that as an actor he is central to the moment and central to the production of the film, whereas Finney, who is similarly central to Danny's moments, doesn't seem to know there is a film at all. He has become so like Danny, who doesn't seem aware there is a social world around him, who is borne away on his own blindly hungry wave, as to be Danny. This is perhaps endless virtuosity, a hungry phenomenon that devours all the space around. The characterization perfectly demands a performance like this, the character himself being, in Finney's "absence," the primary virtuoso.

There is a quite different sense in which virtuosity can be thought to "end," however. When acting is supplanted by modeling, a performer's embodied skill replaced by a systematic technical effect, all of the visual array may become virtuosic in the simple sense of especially attention-grabbing, emphatically abnormal, and rhapsodically irrational. We can come to believe in surface-configured-for-screen, a graphic virtuosity that eclipses actorial performance:

- Micro-detail, hitherto invisible, can be rendered with extreme articulateness. Reflections in shiny surfaces (as in *Minority Report* [2002]), activity inside miniature frames within the frame (as in *2001: A Space Odyssey* [1968]), extreme fidelity in reproduction of the notably slender or tiny, such as hair (as in *Monsters, Inc.* [2001]), multiplication of beings or objects in prodigious quantity (*Lord of the Rings: The Two Towers* [2002]; *2012* [2009]).

- New forms of movement can be described (even opened to vicarious "participation") that contradict the laws of gravity (*The Space Between Us* [2017]), or exceed the limits of the body (*Ant-Man* [2015]), or achieve a speed that would be considered dangerous off the screen (*Speed Racer* [2008]) or would be impossible to achieve with live actors in real space because of the limits of insurance policies (*X-Men 2* [2003]).

- The screen can offer a host of specially designed "realities": alien beings (*Jurassic World* [2015]; *Avatar* [2009]; *The Shape of Water* [2017]); irregular places containing conventional objects (*Pirates of the Caribbean: The Curse of the Black Pearl* [2003]) or unconventional objects in regular places (*Close Encounters of the Third Kind* [1977]); recognizable earthling creatures impossible to photograph (*Life of Pi* [2012]; *Rise of the Planet of the Apes* [2011]), or impossible environments (*Prometheus* [2012]; *Sin City* [2005]).

- Special objects can "come to life" much as one saw in animation with Mickey Mouse's broom (*Fantasia* [1940]): magical transforms,

for example (*Harry Potter and the Sorcerer's Stone* [2001]),
eloquently speaking animals (*Doctor Dolittle* [1998]; *The Jungle
Book* [2016]), mundane infrastructure nefariously morphing (the tile
floor in *Terminator 2* [1991]).

- Historically relevant mortal scenes can be revivified to permit
  reenactment (*Titanic* [1997]) or the establishment of fictional
  narrative in realistic territory (*Changeling* [2008], *The Great Gatsby*
  [2013], *Carol* [2015]).

In films using any or all of these modes, the expense of technical achievement
(personnel hours, sophisticated equipment) can be mortgaged against
anticipated profit to be gained from viewers eager to pay for the chance
to see technical rendering. Acting fades and rendering becomes the new
virtuosity. Once technique has elevated it to the plateau of awareness, by
way of exaggeration, surprising representation, and thrilling movement and
color, film itself becomes the object of cinematic perception, and virtuosic
performance, to the degree that it survives, passes into the domain of
technical experts. A similar takeover of cinematic performativity by technical
expertise happened in the major studios in the period 1927–32, as, sound
making its way into movies, engineers from Westinghouse and General
Electric used their oscilloscopes to help determine which actors would be
terminating their careers and which moving forward into a talking future.
Who, today, does mo-cap well; who looks especially good with green-screen
effects?

The triumph of *technology as acting*, so far, has been mo-cap rendering,
which I analyze to some extent in *Moment of Action* and to which in their
books *Digital Visual Effects in Cinema* and *Making Believe* Stephen Prince
and Lisa Bode give extended attention. With mo-cap, a living performer
(Andy Serkis for Gollum and Caesar the Ape in the *Rings* and *Planet of
the Apes* franchises, Jeff Bridges for *TRON: Legacy* [2010]) is fitted with
a large array of LED lights covering the skin-tight gray or colorless suit
he is wearing. He performs the scene as a kind of dance inside a bounded
space called the "Volume." With a cream or latex paint marker dots are also
laid onto the face. Cameras running from an overhead grid track the balls
through space, making a "data cloud." Mo-cap finally relies on a variant of
the traveling matte technique, today the green screen, making possible the
central moving object's configuration, by digital artists, as virtually any kind
of creature or object, the living performer constituting only the base skeletal
structure upon which the ultimate "performative surface" will be laid. While
mo-cap filming on set demands extraordinary athletic capacity and dancer-
like facility in movement, and very often a lively imagination (because scene
partners and vital props are excluded in filming, to be "filled in" later), it is
finally not the mo-cap performer who is "in performance." The virtuosity
in front of the camera, such as it is, will be entirely hidden by the fictional

surface, laid on with ever-increasing subtlety so as to trick the eye of viewers looking for evidence of the labor. This "viewing eye" is predicted and known by producers and filmmakers as the cultured receptor of such effects, the viewing experience now converted into a game in which recognizing and revealing professional secrets is a central value. Rather than falling for effects, watchers now wish to pointedly—and rationally—appreciate and decode them. And the effects master is the virtuoso.

A new skepticism is thus born with digital effects, differing in structure and format from any viewer's potential doubt as to the "reality" of the cinematic world. Doubt is joined to the movement away from the everyday and into the viewing domain, the transformation of the viewer. While any actor in performance could be decoded as merely a worker pretending to a play, the engaged viewer does not generally see film performance this way, indeed a willing rejection of analysis is part of what the viewer donates to the film experience. The new "skepticism" is founded on keeping up with the Joneses, the Joneses in this case being the engineering team devising and executing the computer-based world of the film, a team entirely accepted (even revered) as secretly present and at work. The new "pleasure" comes in detecting and knowing about developing techniques, reading about them in offscreen publications, talking about them with friends, and in general holding filmmakers who work digitally up to new standards of achievement all the time.

David Conley, the genius behind the tiger in *Life of Pi,* the ape in *Rise of the Planet of the Apes,* and much else on contemporary screens, reflected to me that "Some actors absolutely despise the [mo-cap] process, and don't want to have anything to do with it" (see Pomerance, *Moment* 45). I find in this reflection something profound and moving. That an actor might exist who doesn't "want anything to do with" mo-cap suggests a separation between computerized presentation and embodied performance, a sense at least some actors have that what they do when they are in role is radically different from offering a skeletal substructure of reliably verisimilar movement and posture. They do not see themselves as dancing mannequins—only a step away from the automata of the eighteenth century.

In virtuosic acting, the standards of achievement are not, nor have ever been, rooted in mechanism, extrinsic impression-fostering, mannerism. Standards are invariably personal: idiosyncratic to the emotions and physique of the performer, in and of the moment, and relevant to the emergent contingent context of the playfulness. The virtuosity only appears spontaneous, as performers must know in advance, to some degree, what they will do and when they will do it; but in any virtuosic performance there is bound to be real spontaneity, real improvisation, the springing and blossoming of phrasing being one of virtuosity's constitutive characteristics. (We may love to imagine that stage performance occupies a real living moment while cinematic performance, recorded on film, thus replayable, abstracts *out of* the living flow; but this is hardly fully true; actors in front of the camera are living their lives, take by take, as they work, and the record—the film—is based on, and contains, this actual, visible living.) How an actor can stand out virtuosically, to what degree, and to what end all vary with context, as does the music of the virtuosity and its eventual dissolution into silence.

CODA

A Thought of Conclusion

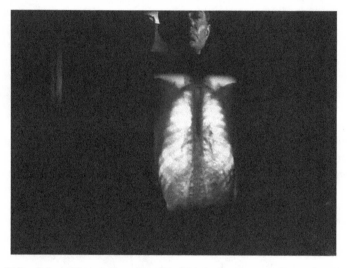

FIGURE 45 *Detail, James Mason in* Bigger Than Life *(Nicholas Ray, Twentieth Century Fox, 1956). Digital frame enlargement.*

In 1933 William Butler Yeats, not only a loyal citizen of the stage community but one of our greatest poets, published "The Circus Animals' Desertion," with these lines:

Players and painted stage took all my love
And not those things that they were emblems of.

How very effortlessly could this be read in a kind of reflective chagrin, and interpreted along the lines of Louis Malle's *My Dinner with André* (1981) where a disturbing echo sounds of Ingmar Bergman's *Autumn Sonata* (1978) in which the character played by Ingrid Bergman says, "I always lived in my art, not in my life." One might feel regret in having committed oneself fully to performance, thus to the delicate frame in which performance lives, as though in mundane reality some shining hope resides to which one should properly, instead, have attended. Things more important than pictures of things. Life more important than performance.

These pages have intentionally addressed interesting complications of performance and one's commitment to it; of virtuosic performance and its limits. Much has been written by numerous scholars and aficionados about one special feature of screen performance, inevitably present in virtuosic moments but there to be seen at other moments of acting as well: that the actor *as a person* is not experienced, so that the character as a person can be. We meet the character, but the character only. Albeit watching with care we encounter only a stranger.

Vivian Sobchack has given considerable attention to the problem of what we might call the stratification of being in cinematic performance in her essay, "Being on the Screen." And my own *Johnny Depp Starts Here* also attends to the confounding effect of the actor's invisible inaccessible personal being. In these present pages I have invoked the mystery several times. That our every touch upon a film character reaches an apogee where he or she is recognizable as surface, not a superficial skin but only a picture of superficial skin, a screen for reflecting light. The virtuosic performance is stunning partly because it invokes the presence of a motivating genius, a spirit of unbounded capability mobilizing and animating it, if invisibly so, except that it is only the result of the mobilization and animation that is plainly on view. The character and the actor, then. But beneath that actor— not only a person engendering this "living" being for us (an exchange value for the audience) but also a contracted worker directed, supervised, shaped, and paid (a use value for the producer)—lives a person who one day in the past made the decision to become the performer he or she is today: a citizen *who transformed him- or herself into* an actor. And while the actorial presence below or behind the character is virtually impossible to discern with surety, the citizen beneath that actor is utterly unknown to the greater audience.

And as we are enchanted by the surface of presentation, we can only speculate as to what makes it glow. Throughout this analysis, it has been taken as a foregone conclusion that of course the deeper structure is something dark and beyond us, a zone and formation that can only be surmised; that what we are given in the virtuosic moment, for all its sparkle and power, is a mere hint. These chapters have attempted to sketch a number of the facets and contingencies of virtuosic performance: the sorts of challenge that face the performer, the nuances of carriage and execution that must be available to the audience.

There is a notable case, however, in which the axiomatic principle of the singularly visible surface is up for grabs.

In *Bigger Than Life* (1956) there is a brief but important scene in which James Mason, as Ed Avery, seriously ill and in consultation with medical personnel, is being administered a barium flouroscopy. With shirt off he stands behind a device with a screen in front and swallows a substance on command. As the substance descends his esophagus we can see the action on the machine's screen within the film screen. A view, purportedly, not merely of the world beneath Ed Avery's surface but also of the world beneath James Mason's. The secret inside, the system heretofore held away from our view.

Nicholas Ray, Mason, and the crew could have effected this moment in two different ways. An animation could have been devised, produced, and then projected either inside the fluoroscope or else through a matte superimposition effected in the optical printer. With such an arrangement we would here be seeing *the effect of* a fluoroscopy; action as indication. Or else—and for lovers of acting I think this "or else" will resonate very loudly—Mason could have swallowed some substance—any substance—that would function just as barium does—perhaps even barium—and been fluoroscoped actually, while our friend the camera watched. A camera rehearsal with lighting would have been sufficient to ensure the visibility of the screen image. And, since in the mid-1950s many people swallowed barium diagnostically even when there turned out to be nothing wrong with them, surviving the moment wouldn't have been problematic for the actor (the actor, I ought to note here, who was simultaneously the producer of the film, the man paying for the technical arrangements Nicholas Ray wanted). This would have been a fluoroscopy per se. Action as reality.

To be sure, however the shot is made some illusion, false or true, is produced of the human interior onscreen: either a character and an actor at once or else a character's surface wedded to his own (fictively manufactured) inside.

If there was any filmmaker who might have been interested in the layering of being that accompanies actors donning characters, that person is Nicholas Ray (see his *I Was Interrupted*) so it is not unthinkable, actually, that he might have come up with the idea of filming the moment "live." To produce an animated, extraneous piece of film that could be used for optical printing would have cost additional money and time. And Mason was well known as a serious actor who always wanted to reinvent and rediscover himself, so that the idea of his agreeing to a "direct" way of filming this moment is not unthinkable either. Ray adored working with him. "James Mason just needed the key or the freshening up of an idea. He is the most constantly improving actor in the business. A beautiful man, beautiful actor" (106).

At least biologically, because it is intended to seem exceptionally revealing this is a virtuosic moment, one that might have been struck through film tricks or struck simply and directly, in live action. Our broad conviction in character as cover dims a hypothesis of realism, however. We attach ourselves to covers and coverings, to the impossibility of getting "backstage." Thus, there must have been some effects technique in use here. Nowadays, after all, we are forever searching for *some effects technique.*

I raise this scene for consideration because, as I am reliably informed by an insider, it was indeed filmed with an actual fluoroscope in real time. Watchers of the film do see the actual, real, living, embodied, *and hitherto entirely inaccessible interior* of James Mason, the actor's deepest self, directly presented onscreen. This may be the only instance in cinema where such a revelation is made available to such depth. Ed Avery is here with the doctor; James Mason the actor is here being Ed Avery; and James Mason the civilian is here with barium going down his throat. One clearly sees the character Ed, sheepish and obedient, and, when he takes off his shirt, the actor Mason, and then, in the fluoroscope, James Neville Mason (1909–1984) who became "James Mason" (and made a film debut in *Late Extra* [1935]).

One can look at the screen image in much the same way that the onscreen "doctor" looks at the fluoroscope, through direct and intimate involvement with an interior. Doctors cannot be absolutely certain when they look and diagnose; and nor can we. But our senses have traveled to the interior.

Here before us, murky yet glowing, is not just a brilliant performance of life, not just an acted simulacrum, even a virtuosic simulacrum, but life itself. Liszt's expostulation, "*Le concert c'est moi!*" now made flesh: the performance is me, or I am the performance, me, all of me, I: everything that I am. If James Mason—the actor, the character, the man, all of them together—indubitably breathed and thought his path through every scene he played, still, here at this marvelous screen moment is something more vital still, the presence of the "I" openly, virtuosically laid before us at the same time as the presence of the character.

Yet who could believe that fluoroscope screen reveals the quick essence of a man's life? Who could feel one had reached a destination, or touched a treasure? Who could believe in being at the heart of darkness, even if one were? And there lies, opened before us, the very great mystery of cinema: that we see and cannot see simultaneously. That our prize, as one after another the cloaking curtains of performance are pulled aside, is not a sacred presence but a riddle, not a layer but a lens.

REFERENCES

Aaron, Stephen. *Stage Fright: Its Role in Acting*. Chicago: University of Chicago Press, 1986.

Bazin, André. "The Ontology of the Photographic Image," in *What Is Cinema?*, Vol. 1. Trans. Hugh Gray. Berkeley: University of California Press, 2005, 1–16.

Becker, Howard S. *Outsiders: Notes on the Sociology of Deviance*. New York: Free Press, 1963.

Benjamin, Walter. *Charles Baudelaire: A Lyric Poet in the Era of High Capitalism*. London: Verso, 1997.

Bernhardt, Sarah. *My Double Life: The Memoirs of Sarah Bernhardt*. Trans. Victoria Tietze Larson. Albany: SUNY Press, 1999.

Bode, Lisa. *Making Believe: Screen Performance and Special Effects in Popular Cinema*. New Brunswick, NJ: Rutgers University Press, 2017.

Bottomore, Stephen. "The Panicking Audience? Early Cinema and the 'Train Effect,'" *Historical Journal of Film, Radio and Television* 19: 2 (1999), 177–216.

Brownlow, Kevin. *David Lean: A Biography*. New York: St. Martin's Press, 1996.

Burke, Kenneth. *A Grammar of Motives*. Berkeley: University of California Press, 1969.

Burton, Richard. *The Richard Burton Diaries*. Ed. Chris Williams. New Haven: Yale University Press, 2012.

Butler, Judith. *Gender Trouble*. London: Routledge, 2006.

Caillois, Roger. *Man, Play and Games*. Trans. Meyer Barash. Urbana: University of Illinois Press, 2001.

Caine, Michael. *Acting in Film: An Actor's Take on Movie Making*. Rev. and exp. edn. New York: Applause, 1997.

Cavell, Stanley. *The World Viewed: Reflections on the Ontology of Film*. Enl. edn. Cambridge, MA: Harvard University Press, 1979.

Cavell, Stanley. *Themes Out of School: Effects and Causes*. Chicago: University of Chicago Press, 1988.

Clark, Danae. *Negotiating Hollywood: The Cultural Politics of Actors' Labor*. Minneapolis: University of Minnesota Press, 1995.

Corbin, John. "'The Play,' review of *Hamlet*," *New York Times* (17 November 1922), 22.

Davis, Ronald L. "Interview with Fred Astaire, July 31, 1976," Southern Methodist University Collection of Ronald L. Davis Oral Histories on the Performing Arts, No. 21, Margaret Herrick Library, Academy of Motion Picture Arts and Sciences, Beverly Hills.

Desjardins, Mary. "Not of Hollywood: Ruth Chatterton, Ann Harding, Constance Bennett, Kay Francis, and Nancy Carroll," in Adrienne L. McLean, ed.,

Glamour in a Golden Age: Movie Stars of the 1930s. New Brunswick, NJ: Rutgers University Press, 2010, 18–43.

Douglas, Mary. *Purity and Danger: An Analysis of Concepts of Pollution and Taboo*. London: Routledge & Kegan Paul, 1966.

Duckett, Victoria. *Seeing Sarah Bernhardt: Performance and Silent Film*. Urbana: University of Illinois Press, 2015.

Dutton, Denis. *The Art Instinct: Beauty, Pleasure, & Human Evolution*. New York: Oxford University Press, 2009.

Feuer, Jane. "The Self-Reflexive Musical and the Myth of Entertainment," in Barry Keith Grant, ed., *Film Genre Reader IV*. Austin: University of Texas Press, 2012, 543–57.

Fishgall, Gary. *Pieces of Time: The Life of James Stewart*. New York: Scribner's, 1997.

Flynn, Gillian. *Gone Girl*. Final Shooting Script, August 29, 2013. Los Angeles: Twentieth Century Fox.

Frascella, Lawrence, and Al Weisel. *Live Fast, Die Young: The Wild Ride of Making Rebel Without a Cause*. New York: Simon & Schuster, 2005.

Fuller, Buckminster. "Vertical is to Live—Horizontal is to Die," *The American Scholar* 39: 1 (Winter 1969–70), 27–47.

Gabbard, Glen O. "Further Contributions to the Understanding of Stage Fright: Narcissistic Issues," *Journal of the American Psychoanalytical Association* 31, 423–41.

Gerth, Hans, and C. Wright Mills, trans. and eds. *From Max Weber: Essays in Sociology*. Oxford: Routledge, 1991. Originally 1948.

Goffman, Erving. *The Presentation of Self in Everyday Life*. Garden City, NY: Doubleday Anchor, 1959.

Goffman, Erving. *Asylums*. Garden City, NY: Doubleday Anchor, 1964.

Goffman, Erving. *Frame Analysis: An Essay on the Organization of Experience*. New York: Harper and Row, 1974.

Goffman, Erving. *Gender Advertisements*. New York: Harper and Row, 1976.

Goffman, Erving. *Forms of Talk*. Philadelphia: University of Pennsylvania Press, 1981.

Goodman, Paul. *Speaking and Language: Defence of Poetry*. New York: Random House, 1972.

Gordon, Mel. *Lazzi: The Comic Routines of the Commedia dell'Arte*. New York: Performing Arts Journal Publications, 1992.

Grant, Barry Keith. *Invasion of the Body Snatchers*. London: BFI, 2010.

Gunning, Tom. "An Aesthetic of Astonishment: Early Film and the Incredulous Spectator," in Linda Williams, ed., *Viewing Positions: Ways of Seeing Film*. New Brunswick, NJ: Rutgers University Press, 1995, 114–33.

Hagen, Uta (with Haskel Frankel). *Respect for Acting*. New York: Wiley, 2008.

Hahn, Reynaldo. *Sarah Bernhardt, Impressions*. Trans. Ethel Thompson. London: E. Mathews and Marrot, 1932.

Halberstam, David. *The Fifties*. New York: Fawcett, 1993.

Haralovich, Mary Beth. "Selling *Mildred Pierce*: A Case Study," in Thomas Schatz, ed., *Boom and Bust: American Cinema in the 1940s*. Berkeley: University of California Press, 1999, 196–202.

Higashi, Sumiko. *Stars, Fans, and Consumption in the 1950s: Reading Photoplay*. New York: Palgrave Macmillan, 2014.

Johnson, Bruce. *Miracles and Sacrilege: Roberto Rossellini, the Church, and Film Censorship*. Toronto: University of Toronto Press, 2008.

Kynaston, David. *Family Britain: 1951–57*. London: Bloomsbury, 2010.
Lehman, Peter. *Running Scared: Masculinity and the Representation of the Male Body*. New edn. Detroit: Wayne State University Press, 2007.
Lowenstein, Adam. *Shocking Representation: Historical Trauma, National Cinema, and the Modern Horror Film*. New York: Columbia University Press, 2005.
Lugowski, David M. "Norma Shearer and Joan Crawford: Rivals at the Glamour Factory," in Adrienne L. McLean, ed., *Glamour in a Golden Age: Movie Stars of the 1930s*. New Brunswick, NJ: Rutgers University Press, 2011, 129–52.
Mann, William. *Kate: The Woman Who Was Katharine Hepburn*. London: Faber & Faber, 2007.
McLean, Adrienne L. "Wedding Bells Ring, Storks Are Expected, the Rumors Aren't True, Divorce Is the Only Answer: Stardom and Fan-Magazine Family Life in 1950s Hollywood," in Murray Pomerance, ed., *A Family Affair: Cinema Calls Home*, London: Wallflower, 2008, 277–90.
McLean, Adrienne L. *Glamour in a Golden Age: Movie Stars of the 1930s*. New Brunswick, NJ: Rutgers University Press, 2011.
McLean, Adrienne L. "Introduction: Stardom in the 1930s," in Adrienne L. McLean, ed., *Glamour in a Golden Age: Movie Stars of the 1930s*. New Brunswick, NJ: Rutgers University Press, 2011, 1–17.
Meisner, Sanford (with Dennis Longwell). *On Acting*. New York: Vintage, 1987.
Méliès, Georges. "En marge de l'histoire du cinématographe," part 6, *Ciné-Journal* (10 September 1926), 9.
Monush, Barry. *The Encyclopedia of Hollywood Film Actors*. N.p.: Applause Theater and Cinema Books, 2003.
Moral, Tony Lee. *Hitchcock and the Making of Marnie*. Lanham, MD: Scarecrow, 2002.
Ohmer, Susan. "Jean Harlow: Tragic Blonde," in Adrienne L. McLean, ed., *Glamour in a Golden Age: Movie Stars of the 1930s*. New Brunswick, NJ: Rutgers University Press, 2011, 174–95.
Oldenburg, Claes. *Proposals for Monuments and Buildings, 1965–69*. Boston: Big Table, 1969.
Ortega y Gasset, José. "On Point of View in the Arts," in *The Dehumanization of Art and Other Essays on Art, Culture, and Literature*. Princeton: Princeton University Press, 1968, 105–30.
Pearce, Robert. *1930s Britain*. Botley, Oxford: Shire, 2010.
Pirandello, Luigi. *Shoot! The Notebooks of Serafino Gubbio, Cinematograph Operator*. Trans. C. K. Scott Moncrieff. Chicago: University of Chicago Press, 2005, originally 1926.
Pomerance, Murray. *An Eye for Hitchcock*. New Brunswick, NJ: Rutgers University Press, 2004.
Pomerance, Murray. *Johnny Depp Starts Here*. New Brunswick, NJ: Rutgers University Press, 2005.
Pomerance, Murray. *The Horse Who Drank the Sky: Film Experience Beyond Narrative and Theory*. New Brunswick, NJ: Rutgers University Press, 2008.
Pomerance, Murray. *The Eyes Have It: Cinema and the Reality Effect*. New Brunswick, NJ: Rutgers University Press, 2013.
Pomerance, Murray. *Marnie*. London: BFI, 2014.

Pomerance, Murray. *The Man Who Knew Too Much.* London: BFI, 2016.

Pomerance, Murray. *Moment of Action: Riddles of Cinematic Performance.* New Brunswick, NJ: Rutgers University Press, 2016.

Pomerance, Murray. "Tilda Swinton in *I Am Love*," in Murray Pomerance and Kyle Stevens, eds., *Close-Up: Great Cinematic Performances: Vol. 2: International.* Edinburgh: Edinburgh University Press, 2018, 238–48.

Pomerance, Murray. "Twelve Memoranda for Jerrylewising," *Kino Slang Blogspot,* January 31, 2018. Online at kinoslang.blogspot.com/2018/01 (accessed December 21, 2018).

Prince, Stephen. *Digital Visual Effects in Cinema: The Seduction of Reality.* New Brunswick, NJ: Rutgers University Press, 2011.

Prynne, William. *Histriomastix.* New York: Garland Publishing, 1974; originally 1633.

Ray, Nicholas. *I Was Interrupted: Nicholas Ray on Making Movies.* Ed. Susan Ray. Berkeley: University of California Press, 1993.

Rousseau, Jean-Jacques. *Politics and the Arts: Letter to M D'Alembert on the Theatre.* Trans. Allan Bloom. Glencoe, IL: Free Press, 1960.

Sartre, Jean-Paul. "Preface: 'A Victory,'" in Henri Alleg, ed., *The Question.* Lincoln: University of Nebraska Press, 2006, xxvii–xliv.

Schivelbusch, Wolfgang. *The Railway Journey: The Industrialization of Time and Space in the Nineteenth Century.* Berkeley: University of California Press, 2014.

Sellers, Robert. *Peter O'Toole: The Definite Biography.* New York: St. Martin's Press, 2015.

Shaw, George Bernard. "Prologue," in *Caesar and Cleopatra.* Whitefish, MT: Kessinger, 2010, 3–8.

Skinner, Cornelia Otis. *Madame Sarah.* New York: Houghton Mifflin, 1967.

Sobchack, Vivian. "Thinking through Jim Carrey," in Murray Pomerance and John Sakeris, eds., *Closely Watched Brains.* Boston: Pearson, 2001, 199–213.

Sobchack, Vivian. "Being on the Screen: A Phenomenology of Cinematic Flesh, or the Actor's Four Bodies," in Jörg Sternagel, Deborah Levitt, and Dieter Mersch, eds., *Acting and Performance in Moving Image Culture: Bodies, Screens, Renderings.* Bielefeld: Transcript, 2012, 429–446.

Stanislavsky, Konstantin. *An Actor Prepares.* New York: Routledge, 1989.

Stevens, Kyle. "Michel Serrault in *La Cage aux folles*," in Murray Pomerance and Kyle Stevens, eds., *Close-Up: Great Cinematic Performances Vol. 2: International.* Edinburgh: Edinburgh University Press, 2018, 149–60.

Stevenson, Robert Louis. "The Strange Tale of Dr. Jekyll and Mr. Hyde," online at www.gutenberg.org/files/43/43-h/43-h.htm#link2H_4_0002 (accessed December 21, 2018).

Taubman, Howard. "Richard Burton as Hamlet: Gielgud Production at the Lunt-Fontanne," *New York Times* (10 April 1964), 30.

Toles, George. Personal conversation. March 2018.

Truffaut, François. *Journal of* Fahrenheit 451. In *Scénario de* La nuit américaine, Paris: Petit bibliothèque des Cahiers du cinéma, 2004, 111–90.

Unsigned Note, December 9, 1963, regarding casting of Louise Latham in *Marnie,* Robert Boyle File 435, Alfred Hitchcock Collection, Margaret Herrick Library, Academy of Motion Picture Arts and Sciences, Beverly Hills.

Wikander, Matthew H. *Fangs of Malice: Hypocrisy, Sincerity, & Acting.* Iowa City: University of Iowa Press, 2002.

Williams, Chris, ed. *The Richard Burton Diaries.* New Haven: Yale University Press, 2012.

Wilson, Frank R. *The Hand: How Its Use Shapes the Brain, Language, and Human Culture.* New York: Pantheon, 1998.

Winwar, Frances. *Wingless Victory: A Biography of Gabriele d'Annunzio and Eleonora Duse.* New York: Harper, 1956.

Wood, Robin. "Art and Ideology: Notes on *Silk Stockings*," *Film Comment* 11: 3 (May–June 1975), 28–31.

Wyatt, Justin. *High Concept: Movies and Marketing in Hollywood.* Austin: University of Texas Press, 1994.

INDEX

Italics indicate images. Dates are given for film and television performers.

CA PROFICIENCY 1

FINANCE TOOLKIT

Published by
Chartered Accountants Ireland
Chartered Accountants House
47–49 Pearse Street
Dublin 2
www.charteredaccountants.ie

© The Institute of Chartered Accountants in Ireland 2012

First published 2006
Reprinted with corrections 2010; reprinted 2012, 2014.

This publication is designed to provide accurate and authoritative information in regard to the subject matter covered. It is provided on the understanding that the Institute of Chartered Accountants in Ireland is not engaged in rendering professional services. The Institute of Chartered Accountants in Ireland disclaims all liability for any reliance placed on the information contained within this publication and recommends that if professional advice or other expert assistance is required, the services of a competent professional should be sought.

ISBN: 978-1-908199-40-9

Typeset by Compuscript
Printed and bound by eprint, Dublin

CONTENTS

INTRODUCTION

The CAP1 Finance syllabus is a comprehensive programme that will introduce you to the key building blocks of corporate finance. The primary sources are your core text books by Anne-Marie Ward: *Finance: Theory and Practice* and *An Introduction to Personal Finance*, which detail all the areas of the course with which you need to be familiar. In addition, you will attend lectures, be asked to complete home assignments by your lecturer and take a mock exam after Christmas.

Finance is a very practical subject and the best way to learn (and pass!) this subject is to attempt as many questions as possible. Try to cover all the questions in the core text books and use this book to help reinforce what you have learned already. Past exam questions, arranged by topic, are reproduced in this Toolkit, and suggested solutions are available through your lectures or from the Institute. Full exam papers may be viewed at www. charteredaccountants.ie.

'Storyline' – An Introduction

In the Finance Toolkit you will take on the role of "Chris", a fictitious trainee chartered accountant. Chris's job entails specific responsibilities for three clients detailed below. As you work through the material in each of the subject areas, you will be asked to attempt tasks presented to Chris on behalf of each of these clients. These tasks are designed to help you apply the knowledge and skills required for your professional examinations.

You should treat these simulations as though they are real-life tasks. Try to put yourself in Chris's position – considering how you might respond to the client, where you might go to get information and when you might ask for help.

SECTION ONE

'STORYLINE' CASE STUDY

Background

You are Chris, a trainee accountant with Shield Kenwick, Chartered Accountants & Registered Auditors. Your manager is one of the partners, Mr Ryan. You have just received the following memo from Mr Ryan.

SHIELD KENWICK
CHARTERED ACCOUNTANTS &
REGISTERED AUDITORS

INTERNAL MEMO

To: Chris
From: Mr Ryan
Date: xx October 2xxx
Re: Update following six-month review meeting

At your recent review meeting we agreed that you are ready to take on some extra responsibility and that you should have further direct exposure to clients. I have considered how this might be best achieved, and have decided the following:

Jane Dough – The Dough House

Jane Dough is a new client, starting up a new business. As part of your duties you will be the first point of contact and reference for any queries from Jane. In particular, you will be responsible for the preparation of Jane's books and records, income tax, PAYE and VAT returns. These will be signed off by me in the usual way. I have included background notes on Jane in **Appendix 1**. Jane also mentioned that she is interested in the activities of a local producers' group, called Poulenc Partnership. I have included their details here in **Appendix 2,** in case you require them at a later point.

Continued

MCL Limited

As part of your duties, you have been seconded one day per week as assistant management accountant to a busy manufacturing company that is a client of the firm. Shield Kenwick provides general support and advice, along with accounting and taxation services, to this client. We do not carry out the statutory audit. The company, MCL Limited, is family owned and you will report directly to the Finance Director, Mike Smithers, while at the office. Additionally, I would hope that you will come directly to me with specific queries which you would like to discuss. I have included some basic background information on MCL in **Appendix 3**.

I anticipate that these responsibilities should help to address some of the areas of concern we had in relation to the competencies identified in the Online CA Diary. I suggest we keep the process under review over the next six to 12 months.

Having agreed to Mr Ryan's suggestions, you return to your desk and continue work.

Appendix i: Jane Dough – The Dough House

On 1 January 2008, Jane Dough established a new business, a coffee and pastry shop, known as "The Dough House". In the future, Jane hopes to also sell local pottery and produce on a small scale. Jane had identified suitable premises in a busy part of town which did not appear to be particularly well serviced by coffee and pastry shops. While Jane has extensive experience working in a coffee shop environment, having been assistant manager in a similar shop for several years, she has never owned or run her own business before.

On 1 January 2008, Jane withdrew €/£5,000 from her own savings and her husband John's great-aunt gave her €/£10,000 as a gift to put towards opening the Dough House. Jane opened a separate bank account for the Dough House, lodging €/£14,500 to the account and retaining €/£500 as petty cash. Jane then signed the deeds on the Dough House's new premises, which were for sale at €/£50,000, drew down a mortgage with a local Building Society for €/£45,000 and paid the balance due for the premises from the business's new bank account. The mortgage is repayable over 20 years and the repayments, which are due at the end of each month, are fixed at €/£250 per month.

While Jane had taken redundancy from her previous employer, the redundancy payment is not expected for some months due to circumstances outside her control.

Jane will need help at lunch time and weekends in The Dough House, and her nephew and niece have agreed to help, so long as they are paid in cash. They are 14 and 17 respectively. Additionally, Jane's husband John has agreed to help whenever possible. Jane is uncertain whether or not she needs to register as an employer.

Continued

Jane and John have two young children, and her husband's incapacitated great-aunt lives with them. John is not employed as he cares for their two children on a full-time basis at home. However, he does have an interest in some rental properties and a small share portfolio. Jane and John have always tried to save a percentage of their income and these savings are kept in a variety of accounts: Credit Union Account, Deposit Account and SSIA. In addition, Jane and John each have a personal pension, life assurance (with critical illness), permanent health insurance (PHI) and are members of VHI.

APPENDIX 2: THE POULENC PARTNERSHIP

The Poulenc Partnership is a group of artisans who make and sell local produce and crafts through farmers' markets, seasonal fairs and independent coffee shops. The partnership has been in existence for approximately eight years and there are currently five partners. The partners share all income and costs, with individual products being sold into the partnership at an agreed price and then sold on to third parties. The current partnership structure is as follows:

- Marie Louise Phillips (25%) – potter and clay-worker;
- Joseph Phillips (father of Marie Louise) (15%) – basket weaver;
- Christopher Pringle (20%) – food producer (preserves, cakes, biscuits etc.) using local ingredients;
- Caiti Pollen (25%) – craft worker (jewellery from local materials and wrought-iron items (candlesticks, tables, fire irons etc.); and
- Ellen Peterson (15%) – public relations and marketing professional, and the only partner who draws a salary.

While Joseph Phillips hopes to retire during 2009, he may continue to sell some of his baskets to the partnership.

Jane has been invited to join The Poulenc Partnership, with effect from 1 July 2009, purchasing Joseph Phillips' 15% interest in return for an investment of €/£50,000.

As the Poulenc Partnership is now a client of the firm, Jane has deferred making a decision about joining the partnership until its accounts for the year ended 31 December 2008 have been finalised.

The existing partners have indicated that there are plans to review the partnership structure at the end of 2009.

APPENDIX 3: MCL LIMITED

MCL Limited is a large, privately-owned company. It was founded in the 1970s by Matthew Smithers and is still owned by the Smithers family. There has been no change in the ordinary share capital of the company for a number of years and the shareholdings are as follows:

Continued

Member	Role	Current Shareholding
Matthew and Maureen Smithers	Founders	8%
Matthew Jnr	CEO	22%
Michael	Finance Director	22%
Martina	Production Director	22%
Millie	Sales and Marketing Director	22%
Mervin (based in New York)	not involved in the company	4%

Matthew Jnr, Michael, Martina and Millie are the only children of Matthew and Maureen. Mervin is Matthew Snr's brother and not directly involved in the company. There are no other directors.

MCL is a textiles company that is involved in producing standard fabric dyes and weaving natural fibre fabrics for use in a variety of home furnishings. The dyes produced are used to dye yarns in-house (but could also be sold directly to third parties). The majority of the woven fabrics are exported to the UK and mainland Europe. However, there is also a core Irish market.

MCL has a large work force which includes: general operatives; weavers (general and skilled); stores team; administration team; and sales and distribution team. Although the company has performed well in the past, it has come under increasing pressure in the last two years.

TOPIC 1: FINANCIAL ENVIRONMENT

Jane Dough Meeting – 1 January 2009

Jane Dough arranges an appointment to see Chris to discuss her plans for the business. At this stage she has secured a lease and work is underway to fit out the coffee shop. Although Jane has plenty of experience working in the coffee shop business, this is her first time as a business owner.

Chris begins by asking Jane what her goals are for the business and how she hopes to achieve these goals. Jane thinks about it and lists her three goals for the Dough House in order of importance:

1. surviving the first year;
2. making a big enough profit to provide a living for her family; and
3. providing a service to the community.

Family members have warned her that most businesses fail in their first year, so she feels that if she can get through this year the business has a great chance of success. Obviously, the business needs to do more than survive; it needs to pay for Jane and her family to have a decent standard of living. She would also like to provide a service to her community. By selling local pottery and produce, Jane feels that she would be giving something back to the town. Her strategy for achieving these goals is to set up in a busy part of town where there is little competition; keep costs low by hiring as few employees as possible and persuade the owner of the building to pay for the coffee shop fit-out.

Chris is impressed by the business acumen that Jane is already clearly displaying. However, he asks Jane to focus on one clear goal for the business now and in the future. Very simply, Chris outlines that, when running a business, whether as owner or manager, she should always focus on one clear goal: "Maximise the value of the firm to the owner(s)."

In Jane's case she is the owner of her business and every decision she takes should be focused towards this one clear goal. This does not mean she cannot provide a service to the community. She can, as long as it increases the value of business it is the right decision. While the goal of maximising the value of the firm is linked to maximising profit and business survival, chasing either of these goals can have other negative repercussion on the business. Chris explains that by focusing on surviving the first year she may not invest in equipment which will maximise long-term value to the business. Likewise, by focusing on profit she might under-invest in customer satisfaction and other longer term intangible assets.

Jane then goes on to outline her concerns that the health of her business may be overly dependent on the state of the economy. This sort of discussion has always bored her in the past but as her livelihood now depends upon economic factors she has begun to take a keen interest.

Finding all of the economic commentary in the newspapers confusing and often contradictory she asks Chris to outline the current state of the economy and the type of economic factors she should keep an eye on to ensure the health of her business going forward.

Task 1

Note the macro-economic factors that will affect the Dough House's success under the broad headings of inflation, economic growth, consumer spending and interest rates.

Having reassured Jane that it is currently a very favourable economic climate to be starting a new business, Jane thanks you for your advice and goes back to the Dough House to meet the plumber who is due to install the new washroom.

MCL Limited Meeting – 10 January 2009

On his first day in MCL Limited, Chris has a meeting with Mike Smithers, a significant shareholder and the firm's finance director. Mike provides Chris with documents prepared by MCL Limited's auditors reviewing the performance of the business over the past two years. During this period the business has come under increasing pressure. While revenue growth and gross margins have remained healthy, rising costs and increasing low-cost competition have had a very negative effect on net margins:

MCL Limited: Performance 2007 and 2008

	2007	2008
Sales	€1m	€1.5m
Gross Profit	€300k	€450k
Gross Margin	30%	30%
Net Profit	€100k	€75k
Net Margin	10%	5%

Mike explains that during the last two years Ireland has undergone tremendous economic growth which has been great for Irish sales, but this period of growth has been accompanied by many negatives. As a member of the European Union, Ireland has for the past couple of years had excessively low interest rates. Interest rates are set by the European Central Bank to stimulate growth across the Eurozone. Because Europe's two big economies, Germany and France, are experiencing below par growth the rates are kept low to stimulate these economies. Although Ireland is experiencing above average economic growth we are still on the same low rates as the rest of Europe. The effect of these too low rates is to increase inflation in Ireland.

For MCL Limited this is bad for two reasons:
1. The company is producing in Ireland where costs are rising.
2. It is exporting the majority of its products to the United Kingdom and Continental Europe where inflation is lower, meaning MCL Limited cannot increase its selling prices as fast as its expenses rise. This has led to a big drop in net profit margins.

The economic growth in Ireland has caused other problems. It has led to a significant scarcity of skilled workers. The accomplished weavers whom MCL Limited employs are in constant demand from competitors and this is driving up the wage bills. All of MCL Limited's employees are based in Ireland so at present they are at a big competitive disadvantage against companies who outsource their manufacturing operations abroad.

If this was not bad enough for MCL Limited, the last two years has seen a big increase in competition from abroad. Mike explains that if you go to any department store in Ireland and look at the country of manufacture you will see the names of countries with much lower costs than Ireland. Many of these fabrics are manufactured in Eastern Europe or Asian countries where costs are much lower. Imports from Asian countries have also become more competitive due to the strength of the Euro currency. What Mike Smithers is now considering is how to improve the efficiency and profitability of the firm's operations. Two options which have been raised are to either invest in more sophisticated plant, or consider outsourcing their manufacturing abroad. The new equipment on the market is more automated so this could reduce the wage bill. The Smithers family is not keen on outsourcing. The business was built up by the family in their home town and the founders would not be happy to discontinue manufacturing in Ireland.

Having reviewed the current operational challenges facing the business, Mike Smithers gives Chris his first task in his new role. Mike explains that this is a very sensitive issue as there has been some disagreement between minority shareholders about the future of the company. He gives Chris a chart with the current management structure. This structure evolved over time and was never formally reviewed. As the company has grown Mike feels that it may be time to review their corporate governance structures and perhaps adapt some best practice from publicly quoted companies. This would make it clearer how decisions are made within the firm and help to resolve disputes amongst shareholders.

Current Structure of MCL Limited Management and Ownership Structure

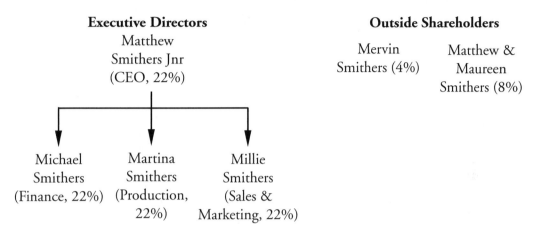

Chris discusses this with Mr Ryan and prepares a memo outlining how MCL fares relative to best practice.

MEMO

Attn: **Michael Smithers (Finance Director)**
Memo: Corporate Governance Best Practice
From: Chris
Date: 31 January 2009

I have spoken to the partner, Mr Ryan, in my accounting practice and he provided a summary of the *UK Corporate Governance Code*, which is the recommended best practice for UK-listed publicly limited companies. I have used this document to highlight the discrepancies with the current corporate governance structures implemented by MCL Limited.

Before beginning it is very important to note that the *UK Corporate Governance Code* is written for publicly quoted companies where the managers may not have a significant stake in the company. This is not the case for MCL Limited. All of the executive directors have a significant stake in the business. Theoretically, this aligns their interests with those of other shareholders. Despite this caveat there are three smaller shareholders, Matthew, Maureen and Mervin Smithers who have significant stakes in the business and are not currently represented. As company law states that all shareholders must be treated equally in access to information, it is important that their interests are represented.

Continued

BOARD OF DIRECTORS

The *UK Corporate Governance Code's* first key principle is that every company, in addition to its executive management team, should be headed by a board of directors, which collectively is responsible for the success or failure of the company. The responsibilities of the board of directors should be clearly divided from the day-to-day running of the company's business. This would generally mean having a Chairman of the Board and a separate Chief Executive Officer. The board should include a balance of executive and non-executive directors, and all directors should be appointed in a fair way. If this process is followed no individual or small group of individuals can dominate the board's decision-taking. The final key points made by the *UK Corporate Governance Code* in relation to the Board of Directors are concerned with the quality and timeliness of information supplied to the board, evaluation of the board's performance and changing the composition of the board at regular intervals.

Currently MCL Limited has four directors all of whom have executive roles in the firm. Currently, MCL Limited has no board of directors, no non-executive directors and no Chairman.

REMUNERATION

The *UK Corporate Governance Code* also provides guidance on remuneration policies for executive and non-executive directors. The level of remuneration should be high enough to attract, retain and motivate directors, but the company should be careful not to pay more than necessary. In addition, the *UK Corporate Governance Code* recommends that a significant proportion of executive directors' remuneration should be structured so as to link rewards to corporate and individual performance. Policies on executive remuneration and for fixing the remuneration packages of individual directors should be set in a formal, transparent way and no director should be involved in deciding his or her own remuneration.

Currently, MCL Limited only has executive directors. Their remuneration is entirely in salary and benefits and is set by the Chief Executive, Matthew Jnr, who also sets his own salary. As all of the executive directors have significant shareholdings, it seems reasonable that their compensation is not directly linked to firm performance. However, it is difficult to justify to an outsider the lack of a clear procedure for setting remuneration packages.

ACCOUNTABILITY, AUDIT AND RELATIONS WITH SHAREHOLDERS

The *UK Corporate Governance Code* also sets out the accountability and audit responsibilities of a board of directors. The board should present a balanced and understandable

Continued

assessment of the company's position and prospects to all shareholders. Internal controls should be sound and safeguard shareholders' investment and the company's assets. The board should also establish formal and transparent arrangements for considering how they should apply the financial reporting and internal control principles and for maintaining an appropriate relationship with the company's auditors. There should be regular dialogue with shareholders. This should be based on the mutual understanding of objectives for the firm. The board as a whole has responsibility for ensuring that this dialogue takes place.

At this time MCL Limited has no formal procedure on accountability and audit. Once a year, a set of audited accounts is produced. These are then disseminated to the management team. None of this information is sent to other shareholders.

Recommendations

The *UK Corporate Governance Code* provides excellent guidance for both Public and Private Companies where there is a separation of ownership and control. As MCL Limited falls into this second category I would recommend implementing many of the recommendations. Acknowledging that implementing some of these issues may be costly I have the following suggestions:

1. Appoint the other shareholders as non-executive directors. The board should meet regularly and comprise the four executives and three non-executives directors.
2. Consider appointing an independent non-executive eighth director. This would provide a balance between executive and non-executive directors.
3. Appoint one of the founders, Matthew or Maureen Smithers, as Chairman of the Board. By having a non-executive director as Chairman of the Board of Directors this will ensure that the interests of the minority shareholders are well represented.
4. Appoint a remuneration committee made up of executive and non-executive board members to decide formal policy on executive and non-executive remuneration.
5. Carry out a review of the internal controls and risk management of MCL Limited.
6. Provide timely accounting information to all members of the board.

Implementing these recommendations should be relatively low cost and greatly reduce agency costs and conflicts among executive and non-executive shareholders.

Jane Dough Telephone Call – 5 February 2009

Ethical Dilemma

Jane telephones Chris looking for guidance on a few issues:

1. A local businessman in the town, Sam Jones, has non-EU workers available to work in the Dough House at a rate of €4 per hour. These people have a low level of English

but Sam explains that they would be useful working in the kitchen of the Dough House. While Jane is attracted by the low wages she is unsure whether to hire them.

2. Currently, Jane is using CityClean, a local recycling company, to deal with her waste disposal. However, she is aware of an unlicensed dump at the edge of the town that will take all of her waste at a fraction of the cost. Again, she is unsure what to do.

Task 2

Outline the correct ethical response to Jane's queries.

MCL Limited Meeting with Mike Smithers – 9 February 2009

Having reviewed the memo on corporate governance and its recommendations, Mike Smithers wants Chris to clarify whether MCL Limited faces any potential issues. Mike outlines to Chris how major decisions are taken in the company:

"Basically, the CEO Matthew Jnr makes the decisions. From time to time one of the other executive directors questions him but he is a tough nut. We are all members of the same family and Matthew Jnr was always the tough one. None of the rest of us ever really stood up to him."

Task 3

Drawing on this conversation and the conversation between Chris and Mike Smithers on 10 January, identify any potential corporate governance issues facing MCL Limited.

TOPIC 2: INVESTMENT DECISIONS

Jane Dough Telephone Call – 2pm, 15 February 2009

Jane telephones to ask some advice. She has been given an investment opportunity by a trusted friend, David. David requires an investment of €1,000 today and will repay €1,200 in one year's time. David reckons that similar risk investments offer a return of 10%.

Before Chris attempts to advise Jane, he decides to ask Mr Ryan for his thoughts on the matter. Mr Ryan reminds Chris that: "A Euro today is worth more than a Euro tomorrow."

This is because we can invest a Euro received today and get interest on it. This is often referred to as the time value of money.

In order to work out whether it is better for Jane to have €1,000 today or €1,200 in one year's time we need to express both alternatives in today's terms. To do this we must calculate the present value of the alternatives.

To calculate the present value we use the following formula:

$$PV = C_t/(1 + r)^t$$

Where

PV = Present Value
 C$_t$ = Cash flow received in time period t.
  r = Opportunity cost of capital. This is the return foregone by investing in the project rather than similar risk securities.
  t = time period

Task 4

Decide whether Jane should make the investment and put a note on the file showing the workings.

Telephone Call with Jane Dough – 2pm, 16 February 2009

Jane telephones again. She understands the calculations and that €1,091.91 is greater than €1,000 but wonders where the opportunity cost of capital of 10% came from.

Chris once again turns to Mr Ryan for his thoughts on the matter. Mr Ryan explains how this highlights a second fundamental rule of finance: "A safe Euro should always be worth more than a risky Euro as it is guaranteed."

Most investors will avoid risk when they can do so without sacrificing return. The opportunity cost of capital we use to calculate our present values depends on the riskiness of the investment opportunity.

Task 5

Determine whether the outcome would be different if the opportunity cost of capital was 5% or 25% using the financial principles as outlined.

Telephone Call with Jane Dough – 2pm, 30 February 2009

Jane has had a nice surprise. She had entered the coffee shop owners' annual prize draw. This morning she discovered that she has won. She now needs to choose her prize. She has the following options:

1. €3,900 received immediately.
2. €1,000 in year 1, €1,000 in year 2, €1,100 in year 3 and €1,200 in year 4.
3. €180 to be received at the end of every year forever.
4. €100 received next year growing at a rate of 3% per annum forever.

The relevant opportunity cost of capital is 5%.

Task 6

Calculate which of the four options Jane should choose to maximise the value of her prize.

Telephone Call with Jane Dough – 2pm, 15 March 2009

The business has now been running for three months quite profitably and Jane has arranged another meeting with Chris at 2pm on the 15 March. Jane is considering investing in a new coffee machine and wants Chris to advise her on whether it will add value to the business. Over the telephone on the previous day she provided Chris with some information on the new machine which he has noted down as follows:

> *Jane is always reminding herself to focus on maximising the value of the firm. Consequently Jane is considering investing in a new coffee machine for the Dough House. She has been contacted by the La Riva sales representative who has demonstrated their new range of state-of-the-art coffee machines. The machine grinds the coffee beans and makes everything from an espresso to a double dry extra hot latte automatically. The machine is expensive. It costs €25,000 payable upfront and has a useful life of 10 years. However, the machine is capable of running at a far higher capacity than the existing Dough House machine and La Riva estimates that on every cup of coffee she will save about 5c, from electricity, labour and other efficiencies. Jane estimates that she currently sells on average 200 cups of coffee per day and is open 300 days per year. She calculates this as an annual saving of €3,000. Over 10 years this gives a total saving of €30,000. As this is in excess of the €25,000 initial outlay Jane thinks it will add value to her business to the tune of €5,000. However, she is not sure if she got this right.*

Chris met with Mr Ryan to review this information, and took the following notes:

> ### Notes from Meeting with Mr Ryan – 9am, 16 March 2009
>
> *We first need to work out the annual savings using the new machine:*
>
> | | |
> |---|---:|
> | Cups per annum | 60,000 |
> | Saving per cup | × 5c |
> | Saving per annum | €3,000 |
>
> *Next we need to calculate the present value of these savings. The savings are an equal amount per annum for a set number of years and we call this an annuity. To calculate the present value of an annuity we use the following formula:*
>
> $$PV = C \times [1/r - 1/r \, (1 + r)t]$$
>
> *Alternatively, I can use annuity factor tables which contain the value of €1 received every year for a certain number of years and these make our calculations much easier. Mr Ryan*
>
> *(Continued)*

explained that the interest rate used to calculate the annuity depends on the riskiness of the project. He estimated that for the coffee machine an appropriate cost of capital would be 10%.

Present Value of Annual Savings:

Saving Per Annum	€3,000
Annuity Factor10, 10%	×6.145
Present Value of Savings	€18,435

So the €3,000 per annum saved over the next 10 years is worth €18,435 in today's terms. Therefore the net present value of buying the new machine can be calculated as:

NPV = PV – Initial Investment
NPV = 18,435 – 25,000 = €(6,565).

Mr Ryan explained that buying this new machine will actually reduce the value of the Dough House by €6,565.

Assuming all cash flows occur at year end, I can then calculate how many cups of coffee Jane would have to sell per day in order to justify buying the machine.

Present Value of Savings Required	25,000
Annuity Factor	6.145
Savings per annum	4,068
Savings per cup	5c
Number of cups per annum	81,367
Number of Days Open per annum	300
Cups per day	271

In order to justify buying the machine the Dough House would have to be selling at least 271 cups of coffee on average per day.

Meeting with Jane Dough – 2pm, 16 March 2009

At 2pm, Jane arrives into Shield Kenwick and sits down to discuss the La Riva coffee machine. Chris clearly explains to Jane that purchasing the coffee machine today will actually lead to a reduction in value of her business of €6,500. In order to justify buying the machine she would need to be selling over 270 cups per day on average. Chris advises her to reconsider the investment.

Jane understands that the La Riva machine is not viable but asks Chris to consider an alternative machine which she did not discuss with him previously. It is made by a competitor, Coffee Inc. It costs €10,000 with €5,000 payable upfront and €5,000 payable after one year, and has a useful life of 10 years. However, the machine is also capable of running at a higher capacity than the existing Dough House machine and Coffee Inc estimates that on every cup of coffee she will save about 4c, from electricity, labour and other efficiencies.

Task 7

Evaluate whether Jane should go ahead with the purchase of the Coffee Inc machine using the relevant information from the previous example.

MCL Limited Meeting (Investment Appraisal) – 20 March 2009

Mike Smithers was very impressed by the work prepared on corporate governance. He has shown the document to the other executive directors and they are meeting next month to consider implementing the recommendations. Mike now wants Chris to review best practice for investment appraisal and prepare a memo for the management team on alternative approaches, using the new investment in plant to illustrate the best form of investment appraisal.

Specifically, Mike would like Chris to begin by calculating the Net Present Value of the project. Chris should also test the sensitivity of this analysis to changes in the discount rate. He then wants Chris to go on and calculate the:

1. Payback
2. Discounted Payback
3. Accounting Rate of Return
4. Internal Rate of Return

Finally, he wants Chris to highlight the disadvantages of each relative to Net Present Value. As the prerequisite for this, he supplies the following data regarding details of new plant:

As part of the drive to reduce costs and increase profitability the company is considering investing in new manufacturing equipment. This equipment will require a large initial outlay and will result in positive cash inflows for the four-year useful life. MCL Limited commissioned and paid for a report by management consultants last year at a cost of €25,000 which forecast the following information on the equipment:

1. The equipment will cost €2 million, will have a residual value after four years of €200,000 and will be depreciated at 25% per annum on a straight-line basis. Capital allowances can be claimed at 15% per annum straight line.
2. Annual savings on labour are initially €150k growing at a rate of 5% per annum for each of the next three years.
3. Production Efficiencies of €500k per annum in Year 1 growing at 3% per annum thereafter.
4. The CEO intends allocating €100k per annum of existing head office costs to the new machinery.
5. The new plant requires an additional investment of €50k in working capital. This will be recovered at the end of the four years.
6. The area where the plant will be located is currently let out to a local business for €25,000 per annum.
7. MCL Limited pays corporation tax at a rate of 12.5% payable one year in arrears.

Note: assume that all cashflows occur at year end. As MCL Limited does not have an estimate of its cost of capital you can assume it is 10%. This assumption is based on a valuation of MCL Limited carried out three years ago.

Task 8

Prepare a Memo for the management team describing the key points to watch for when carrying out investment appraisals.

Task 9

Calculate the NPV of the proposed project.

Task 10

Test the sensitivity of the NPV analysis using discount factors of 5% and 15%.

Task 11

Draft a briefing note on the alternatives to NPV, as outlined by Mike, and outline the disadvantages of each. The note should include calculations.

Task 12

Draft a note of your recommendation on the proposed project and your advice as to which method of investment appraisal should be adopted by MCL for future projects.

MCL Limited Meeting (Investment Appraisal) – 15 May 2009

Mike Smithers, who is very impressed by the information that Chris has submitted, has received a request from one of the factory managers to purchase a new piece of equipment. The details of this machine include some information on inflation. Mike has asked Chris to prepare another NPV analysis to assess whether MCL should purchase the equipment.

The machine costs €100k and has a useful life of three years. The real revenues are €400k per annum for three years. The real costs are €350k per annum for three years. The relevant nominal discount rate is 15.5% and the general inflation rate is 5%.

Chris has asked Mr Ryan to explain how inflation impacts when calculating NPV. As Mr Ryan is on his way to the Chartered Accountants Ireland Annual Conference, he prepares a memo explaining this, for Chris to review.

INTERNAL MEMO

Attn: Chris
Memo: Investment Appraisal of New Machine for MCL and the impact of inflation
From: Mr Ryan
Date: 31 May 2009

We must always remember to be consistent in how we handle inflation. We must use nominal interest rates to discount nominal cash flows and real interest rates to discount real cash flows.

In the example here I have assumed the general inflation rate applies to both revenue and costs. You will get the same results, whether you use nominal or real figures. You can calculate real discount rates and nominal cash flows using the following formulae.

$$\text{Real Rate} = \frac{1 + \text{nominal rate}}{1 + \text{inflation rate}} - 1$$

$$\text{Nominal cash flow} = \text{Real cash flow} \times (1 + \text{inflation rate})^t$$

To calculate the Net Present Value of this project we begin by assuming costs and revenues are both subject to 5% inflation.

(i) As we are dealing with real cash flows we will convert our nominal discount rate into a real discount rate.

      Nominal Rate: 15.50%
      General inflation Rate: 5%

$$\text{Real Rate} = \frac{1 + \text{nominal rate}}{1 + \text{inflation rate}} - 1$$

$$\text{Real Rate} = \frac{1 + 15.5\%}{1 + 5\%} - 1$$

$$\text{Real Rate} = 10\%$$

As in part (ii) they are subject to different rates of inflation, we will discount costs and revenues separately.

Continued

(ii)

	0	All figures in 1	€000s 2	3
Revenues		400	400	400
DF 10%		0.909	0.826	0.751
		363.6	330.4	300.4
Costs		−350	−350	−350
DF 10%		0.909	0.826	0.751
		−318.15	−289.1	−262.85
Machine Cost	−100			
Total DCF	−100	45.45	41.3	37.55
NPV	24.3			

As the NPV is positive, MCL should proceed with the project. However, before reverting to MCL, I believe you should recalculate the information under the assumption that costs will rise faster than revenues. I suggest using a 7% p.a. inflation rate for costs.

Task 13

Calculate the NPV of the proposed project, assuming costs are subject to 7% pa inflation while revenues increase at the same rate as general inflation. Make a recommendation as to whether MCL should proceed with the proposal under these conditions.

Jane Dough Meeting (Working Capital Management) – 15 June 2009

Jane telephones Chris to arrange another meeting. The Dough House is having some cash flow problems. She is not sure why but at the end of every month she is quite short of cash. The business is profitable but she has had to arrange an overdraft facility at a rate of 10% with the local bank. Chris is quite concerned about this. For a business which has takings in cash and can take credit from suppliers the Dough House should generally have excess cash at the end of each month. After plenty of discussions with Jane, Chris identifies several problems with the way Jane is managing the working capital of the Dough House. He agrees with Jane that these can be summarised as follows:
1. Her office delivery service. This is a recent innovation where the Dough House is providing in-house coffee and pastries to local businesses. This is very profitable as she can charge higher prices for delivery. However, Jane must invoice the businesses. She is doing this manually and as she is so busy she often takes a couple of weeks before

sending them. Jane's average value of debtors is €20,000 and average value of credit sales per day is €1,000.

2. The second problem concerns her local suppliers. They are small operators and are very keen to be paid quickly. As they need to borrow a delivery van they deliver relatively infrequently at no discount. Being a small business owner herself she has sympathy for them and generally pays cash on delivery. Her average level of creditors is €2,000 and her average value of credit purchases per day is €400.

3. She also must store a lot of raw materials on the premises. Jane's average value of raw materials stock is €12,000 and she use €250 of raw materials on average per day.

4. To maintain staff morale she pays wages at the end of each day.

Task 14

Calculate the Dough House's cash conversion cycle.

Task 15

Prepare a memo for Jane on the subject of working capital management. In the memo you should include reference to:
- how the four issues highlighted by Jane are affecting her cash flow and how she might address them; and
- how making changes to her working capital management can have negative consequences on the business.

(Jane thanks Chris for the advice. He assures her that these are common teething problems in a new business. Jane heads back to work confident that these five easy-to-implement changes will greatly improve the liquidity of her business.)

Jane Dough Telephone Call (Working Capital Management) – 30 June 2009

Jane telephones Chris to ask some advice. She has implemented all of his previous advice regarding debtors, creditors and wages. She has one more question and it concerns the most economic quantity of stock to order. She has calculated that every year she is using 1,500 bags of baking powder. The cost of each delivery (excluding the purchase price) is €1. As she has limited storage space she estimates the annualised cost of holding each unit is 30c. She's not sure how much stock she should purchase each time, given the concerns around working capital management.

Task 16

Calculate the Economic Order Quantity (EOQ) and the total costs of ordering and holding the stocks of baking powder per annum.

MCL Meeting (Working Capital Management) – 15 July 2009

Mike Smithers has decided to leverage on Chris's obvious skills and sets him his next task relating to working capital management. In the past they have managed working capital on an ad hoc basis. Over the next two months Mike Smithers wants Chris to review the company's current budget forecasts and suggest how they might best manage their working capital requirements next year. The company is forecasting a sharp slowdown in sales at the end of this year. Mike thinks that this will negatively affect their short-term cash flow at the start of next year.

Mike has provided Chris with the following information to prepare a quarterly cash budget for next year.

1. Sales are forecast as follows:

All figures in €000s

	Q1	Q2	Q3	Q4
Sales	155	161.25	231	206

MCL receives 80% of cash from sales in the quarter incurred and 20% of sales in the following quarter. Sales in Q4 of the current year are forecast to be €180,000.

2. Purchases are forecast as follows:

All figures in €000s

	Q1	Q2	Q3	Q4
Purchases	120	110	100.0	115.0

MCL pays 100% of creditors in the quarter following purchase. Purchases in Q4 of the current year are forecast to be €130,000.

3. MCL is forecast to receive cash from sale of investments of €25,000 in Q3 next year.

4. All other expenses outlined below are paid in the quarter incurred:

All figures in €000s

	Q1	Q2	Q3	Q4
Current Expenses	60.0	60.0	60.0	60.0
Capital Expenditure	5.0	2.6	11.0	13.0
Interest	2.0	2.0	2.0	1.6
Dividends	2.0	2.0	2.0	2.0
Taxes	4.0	4.0	5.0	6.0

Note that interest includes the cost of outstanding long-term debt but does not include any additional borrowing to meet cash requirement next year.

5. MCL must maintain a minimum cash balance of €10,000 at the end of each quarter.

Task 17

Using the information above, prepare a memo for Mike which includes a cash budget (in the format of Cash Sources less Cash Uses) for each of the four quarters of next year. Include an estimation of any short-term financing requirements.

Attn: Chris
Memo: Working Capital Management
From: Mike Smithers
Date: 15 August 2009

Well done. You have done a great job preparing the cash budget. I have spoken to our bankers and discussed our various options with the management team. I believe we have the following options to address our short-term financing needs.

1. We can get a short-term bank loan at a rate of 10% per annum. This loan is for amounts up to €20,000. Above this amount we must pay a rate of 20%.
2. We can stretch our payments to creditors. This will cost 3% per quarter. I estimate that the maximum we can stretch is €20k.
3. We can offer discounts to our suppliers. This will cost us the equivalent of 4% per quarter. I estimate that this discount will bring in €20k in cash early.

When you are in the office on Friday, I would be obliged if you could work on a financing plan which would make the best use of these options.

Task 18

Prepare a financing plan based upon the budget above using the financing options in order of cost. Be sure to include the costs of the financing options.

TOPIC 3: FINANCING DECISIONS

MCL Limited Meeting (Financing decisions) – 5 September 2009

Again Michael Smithers is incredibly impressed by the work Chris has carried out. The company has already begun implementing the recommendations for managing working capital for next year and Mike has intimated that he would like Chris to get involved with some of the discussions around capital structure. Chris realises that his knowledge is fairly skimpy (to say the least) in this area, and decides to put in some advance study on the subject. He asks Mr Ryan to talk him through some of the basics of capital structure.

Notes: Meeting with Mr Ryan – 15 September 2009

Mr Ryan began by explaining the traditional view of capital structure before going on to explain the weaknesses with the traditional model and the effect of taxes on capital structure.

TRADITIONAL MODEL

The traditional model was based on the premise that debt is cheaper than equity. Replacing equity with debt will lower your cost of capital. This will be compensated in part by an increase in the cost of the remaining equity. However, up to a point, you can reduce your cost of capital and thereby increase the company's value by replacing equity with debt. **There is an optimal capital structure which a company should attempt to achieve.**

PROBLEM WITH THE TRADITIONAL EXPLANATION – MODIGLIANI AND MILLER (NO TAXES)

Modigliani and Miller, assuming zero taxes, proposed that the traditional view conveniently fits what happens in practice, but is based on a false premise: that the act of borrowing money is sufficient to increase a firm's value.

The value of a levered firm is equal to the value of an unlevered firm with identical expected cash flows.

Consider a situation where a company earns €1,500 this year and has zero debt. The company's shares trade at €10 each and there are 1,000 in issue. Two alternatives:

1. *The company tries to increase firm value by issuing €5,000 of debt @ 10% interest rate to repurchase 500 shares at €10.*
2. *If the company borrows nothing and an individual who has one share instead borrows €10 to buy an additional share in the company, consider the outcome.*

1. *The company tries to increase firm value by issuing €5,000 of debt @ 10% interest rate.*

	Old Situation	*New Situation*
Number of Shares	*1000*	*500*
Price per share	*€10*	*€10*
Market Value of Shares	*€10,000*	*€5,000*
Debt @ 10%	*0*	*5,000*
Operating Income	*1,500*	*1,500*
Interest		*500*
Earnings per share	*1.50*	*2*
Return on shares	*15%*	*20%*

(Continued)

2. *If the company borrows nothing and an individual who has 1 share instead borrows €10 to buy an additional share in the company, consider the outcome.*

	Old Situation	*Borrows €10 and buys share*
Number of Shares	1	
Price per share	€10	€10
Market Value of Shares	€10	€20
Debt @10%	0	€10
Income before interest	1.50	3
Interest		1
Earnings	1.50	(3−1) = 2
Return	15%	20%

To conclude, as an individual can replicate anything a company can do regarding leverage it is impossible for a company to increase firm value by borrowing more money (assuming zero taxes).

TAXES – MODIGLIANI & MILLER

Modigliani and Miller then went on to propose an alternative hypothesis after relaxing the assumption of no taxes. For this second hypothesis they assumed that interest on debt is tax deductible.

The value of a levered firm is greater than the value of an otherwise identical unlevered firm by the amount of debt multiplied by the tax rate.

THEORY OF TAX SHIELD – EXAMPLE

- *Two companies, one levered (L), one unlevered (U).*
- *Both have EBIT of €1,000.*
- *U has debt of €1,000 @ interest of 8% per annum.*
- *Tax rate = 20%.*
- *Cost of capital = 8%.*
- *No growth.*

Calculate both companies' income attributable to shareholders (i.e. profit after interest and tax).

(Continued)

All figures in €000s

	U	L
Extract from Balance Sheet		
Debt @ 8%	0	1,000
Extract from Profit and Loss Account		
EBIT	1,000	1,000
Interest	0	80
Profit Before Tax	1,000	920
Tax @ 20%	200	184
Income Attributable to Shareholders	800	736

Total income to stock and bondholders is:

All figures in € thousands

	U	L
Stockholders	800	736
Bondholders	0	80
Total	800	816

Therefore, there is an interest tax shield per annum of €16 by having Debt in Capital Structure.

What is the PV of this tax shield?

$$PV = \frac{C}{r}$$

$$PV = 16/8\% = €200$$

MCL Limited Meeting (Financing Decisions) – 30 September 2009

After spending several hours on the subject, Chris is now pleased that he has mastered the basics of Capital Structure. When he meets Mike the following week, Mike notes that he has finished reviewing the investment appraisal reports and is convinced that Net Present Value is the best way to appraise their investment in the new Plant. However, he is concerned about the assumptions Chris raised in the report relating to the cost of capital. (The cost of capital used was out of date as it was taken from a three-year-old valuation report conducted by the firm's auditors.)

He now wants Chris to review the company's capital structure and estimate their current weighted average cost of capital. He also wants Chris to outline any drawbacks or weakness he can identify in the methodology used to estimate the cost of capital.

Before attempting this exercise, Chris asks Mike to give him any background information he can. Mike has obtained the following information for Chris:

INFORMATION ON MCL LIMITED CAPITAL STRUCTURE

MCL's auditors have estimated the total market value of MCL Limited's equity at €8m and the total market value of the debt at €2 million.

In order to estimate a weighted average cost of capital for the company I am told that you must first estimate a cost of equity and a cost of debt. As MCL Limited is not publicly quoted I have identified comparable publicly quoted companies to get information to calculate an appropriate cost of equity for MCL Limited. There are only two competitors of MCL Limited which have a stock exchange listing, Knitwear PLC and Apparel Manufacturing PLC. Both Knitwear PLC and Apparel PLC have similar capital structure to MCL Limited.

Finally, MCL faces a marginal tax rate of 12.5% and makes annual interest payments on debt of €160,000.

Chris has asked one of the experienced partners for the appropriate data for Apparel Manufacturing PLC and Knitwear PLC. She has left a message on his phone stating that Apparel has an equity market Beta of 1.25. The market return is 10% and the risk-free rate of interest is 4%. Knitwear PLC has a dividend yield of 4% and a long-term growth rate in dividends of 7.5%.

Task 19

Calculate an appropriate Weighted Average Cost of Capital (WACC) for MCL, based on the information you have gathered. State any limitations of the WACC model.

MCL Limited Meeting (Financing Decisions) – 10 October 2009

Mike Smithers has finished reviewing the Weighted Average Cost of Capital calculations and is happy with the result. However, previously, he left out one vital piece of information. The company will have to raise additional funding to finance the plant. This new funding will affect the capital structure of MCL Limited.

He mentions that to finance the investment in new machinery MCL Limited needs to find additional funding. He explains the principles and assumptions behind the funding in MCL.

Ideally, we should match the source and use of this funding by duration. Funding is usually classified by duration:

Short Term – Under two years, e.g. bank overdraft, short-term loans, factoring and invoice discounting
Medium Term – two to seven years, e.g. term loan, hire purchase and instalment credit, leasing
Long Term – Over seven years, e.g. equity finance and debt finance

As the savings from the investment in machinery are spread over a four-year period it makes sense to match this payoff with a medium-term source of funds. The management team believes a term loan is the most advantageous way to finance the machinery.

This new loan will be at a rate of interest of 8% and will increase MCL Limited's debt/value ratio to 40%.

Task 20

Calculate the impact that these changes will have on MCL Limited's cost of capital. Mike is pleased to hear that the revised WACC is quite close to the cost of capital used to assess the investment in the new machinery. He mentions that he has recalculated the NPV with the new WACC and it is still generating a positive NPV of €54,200, indicating that MCL should still go ahead.

MCL Limited Meeting (Financing Decisions) – 20 October 2009

Mike Smithers is happy with the memo that Chris has prepared but would like to explain some of the key principles in this area to the rest of the management team. He asks Chris

---

Task 21

Prepare a short memo for Mike outlining:

1. Portfolio Theory
2. The Capital Asset Pricing Model
3. Efficient Markets Hypothesis

MCL Limited Meeting (Financing Decisions) To Assess the Financial Position of MCL Limited – 5 November 2009

Mike Smithers is considering further expansion of MCL Limited. However, he is not sure how the bank will react to any requests for further funding.

MCL LIMITED RELEVANT FINANCIAL INFORMATION

	2008 €
Extracts from Income Statement	
Sales	1,637,600
Cost of Sales	854,940
Depreciation	23,100
EBIT	286,200
Interest	36,829
Net Income	199,371
Dividends	0

Extracts from Statement of Financial Position

	2008 €
Debtors	99,940
Stock	91,255
Current Assets	206,418
Debtors	99,940
Total Assets	837,043
Current Liabilities	77,233
Book Value of Equity	709,810
Market Values	
Market Value Debt	8,000,000
Market Value Equity	2,000,000

Task 22

Prepare a memo for Mike outlining how the bank might measure the current financial position of MCL Limited.

MCL Limited Meeting (Financing Decisions) Long-Term Financing Options – 20 November 2009

Mike Smithers is also concerned about the financing options for MCL Limited in the future. At some stage one or more of the shareholders may want to sell out. None of the other shareholders has the resources to buy them out. He has asked Chris to accompany him to see BIA Corporate Finance, the corporate advisors, in Dublin. The corporate advisors are suggesting that MCL Limited could raise finance from banks, venture capitalists or in the longer term perhaps the capital markets. They will meet with Dave Sheehan, one of the partners in BIA Corporate Finance, and Mike would like Chris to write a follow-up memo, particularly noting:

1. What role banks and institutional investors could play in providing finance to MCL Limited.
2. Describe the nature and role of capital markets. Outline the principal alternative security types (equity, preference shares and debentures), their characteristics and situations where they are suitable.
3. Demonstrate an understanding of the role of venture capital. Outline the requirements of a venture capitalist in terms of assessment of investment criteria and exit routes.

MEMO

Attn: **Michael Smithers (Finance Director)**
Memo: **MCL Limited Long-Term Financing**
From: **Chris**
Date: **25 November 2009**

Following discussions with Dave Sheehan of BIA Corporate Finance, I have prepared the following document on long-term financing options. This document simply summarises the key points.

THE ROLE BANKS AND INSTITUTIONAL INVESTORS COULD PLAY IN PROVIDING FINANCE TO MCL LIMITED

Banks and Institutional investors can play an important role by providing funds in several ways, through bank debt, equity investment and capital markets. Banks take money on deposit from savers and lend it out to individuals and corporations in order to generate profits. Institutional investors raise cash from investors who wish to grow their investments (e.g. for their pension) and provide it to the firm: (1) the financial manager in the firm has a demand for funds which he invests in the firms operations; (2) this investment generates cash from operations; (3) which are returned to the investor (4b) (via dividends and interest payments) or reinvested in the firm to provide capital gains to the investor (4a).

Continued

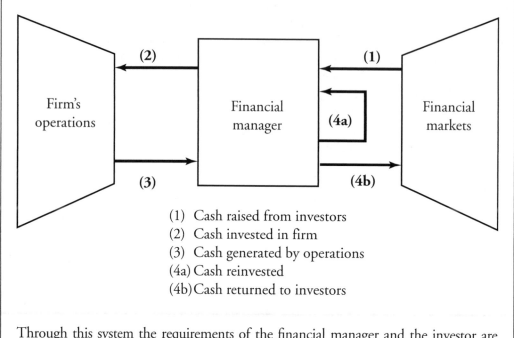

(1) Cash raised from investors
(2) Cash invested in firm
(3) Cash generated by operations
(4a) Cash reinvested
(4b) Cash returned to investors

Through this system the requirements of the financial manager and the investor are catered for. The financial manager has the funds to grow the business and the investor is provided with a return on his investment commensurate with the risk of the business.

28 November 2009 (over coffee!)

Mike has been discussing his uncle's ventures into stocks and shares and has admitted that he would be interested in learning to "play the market" himself. He admits that he is not sure of the differences between equities and bonds, and wonders if you would draft him a short explanation.

Task 23

For each of equities/shares and bonds, explain what is meant by the term and give the principal characteristics.

28 November 2009 (over coffee!)

Mervin Smithers has approached you and wonders if you could prepare a note on Venture Capitalism for the Management Team. He has found the information you have given to Mike over the last number of months very useful and is hoping you can help him out. He would prefer to get the information in "bullet points".

Task 24

Write a short list of bullet points for Mervin, describing the role of venture capital. Outline the requirements of a venture capitalist in terms of assessment of investment criteria and exit routes.

TOPIC 4: FINANCE AND THE INDIVIDUAL

Jane Dough Meeting – 5 December 2009

Jane arranges another appointment to see Chris. On this occasion she wants to see Chris for personal finance advice. The business is now operating quite profitably. She has implemented the working capital suggestions and she now has excess cash at the end of every month. As suggested she is depositing this in a high interest on demand account and this is adding nicely to the bottom line. The coffee business is steadily increasing.

After recapping the year's progress they focus on the purpose of this meeting. Being so busy Jane's personal finances have been neglected. She has made few changes since she went from being an employee 12 months ago to being self-employed. Chris asks her to write down all of her and John's savings and investments.

LIST OF PERSONAL INVESTMENTS

Credit Union Account (r = 4%)	€15,000
Deposit Account (r = 1%)	€20,000
SSIA (maturing this month)	€25,000
Personal pension	€40,000
Interest in rental properties (yielding 2%)	€50,000
Small Share portfolio valued at	€15,000
(average 5 year return 10% per annum)	

The couple are also contributing to	Net per annum
Life assurance (critical illness)	€2,000
Permanent health insurance	€1,000
Voluntary health insurance	€2,500

Chris's first concern is that the couple may be over-insured. Jane has brought the policies, and the life assurance and permanent health insurance provide comprehensive cover for loss of earnings should she become sick or incapacitated. The Voluntary Health Insurance covers everything in the Permanent Health Insurance policy. Jane decides to cancel the Permanent Health Insurance. This will save her €1,000 net per annum.

Chris is also concerned that the €20,000 Jane has in the deposit account is earning a gross return of only 1%. The €15,000 in the Credit Union is getting a better rate of interest of 4%. Chris points out that this is less than the rate of inflation and she is losing in real terms by leaving her money in either account. They agree that she needs to have cash available so maintains a balance of €30,000 in the credit union account. The couple already has a reasonable exposure to the property market and a small exposure to the stock market. Jane decides to put the remainder towards the stocks and share portfolio through a low fee online account. As Jane will not need to access this money for at least five years she is confident that it will provide a return at least in excess of the rate of inflation. They will continue contributing to the personal pension as this is a very tax efficient form of saving.

Revised List of Personal Investments

Credit Union Account (r = 4%)	€30,000
Personal pension	€40,000
Interest in rental properties (yielding 2%)	€50,000
Share portfolio valued at (average 5-year return 10% per annum)	€45,000
The couple are also contributing to:	Net per annum
Life assurance (critical illness)	€2,000
Voluntary health insurance	€2,500
Additional Contribution to the personal pension	€1,000

Satisfied that her personal finances are in order, Jane goes back to the Dough House to bake mince pies for the Christmas shopping rush.

Jane Dough Telephone Call – 8 December 2009

Jane telephones Chris excitedly. To celebrate the first year anniversary of the business her uncle, Tom, has offered to make an investment of €5,000 in one of two companies on her behalf. He heard on the rumour mill that both of these companies are going to "do really well". He has provided Jane with some financial information comparing the current performance of the two businesses. She asks Chris if he can assess the relative performance of the companies from this information.

Financial Information

All figures in €000

	Company 1	Company 2
Sales	532.1	2,265.3
Net Profit	105.7	125.2
Capital Employed	959.7	2,918.3
Current Assets	345.1	1,305.4

Current Liabilities	211	1,146.0
Stock	56.2	573.5
Long-term Debt	367.8	1,233.9
Debtors	191.6	623.3
Share Price Information		
Stock Price	11.3	22.2
Earnings per Share	0.574	1.076
Dividend per Share	0.24	0.11

Task 25

Prepare a ratio analysis of the two companies and conclude whether either company should be further considered as an investment vehicle for Jane.

MCL Limited Meeting – 15 December 2009

Matthew Jnr, the CEO, drops into Chris's office. He had been rereading the memos that Chris has prepared throughout the year and is very impressed. However, on this occasion he wants to discuss his personal investments. Matthew Jnr has been investing in the stock market for five years. Originally he approached it as a bit of fun but has now begun to take it more seriously. Matthew Jnr has to date taken an ad hoc approach to investing but would like to take a more formal approach. He currently has a portfolio worth €100,000 equally divided amongst 20 stocks listed in the UK. His portfolio has provided an average return of 6% per annum over the last five years while the FTSE All Share has returned 8%. Matthew is disappointed by this as he would like to get higher returns and is happy to take a risk.

His stockbroker has sent him some information on two companies, Bellweather PLC and Jones PLC. Matthew Jnr wants Chris to tell him which would be more suitable to add to his portfolio. He gives Chris the following information on the stock and asks Chris to email him with his advice.

	Bellweather PLC	Jones PLC
Correlation with Existing Portfolio	0.10	1.0
Market Beta	1.25	0.75
Risk-Free Rate of Interest	4%	

Before attempting any calculations, you read the memo prepared for you by Mr Ryan before he left the office yesterday.

MEMO

Attn: **Chris**
Subject: Implications of portfolio theory and the capital asset pricing model
            for Matthew Jnr's existing portfolio
From: **Mr Ryan**
Date: **14 December 2009**

Portfolio theory recommends that investors hold a diversified portfolio of shares, so as to eliminate firm specific risk. This can be achieved by holding a portfolio of at least 12 to 15 shares with uncorrelated returns or an index tracking fund. As Matthew's existing portfolio contains 20 stocks this would suggest he is adequately diversified and is not overly exposed to bad news from one specific firm.

The CAPM indicates that an investor should not expect to earn a premium for incurring specific risk as they can be diversified away (as is the case in this portfolio). Investors can however expect a reward for incurring market risk. This is the case as market risk is unavoidable, even for those investors holding a diversified portfolio of shares. The market risk of a share or portfolio is generally expressed as its market beta or β.

The CAPM states that the expected return on share i can be expressed as follows:

$$E(R_i) = R_f + \beta_i (E(R_m) - R_f)$$

Where:
$E(R_i)$ = Expected Return from holding stock i
R_f = Risk-free rate of interest
$E(R_m)$ = Expected return on the market portfolio

Thus, when investing on the stock market, the CAPM would advise to hold a diversified portfolio, whose beta factor is consistent with the investor's attitude to risk. Matthew has indicated that he would like to take risk. The CAPM suggests that he should hold a portfolio with a $\beta > 1$ to receive a return greater than the market portfolio and a $\beta < 1$ to receive a return less than the market portfolio.

If one looks at the historical return of the existing portfolio we can get an estimate of the portfolio's β.

$$R_i = R_f + \beta_i (R_m - R_f)$$

$$6\% = 4\% + \beta i (8\% - 4\%)$$

This would suggest the β of the existing portfolio is 0.5. As he is seeking higher returns the CAPM would indicate that he should adjust his portfolio to increase the market risk and consequent expected return.
You should also note that the correlation coefficient (ρ) depicts the strength of the relationship between two shares returns. Correlation coefficients range between

(Continued)

−1 and +1. −1 indicates, they have an extremely strong negative relationship. If one increases by 1%, the other will decrease by 1%. +1 indicates, they have an extremely strong positive relationship. If one increases by 1%, the other will increase by 1%. The lower the correlation coefficient between the returns on two companies, the greater is the scope for risk reduction, through diversification.

Task 26

Calculate the expected return from investing in Bellweather PLC and Jones PLC and recommend which stock would be more suitable for Matthew to invest in.

SECTION TWO

FORMULAE AND TABLES

TABLES

Present Value Tables

Periods					Discount rates (r)					
(n)	1%	2%	3%	4%	5%	6%	7%	8%	9%	10%
1	0.990	0.980	0.971	0.962	0.952	0.943	0.935	0.926	0.917	0.909
2	0.980	0.961	0.943	0.925	0.907	0.890	0.873	0.857	0.842	0.826
3	0.971	0.942	0.915	0.889	0.864	0.840	0.816	0.794	0.772	0.751
4	0.961	0.924	0.888	0.855	0.823	0.792	0.763	0.735	0.708	0.683
5	0.951	0.906	0.863	0.822	0.784	0.747	0.713	0.681	0.650	0.621
6	0.942	0.888	0.837	0.790	0.746	0.705	0.666	0.630	0.596	0.564
7	0.933	0.871	0.813	0.760	0.711	0.665	0.623	0.583	0.547	0.513
8	0.923	0.853	0.789	0.731	0.677	0.627	0.582	0.540	0.502	0.467
9	0.914	0.837	0.766	0.703	0.645	0.592	0.544	0.500	0.460	0.424
10	0.905	0.820	0.744	0.676	0.614	0.558	0.508	0.463	0.422	0.386
11	0.896	0.804	0.722	0.650	0.585	0.527	0.475	0.429	0.388	0.350
12	0.887	0.788	0.701	0.625	0.557	0.497	0.444	0.397	0.356	0.319
13	0.879	0.773	0.681	0.601	0.530	0.469	0.415	0.368	0.326	0.290
14	0.870	0.758	0.661	0.577	0.505	0.442	0.388	0.340	0.299	0.263
15	0.861	0.743	0.642	0.555	0.481	0.417	0.362	0.315	0.275	0.239

	11%	12%	13%	14%	15%	16%	17%	18%	19%	20%
1	0.901	0.893	0.885	0.877	0.870	0.862	0.855	0.847	0.840	0.833
2	0.812	0.797	0.783	0.769	0.756	0.743	0.731	0.718	0.706	0.694
3	0.731	0.712	0.693	0.675	0.658	0.641	0.624	0.609	0.593	0.579
4	0.659	0.636	0.613	0.592	0.572	0.552	0.534	0.516	0.499	0.482
5	0.593	0.567	0.543	0.519	0.497	0.476	0.456	0.437	0.419	0.402
6	0.535	0.507	0.480	0.456	0.432	0.410	0.390	0.370	0.352	0.335
7	0.482	0.452	0.425	0.400	0.376	0.354	0.333	0.314	0.296	0.279
8	0.434	0.404	0.376	0.351	0.327	0.305	0.285	0.266	0.249	0.233
9	0.391	0.361	0.333	0.308	0.284	0.263	0.243	0.225	0.209	0.194
10	0.352	0.322	0.295	0.270	0.247	0.227	0.208	0.191	0.176	0.162
11	0.317	0.287	0.261	0.237	0.215	0.195	0.178	0.162	0.148	0.135
12	0.286	0.257	0.231	0.208	0.187	0.168	0.152	0.137	0.124	0.112
13	0.258	0.229	0.204	0.182	0.163	0.145	0.130	0.116	0.104	0.093
14	0.232	0.205	0.181	0.160	0.141	0.125	0.111	0.099	0.088	0.078
15	0.209	0.183	0.160	0.140	0.123	0.108	0.095	0.084	0.074	0.065

	21%	22%	23%	24%	25%	26%	27%	28%	29%	30%
1	0.826	0.820	0.813	0.807	0.800	0.794	0.787	0.781	0.775	0.769
2	0.683	0.672	0.661	0.650	0.640	0.630	0.620	0.610	0.601	0.592
3	0.565	0.551	0.537	0.525	0.512	0.500	0.488	0.477	0.466	0.455
4	0.467	0.451	0.437	0.423	0.410	0.397	0.384	0.373	0.361	0.350
5	0.386	0.370	0.355	0.341	0.328	0.315	0.303	0.291	0.280	0.269
6	0.319	0.303	0.289	0.275	0.262	0.250	0.238	0.227	0.217	0.207
7	0.263	0.249	0.235	0.222	0.210	0.198	0.188	0.178	0.168	0.159
8	0.218	0.204	0.191	0.179	0.168	0.157	0.148	0.139	0.130	0.123
9	0.180	0.167	0.155	0.144	0.134	0.125	0.116	0.108	0.101	0.094
10	0.149	0.137	0.126	0.116	0.107	0.099	0.092	0.085	0.078	0.073
11	0.123	0.112	0.103	0.094	0.086	0.079	0.072	0.066	0.061	0.056
12	0.102	0.092	0.083	0.076	0.069	0.063	0.057	0.052	0.047	0.043
13	0.084	0.075	0.068	0.061	0.055	0.050	0.045	0.040	0.037	0.033
14	0.069	0.062	0.055	0.049	0.044	0.039	0.035	0.032	0.028	0.025
15	0.057	0.051	0.045	0.040	0.035	0.031	0.028	0.025	0.022	0.020

Annuity Table

Periods   **Discount rates (r)**

(n)	1%	2%	3%	4%	5%	6%	7%	8%	9%	10%
1	0.990	0.980	0.971	0.962	0.952	0.943	0.935	0.926	0.917	0.909
2	1.970	1.942	1.913	1.886	1.859	1.833	1.808	1.783	1.759	1.736
3	2.941	2.884	2.829	2.775	2.723	2.673	2.624	2.577	2.531	2.487
4	3.902	3.808	3.717	3.630	3.546	3.465	3.387	3.312	3.240	3.170
5	4.853	4.713	4.580	4.452	4.329	4.212	4.100	3.993	3.890	3.791
6	5.795	5.601	5.417	5.242	5.076	4.917	4.767	4.623	4.486	4.355
7	6.728	6.472	6.230	6.002	5.786	5.582	5.389	5.206	5.033	4.868
8	7.652	7.325	7.020	6.733	6.463	6.210	5.971	5.747	5.535	5.335
9	8.566	8.162	7.786	7.435	7.108	6.802	6.515	6.247	5.995	5.759
10	9.471	8.983	8.530	8.111	7.722	7.360	7.024	6.710	6.418	6.145
11	10.37	9.787	9.253	8.760	8.306	7.887	7.499	7.139	6.805	6.495
12	11.26	10.58	9.954	9.385	8.863	8.384	7.943	7.536	7.161	6.814
13	12.13	11.35	10.63	9.986	9.394	8.853	8.358	7.904	7.487	7.103
14	13.00	12.11	11.30	10.56	9.899	9.295	8.745	8.244	7.786	7.367
15	13.87	12.85	11.94	11.12	10.38	9.712	9.108	8.559	8.061	7.606

(n)	11%	12%	13%	14%	15%	16%	17%	18%	19%	20%
1	0.901	0.893	0.885	0.877	0.870	0.862	0.855	0.847	0.840	0.833
2	1.713	1.690	1.668	1.647	1.626	1.605	1.585	1.566	1.547	1.528
3	2.444	2.402	2.361	2.322	2.283	2.246	2.210	2.174	2.140	2.106
4	3.102	3.037	2.974	2.914	2.855	2.798	2.743	2.690	2.639	2.589
5	3.696	3.605	3.517	3.433	3.352	3.274	3.199	3.127	3.058	2.991
6	4.231	4.111	3.998	3.889	3.784	3.685	3.589	3.498	3.410	3.326
7	4.712	4.564	4.423	4.288	4.160	4.039	3.922	3.812	3.706	3.605
8	5.146	4.968	4.799	4.639	4.487	4.344	4.207	4.078	3.954	3.837
9	5.537	5.328	5.132	4.946	4.772	4.607	4.451	4.303	4.163	4.031
10	5.889	5.650	5.426	5.216	5.019	4.833	4.659	4.494	4.339	4.192
11	6.207	5.938	5.687	5.453	5.234	5.029	4.836	4.656	4.486	4.327
12	6.492	6.194	5.918	5.660	5.421	5.197	4.988	4.793	4.611	4.439
13	6.750	6.424	6.122	5.842	5.583	5.342	5.118	4.910	4.715	4.533
14	6.982	6.628	6.302	6.002	5.724	5.468	5.229	5.008	4.802	4.611
15	7.191	6.811	6.462	6.142	5.847	5.575	5.324	5.092	4.876	4.675

	21%	22%	23%	24%	25%	26%	27%	28%	29%	30%
1	0.826	0.820	0.813	0.806	0.800	0.794	0.787	0.781	0.775	0.769
2	1.509	1.492	1.474	1.457	1.440	1.424	1.407	1.392	1.376	1.361
3	2.074	2.042	2.011	1.981	1.952	1.923	1.896	1.868	1.842	1.816
4	2.540	2.494	2.448	2.404	2.362	2.320	2.280	2.241	2.203	2.166
5	2.926	2.864	2.803	2.745	2.689	2.635	2.583	2.532	2.483	2.436
6	3.245	3.167	3.092	3.020	2.951	2.885	2.821	2.759	2.700	2.643
7	3.508	3.416	3.327	3.242	3.161	3.083	3.009	2.937	2.868	2.802
8	3.726	3.619	3.518	3.421	3.329	3.241	3.156	3.076	2.999	2.925
9	3.905	3.786	3.673	3.566	3.463	3.366	3.273	3.184	3.100	3.019
10	4.054	3.923	3.799	3.682	3.571	3.465	3.364	3.269	3.178	3.092
11	4.177	4.035	3.902	3.776	3.656	3.543	3.437	3.335	3.239	3.147
12	5.278	4.127	3.985	3.851	3.725	3.606	3.493	3.387	3.286	3.190
13	4.362	4.203	4.053	3.912	3.780	3.656	3.538	3.427	3.322	3.223
14	4.432	4.265	4.108	3.962	3.824	3.695	3.573	3.459	3.351	3.249
15	4.489	4.315	4.153	4.001	3.859	3.726	3.601	3.483	3.373	3.268

FORMULAE

Adjusted present value

$$APV = Vu + Dt - \text{PV of issue costs}$$

Capital asset pricing model

$$r_j = r_f + \beta(r_m - r_f)$$

Dividend valuation model (no growth – finding the value of equity)

$$P_0 = \frac{D_1}{Ke}$$

Dividend valuation model (no growth – finding the cost of equity)

$$Ke = \frac{D_1}{P_0}$$

Dividend valuation model (with growth – finding the cost of equity)

$$Ke = \frac{D_0(1 + g)}{P_0} + g$$

Dividend valuation model (with growth – finding the value of equity)

$$P_0 = \frac{D_0(1 + g)}{Ke - g}$$

Economic batch quantity

$$EBQ = \sqrt{\frac{2FU}{CP(1 - d/r)}}$$

Economic order quantity model

$$EOQ = \sqrt{\frac{2FU}{CP}}$$

Equivalent annual annuity

$$\text{Annual annuity equivalent of the NPV} = NPV \times \frac{i}{1 - (1 + i)^{-n}}$$

Growth in dividends (using historic actual dividend information)

$$g = \sqrt[y]{\frac{D_{t0}}{D_{t0 - y}}} - 1$$

Growth (using retentions)

$$g = br$$

Interpolation (IRR)

$$\text{IRR rate} = \text{Rate 1} + \frac{\text{NPV 1 (Rate 2} - \text{Rate 1)}}{\text{NPV 1} - \text{NPV 2}}$$

Irredeemable debt (market value of debt)

$$D = \frac{i}{K_d}$$

Irredeemable debt (cost of debt)

$$K_d = \frac{i(1 - t)}{D}$$

Nominal discount rate

$$\text{Nominal discount rate} = ((1 + \text{Real rate}) \times (1 + \text{Inflation rate})) - 1$$

Preference share (cost)

$$K_P = \frac{D_1}{P_p}$$

Redeemable bonds (market value)

$$P_0 = \frac{I_1}{(1 + K_d)} + \frac{I_2}{(1 + K_d)^2} + \dots \frac{R_n}{(1 + K_d)^n}$$

Redeemable bonds (cost/return)

$$K_d = \frac{I_1}{P_0} + \frac{(R - P_0)/n}{P_0}$$

Standard deviation

The square root of the variance (σ^2), which is:

$$\sigma^2 = (X_1 - Y)^2 p_1 + (X_2 - Y)^2 p_2 \dots \dots (X_n - Y)^2 p_n$$

Untraded debt (cost)

$$K_{dt} = i(1 - t)$$

Weighted Average Cost of Capital (WACC)

$$\text{WACC} = \frac{E(Ke)}{(D + E)} + \frac{D(Kd(1 - t))}{(D + E)}$$

Annualised cost of discount

$$\frac{d}{100 - d} \times \frac{365}{(\text{reduction in receivables/debtors days})}$$

SOLUTIONS TO TASKS FROM 'STORYLINE' CASE STUDY

Solution Task 1

Inflation

Jane has already identified costs as something she is trying to minimise. Chris separates these costs into raw materials, wages and overheads. Currently raw material prices are rising significantly. Currently the rate of inflation in Ireland is 5% per annum. Wages are rising at a high rate of 6% and with high energy prices overheads are also rising. Jane must keep a close eye on these cost increases. If they rise significantly she must pass on the rise to consumers in the form of price increases. This is the only way to maintain her profit margins.

Economic Growth

The economy is currently growing at a rate of 4% per annum. This is an ideal level of growth for setting up a new business. Over the last 10 years growth in Ireland has varied from 2% to 6%. Few economists are forecasting a decrease in economic growth or a recession for the next couple of years so the business environment should remain healthy.

Consumer Spending

This rate of growth links directly to consumer spending. As spending money in a coffee shop is a luxury, it is very sensitive to economic growth. As long as economic growth remains strong people will have money in their pocket and Jane should be able to grow the Dough House's business.

Interest Rates

Finally, the level of interest rates is very important. It affects economic growth and also affects her savings and borrowings. As interest rates rise economic growth is constrained and as interest rates fall the level of economic growth generally increases. Because interest rates are currently low relative to historical levels it is likely they will gradually rise in the future. This may constrain economic growth but policy makers are careful not to increase interest rates too quickly. One advantage of rising interest rates is that Jane has significant savings. At the moment these are earning low rates of interest. As interest rates rise these savings will grow faster.

Solution Task 2

- Employing non-EU workers – this is an area which is not clear cut but we should seek to satisfy ourselves that these workers are receiving the minimum standards required by law. €4 is less than the minimum wage. Jane must always observe this law.
- Unlicensed waste disposal – this is an issue which can generate significant fines and very bad publicity. It is ethically wrong and Jane should never use unlicensed companies in this area.

Solution Task 3

As outlined in the previous memo, dated 31 January 2009, the issue is essentially one of the absence of proper corporate governance procedures that would offset the dominance of the chief executive. The main issues are as follows:
- Dominant chief executive. Matthew Jnr seems to be particularly dominant and, though he is not a majority shareholder, he seems to essentially run the company his way.
- Concentrated ownership and management of the company. The ownership of the company is concentrated among a close group of family members. This can lead to disharmony among the shareholders and a lack of clarity of purpose for management.
- No independent/outside board members. All of the board members are from the family. Bringing in an experienced outside board member would give additional perspective to the business.
- Little communication with minority shareholders. As highlighted previously, all shareholders should be treated equally within the firm. There is generally no valid reason for not providing information to outsider shareholders.
- Little representation of minority shareholder interests. Again, as outlined previously, the minority shareholders have no representation in the management of the company.

Solution Task 4

- €1,000 to be paid today.
- €1,200 to be received in one year's time. We must calculate the present value of this cash flow.

$$\mathbf{PV = C_t/(1 + r)^t}$$
$$PV = 1200/(1 + 10\%)^1$$
$$PV = 1{,}090.91$$

- €1,200 to be received in one year's time is the same as having €1,090.91 today.

- As €1,090.91 is greater than €1,000 it is optimal for Jane to invest with Chris.
- By making this investment, Jane will be €90.91 better off than if she kept her €1,000 today. This "investment profit" is usually referred to as the Net Present Value (NPV).

Solution Task 5

$r = 25\%$
$PV = C_t/(1 + r)^t$
$PV = 1200/(1 + 25\%)^1$
$PV = 960$

€1,200 to be received in one year's time is the same as receiving €960 today given an opportunity cost of capital of 25%. Remember the initial investment is €1,000. As Jane will be receiving less than she is paying out in today's terms it is no longer worth her investing. The NPV of the investment is now negative.

$NPV = 960 - 1,000 = (40)$
$r = 5\%$
$PV = Ct/(1 + r)_t$
$PV = 1200/(1 + 5\%)^1$
$PV = 1,142.86$

€1,200 to be received in one year's time is the same as receiving €1,142.86 today given an opportunity cost of capital of 5%. As her initial investment is €1,000 she will be receiving more than we are paying out in today's terms. It is worth Jane investing. The NPV of the investment is NPV = 1,142.86 − 1,000 = 142.86.

Solution Task 6

1. The present value of alternative 1 is €3,900.
2.

	Y0	Y1	Y2	Y3	Y4
	NIL	1,000	1,000	1,100	1,200
Disc @ 5%		**.952**	**.907**	**.864**	**.823**
	NIL	952	907	950.4	987.6

$NPV = €3,797$

3. The third option where a cash flow is received every year forever is called a perpetuity. The present value of a perpetuity is calculated using the following formula:

$PV = C_1/r$

For option 3 the present value is given by

$PV = 180/5\%$
$PV = 3,600$

The present value of option 3 is €3,600.

4. The fourth option where a cash flow grows at a certain rate every year forever is called a growing perpetuity. The present value of a growing perpetuity is calculated using the following formula.

$$PV = C_1/(r - g)$$

For option 4 the present value is given by

$$PV = 100/(5\% - 3\%)$$
$$PV = 5,000$$

The present value of option 4 is €5,000.

Therefore, Jane should take the fourth alternative as this has the largest present value.

Solution Task 7

Annual saving from using the new machine under the assumptions of the Dough House being open 300 days per annum and serving 200 cups per day.

Cups per annum	60,000
Saving per Cup	× 4c
Saving per annum	€2,400

Using the cost of capital, which Mr Ryan provided, of 10% and again assuming all cash flows occur at year end

Present Value of Annual Savings

Saving Per Annum	€2,400
Annuity Factor 10, 10%	6.145
Present Value of Savings	€14,748

So the €2,400 per annum saved over the next 10 years is worth €14,748 in today's terms. Therefore the net present value of buying the new machine can be calculated as

$$NPV = PV - \text{Initial Investment}$$
$$NPV = 14,748 + (5,000) + (4,545) = 5203$$

The investment opportunity has a positive Net Present Value of €5,203 and Jane should go ahead with it.

Solution Task 8

Attn: Michael Smithers (Finance Director)
Memo: Investment Appraisal of New Plant
From: Chris
Date: 31 April 2009

One must be careful when you are using net present value as it depends only upon future cash flows. There are several key points to watch out for when carrying out Net Present Value Investment Appraisal.

1. Do not confuse cash flows with accounting profit.
   Accountants adjust cash flows in two main ways:
   - Accruals and prepayments (the matching principle). We are interested in when the cash flow actually happened.
   - Accountants deduct current expenses but depreciate capital expenses; we will not distinguish between the two.
2. Do not confuse average with incremental payoffs.
   - Managers are often reluctant to "throw good money after bad". Occasionally an incremental cash flow makes a loser a winner.
3. Include all incidental effects.
   - e.g. A new bit of rail track may be negative NPV on its own, but if all the additional train travel is included it may be positive.
4. Do not forget working capital requirements.
   - Net working capital is the difference between a company's short-term assets and liabilities. Most projects include a working capital investment which should be included in NPV calculations.
   - Working capital = inventory + accounts receivable – accounts payable.
5. Forget sunk costs.
   - Sunk costs are past and irreversible outflows. They should be forgotten when evaluating the NPV of a project today.
6. Include opportunity costs.
   - If you need to use a machine you own for a project which over its life will earn €100,000, and the machine could be sold today for €100,000, is it worthwhile undertaking the project?
7. Beware of allocated overhead costs.
   - Beware of loosely allocated overheads to a project.

Solution Task 9

Net Present Value Calculations

All figures in €000s

Year	Note	0	1	2	3	4	5
Equipment	2	−2,000				200	
Labour	4		150	157.5	165.4	173.7	
Efficiencies	5		500	515	530.5	546	
Working Cap	7	−50	50				
Rent foregone	8		−25	−25	−25	−25	
Tax	9			−40.6	−43.4	−46.4	+25.6
Cash Flow		−2,050	625	606.9	627.5	898.3	+25.6
DF @ 10%		1	0.909	0.826	0.751	0.683	0.621
DCF		−2,050	568.1	501.3	471.3	613.5	15.9

Net Present Value = €120,100 positive. Thus, it is worth investing.

NOTES TO THE NET PRESENT VALUE CALCULATIONS

1. MCL Limited commissioned and paid for a report by management consultants last year at a cost of €25,000. *Answer* This is a **sunk cost**. It was paid for last year. We are only interested in incremental cashflows so this is excluded from the net present value calculations below.

2. The equipment will cost €2 million, will have a residual value after four years of €200,000 and will be depreciated at 25% per annum on a straight line basis. *Answer* We are only interested in incremental cashflows. We must pay out a cash-flow of €2 million today, and will receive a cash inflow of €200,000 in four years' a time.

3. Capital allowances can be claimed at 15% per annum straight line. *Answer* These capital allowances are not incremental cash-flows. However they are relevant to our tax calculation and are included in note 9.

4. Annual savings on labour are initially €150k growing at a rate of 5% per annum for each of the next three years. *Answer* Labour is an incremental cashflow and we must include it as follows:

All figures in €000s

	1	2	3	4
Labour	150	157.5	165.4	173.7

5. Production Efficiencies of €500k per annum in year 1 growing at 3% per annum thereafter. *Answer* Production efficiencies are incremental and must be included.

All figures in €000s

	1	2	3	4
Efficiencies	500	515	530.5	546

6. The CEO intends allocating €100k per annum of existing head office costs to the new machinery. *Answer* Beware of allocated overheads. These are not incremental cash-flows and should not be included in the Net Present Value calculations.

7. The new plant requires an additional investment of €50k in working capital. This will be recovered at the end of the four years.

8. The area where the plant will be located is currently let out to a local business for €25,000 per annum. *Answer* We are going to miss out on €25,000 per annum in Years 1 to 4. This is an opportunity cost and should be included as follows.

All figures in €000s

	1	2	3	4
Rent foregone	25	25	25	25

9. MCL Limited pays corporation tax at a rate of 12.5% payable one year in arrears.

Answer:

	All figures in €000s			
	1	**2**	**3**	**4**
Labour Saving	150.0	157.5	165.4	173.7
Energy Saving	500.0	515.0	530.5	546.4
Capital Allowances	−300	−300	−300	−300
Balancing allowance				−600
Rent Foregone	−25	−25	−25	−25
Profit	325.0	347.5	370.9	(204.9)
Tax payable (recoverable) @ 12.5%	40.6	43.4	46.4	(25.6)

Balancing allowance is cost (2,000 − disposal value 200) less allowances claimed to date.

Solution Task 10

Sensitivity Analysis

To test the sensitivity of this analysis to changes in the discount rate we take the final three rows from the NPV analysis above. By inputting the discount factors from different discount rates we can assess the effect on NPV. We will try two discount rates, 5% and 15%.

Cash Flow	−2050	625	606.9	627.5	898.3	+25.6
DF @ 5%	1	0.952	0.907	0.864	0.823	0.784
DCF	−2,050.0	595.0	550.5	542.21	739.3	+20.1

Net Present Value = €397.100

Cash Flow	−2050	625	606.9	627.5	898.3	25.6
DF @ 15%	1	0.870	0.756	0.658	0.572	0.497
DCF	−2,050.0	543.8	458.9	412.8	513.8	12.7

Net Present Value = (€−108.000)

The project is very sensitive to changes in the discount rate. At a discount rate of 5% it generates a positive NPV of €397.100. This drops to about €120k with a discount rate of 10% and becomes negative (€108.000) at a discount rate of 15%. Below we will see how to calculate the break-even discount rate (Internal Rate of Return) of the project.

Solution Task 11

Alternatives to NPV

There are several alternatives to Net Present Value such as Payback, Discounted Payback, Accounting Rate of Return and Internal Rate of Return. All of these alternatives have drawbacks relative to Net Present Value. I have calculated each of these below and illustrate their shortcomings.

Payback

The payback period of a project is the number of years it takes before the cumulative forecasted cash flow equals the initial outlay. The payback rule says only accept projects that "payback" in the desired timeframe.

The total initial investment in year 0 is €2,050,000. To calculate the payback period we calculate the accumulated cash-flows.

All figures in €000s

	0	1	2	3	4	5
Cashflow	−2,050	625	606.9	627.5	898.3	+25.6
Accumulated Cashflow	−2,050	−1,425	−818.1	−190.6	707.7	733.3

We can see that the payback of the initial investment occurs in Year 4. Therefore the payback period is four years.

Disadvantages of payback:
1. This method does not provide a clear criterion for accepting/rejecting a project.
2. It also does not take into account the time value of money or the opportunity cost of capital.
3. Payback ignores cash-flows beyond the payback period.

Discounted Payback

Discounted payback is a variation of the payback rule which takes into account the time value of money. To calculate the discounted payback period all cashflows are discounted at the opportunity cost of capital and the accumulated discounted cashflow is calculated. The discounted payback period is the number of years it takes for the initial investment to be recouped in present value terms.

All figures in € thousands

	0	1	2	3	4	5
DCF	−2,050	568.1	501.3	471.2	613.5	15.9
Accumulated DCF	−2,050	−1,481.9	−980.6	−509.4	104.1	120

We can see that the discounted cashflow payback of the initial investment occurs in Year 4. Therefore the payback discounted payback period is four years.

Disadvantages:
1. This method does not provide a clear criterion for accepting/rejecting a project.
2. It ignores cashflows beyond the payback period.

Accounting Rate of Return

This method ranks projects according to their ARR or return on investment (ROI). There are a couple of definitions:

Annual Accounting Rate of Return

$$\frac{\text{Average annual project profits (pre or post tax)}}{\text{Average or initial investment outlay}}$$

Accounting Rate of Return

$$\frac{\text{Total Project Profits (pre or post tax)}}{\text{Average or Initial Investment Outlay}}$$

All figures in €000s

	1	2	3	4	Total
Labour Saving	150.0	157.5	165.4	173.7	
Energy Saving	500.0	515.0	530.5	546.4	
Rent Foregone	−25.0	−25.0	−25.0	−25.0	
Depreciation	−450.0	−450.0	−450.0	−450.0	
Profit before Tax	175.0	197.5	220.9	245.1	838.5
Less: Tax @ 12.5%	−40.6	−43.4	−46.4	+25.6	
Profit after Tax	134.4	154.1	174.5	270.7	733.7

- The total profit before tax on the project is €838.5k.
- The average annual profit before tax equals €838.5k/4 = €209.6k.
- The total profit after tax on the project is €733.7k.
- The average annual profit after tax equals €733.7k/4 = €183.4k.
- The initial investment in the project is €2,050,000.

Therefore:

1. The annual accounting rate of return (before tax)

$$= 209,600/2,050,000 = 10.2\%.$$

2. The annual accounting rate of return (after tax)

$$= 183,400/2,050,000 = 8.95\%.$$

Note 1: Alternatively the average investment ARR could have been used.
Note 2: An assumption has been made that the "rent foregone" is an accounting adjustment. It could be argued that this is a notional accounting entry and should be omitted.

Whichever approach is adopted it is important that you state your assumptions in the examination.

3. The accounting rate of return (pre tax)

$$= 838,500/2,050,000 = 40.9\%$$

4. The accounting rate of return (post tax)

$$= 1,018,300/2,050,000 = 49.7\%$$

Disadvantages of the Accounting Rate of Return:

1. Accounting Rate of Return is based on project profits not cashflows.
2. ARR considers average rates of return, ignoring the time value of money.
3. There are different definitions making comparison difficult.
4. The accept-reject decision is often relative to firm's existing projects. A company may reject profitable projects just because they are not as profitable as existing projects.
5. ARR is not based on an opportunity cost of capital.
6. There is also a danger that the Accounting Rate of Return might erroneously be compared to the opportunity cost of capital. In this case the project would be rejected (ARR = 8% < 10%) when in fact it generates a positive net present value.

Internal Rate of Return

The Internal rate of return is defined as the discount rate at which the NPV of a project is equal to zero. The decision rule is that a project should be accepted if its IRR>Opportunity Cost of Capital.

$$\frac{-2050}{(1 + IRR)^0} + \frac{625}{(1 + IRR)^1} + \frac{606.9}{(1 + IRR)^2} + \frac{627.5}{(1 + IRR)^3} + \frac{898.3}{(1 + IRR)^4} + \frac{25.6}{(1 + IRR)^5}$$
$$= 0$$

To calculate the IRR we start with a reasonable estimate of r, in this case 15%.

$$\frac{-2050}{(1 + 15\%)^0} + \frac{625}{(1 + 15\%)^1} + \frac{606.9}{(1 + 15\%)^2} + \frac{627.5}{(1 + 15\%)^3} + \frac{898.3}{(1 + 15\%)^4} + \frac{25.6}{(1 + 15\%)^5}$$
$$= +108K$$

As this is a negative Net Present Value we know that our estimate of 15% is too high. We therefore try a lower estimate of 10%.

$$\frac{-2050}{(1 + 10\%)^0} + \frac{625}{(1 + 10\%)^1} + \frac{606.9}{(1 + 10\%)^2} + \frac{627.5}{(1 + 10\%)^3} + \frac{98.3}{(1 + 10\%)^4} + \frac{25.6}{(1 + 10\%)^5}$$
$$= +120.1K$$

As this Net Present Value is positive we know that 10% is too low. The IRR lies between 10% and 15%. We can use the following formula to interpolate the correct IRR.

$$r_{low} + \frac{NPV_{low} \times (r_{high} - r_{low})}{NPV_{low} - NPV_{high}}$$

where

r_{low} = the estimate of the IRR that produces a negative NPV
NPV_{low} = the NPV calculated using r_{low}
r_{high} = the estimate of the IRR that produces a positive NPV
NPV_{high} = the NPV calculated using r_{high}

From above

$r_{low} = 15\%$
$NPV_{low} = -108.0$
$r_{high} = 10\%$
$NPV_{high} = 120.1$

$$10\% + \frac{120.1 \times (15\% - 10\%)}{120.1 + 108}$$

In this situation the IRR of the project = 11.6%. As this is greater than the opportunity cost of capital (10%) the project should go ahead.

Disadvantages of Internal Rate of Return:
These include:
- It is not reliable when choosing between mutually exclusive projects.
- A project does not necessarily have one IRR. Depending on the sign and size of the cash flows there may be several IRRs.
- IRR does not take into account the scale of a project.

Advantages of Net Present Value

The advantages of NPV over these other investment appraisal techniques are that (1) unlike Accounting Rate of Return it is based on cash flows rather than accounting numbers; (2) unlike Accounting Rate of Return and Payback, NPV takes into account the time value of money; (3) unlike Accounting Rate of Return and Payback it provides a clear accept-reject decision; (4) unlike Accounting Rate of Return and Payback, NPV is based on the opportunity cost of capital which takes into account the risk of the project; and (5) unlike IRR it takes into account the scale of a project.

Solution Task 12

Recommendations
1. As the new machine will generate a positive Net Present Value, I recommend that we should go ahead with the project.
2. In future all investment appraisals should be carried out using the Net Present Value investment appraisal technique.
3. MCL Limited needs to review the company's capital structure and generate an up-to-date estimate of the cost of capital.

Solution Task 13

Revenues are still subject to 5% inflation but now costs are subject to 7% inflation. We now have two real discount rates, a revenue real discount rate and a cost real discount rate. To calculate the cost real discount rate we use the formula from above.

Nominal rate   15.50%
Cost inflation rate   7%
Cost real rate   8% (rounded up) $((1.155/1.07) - 1)$

All figures in €000s

	0	**1**	**2**	**3**
Revenues		400	400	400
DF 10%		0.909	0.826	0.751
		363.6	330.4	300.4
Costs		−350	−350	−350
DF 8%		0.926	0.857	0.794
		−324.1	−299.95	−277.9
Machine	−100			
Total DCF	−100	39.5	30.45	22.5
NPV −7.55				

As costs are subject to a higher inflation rate the Net Present Value is now negative. MCL should no longer proceed with the project.

Solution Task 14

Cash Conversion Cycle = Stock Conversion Period + Debtor Conversion Period − Credit Period Granted by Suppliers
Stock Conversion Period (days) = Average Value of Stock/Average Value of Stock Used per Day
Debtor Conversion Period (days) = Average Value of Debtors/Average Value of Credit Sales per Day
Creditor Conversion Period (days) = Average Value of Creditors/Average Value of Credit Purchases per Day
For the Dough House the relevant ratios are:
Stock Conversion Period = 12,000/250 = 48 days
Debtor Conversion Period = 20,000/1,000 = 20 days
Creditor Conversion Period = 2,000/400 = 5 days
Cash Conversion Cycle = Stock Conversion Period + Debtor Conversion Period − Credit Period Granted by Suppliers
Cash Conversion Cycle = 48 + 20 − 5 = 63 days
This gives a total cash conversion cycle of 63 days. This is more than two months.

Solution Task 15

To: Jane Dough
From: Chris, Shield Kenwick
Re: Working Capital Management
Date: 15 June 2009

Further to our conversation about working capital management, I have calculated your cash conversion cycle (i.e. the time it takes to recover cash in the business). For the Dough House, this cycle is approximately 63 days (based on the information you gave me).

All of these factors we discussed are contributing to the Dough House's cash flow problems. In order to manage working capital more efficiently, you will need to manage the debtors and creditors better and keep less cash tied up in stock. I have identified several ways in which you might go about achieving this:

1. Formalize the amount of credit you give to your customers and send out invoices much faster.
2. Negotiate a fair period of credit with your suppliers, or alternatively negotiate a discount for early payment.
3. Minimize the amount of stock held on the premises. If you buy in bulk you should negotiate a discount to compensate you for tying cash up in stock.
4. Begin paying wages one week in arrears.
5. Put any excess cash in a high interest on demand account. It is important to get a return on short-term funds.

If implemented, these five actions could greatly improve your working capital position. However, these actions need to be traded off against potential costs of reducing the cash conversion period:

- Reducing the inventory conversion period would mean carrying lower amounts of inventory which could reduce sales. At present it appears you are carrying too much inventory but care must be taken not to reduce it too far.
- Reducing the period of credit allowed to customers could result in the offices buying from alternative coffee vendors, thereby reducing sales.
- Paying wages in arrears may make staff recruitment and retention more difficult.
- Increasing the credit taken from suppliers may cause deterioration in the relationship with them. This could lead to a loss of supply.

I hope these points are useful to you. Please give me a call if you would like to discuss the issue further.

Solution Task 16

$$EOQ = \sqrt{(2 \times FU/CP)}$$

Where
U = Annual Usage of the inventory item
F = Cost of placing an order
CP = Cost of holding one unit of stock for one year

$$EOQ = \sqrt{(2 \times 1{,}500 \times 1/0.30c)} = 100 \text{ units}$$

The total cost = the annual ordering cost + the cost of holding stock
The annual ordering cost = Number of orders per year × cost of each order
The annual ordering cost = U/Q × F, where Q = Order quantity
For Jane the annual ordering cost = 1,500/100 × 1 = €15
The cost of holding stock = Average stock level (in units) × Cost of holding each unit per year
The cost of holding stock = Q/2 × CP
For Jane the cost of holding stock = 100/2 × 0.30 = €15
For Jane the total cost = €30

Solution Task 17

Attn: Michael Smithers (Finance Director)
Memo: Working Capital Management
From: Chris
Date: 30 July 2009

I have prepared the following cash budget to illustrate next year's short-term financing requirements. Due to the sharp slowdown in sales we have a significant shortfall in (sources – uses) of cash in Q1 and Q2. The situation recovers in Q3 and Q4, so MCL Ltd needs to find sources of short-term finance.

155 x 80% + 180 x 20%	161.25 x 80% + 155 x 20%	231 x 80% +161.25 x 20%	206 x 80% + 231 x 20%
↓	↓	↓	↓

Table 1: MCL Ltd Forecasted Cash Budget for next year

	Q1	Q2	Q3	Q4
Sources of Cash				
Collections from Debtors	160.0	160.0	217.0	211.0
Other	0.0	0.0	25.0	0.0
Total Sources	160.0	160.0	242.0	211.0

Uses of Cash

Payments to Creditors	130.0	120.0	110.0	100.0
Current Expenses	60.0	60.0	60.0	60.0
Capital Expenditure	5.0	2.6	11.0	13.0
Interest	2.0	2.0	2.0	1.6
Dividends	2.0	2.0	2.0	2.0
Taxes	4.0	4.0	5.0	6.0
Total Uses	203.0	190.6	190.0	182.6
Sources minus Uses	(43.0)	(30.6)	52.0	28.4

Calculation of short-term financing requirements

Cash at start of period	10.0	(33.0)	(63.6)	(11.6)
Change in cash	(43.0)	(30.6)	52.0	28.4
Cash at end	(33.0)	(63.6)	(11.6)	16.8
Min. Cash Balance	10.0	10.0	10.0	10.0
Cumulative Financing Requirement	43.0	73.6	21.6	(6.8)

Should you wish to discuss this further, I would be happy to call out to you at your convenience. *(Note for students – assume that the minimum cash balance of €10 at the beginning of Q1 is present at the end of the previous quarter.)*

Solution Task 18

Attn: Mike Smithers
Memo: Working Capital Management
From: Chris
Date: 30 August 2009

I have prepared the following financing plan based upon the budget above. I have assumed that MCL will take the financing options in order of cost, i.e. bank loan @ 10% p.a., stretch payables @ 12% p.a., shorten receivables @ 16% p.a., bank loan @ 20% p.a.

Table 2: MCL Limited Financing Plan

	Q1	Q2	Q3	Q4
New Borrowing				
Bank loan @ 10%	20.0	0.0	0.0	0.0
Bank loan @ 20%	0.0	14.8	0.0	0.0
Stretch payables	20.0	20.0	7.7	0.0
Shorten receivables	3.0	20.0	0.0	0.0
Total	43.0	54.8	7.7	0.0
Repayments				
Bank loan @ 10%	0.0	0.0	0.0	20.0
Bank loan @ 20%	0.0	0.0	14.8	0.0
Payables	0.0	20.0	20.0	7.7
Receivables	0.0	3.0	20.0	0.0
Total Cash Raised	43.0	31.8	(47.1)	(27.7)

Interest Payments

Bank loan @ 10%	0.0	0.5	0.5	0.5
Bank loan @ 20%	0.0	0.0	0.7	0.0
Stretch payables	0.0	0.6	0.6	0.2
Shrink receivables	0.0	0.1	0.8	0.0
Net interest paid	0.0	1.2	2.6	0.7
Cash Required for Operations	43.0	30.6	(52.0)	(28.4)
Total Cash Raised	43.0	31.8	(47.1)	(27.7)

In Q1 you have a short-term financing requirement of €43k. MCL should take out a bank loan of €20k and stretch payables by €20k. You will also have to shorten receivables by €3k. This will cover the shortfall of €43k in Q1. However this financing will incur interest in Q2 of:

Bank loan €20k @ 10%/4	= 0.5k
Stretch Payables €20k @ 3%	= 0.6k
Shrink Receivables €3k @ 4%	= 0.1k
Total Interest	€1.2k

The total short-term financing requirement in Q2 is €31.8k, made up of €30.6k cash required from operations plus interest of €1.2k. To finance this you will have to stretch payables by €20k, shorten receivables by €20k and take out a loan of €14.8k @ 20%.

This financing will incur interest in Q3 of €2.6k. However, in Q3 there should be a cash surplus of €52k from operations and this can be used to repay the bank loan @ 20%. In Q3 it will still be vital to stretch payables by €7.7k.

Finally in Q4 there will be interest of €0.7k from financing in Q3. A cash surplus of €28.4k from operations can be used to repay the bank loan at 10%. There will be no need to stretch payables. I hope this table clearly shows how MCL can manage its short-term financing requirements for next year.

Solution Task 19

To calculate the cost of capital, use the Weighted Average Cost of Capital (WACC) Formula.

$$\textbf{WACC} = \textbf{k}_E \, \frac{\textbf{E}}{\textbf{D} + \textbf{E}} + (1 - \textbf{T})\textbf{kd} \, \frac{\textbf{D}}{\textbf{D} + \textbf{E}}$$

Where
WACC = Cost of Capital
k_E = Cost of Equity
k_D = Cost of Debt
T = Tax Rate
D = Amount of Debt in Capital Structure
E = Amount of Equity in Capital Structure

Measuring the Various Costs

(a) Measuring the Cost of Debt

This can be approximated by the following calculation:

$$\text{Current Yield} = \frac{\text{Total Coupon per annum}}{\text{Price}}$$

However this method ignores future coupon payments and the maturity repayment. The more correct way is to calculate the Yield to Maturity.

$$\text{Price} = \sum_{t=1}^{N} \frac{C}{(1 + k_D/n)} + \frac{X}{(1 + k_D/n)^N}$$

Where
N = Number of coupon payments remaining
C = Actual monetary payment
X = Maturity Value
n = Number of coupon payments per annum
k_D = Yield to maturity (Cost of Debt)

For MCL Limited we know that the total value of their debt is €2m and their annual interest payments are €160,000. We do not have enough information to calculate the yield to maturity so instead we calculate the current yield.

$$\text{Current Yield} = \frac{\text{Total Coupon per annum}}{\text{Price}}$$

$$\text{Current Yield} = 160,000/2,000,000 = 8\%$$

(b) The Cost of Equity

There are two main ways to calculate the cost of equity

(i)   CAPM

$$k_E = R_f + b \,(R_m - R_f)$$

(ii) Dividend Valuation Model
      Here D_0 is the current dividend
      G = the estimated growth rate
      P_0 = the current share price

$$P_0 = D_0 \frac{(1 + G)}{(k_E - G)}$$

We can rearrange as

$$k_E = D_0/P_0 + g$$

The cost of equity is equal to the dividend yield plus the long-term growth rate in dividends.

The next step is to estimate the cost of equity. From financial sources I have estimated that the appropriate risk-free rate of interest is 4% and the appropriate market risk premium is 10%. Apparel PLC has a similar capital structure to MCL Limited and has an equity market beta of 1.25.

I can therefore use the Capital Asset Pricing Model to estimate the cost of equity for MCL Limited.

$$k_E = R_f + b (R_m - R_f)$$
$$k_E = 4\% + 1.25[10\% - 4\%] = 11.5\%$$

We can check this k_E using information from Knitwear PLC. We are told that this company pays a dividend yield of 4% and has a long-term growth rate in dividends of 7.5%.

$$k_E = D_0/P_0 + g$$
$$k_E = 4\% + 7.5\% = 11.5\%$$

Our existing long-term debt is costing 8% per annum on average and we face a marginal tax rate of 12.5% per annum.

$$WACC = k_E \frac{E}{D + E} + (1 - T)K_D\frac{D}{D + E}$$
$$WACC = 11.5\% \times 8m/(8m + 2m) + 8\% \times (1 - 12.5\%) \times 2m/(8m + 2m) = 10.6\%$$

I have therefore estimated the MCL Limited weighted average cost of capital to be 10.6%.

Weakness of the WACC model

- This measures the cost of capital for the company as a whole and assumes that each project has exactly the same debt/equity ratio as the overall company debt/equity ratio.
- Furthermore, as NPV calculations are forward looking, using WACC assumes that this specific capital structure will be maintained throughout the life of the project.
- How large is the equity risk premium?
- What is the correct risk-free rate to use?
- How reliable is the CAPM beta?
- Different costs of capital for different projects.

Solution Task 20

This new funding will affect the capital structure of MCL Limited. The new loan will be at a rate of interest of 8% and will increase MCL Limited's debt/value ratio to 40%. These changes will affect MCL Limited's cost of capital.

To calculate the revised Weighted Average Cost of Capital to assess this project we need to follow three steps.

Step 1. Calculate the opportunity cost of capital using existing weights.

Opportunity Cost of Capital
$$k_c = k_e \times E/(D + E) + k_d \times D/(D + E) = 10.8\%$$
$$k_c = 11.5\% \times 80\% + 8\% \times 20\% = 10.8\%$$

Step 2. Using the new cost of debt and leverage, calculate the new cost of equity.
$$k_e = k_c + (k_c - k_d*)D/E* = 12.7\%$$

Where
k_d^* = the new cost of debt
D/E^* = the new debt/equity ratio
$k_e = 10.8 + (10.8 - 8\%)40/60 = 12.7\%$

Step 3. Recalculate the WACC at the new financing weights.

$$WACC = k_E \frac{E}{D + E} + (1 - T)K_D \frac{D}{D + E}$$

$$WACC = 12.7\% \times 60\% + 8\% \times 40\% \times (1 - 12.5\%) = 10.4\%$$

Solution Task 21

Attn: Michael Smithers (Finance Director)
Memo: Portfolio Theory, CAPM, Efficient Markets Hypothesis
From: Chris
Date: 25 October 2009

Portfolio Theory

The major lessons of portfolio theory are:
1. Investors should diversify. It has been shown that by diversifying one's returns across a number of different securities one can reduce risk (standard deviation of returns) without sacrificing expected return.
2. The lower the correlation coefficient between the returns on two companies, the greater is the scope for risk reduction through diversification.
3. Different investors will have different preferences regarding the trade-off between risk and return, but all will be interested in maximising returns relative to risk.
4. Given the existence of a risk-free asset each investor may have his own unique optimal risky portfolio.

Investors are observed to diversify in practice. However, the appropriateness or otherwise of portfolio theory is largely dependent on the assumption that investors are only interested in expected return and standard deviation.

It is clear that investors are interested in return and risk, but the use of standard deviation as a measure of risk can be questioned, particularly if returns have been skewed rather than being symmetric distributions.

Overall, the assumptions of the theory are a reasonable approximation of reality and the widespread application of portfolio theory is evidence of its usefulness.

Capital Asset Pricing Model (CAPM)

When talking about portfolio theory we noted that investors require compensation for taking on additional risk, through the expectation of additional returns. Thus, in a competitive market, assets with higher risk should offer greater returns. Specifically, we might expect that the return on an asset i could be described by the following equation.

$$R_i = R_f + \text{risk premium}$$

Where:
R_i = Return on asset i
R_f = Risk-free rate of interest

Equation 1 simply states that the required return on any asset consists of two parts. Firstly, a rate of return to compensate for the time value of money, and secondly, a risk premium. If we could link the risk premium with the risk of the asset we could determine the required rate of return of any asset. This is precisely what the CAPM seeks to do. What we are seeking is a simple model in the form:

$$\text{Cost of capital} = \text{Risk-free rate} + \text{Risk premium}$$

We turn to the capital markets to determine the appropriate risk premium.

Assumptions of the CAPM
1. All investors have the same investment opportunity set.
2. All investors have the same information and use it in the same way.
3. All investors have the same risk-free rate of interest for borrowing and lending.
4. All investors have the same views on the prospects of each security.
5. All investors have the same decision-making horizon – one period model.

The market portfolio m therefore serves as a benchmark for the assessment of risk and return. Any investment having the same risk as the market portfolio must yield at least the same expected return $E(r_m)$.

Security Market Line

We are looking for an expression in the form:

$$E(R_i) = \text{risk-free rate} + \text{risk premium}$$

Where $E(R_i)$ = expected return on any asset i regardless of whether it is efficient or inefficient

If i is the risk-free asset then

$$E(R_i) = R_f$$

If i is the market portfolio then

$$E(R_i) = E(R_m) = R_f + [E(R_m) - R_f]$$

We can include an additional component βi to create the expression below:

$$E(R_i) = R_f + \beta_i[E(R_m) - R_f]$$

This is the Security Market Line, or the Capital Asset Pricing Model.

For 1 and 2 to still hold, then
$\beta_i = 0$ for the risk-free asset
$\beta_i = 1$ for the model portfolio

What exactly does β_i signify?

βi is a measure of the market risk of an asset. Market risk of an asset is the risk that it brings to the market portfolio (which is the investor's portfolio of risky assets).

It can also be interpreted as the sensitivity of the returns on an investment to returns on the market portfolio. If the returns on the market portfolio change by 2%, then the expected return on share i will change by ($2\% \times \beta_i$).

Efficient Market Hypothesis (EMH)

The EMH implies that if new information is revealed about the firm it will be incorporated into the share price rapidly and rationally with respect to the share price movement and the size of the share price movement. As current and past information is quickly reflected in share prices there is an absence of abnormal profit-making opportunities.

Three core principles of EMH

1. Investors are rational and hence value securities rationally.
2. Even if investors are not rational, their irrationality-inspired trades of securities are random and the effects of irrationality should cancel each other out.
3. If, by chance, the majority of investors are irrational in similar ways and push securities away from fair value then arbitrageurs will enter the market to profitably push prices back to fair value.

Market Efficiency Example

For instance, BMW announces at 10 am that it has a prototype electric car which will cost £10,000, has the performance of a petrol car and will run for 500 miles before requiring a low cost re-charge. Investors will try to assess the change in the value of the share and see whether this prototype will increase or decrease the value of BMW and by how much. If the overwhelming market opinion is that this news is positive for BMW, in an efficient market the share price will almost instantaneously move to a new higher share price.

The black line shows an efficient response to BMW's announcement. The share price instantaneously adjusts to the new level. There are four other possibilities if the assumption of efficiency is relaxed. (1) Leak of info by BMW's management brings other buyers in before the announcement is made. (2) There is an overreaction to the announcement and the share price rises too far (a bubble) before drifting lower (deflating). (3) There is a slow reaction to the news. (4) The share price fails to rise at all to its efficient level.

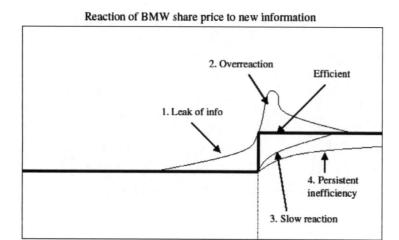

Reaction of BMW share price to new information

Value of the efficient market

1. Encourages share buying. People do not like buying over-valued assets or an asset which is inefficiently priced. People do not like uncertainty. Market efficiency helps towards raising money from investors.
2. Gives correct signals to company management. Aim of the manager is to maximise the value of the firm. If share prices do not correctly reflect the true value maximising behaviour of management this will lead management to make inappropriate decisions. Management also use the share price to work out the correct cost of capital. If share price is wrongly valued this will lead to inappropriate investment decisions.
3. Helps for resource allocation. Capital in the economy should be allocated to companies which are performing well, this will lead to increases in economic growth. If poorly performing companies have high valuations they will be able to issue new shares, attracting money which should be allocated elsewhere, leading to lower economic growth.

Solution Task 22

Attn: Michael Smithers (Finance Director)
Memo: MCL Limited Financial Position
From: Chris
Date: 15 November 2009

I have prepared the following report assessing MCL Limited's financial position to illustrate the types of information that your bankers will look at when assessing any requests for further debt.

1. How much has the company borrowed?

The company's bankers want to make certain that MCL Limited does not borrow excessively. If the company wants to take out a new loan the lenders will scrutinize several measures of whether the company is borrowing too much and will demand it keep its debt within certain bounds. These limits are generally set using financial ratios.

$$\text{Debt--Equity} = \frac{\text{Market Value Long-Term Debt}}{\text{Market Value Equity}}$$

$$= 2,000,000/8,000,000 = 25\%$$

$$\text{Cash Cover} = \frac{\text{EBIT} + \text{Depreciation}}{\text{Interest}}$$

$$= (286,200 + 23,100)/36,829 = 8.4 \text{ times}$$

$$\text{Gearing} = \frac{\text{Long-Term Debt}}{(\text{Long-Term Debt} + \text{Equity})}$$

It is not possible to calculate the gearing ratio as the balance sheet does not provide the book values of long-term debt and equity. However, using market values, the gearing ratio is €8m/€10m = 80%, which is extremely high.

2. How liquid is the company?

MCL Limited's bankers will also keep an eye on the short-term financial position. This is known as the liquidity of the company and can be assessed with the following ratios.

$$\text{Current Ratio} = \frac{\text{Current Assets}}{\text{Current Liabilities}} = 206,418/77,233 = 2.67$$

$$\text{Acid Test Ratio} = \frac{\text{Current Assets} - \text{Stock}}{\text{Current Liabilities}}$$

$$= (206,418 - 91,255)/77,233 = 1.49$$

3. How efficiently are they using the company's assets?

Understanding the investment in fixed assets and working capital that is needed to support MCL Limited's current activities will help to uncover any inconsistencies in borrowing plans. Efficiency is calculated using the following ratios.

$$\text{Asset Turnover} = \frac{\text{Sales}}{\text{Total Assets}} = 1,637,600/837,043 = 1.96$$

Days in Stock = Stock/(Cost of Sales/365) = 91,255/(854,940/365) = 39 days

4. How profitable is the company?

Bankers are also going to be concerned about whether MCL Limited has the profitability levels to support debt and meet interest payment. This can be assessed using the following ratios.

$$\text{Margin} = \frac{\text{Net Income}}{\text{Sales}} = 199{,}371/1{,}637{,}600 = 12\%$$

$$\text{Return on Equity} = \frac{\text{Net Income}}{\text{Book Value of Equity}} = 199{,}371/709{,}810 = 28\%$$

$$\text{Return on Equity} = \frac{\text{Net Income}}{\text{Market Value of Equity}} = 199{,}371/8{,}000{,}000 = 2.5\%$$

$$\text{Payout Ratio} = \frac{\text{Dividends}}{\text{Earnings}} = \text{No Dividend in 2007}$$

Solution Task 23

Briefing Note: Mike Smithers
Equities/Shares

Definition

Equity securities, also known as common stocks or shares, represent ownership in a corporation. Each share entitles its owner to one vote on matters of corporate governance (e.g. the election of the board of directors) and to a share in the profits of the corporation. The corporation is typically managed by a group of professional managers on behalf of the shareholders. The shareholders then elect a board of directors to oversee these professional managers.

Share characteristics

The two key characteristics of common stock ownership are its residual claim and limited liability features. Residual claim means that shareholders have claim to the portion of profits which remain after the interest and taxes have been paid. The bigger the profits the bigger the residual claim. Limited liability means that the most shareholders can lose in the case of bankruptcy of the corporation is their original investment. Although they are the owners of the corporation, shareholders are not personally liable for the debts of the firm at liquidation.

Bonds

The bond market is composed of longer-term borrowing or debt instruments. This market includes government and corporate debt instruments. This market is often referred to as the fixed income market as these instruments generally pay fixed interest rates.

Bond characteristics

A bond is a security that is issued in connection with a borrowing arrangement. The borrower sells a bond to the lender to raise cash, and the bond is an IOU. The arrangement obligates the issuer to make specified payments to the bondholder on specified dates. When the bond matures the bond's face value is repaid to the bond holder. The coupon rate for the bond serves to determine the interest payment. The annual payment is the coupon rate times the face value.

The return to a bondholder comes in the form of income and capital gains. The income comes from the coupon but bond prices also change affecting capital gains/losses. As bonds pay a fixed interest payment, if interest rates rise, bond prices fall. Likewise, if interest rates fall the bond price will increase.

Solution Task 24

Briefing Note for Mervin Smithers: Venture CapitalVenture capitalists provide funds for privately owned firms with high growth potential.

- Venture capitalists look for high-risk investments and expect a high return of 50 to 80% per annum or five to eight times the initial equity investment over five to seven years.
- Many investments by venture capitalists will fail. The failure rate could be as high as 20%.
- Venture capitalists generally take a 20 to 30% share of equity. They do not look for a controlling interest.
- However, when providing an investment, venture capitalists take special rights to appoint a number of directors.
- They often take additional rights to make changes to the board depending on poor firm performance.
- Venture capitalists always have a clear target for exit route and date. At this point they can recoup their investment generally through:
    - o The sale of the stake or the entire company to another firm
    - o The flotation on the stock market.

Solution Task 25 Financial analysis of Company 1 and Company 2

	Company 1	Company 2
Profitability		
Net Profit Margin		
$\dfrac{\text{Net Profit}}{\text{Sales}} \times 100$	$\dfrac{105.7}{532.1} \times 100$	$\dfrac{125.2}{2,265.3} \times 100$
	19.9%	5.5%

Return on Capital Employed

$$\frac{\text{Profit}}{\text{Capital Employed}} \times 100 \qquad \frac{105.7}{959.7} \times 100 \qquad \frac{125.2}{2{,}918.3} \times 100$$

$$11\% \qquad\qquad 4.3\%$$

Company 1 is clearly more profitable for the half year than Company 2 with far superior profitability.

Liquidity

	Company 1	Company 2
Current Ratio		

$$\frac{\text{Current Asset}}{\text{Current Liabilities}} \qquad \frac{345.1}{211} \qquad \frac{1{,}305.4}{1.146.0}$$

$$1.6{:}1 \qquad\qquad 1.1{:}1$$

Acid Test Ratio

$$\frac{\text{Current Assets} - \text{Stock}}{\text{Current Liabilities}} \qquad \frac{345.1 - 56.2}{211} \qquad \frac{1{,}305.4 - 573.5}{1{,}146}$$

$$1.4{:}1 \qquad\qquad 0.6{:}1$$

Company 1 also appears to be in a better position regarding liquidity. They are doing a better job of managing their short-term assets and liabilities.

Gearing

	Company 1	Company 2
Debt/Capital Employed		

$$\frac{\text{Long-term Debt}}{\text{Capital Employed}} \times 100 \qquad \frac{367.8}{959.7} \times 100 \qquad \frac{1{,}233.9}{2{,}918.3} \times 100$$

$$38\% \qquad\qquad 42\%$$

Both companies have similar levels of gearing. These are both at reasonable levels. A closer examination of Company 1 accounts reveals they are gradually decreasing this gearing over time.

Efficiency

	Company 1	Company 2
Debtors' days		

$$\frac{\text{Debtors}}{\text{Credit Sales}} \times 182.5 \text{ days} \qquad \frac{191.6}{532.1} = 65 \text{ days} \qquad \frac{623.3}{2{,}265.3} = 50 \text{ days}$$

Unfortunately, we have no information on purchases so cannot calculate creditors' days. Company 1 appears to be extending more credit to their debtors than Company 2 although the difference is marginal.

Market Value Ratios

	Company 1	**Company 2**

P/E Ratio

$$\frac{\text{Stock Price}}{\text{Earnings per Share}} \qquad \frac{11.3}{0.574} = 19.7 \qquad \frac{22.2}{1.076} = 20.7$$

$$\frac{\text{Dividend per share}}{\text{Stock Price}} \qquad \frac{0.24}{11.3} = 2\% \qquad \frac{0.11}{22.2} = 0.5\%$$

Company 1 pays a higher dividend and their valuations appear similar. This is surprising given the much better financial performance of Company 1 over the six-month period.

Conclusion

Given the limited information provided we should not reach strong conclusions. However, the superior performance of Company 1 relative to Company 2 would justify more research.

Solution Task 26

Expected Return on Bellweather PLC

$E(R_i) = R_f + \beta_i (E(R_m) - R_f)$
$4\% + 1.25(8\% - 4\%) = 9\%$

Expected Return on Jones PLC
$E(R_i) = R_f + \beta_i (E(R_m) - R_f)$
$4\% + 0.75(8\% - 4\%) = 7\%$

Bellweather PLC is more suitable for Matthew's portfolio as:

1. Bellweather PLC has a lower correlation with the existing portfolio so it will have a greater diversification benefit than Jones PLC.
2. Bellweather also offers a higher expected return than Jones PLC and this is in line with Matthew's attitude to risk and return.